ESSENTIALS

of Cash Management

Sixth Edition

D0506578

Co-Editors:

Peter S. Adam
Principal
Adam & Associates

William A. Harrison
President
Harrison Consulting Group

Associate Editors:

W. Steven Culp, CCM, CPA, Chair
Mary I. Adams, CCM
Kent W. Crocombe, CCM
Terry S. Maness, CCM
Dennis W. Reedy, CCM
Margaret L. Weber, CCM
David A. Wikoff, Ph.D., CCM

A publication of the Association for Financial Professionals

**Association for
Financial Professionals**

All inquiries should be addressed to:

Communications Department
Association for Financial Professionals
7315 Wisconsin Avenue, Suite 600 West
Bethesda, Maryland 20814

ISBN 0-9614799-7-3

CONTENTS

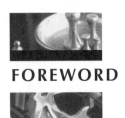

FOREWORD

In recent years, the practice of cash management has undergone significant changes as a result of enhancements in technology, increased globalization, growing market volatility, corporate pressures to enhance shareholder value, and a host of regulatory and legislative initiatives. Never before has managing cash presented so many challenges and so many opportunities.

These changes are reflected in the **Essentials of Cash Management, Sixth Edition**. Developed by treasury practitioners as the body of knowledge in cash and treasury management, this Sixth Edition has been updated and expanded, with special emphasis on critical areas such as the payments system, information technology management, electronic commerce, financial risk management, and international treasury management.

As in previous editions, **Essentials of Cash Management, Sixth Edition** also features questions and answers to help readers test their understanding of the information presented in each chapter, as well as a glossary of key cash and treasury management terms. The 16 chapters of **Essentials of Cash Management** cover the entire scope of cash management as well as many of the additional functions of treasury management, ranging from the role of cash management in finance to the latest developments in financial risk management.

Although the primary use of **Essentials of Cash Management** is as a study guide for the Certified Cash Manager (CCM) exam, it is also a valuable resource for anyone who wishes to enhance his or her knowledge of cash and treasury management. In addition, it is a handy reference tool for seasoned treasury executives, vendors of treasury management products, and college students and faculty interested in learning about cash management.

Essentials of Cash Management, Sixth Edition reflects the knowledge and expertise of corporate practitioners who worked tirelessly to develop the most comprehensive text in the field of cash and treasury management. We hope it will become essential reading for treasury professionals who wish to enhance their companies' financial performance.

W. Steven Culp, CPA, CCM
Chairman, Body of Knowledge Task Force

EDITORS' ACKNOWLEDGEMENTS

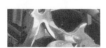

The planning and writing of **Essentials of Cash Management, Sixth Edition** would not have been possible without the hard work and dedication of several talented individuals.

Very special thanks go to members of the Body of Knowledge (BOK) Task Force, chaired by W. Steven Culp. CPA, CCM, Vice President and Assistant Treasurer, Funding and Risk Management, Deutsche Financial Services Corporation. Other BOK members are Mary I. Adams, CCM, Senior Vice President, Chase Bank of Texas, N.A.; Kent W. Crocombe, CCM, Treasurer, Aladdin Industries, Inc.; Terry S. Maness, CCM, Dean, Hankamer School of Business, Baylor University; Dennis W. Reedy, CCM, Director, Treasury Operations, Indiana University; Margaret L. Weber, CCM and David A. Wikoff, Ph.D., CCM, President, End Results, Inc. BOK members were responsible not only for the scope and content of the text, but were also heavily involved in the drafting and editing of new and revised material. The publication reflects their professionalism, expertise and dedication to quality.

We are also deeply grateful to the CCM Review Course faculty for their valuable comments and suggestions for improving the text. CCM Review Course faculty are Michele Allman-Ward, CCM, President, Allman-Ward Associates; Mark Krawczyk, CCM, Principal & CEO, CZYK & Associates; Elizabeth A. Olson, CCM, Senior Consultant, Treasury Strategies, Inc.; Paul Ruggeri, CCM, Principal, Ruggeri Management Consulting; George Schilling, CCM, President, Schilling & Associates, Inc.; Joseph Tinucci, CCM, President, Tinucci & Associates, Inc.; and James Washam, Ph.D., CCM, Assistant Professor of Finance, Arkansas State University.

Other important contributors include Lee Epstein, CEO of both Money Market One and Decision Analytics. Epstein spent considerable time on critiquing the investment chapter, and his valuable input and critical insights greatly enhanced the chapter.

Other people who gave a great deal of their time to the project include Prodyot Samanta, Ph.D., Professor of Economics and Finance at Manhattan College, who wrote the chapter on financial risk management; and Arlene Chapman, CCM, TMA's Director of Payments and Standards, who reviewed the chapters related to electronic commerce and relationship management.

In addition, we would like to thank Rori Ferensic, TMA's Certification Manager, for serving as project manager; Ayo Mseka, TMA's Director of Publications and Creative, who was in charge of the final publishing process; and Courtney R. Tallman, TMA's Graphic Designer and Production Artist, for the design and production of the publication.

Finally, we would like to thank our families for their support and understanding as we faced the rewarding but challenging task of writing **Essentials of Cash Management, Sixth Edition**.

Peter S. Adam, Adam & Associates
William A. Harrison, Harrison Consulting Group

ABOUT THE EDITORS

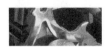

Peter S. Adam is Principal of Adam & Associates. He is an international economic analyst and author of financial articles, government and corporate reports. William A. Harrison is President of Harrison Consulting Group. He is an organizational development consultant and has written numerous reports, handbooks, policy manuals and training courses.

ABOUT TMA

The Treasury Management Association (TMA) is the world's leading professional association representing more than 12,000 treasury executives from 6,500 leading companies and organizations.

TMA enables treasury professionals to perform effectively in a changing business world and prepares them for future challenges through professional development and executive education opportunities, certification programs, career services, publications and technical information, original research, industry standards and representation before legislators and regulators.

Membership in TMA is open to corporate treasury practitioners as well as those who sell products and services to the treasury management profession, such as bankers, consultants, and acedemics. The mission of the Association is enhanced value of the treasury profession through professional knowledge, respect and recognition for the profession, a favorable business environment, and professional conduct.

CHAPTER **1**

The Role of Cash Management in Corporate Finance

OVERVIEW

This chapter establishes the basis for the development of cash management as a separate discipline within a company's financial organization. It also describes how cash management has evolved in response to changes in financial practices and institutional arrangements in the U.S. This chapter introduces a number of terms and concepts that will be developed in more detail later in this book.

LEARNING OBJECTIVES

Upon completion of this chapter and the related study questions, the reader should know:

1. The objectives of cash management

2. How cash management supports major corporate financial objectives

3. The major functions of cash management

4. The place of cash management in the corporate financial organization

5. The historical evolution of cash management in the U.S.

KEY CONCEPTS

1. A Company's Operating Cycle

2. The Cash Flow Timeline

3. Float

4. The Major Objectives of Corporate Finance and Cash Management

5. Evolution of Cash and Financial Management

OUTLINE

I. THE OVERALL CORPORATE OBJECTIVE

A company's primary objective is to maximize shareholder value. Shareholders invest in a company to earn a total return that exceeds that which is available from similar investment alternatives. The efficient management of a company's resources and operations will generate profits that enhance its value to shareholders. Finance and treasury departments ensure timely provision of the cash resources necessary for sustaining a company's ongoing activities. Finance and treasury activities are extremely important aspects of corporate management and are essential to the attainment of a company's overall objectives.

II. CASH MANAGEMENT OBJECTIVES AND THE CASH FLOW TIMELINE

Managing cash is an integral part of a company's overall operations. Cash is required to sustain the operating cycle, and cash managers ensure that a company's operating cycle, as shown in Exhibit 1.1, is adequately financed. Therefore, the objectives of cash management are closely related to the management of the operating cycle.

EXHIBIT 1.1
Operating Cycle

A. Cash Management Objectives

The primary objective of cash management is to utilize cash as efficiently as possible in a manner consistent with a company's overall strategic objectives.

Major objectives of cash management include:

- **Maintaining Liquidity** - Liquidity refers to a company's ability to meet upcoming obligations in a timely and cost effective manner.

- **Optimizing Cash Resources** - Cash managers establish systems that reduce holdings of non-earning cash balances to minimum levels while still providing adequate liquidity. Any excess cash balances are either invested to generate additional income or used to reduce interest expense through the repayment of debt.

- **Financing** - Cash managers assist in obtaining both short- and long-term borrowed funds in a timely manner and at an acceptable cost. These credit facilities are used to fund a company's cash shortages.

- **Managing Risk** - Cash managers help in the monitoring and controlling of a company's exposure to interest rate, foreign exchange, and other risks.

- **Coordinating Financial Functions** - Cash managers help ensure that managers in other areas of the company understand and implement policies that are consistent with cash management objectives.

B. The Operating Cycle and the Cash Flow Timeline

The operating cycle consists of the day-to-day activities pertaining to the purchase of and payment for raw materials, their transformation into saleable goods, their marketing, and the ensuing collection of revenues. From a cash manager's perspective, this basic operating cycle translates into a general cash flow timeline as outlined in Exhibit 1.2. The cash inflows and outflows that occur along the cash flow timeline are rarely for the same amount, nor do they occur at the same time. Given the imbalance and uncertainty of cash inflows and outflows, the challenge for cash management is to ensure that sufficient levels of cash are available at all phases of the cycle.

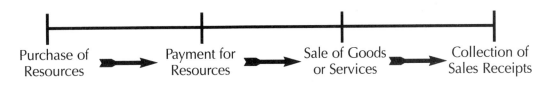

EXHIBIT 1.2
General Cash Flow Timeline

C. Cash Flows

There are three types of cash flows that cash managers must consider:

1. **Cash Inflows** - These are funds collected from customers, obtained from financial sources such as lenders, or received from other payors.

2. **Concentration and Liquidity Management Flows** - These include internal transfers among operating units of a company and between various bank accounts owned by a company. The objective of funds concentration is to systematically create a pool (or pools) of liquid reserves held as cash or invested in cash equivalents.

3. **Cash Outflows** - These are funds disbursed from liquid reserves to vendors, employees, lenders, shareholders, and other payees of the company.

D. Cash Flow Timeline and Float

The cash flow timeline comprises the total time interval from the time resources are purchased at the beginning of a company's operating cycle until the time payment is received for goods or services at the end of a company's operating cycle.

Float is a term that refers to the time interval, or delay, between the start and completion of a specific phase or process that occurs along the cash flow timeline. The various types of float that a company must manage are illustrated in the detailed cash flow timeline in Exhibit 1.3.

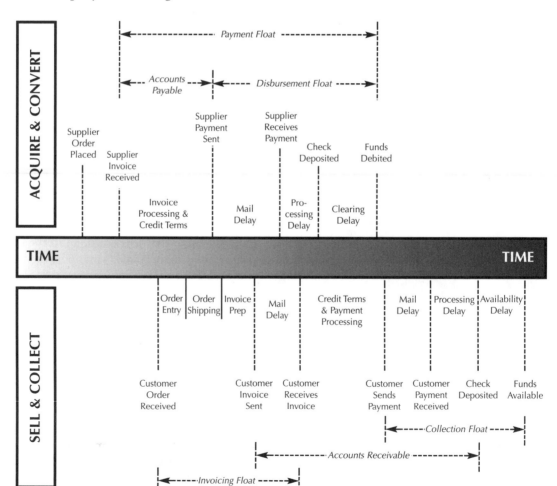

EXHIBIT 1.3
A Company's Cash Flow Timeline

NOTES:
- *assumes payments by check*
- *time periods not to scale*

Different float terms may refer to the same (or similar) time intervals, but their usage varies depending upon whether or not the time period covered is viewed from the perspective of the receiving party (payee) or the sending party (payor). For example, consider the terms collection and disbursement float when a check is sent in payment of an invoice:

- **Receiving Party's (Payee's) Perspective** - Collection float represents the delay between the time a check is mailed and the time the receiving party (payee) receives available funds in their account.

- **Sending Party's (Payor's) Perspective** - Disbursement float represents the delay between the time the check is mailed and the time the funds are charged to the sending party's (payor's) account.

The following are specific types of float that are important to the cash manager:

- **Invoicing Float** - Represents the delay between the purchase of goods or services and the receipt of an invoice by the payor.

- **Payment Float** - Represents the delay between the receipt of an invoice by the payor, including the credit period, and the time the payor's account is charged for the funds sent in payment of the invoice.

A company typically benefits from shortening all types of float associated with cash inflows, and lengthening all types of float associated with cash outflows. In principle this is true, except that companies generally do not extend disbursement float to the point of jeopardizing their vendor relationships. Also, other priorities such as cost containment and access to required management information should be considered in addition to float optimization in developing cash management procedures.

E. Tools of Cash Management

The tools of cash management, as presented in this book, represent various techniques, products, and services that enable a cash manager to manage a company's cash resources more effectively. Informed application of these tools can reduce the time and magnitude of unfavorable float that occurs along the cash flow timeline. An efficient cash management system will generally increase a company's overall liquidity. This increased liquidity not only reduces a company's risk of insolvency but will typically increase its overall profitability.

The practice of cash management is focused on resolving cash shortages or surpluses that occur along the cash flow timeline due to the unsynchronized nature of a company's cash inflows and outflows. This includes involvement in the following day-to-day operations:

- **Collection** - Collecting funds from customers or other payors

- **Concentration** - Concentrating funds where they can be most efficiently utilized

- **Disbursement** - Disbursing funds to vendors, employees, investors, and other payees

- **Information Gathering and Analysis** - Developing and maintaining appropriate information systems

- **Forecasting** - Forecasting future cash flows to predict potential shortages or surpluses

- **Investment** - Investing excess cash balances

- **Borrowing** - Borrowing to meet short-term requirements

- **Managing Financial Relationships** - Managing relationships with banks and other financial service providers

III. THE FINANCE FUNCTION AND FINANCIAL DECISIONS

A company's financial policies and practices significantly influence its cash management operations.

A. The Finance Function

Finance plays a pivotal role in the achievement of a company's major objective of maximizing shareholder value. The principal roles of corporate finance include:

1. **Accounting** - The key role of the accounting function is to record a company's financial activity. This includes the recording of its assets, liabilities, equity, revenues, expenses, and earnings. Most financial statements that are provided to third parties are prepared in accordance with Generally Accepted Accounting Principles (GAAP) as formulated by the Financial Accounting Standards Board (FASB), the organization that oversees U.S. accounting standards. A company may also develop various internal financial reports to assist management with the ongoing operation and control of its business.

2. **Funding** - The funding function involves raising capital to finance a company's operations and capital projects.

3. **Capital Budgeting** - The capital budgeting function involves:

    - Evaluating quantitatively alternative projects in which a company could invest its capital resources. Quantitative factors include costs, profits, and cash flows.

    - Estimating the economic return of projects in relation to one another and in relation to the company's cost of capital.

    - Evaluating qualitative factors of projects. Qualitative factors include such things as how a project fits into a company's core strategy and whether it is an activity in which a company would have a competitive advantage.

B. Corporate Financial Decisions

Important financial decisions a company must make include the following:

1. **Capital Structure** - A company must decide on a desired capital structure, including the relative proportions of debt and equity funding. The optimum mix of debt and equity financing can vary greatly from one company or industry to another.

2. **Investment Decisions** - Companies have limited financial and management resources. Therefore, they must decide what projects are appropriate and how much to invest in them. Such analysis involves estimating both the risks and returns of a given project.

    Investment decisions also encompass divestiture decisions such as the sale of a division, subsidiary, or the discontinuance of a product line because the company's capital resources can be more effectively deployed elsewhere.

3. **Financing Decisions** - A company must weigh several interrelated factors when deciding to raise additional debt or equity to finance its needs. For example, a company's capacity to raise different types of capital is influenced by its perceived risk profile, which in turn is influenced by its existing capital structure. Also a company's projected risk profile based upon a proposed debt or equity offering can influence its ability to market such an offering.

4. **Dividend Decisions** - A company must decide how much of its earnings to distribute as cash dividends to stockholders and how much to retain and reinvest in its operations. This decision is sometimes guided by shareholder expectations, which vary widely and may be dependent on a company's industry or stage of development. Dividend decisions and payouts can also be restricted by covenants contained in a company's debt agreements.

IV. FINANCIAL ORGANIZATION

The structure of a company's financial organization should facilitate the achievement of its overall objectives. Financial organizational structures vary significantly from company to company and industry to industry.

A. Financial Organizational Structure

In a large company, the treasurer and the controller typically report to the Chief Financial Officer (CFO). Some companies have a flatter organizational structure in which all of the following functions report directly to the CFO:

- Treasury

- Accounting

- Information systems

- Audit

- Strategic planning

- Financial analysis

Exhibit 1.4 illustrates how the cash manager typically fits into the financial organization of a large company.

EXHIBIT 1.4

Typical Organization of the Financial Function

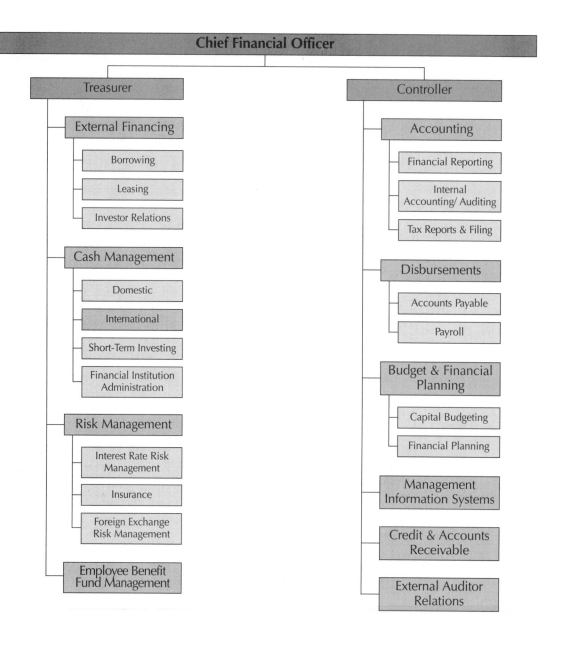

B. Key Roles and Responsibilities

The financial function is generally divided into the following roles and responsibilities:

1.   **Chief Financial Officer (CFO)** - The CFO is normally a member of the top management team, reporting to the Chief Executive Officer (CEO). In a large company, the CFO usually oversees the treasury and accounting functions, and plays an important strategic planning role as the pivotal person in the capital budgeting and investment decision-making process. Selecting and rejecting investment projects is one of the ways a company implements its strategic plan. Final decisions on building a plant, buying or selling a subsidiary, or closing down a product line are typically the responsibility of the CEO or the Board of Directors. However, the CFO plays a central role in presenting and quantifying decision alternatives and measuring the financial results of those decisions once they are implemented.

2. **Treasurer** - The treasurer is usually responsible for arranging external financing, managing relationships with banks and other financial institutions, and overseeing day-to-day liquidity management. Other functions for which the treasurer may be responsible include risk management, managing dividend disbursement, insurance, and pension assets. In a large company, some of these responsibilities may be delegated to an assistant treasurer.

3. **Controller** - The controller is normally responsible for accounts payable, internal accounting, preparation of financial statements, internal auditing, coordination with external auditors, preparation of budgets, tax filings, and monitoring budgeted capital expenditures. In some companies the Management Information Systems Department and Credit Department also report to the controller, whereas in other companies they report to the treasurer.

4. **Internal Auditor** - The internal auditor is responsible for determining that controls and operating procedures are in place to protect a company from losses caused by inefficiency, inaccuracy, or fraud. The internal auditor typically reports directly to the Board of Directors.

5. **Credit Manager** - The credit manager is responsible for preserving and collecting accounts receivable, setting corporate credit policies, approving the extension of credit terms to customers, and establishing information systems to monitor accounts receivable. The credit manager may report to either the controller or treasurer.

6. **Cash Manager** - The cash manager is part of treasury and is concerned primarily with the management of day-to-day cash flows and banking relationships, as detailed in the following section. In a smaller company, these functions may be handled by accounting personnel.

V. THE ROLE OF THE CASH MANAGER

The functions and reporting relationships of cash managers typically are as follows::

A. Cash Management

The responsibilities assigned to the cash manager may vary from company to company, but usually include:

1. **Funds Management**

   • Monitoring the daily cash position

   • Controlling cash balances on deposit at financial institutions

   • Moving funds from concentration accounts or other accounts to where they are needed

2. **Banking System Administration**

   • Managing bank relationships, including compensation for banking services

   • Conducting analytical reviews and feasibility studies of banking services

3. **Liquidity Management**

   • Short-term borrowing

   • Short-term investing

4. **Forecasting**

   • Projecting future cash shortages and surpluses

   • Monitoring the accuracy of prior projections

5. **Systems Design, Implementation, and Evaluation**

   • Analysis, design, implementation, and ongoing evaluation of cash management systems

B. Reporting Relationships

In most companies, the cash manager reports directly or indirectly to the treasurer who, in turn, reports to the CFO. In a small company, the cash manager's job may be a responsibility of the treasurer or assistant treasurer, but in a large company a staff of several people may be devoted to cash management activities.

C. Coordination with Other Internal Functions

Cash management requires teamwork and cooperation with other internal departments of a company. The activities of other departments, such as credit management and accounts payable, have a direct impact on the cash management function. Often these departments report to managers outside the treasury area, such as the controller. Therefore, the cash manager must often interact with these departments and assert informal influence to ensure that overall cash management objectives are met.

VI. DEVELOPMENT OF CASH MANAGEMENT IN THE U. S.

Cash management in the U. S. has been influenced by particular features of the domestic banking system, mail system, and payment conventions. Although these factors are constantly evolving due to changes in legislation, financial trends, and technology, the following are some characteristics that have distinguished the U.S. financial environment:

• Large numbers of banks and other financial institutions

• Limited nationwide branch banking

• Payment of most bills by check

• Extensive use of the mail for payment remittance

Cash management has changed a great deal in the last half century. Prior to 1940, interest rates were low and corporate treasurers did not have a variety of external investment opportunities. There was more money in the banking system than there was loan demand. Banks funded their loans with interest-free Demand Deposit Accounts (DDAs) and invested the excess in safe, low yielding government securities. Banks competed with each other far less than they do today. Interest rates were capped by law. Banks were highly selective in their corporate lending, motivating treasurers to keep large excess balances to protect credit facilities. The remainder of this section provides an overview of the historical trends that have affected cash management. Many of the topics discussed will be covered in greater detail in subsequent chapters.

A. The 1940s and 1950s

Two events in the 1940s and 1950s were notably important to cash management.

1. **The First Lockbox** - A lockbox is a collection system in which a company's customers mail payments to a designated post office box. A third party collects the payments, processes the remittances, and deposits the checks directly into the customer's account. RCA was one of the first companies to arrange this type of collection system in 1947. It was designed to accelerate payments from dealers who were borrowing from RCA to finance their inventory of RCA products.

2. **The Accord and the Government Securities Market** - In 1951, the Federal Reserve Board of Governors reached an historic accord with the U.S. Treasury Department. It gave the Federal Reserve (Fed) the right to pursue an independent monetary policy. The Fed subsequently adopted a policy of purchasing only short-term Treasury bills and stopped purchasing longer-term Treasury notes and bonds. The Treasury no longer had the Fed as a captive investor for notes and bonds and had to rely on a competitive market to raise funds. The Fed's removing itself from the long-term side of the Treasury market also meant that interest rates were now determined as a result of competitive market forces rather than by government action. This marked the birth of a huge market of safe, liquid securities with short-, medium-, and long-term maturities for companies with excess cash.

B. The 1960s

The decade of the 1960s produced several developments that influenced the evolution of cash management.

1. **Negotiable Bank Certificates of Deposit (CDs)** - By 1960, banks needed to buy funds and compete for deposits to support their growing loan portfolios. In 1961, the Fed authorized banks to issue negotiable certificates of deposit. The introduction of CDs provided a new source of funds for banks and an investment instrument for corporations.

2. **Lockbox Models** - Bank-operated lockboxes became increasingly popular as cash managers became more aware of collection float and its related cost. In the late 1960s, a model was developed for studying mail times between one city and another. The model optimized the location of lockbox sites in relation to the disbursement banks and mail points used by payors.

3. **Diversifying Short-Term Investments** - Interest rates continued to rise in the 1960s. Treasurers diversified from low-yielding, liquid government securities into new instruments such as municipal obligations, banker's acceptances, commercial paper, and repurchase agreements.

4. **Managing Bank Balances** - Treasurers managed cash resources more efficiently, reduced idle bank balances, and demanded more bank services for balances on deposit. In response, banks expanded their corporate services and developed formal marketing programs.

C. The 1970s

The runaway inflation of the 1970s and high interest rates that continued from the late 1970s into the 1980s elevated the importance of cash management and prompted a great deal of financial innovation.

1. **Remote Disbursement** - Remote disbursement was designed to take advantage of the inaccessibility of certain banks. These banks, generally located in geographically isolated locations, offered significant float gains to companies that used them for check disbursement. The remoteness of these banks created difficulty in physically presenting checks drawn on them in a timely manner. The Federal Reserve was granting credit to the depositing bank before the check could be collected from the remote bank on which it was drawn. The increased use of remote disbursement throughout the 1970s, coupled with the Federal Reserve's concern over float costs and the financial health of banks used for this purpose, led to programs aimed at discouraging this practice.

2. **Controlled Disbursement** - Controlled disbursement was designed to take advantage of the Federal Reserve's presentment schedule. In a number of banks, the final presentment of checks from the Fed was sufficiently early in the day to enable a company to determine its total daily check clearings and fund this amount. The company could then make investment and/or borrowing decisions knowing there would be no additional clearings against the account that day.

3. **Funds Concentration** - The amounts deposited in local banks were reported by the depositing units to third-party service providers. The information was consolidated and relayed to the concentration bank, which created a depository transfer check (DTC) to transfer funds from the local banks into a concentration account. Today, DTCs have been replaced largely by electronic depository transfers (EDTs).

4. **Bank Balance Reporting** - Banks began to offer services to gather and store bank balance and transaction information which companies could access directly. Information from multiple banks could be consolidated into a single report.

5. **Transaction Detail and Real-Time Reporting** - Customers began to get detailed transaction information on bank services. Banks offered information such as inbound wire transfer amounts with accompanying reference information during the same working day in which they were received. Methods were developed for customers to initiate funds transfers and other transactions using terminals in their offices.

6. **Electronic Payments** - Electronic payment alternatives began to be developed using the Automated Clearing House (ACH). The primary applications were direct deposit of payroll and collection of life insurance premiums.

7. **Commercial Paper (CP)** - Large corporations increased their borrowing by issuing short-term promissory notes, known as commercial paper. Issuing CP directly in the money markets was less expensive than borrowing from banks.

D. The 1980s

The 1980s were a decade of deregulation that continued into the 1990s and had a great impact on cash management.

1. **Depository Institutions Deregulation and Monetary Control Act (1980)** - Also known as the Monetary Control Act, this was the most comprehensive banking legislation since the 1930s. It paved the way for a number of changes which were destined to have an impact on bank services and prices for years to come. (See Chapter 3, The U.S. Financial Environment.)

2. **Noon Presentment and Payor Bank Services** - In 1983, the Fed accelerated its presentment schedule by making second presentments later in the day as part of the float-reduction program mandated by the Monetary Control Act.

3. **Electronic Corporate-to-Corporate Payments** - Banks began to promote corporate trade payments through the ACH. Companies understood the efficiency of electronic payments, but many were reluctant to give up disbursement float.

4. **Electronic Commerce (EC) and Electronic Data Interchange (EDI)** - EC is the exchange of business information from one organization to another in some type of electronic format and includes facsimile (fax), electronic mail (e-mail), and EDI communications. EDI is a formalized computer-to-computer communication for routine business transactions in a standard format. Financial EDI (FEDI) is EDI related to payments. The introduction of these new technologies has caused significant changes in treasury and cash management operations.

5. **Use of Personal Computers (PCs)** - The introduction of the PC led banks and software firms to develop the treasury workstation. Software was developed to retrieve information automatically from banks and compile it into consolidated reports. The electronic spreadsheet replaced the paper spreadsheet.

6. **Integration of International Financial Markets** - Worldwide integration resulted from the global expansion of companies and banks and the development of international financial centers. Computer and communications technology played a crucial role in forging these links, in facilitating the enormous funds flows, and in increasing the importance of foreign exchange management. The Eurodollar market, developed initially in the 1960s, was based on the accumulation of U.S. dollars on deposit in financial institutions outside the U.S. This market broadened into the Eurocurrency market, part of the worldwide offshore currency market.

7. **Financial Product Innovation** - In the early 1980s, a number of capital market innovations were introduced. These new products included interest rate and currency swaps, futures, options, and asset-backed securities.

8. **Bank Creditworthiness** - Several events occurred that raised concerns about the creditworthiness of banks. The Federal Reserve became concerned about the impact that a major bank failure would have on the payments system. Banks shared this concern because of their exposure to interbank settlement risk. Treasurers, who had previously shown little interest, started to scrutinize the financial condition of their banks.

   A key factor in judging a bank's creditworthiness is its level of capital. Concerns about bank failures at the time prompted development of capital adequacy ratios that could be used on a global basis in evaluating a bank's relative financial condition.

9. **Cash Management Ethics** - In the early 1980s, the E.F. Hutton Company was involved in a widely discussed case concerning fair bank compensation. By channelling check deposits from Hutton branches through unsophisticated banks that treated ledger balances as though they were available balances, Hutton was effectively able to borrow interest-free from the banks. This case helped focus attention on the ethical application of cash management practices.

E. The 1990s

Technological and legal trends of the 1980s continued into the 1990s.

1. **Payments System Risk** - Payments system risk became a concern because of the increasing volume of money transfers through Fedwire, the Clearing House Interbank Payments System (CHIPS), and the ACH. The Federal Reserve has taken numerous steps to reduce this risk.

2. **Electronic Payment of State and Federal Taxes** - The federal government, most state governments, and many local governments require the electronic payment of sales, withholding, income, and other taxes above a certain dollar limit. Electronic filing of tax returns and information is also offered by many government tax authorities.

3. **Interstate Banking** - Government regulations prohibiting interstate banking and branching are gradually being removed. The Interstate Banking and Branching Efficiency Act of 1994 permitted banks to operate fully integrated banking systems nationwide beginning in June 1997.

4. **Derivatives** - Advances in technology and financial theory have given rise to an astounding variety of complex financial instruments known as derivatives (securities whose value is determined by another security, index, or financial value). Derivative products allow corporate treasurers to hedge risks more precisely but may be difficult to analyze and can be extremely volatile.

5. **Technology** - Technological developments such as the Internet have extended and enhanced the use of electronic commercial payment and financial information systems.

6. **Security Concerns** - The growing use of telecommunications equipment for transmission of financial transactions, and equipment that can copy documents such as checks with unprecedented clarity, has necessitated development of safeguards to maintain systems security and to prevent transaction fraud. There are various technological and organizational countermeasures that companies and financial institutions can implement to prevent fraud and electronic defalcations.

7. **Globalization** - The reduction and removal of tariffs and legal and regulatory impediments to international trade and financial activity have "globalized" finance. Agreements such as NAFTA and the Maastricht Treaty hold the prospect of knitting the world's capital markets into one integrated market.

8. **Payment Cards** - The use of purchase and procurement cards has transformed the way many companies pay for their small-dollar purchases. Miniaturization of electronic components into chips that can store enormous amounts of information has also led to the development of smart cards.

9. **Year 2000 Compliance** - Companies and financial institutions have expended a tremendous amount of time and resources to ensure that their management information systems are capable of processing dates beyond December 31, 1999. Most software and many hardware systems require significant reprogramming or other modifications to enable recognition of dates in the year 2000 and beyond.

10. **European Economic Union** - The signing of the Maastricht Treaty has provided a timetable for the formation of the Economic and Monetary Union (EMU). When completed, the EMU will consolidate most European countries into a single economic unit that will share a common currency called the euro.

VII. CURRENT TREASURY ENVIRONMENT

The historical factors previously mentioned have played a significant role in shaping and reshaping the corporate financial function. Treasury and cash management operations are undergoing rapid change due to various trends, including:

A. Quality Management

The issue of quality has become an integral part of the overall corporate environment. Treasury departments have not been immune to this trend and are continuously challenged to produce quality results at an acceptable cost and assist other corporate departments in quality management as well.

B. Reorganization of Treasury Operations

As the treasury function has evolved, treasury professionals have continually endeavored to effectively use available resources to attain both financial and overall corporate objectives. A number of developments have prompted a re-examination of how treasury is organized, how it functions, and the efficiency with which it operates. In many cases the restructuring of treasury operations has resulted in downsizing. Technological developments allow fewer people to accomplish more. Recasting treasury operations typically involves the following corporate practices:

1. **Re-engineering** - The concept of re-engineering involves a radical redesign of a particular business process with the goal of continuous process improvement. The redesign of treasury operations may include restructuring or eliminating traditional treasury processes.

2. **Benchmarking** - In the process of re-engineering the treasury function, it is valuable to seek out examples of other companies that have successfully redesigned their operations. The best practice in a given field serves as a benchmark that can be used to compare and evaluate a company's existing process.

3. **Outsourcing** - One possible outcome of re-engineering the treasury operation may be the decision to have an outside provider perform part, or all, of a business function. This is known as outsourcing. For example, a company may decide to outsource its disbursement processing. It sends a data file containing payment information to an outside processor. The processor then initiates the specified payments on the company's behalf, using the designated method of payment (such as check or ACH).

VIII. FUTURE FINANCIAL TRENDS

The 21st century will see a continuation of certain present trends and the development of new trends resulting from an ever-changing financial environment. Following are some of the possibilities:

• Certain sources predict the segmentation of the U.S. banking system into two distinct components: one comprised of large nationwide financial institutions offering a wide range of services; the other consisting of small "boutique" institutions specializing in a limited number of banking services.

• Current legislative initiatives to allow the payment of interest on corporate demand deposits could, if passed, significantly change many traditional U.S. cash management practices.

• The increasing use of sophisticated computers and telecommunications systems will continue to be a driving force in shaping the future of treasury management in the global economy.

Questions

These chapter questions are to test and review the information in the text and are not examples of CCM examination questions, nor are they in the examination format.

Answers can be found at the back of the book on pgs. 361-362.

1.   What are the major objectives of cash management?

2.   What is the relationship between the operating cycle and the cash flow timeline?

3.   What are the three general types of cash flows that must be managed?

4.   What is the purpose of using cash management tools?

5.   What are the three principal roles of the finance function?

6.   What are the four important corporate financial decisions?

7.   Who are the key players (besides the cash manager) involved in the finance function?

8.   What are the five cash management functions and responsibilities?

9.   What is float?

10.   What two disbursement products were introduced in the 1970s?

11.   What major piece of banking legislation reshaped cash management in the 1980s?

12.   What are the key issues in the current treasury environment?

CHAPTER **2**

Accounting and Financial Concepts

OVERVIEW

This chapter reviews the basic principles of accounting and finance as they apply to cash management.

LEARNING OBJECTIVES

Upon completion of this chapter and the related study questions, the reader should know:

1. How cash accounting differs from accrual accounting

2. The basic financial statements – the income statement, balance sheet, and statement of cash flows

3. Working capital and its components

4. The basic concepts of finance: interest, the time value of money, liquidity, corporate capital structure, the cost of capital, and capital budgeting

5. How to calculate basic financial ratios

KEY CONCEPTS

1. Cash versus Accrual Accounting

2. Float

3. Interest, Discounting, and Time Value of Money

4. Capital Budgeting, Equity and Debt Financing, Leverage

5. Measuring Liquidity, Working Capital, and Net Working Capital

6. Basic Corporate Performance Measurement

OUTLINE

I. ACCOUNTING CONCEPTS

This section describes the basic accounting concepts on which the system of financial reporting and record-keeping used in the U.S. today is based.

A. Accounting Principles

Accounting provides the data necessary for measuring a company's performance and assessing its financial position. The accounting function records a company's assets, liabilities, shareholder equity, revenues, and expenses, and reports them according to a detailed set of rules called Generally Accepted Accounting Principles (GAAP). These principles are developed, agreed upon, and published in the form of Financial Accounting Standards (FAS) by the Financial Accounting Standards Board (FASB), an independent, self-regulating organization formed in 1973. Although not a government entity, FASB wields great authority.

The Securities and Exchange Commission (SEC), an independent regulatory agency of the United States government, requires companies that issue securities to the public to file financial statements. The SEC enjoys broad powers with respect to prescribing accounting practices and standards for such reports. These are found in its Financial Reporting Releases (FRRs), Regulations S-X, and decisions on cases that have come before the Commission.

The SEC maintains, however, that the private sector should retain the initiative for establishing and improving accounting standards, and it relies on the FASB for this purpose. Financial statements conforming to GAAP are presumed to have the SEC's support.

Adherence to GAAP is important because investors, lenders, and trade creditors rely on consistent financial information for decisions with regard to investing, lending, and provision of credit.

Companies enjoy wide latitude in keeping records for their own internal purposes. There are, however, managerial and cost accounting conventions and norms applicable to most industries and most types of commercial and non-commercial establishments.

B. Cash Versus Accrual Accounting

Some companies record their revenues, expenses, and earnings strictly on the basis of when cash is received or paid out. This is known as cash accounting. In cash accounting, all accounting entries are directly related to a cash inflow or outflow. Sales are recorded as the cash is received and expenses are recorded as they are paid. Small businesses tend to use the cash accounting approach.

The other primary accounting method is accrual accounting. The fundamental difference between cash and accrual accounting is that the latter recognizes revenues as they are earned and expenses as they are incurred, regardless of when the related cash flows occur. With accrual accounting, revenues may be reported but not yet collected, and expenses may have been incurred but not yet paid. It is particularly important for the cash manager, who is mainly concerned with cash flows, to understand the distinction between accounting information and cash flows.

The most important accrual accounting concepts include:

1.   **Income Recognition** - Revenue is recognized when sales are made. When sales are made on credit, accounts receivable are created on the balance sheet. Accounts receivable represent revenues from sales that have been recognized but not yet collected as cash. When funds are collected from the customer, the accounts receivable balance is decreased and the cash balance is increased without any effect on income.

2.   **Cost Recognition** - Product costs incurred in a time period prior to the sale are added to the inventory value. They are not treated as expenses when there is a cash expenditure. In order to match revenues and expenses, costs associated with manufacture are recognized as part of the cost of goods sold in the accounting period in which the sale takes place.

3.   **Capitalized Assets** - Capitalized assets are expected to have lives greater than one accounting cycle and are not fully expensed in the period in which they are acquired. The assets are carried on the balance sheet at their acquisition cost and depreciated in subsequent periods.

4. **Depreciation and Amortization** - Accounting expense connected with a capitalized asset is recognized by depreciation in the case of fixed assets and amortization in the case of long-term intangible assets. With both depreciation and amortization, the cost of the asset is allocated over its allowable life. Neither depreciation nor amortization measures a decline in the actual value of an asset. Both are non-cash expenses; therefore, the income statement for an accounting period understates the cash flow provided by operations by the amount of depreciation expense and/or amortization taken.

5. **Deferred Taxes** - The difference between the time the tax code requires companies to recognize revenues and expenses and the time they are recognized under accrual accounting results in differences between the cash disbursed for income taxes and the tax provision reported on income statements. This difference is recognized as a deferred tax and appears on the balance sheet.

6. **Capital and Dividends** - A number of cash flows, such as capital asset additions, retirements, and dividends, are neither income nor expenses. The addition of capital to the company, through the issuance of debt or the sale of common stock, results in a cash inflow but is not income. The cash outflow for the repayment of principal on a debt obligation is not an expense. The payment of cash dividends to shareholders is a distribution of profits, not an expense.

7. **Management Discretion** - A company has some degree of latitude and must exercise judgment on the allocation of expenses and revenues. There is potential for companies to adjust the value of revenues or expenses under the accrual system. Part of the external auditor's role is to render an opinion that revenue and expense recognition conforms with GAAP. (It is permissible for a company to keep its financial records on a cash basis and adjust them to an accrual basis at the end of reporting periods. Larger corporations seldom do this, however, and for reporting purposes typically use accrual-based accounting methods exclusively.)

C. Accounting for Cash and Float

Cash amounts on a company's books often differ from its bank account balances. There are two reasons for this: checks deposited by a company take time to clear (the interval and amount are known as float), and payees do not present checks issued by the company immediately.

Sometimes a company's cash account will show a negative balance. One way to avoid this is by combining the cash account with another current asset account, such as marketable securities, which may have sufficient balances to offset the cash account's deficit. As an alternative, a company can report checks issued but not yet presented for payment as a liability, such as "drafts payable" or "checks not yet cleared" which will also keep the cash account balance positive.

D. Financial Statements

GAAP requires three statements for reporting financial results: the income statement, the balance sheet, and the statement of cash flows.

1. **Income Statement** - The income statement, or profit and loss statement, is a record of revenues and expenses, as illustrated in Exhibit 2.1. It describes the net change in the amount of shareholder equity resulting from operations over a specified period of time.

   Categories used on the Income Statement include:

   - **Revenues** - Revenues represent the total or gross amount derived from a company's sale of merchandise or services.

   - **Cost of Goods Sold** - The cost of goods sold represents the expense of providing goods and services for sale. It includes labor and material directly used in manufacturing the product that was sold, and indirect, or allocated, manufacturing expenses.

   - **Operating Expenses** - Operating expenses, such as selling or administrative expenses, are necessary for the conduct of the business, but are not tied directly to the production of goods and services.

   - **Depreciation** - Depreciation of fixed assets and amortization of intangible assets are typically considered operating expenses, particularly in manufacturing operations. Neither is a cash outlay.

   - **Operating Profit** - Operating profit, also known as operating income, is the profit after deducting the cost of goods sold and operating expenses from revenues. The term is often used interchangeably with EBIT, earnings before interest and taxes.

   - **Other Income/Expenses** - The income statement may include other income and expenses such as interest income and expense, or currency gains or losses. These are income and expenses that arise from non-operating activities.

   - **Net Income** - Net income is operating profit less the cost of debt financing and income taxes incurred during the accounting cycle, adjusted for other income and expenses.

EXHIBIT 2.1

Sample Year-End Income Statement

Revenues	$ 15,000,000
Less: Cost of Goods Sold	9,200,000
Gross Profit	5,800,000
Less: Operating Expenses	4,000,000
Less: Depreciation	200,000
Operating Profit/EBIT	1,600,000
Less: Interest Expense	300,000
Net Profit Before Taxes	1,300,000
Less: Provision for Income Taxes	450,000
Net Income	**$ 850,000**
Earnings Available for Common Shareholders	$ 850,000
Less: Common Stock Dividends Paid	250,000
Addition to Retained Earnings	$ 600,000
Earnings per Share (100,000 shares outstanding)	$ 8.50

2. **Balance Sheet** - A balance sheet, or statement of financial condition, is illustrated in Exhibit 2.2. It is a snapshot of a company's financial condition. It reports, as of a specific date, the following:

EXHIBIT 2.2

Sample Balance Sheets (Current and Prior Year)

ASSETS

	Current Year	Prior Year	Change
Cash	$ 1,500,000	$ 1,000,000	$ 500,000
Short-Term Investments	1,300,000	1,500,000	(200,000)
Accounts Receivable	1,700,000	1,300,000	400,000
Inventory	2,600,000	2,100,000	500,000
Pre-Paid Expenses	900,000	900,000	0
Total Current Assets	8,000,000	6,800,000	1,200,000
Property, Plant, & Equipment	7,500,000	6,800,000	700,000
Total Assets	**$15,500,000**	**$13,600,000**	**$ 1,900,000**

(Continued)

LIABILITIES AND OWNERS' EQUITY

	Current Year	Prior Year	Change
Accounts Payable	$ 1,600,000	$ 1,200,000	$ 400,000
Short-Term Notes Payable	1,800,000	1,300,000	500,000
Total Current Liabilities	3,400,000	2,500,000	900,000
Long-Term Debt	3,900,000	3,500,000	400,000
Total Liabilities	7,300,000	6,000,000	1,300,000
Common Stock at Par Value	200,000	200,000	0
Paid-In Capital	3,600,000	3,600,000	0
Retained Earnings	4,400,000	3,800,000	600,000
Total Equity	8,200,000	7,600,000	600,000
Total Liabilities & Equity	**$15,500,000**	**$13,600,000**	**$ 1,900,000**

EXHIBIT 2.2

Sample Balance Sheets (Current and Prior Year)

- **Assets** - Assets are the items of value owned by a company. Assets are typically listed at historical cost (not present-day market value) adjusted for depreciation. Assets' depreciated value is shown as their book value. They are usually listed on the balance sheet in order of decreasing liquidity, or convertibility into cash, as follows:

  - **Current Assets** - The basic current assets include cash, marketable securities, accounts receivable, and inventories. Current assets are normally converted to cash within one year, or within the operating cycle. Current assets may also include prepaid expenses such as insurance premiums which are paid in advance.

  - **Fixed Assets** - Fixed assets are a company's investment in property, buildings, machinery, and equipment. Fixed assets (also known as long-term assets or capital assets) cannot be turned into cash as readily as current assets.

  - **Intangible Assets** - Intangible assets are assets that lack physical substance. Examples are goodwill, trademarks, and patents. There is often a high degree of uncertainty concerning the future benefits of intangible assets. They are amortized over their legal or useful life.

- **Liabilities** - Liabilities represent obligations of the firm. They are usually listed on the balance sheet in order of increasing maturity, as follows:

  - **Current Liabilities** - Current liabilities include obligations such as accounts payable, short-term loans, wages payable, taxes payable, and the current portion of long-term debt (all due within one year or within the operating cycle). Accounts payable (also referred to as trade payables) are amounts due to vendors for purchased items. Short-term notes payable are typically short-term bank loans or commercial paper.

◆ **Long-Term Liabilities** - Long-term liabilities are obligations such as term loans, mortgages, and bonds due beyond one year or one operating cycle.

• **Equity** - Shareholder equity represents the owners' position in the company. It is the net book value of the company committed by and belonging to the owners in the form of shareholder capital and retained earnings. Retained earnings represent the increase in shareholder equity that can arise from retention of profits in the company.

The following equation always holds true:

$$\text{Total Assets} = \text{Total Liabilities} + \text{Shareholder Equity}$$

---

3.   **Statement of Cash Flows** - Under accrual accounting, the reporting period when a revenue or expense item is recognized is often different from the reporting period when the corresponding cash transaction takes place. Although the income statement based on accrual accounting is a useful indication of the company's performance, lenders, creditors, and investors are concerned with the company's cash flow because cash, not earnings, repays debt, pays bills, and pays dividends.

The Statement of Cash Flows provides an indication of the sources of a company's cash flow and how it is being used. The statement of cash flows is divided into three sections – Operating, Investing, and Financing Activities.

Exhibit 2.3 shows how a Statement of Cash Flows can be derived from information in the income statement and balance sheet.

To calculate cash flow from operating activities, depreciation and any other non-cash charges are added to net income. Then, changes in accounts receivable and payable are added or subtracted, along with changes in other operating accruals. The total is net cash provided (or used) by operating activities.

Other corporate actions that affect a company's cash flow include:

• Investing activities such as buying and selling plant and equipment and financial instruments, and

• Financing activities, such as issuing or retiring equity or debt.

EXHIBIT 2.3

*Sample
Statement of
Cash Flows*

Cash Flows from Operating Activities		
Net Income		$ 850,000
Adjustments to Reconcile Net Income to Net Cash		
Depreciation	200,000	
Increase in Accounts Receivable	(400,000)	
Increase in Inventories	(500,000)	
Increase in Accounts Payables	400,000	(300,000)
Net Cash Provided (Used) by Operating Activities		$ 550,000
Cash Flows from Investing Activities		
Capital Expenditures	(900,000)	
Decrease in Short-Term Investments	200,000	
Net Cash Provided (Used) in Investing Activities		($ 700,000)
Cash Flows from Financing Activities		
Net Borrowing - Bank Line of Credit Agreement	500,000	
Proceeds from Issuance of Long-Term Debt	400,000	
Dividends Paid	(250,000)	
Net Cash Provided (Used) by Financing Activities		$ 650,000
Net Increase (Decrease) in Cash		
Cash - Beginning of Year	$1,000,000	
Cash - End of Year	1,500,000	
Net Cash Increase (Decrease)		$ 500,000

The statement of cash flows in Exhibit 2.3 shows that the company generated a cash flow from operations of $550,000. Net income provided $850,000, and depreciation was another $200,000, but net changes in balance sheet amounts absorbed $500,000, since inventory and receivables increased by $900,000, while payables increased only $400,000.

Investing activities during the period used $700,000, comprised of $900,000 in capital expenditures offset by a $200,000 decrease in short-term investments.

During the period, the company had a net inflow of $650,000 of cash from financing activities, and total cash increased by $500,000.

E. Auditing and Financial Statement Reliability

Practically all businesses that borrow from banks or require credit produce some form of financial statements conforming to generally accepted formats. While the management of a company is always responsible for the financial statements it issues, not all sets of financial statements are considered equally reliable.

Typically, a company either produces its own financial statements or has a Certified Public Accountant (CPA) or CPA firm do it.

These statements can be audited or unaudited. If the statements are audited, a CPA or a CPA firm has reviewed them for compliance with GAAP using Generally Accepted Auditing Standards (GAAS) as promulgated by the Auditing Standards Board of the American Institute of Certified Public Accountants (AICPA).

Just because a CPA has helped compile a set of financial statements does not mean, however, that they have been audited. If audited, a set of financial statements will include an opinion letter that sets forth both the scope of the CPA's review, and the extent to which the auditing CPA found that the statements are in material compliance with GAAP.

The auditor can render four types of opinions: unqualified, qualified, disclaimed, or adverse.

1. **Unqualified** - In an unqualified opinion, the auditor states that the company's financial statements provide a fair description of the company's financial condition in accordance with GAAP.

2. **Qualified** - In a qualified opinion the auditor notes exceptions concerning compliance with GAAP, such as accuracy of tax liabilities, asset valuation, or accounting inconsistencies.

3. **Disclaimed** - In a disclaimed opinion, the auditor states that the information management presented was insufficient to render an opinion.

4. **Adverse** - In an adverse opinion, the auditor states categorically that the financial statements do not fairly present the financial condition and/or operations of the company in conformance with GAAP.

Generally, investors and creditors give audited financial statements with an unqualified opinion more credence than those that are somehow qualified. Audited financial statements, qualified or not, are usually considered more reliable than those merely compiled by a CPA or issued by a company itself.

F. Working Capital and Net Working Capital

Working capital refers to the funds in a company's current asset accounts – cash, accounts receivable, and inventory. These are the accounts through which cash flows in a company's cash conversion cycle. Net working capital is equal to current assets minus current liabilities such as accounts payable.

II. FINANCIAL CONCEPTS

There are several key financial concepts that cash managers use on a daily basis.

A. Time Value of Money

The time value of money is a fundamental principle of finance. A dollar today is worth more than a dollar tomorrow because a dollar today can be invested to earn a return. Conversely, a dollar tomorrow is worth less than a dollar today because the opportunity to earn interest is foregone. The value of a cash flow at any point in time can be determined by using an appropriate interest rate and the number of time periods involved.

1. **Future Value** - Future value is the value in the future of a sum of money invested today.

Future Value = Value Today x (1+ Interest Rate)$^{\text{Number of Periods}}$

or

$$FV = PV \times (1+i)^n$$

Where:
    FV = Future Value
    PV = Present Value or Value Today
    i　 = Interest Rate
    n　 = Number of Periods

The future value of $100 for two periods at ten percent, compounded annually, is:

$$\text{Future Value } = \$100 \times (1 + .10)^2 = \$100 \times (1 + .10) \times (1 + .10)$$
$$= \$100 \times (1.210) = \$121$$

2. **Present Value** - Present value is today's value of any sum to be received in the future. Present value can be determined by applying an appropriate discount rate to a future cash flow stream. This concept is useful for comparing alternative transactions with cash flows to be received at a future date, or dates, or to determine how much an investor would be willing to pay for an investment that provides a particular future cash flow stream.

For example, assume a company can make an investment that pays $100 at the end of three years. How much is this future payment worth if the appropriate rate of interest is ten percent? This is determined to be $75.13, as follows:

$$\frac{100}{(1 + .10)^3} = \frac{100}{[(1 + .10) \times (1 + .10) \times (1 + .10)]} = \$75.13$$

This equation can also be expressed in the following algebraic format:

$$PV = \frac{FV}{(1 + i)^n}$$

Where:

PV	=	Present Value
FV	=	Future Value
i	=	Interest Rate
n	=	Number of Periods

---

3. **Net Present Value (NPV)** - Net Present Value (NPV) is a calculation of the value today of cash flows at different points in the future.

   The investment and costs associated with the investment are outflows, while return on and of investment are inflows. If the sum of all discounted cash flows (in and out) is positive, then the project or investment has a positive net present value. If the discounted sum is negative, then the project or investment has a negative net present value. If the company were to invest in a project with a positive net present value, then the overall value of the company would increase by the amount of the project's net present value.

   Using the information from the previous example, if the company were to pay $70 to purchase the investment which paid $100 in three years, it would have a net present value of $5.13, calculated as follows:

NPV = Present Value of Cash Inflows − Present Value of Cash Outflows

$$NPV = \frac{100}{(1.10)^3} - \$70$$

NPV = $75.13 − $70.00 = $5.13

B. Discount Rate/Opportunity Cost

In determining present and future values, the interest rate is generally referred to as the discount rate. The discount rate is also known as the opportunity cost because it represents the return a company would expect to earn on alternative investment opportunities. Companies often use their cost of capital as a discount rate for evaluating their project opportunities. In riskier businesses, companies tend to have higher costs of capital and therefore usually use higher discount rates in evaluating their projects. Evaluating a given project with higher discount rates lowers its net present value because each future cash flow is discounted more deeply.

Companies may use different discount rates for different types of projects. Low-risk, short-term projects may be evaluated using a short-term opportunity cost such as the company's short-term borrowing or the return on its short-term investments. High-risk projects are often evaluated using a "risk-adjusted" discount rate that is greater than the company's normal opportunity cost, which factors in the additional risks these projects carry.

C. Capital Structure and Strategy

1. Debt and Equity

Companies rely on two sources of capital:

- Debt, which can include trade credit, bank loans, and other debt instruments, such as commercial paper, notes, or bonds; and/or

- Equity, which connotes ownership.

Each company must choose its own capital structure, the proportion of debt and equity it uses to finance its activities. The following table summarizes and compares the characteristics of both types of capital.

DEBT VS. EQUITY

	DEBT	EQUITY
TYPES	Trade Credit	Common Stock
	Bank Loans	Preferred Stock
	Other Loans	Convertible Preferred Stock
	Commercial Paper	
	Debentures	
	Notes	
	Bonds	
	Convertible Debt Securities	
ACCOUNTING PRESENTATION	Short-Term and Long-Term Liabilities	Common Stock Additional Paid-In Capital Retained Earnings
CHARACTERISTICS	Legally binding obligation	Ownership
	No voting rights	Voting rights
	Requires repayment of principal and interest	Dividends on common stock are optional
	Interest is tax-deductible	Dividends are paid from after-tax profits
	Loan covenants can be restrictive	All cumulative preferred dividends must be paid before dividends paid on common stock

2. **Capitalizing a Company**

To a great extent, capitalizing a company is a market-driven decision. Smaller and startup companies have limited financing alternatives and often rely on the principals involved to supply equity and debt capital. Larger and more established companies have a greater number of financing alternatives.

Generally, equity is more expensive than debt because dividends, unlike interest, are not tax-deductible. Also, investors and financial institutions demand higher returns for risks perceived as greater, and equity has a subordinate claim to debt on a company's assets.

Other factors that affect a company's debt and equity financing alternatives include: industry practice, a company's financial history, earnings variability, capital intensity, barriers to competitive entry, as well as investor predispositions toward risk and reward as demonstrated in the markets for debt and equity.

Companies have the following incentives to finance with debt:

- The after-tax cost of debt is typically lower than the after-tax cost of equity because interest is tax deductible, and debt is senior to equity in a company liquidation.

- Existing shareholders often prefer it because new stock dilutes the proportion of their holdings and diminishes earnings per share.

However, companies capitalized through common equity tend to be considered more stable, in part because they are not required to make dividend payments.

3. **Leverage**

Leverage is the degree to which a company's use of debt or high fixed costs causes earnings to change more rapidly than revenues.

If a company (or project) is leveraged with high levels of debt or has high fixed costs (which provide operating, as opposed to financial, leverage), an increase in revenues produces a proportionately greater increase in pre-tax earnings than if the company (or project) were not leveraged. Leverage is, however, a two-edged sword. In a leveraged company, a decrease in revenue causes a proportionally greater loss of earnings. If, on the other hand, all costs are variable, and the project or company is predominantly financed through equity, the impact of changes in revenues is less pronounced.

The effect of leverage when revenue increases and decreases is illustrated in the following tables:

10% INCREASE IN REVENUE

LEVERAGED COMPANY

	Year 1	Year 2	% Change
Revenues	$100,000	$110,000	+10%
Fixed Costs	75,000	75,000	0%
Variable Costs	5,000	5,500	+10%
EBIT	20,000	29,500	
Interest	5,000	5,000	
Pre-Tax Earnings	$15,000	$24,500	+63.3%

UNLEVERAGED COMPANY

	Year 1	Year 2	% Change
Revenues	$100,000	$110,000	+10%
Fixed Costs	70,000	70,000	0%
Variable Costs	10,000	11,000	+10%
EBIT	20,000	29,000	
Interest	0	0	
Pre-Tax Earnings	$20,000	$29,000	+45%

10% DECREASE IN REVENUE

LEVERAGED COMPANY

	Year 1	Year 2	% Change
Revenues	$100,000	$90,000	-10%
Fixed Costs	75,000	75,000	0%
Variable Costs	5,000	4,500	-10%
EBIT	20,000	10,500	
Interest	5,000	5,000	
Pre-Tax Earnings	$15,000	$5,500	-63.3%

UNLEVERAGED COMPANY

	Year 1	Year 2	% Change
Revenues	$100,000	$90,000	-10%
Fixed Costs	70,000	70,000	0%
Variable Costs	10,000	9,000	-10%
EBIT	20,000	11,000	
Interest	0	0	
Pre-Tax Earnings	$20,000	$11,000	-45%

D. Cost of Capital

Companies try to minimize their cost of capital, which can be calculated based on the cost of equity and after-tax cost of debt. Many companies consider their Weighted Average Cost of Capital (WACC), as expressed in the formula below, to be an appropriate discount rate for evaluating projects whose risk profiles are consistent with the overall risk profile of the company.

$$\text{WACC} = (\text{After Tax Cost of Debt} \times \% \text{ of Debt}) + (\text{Cost of Equity} \times \% \text{ of Equity})$$

Assume the following:

• A company's long-term capital structure is 40% debt and 60% equity

• The company's average cost of debt is 12%

- The company's marginal tax rate is 34%; therefore, the after-tax cost of debt is 12% x (1 – .34) = 7.92%

- Its cost of equity is 16%

The WACC is calculated as follows:

WACC = (.0792 x .40) + (.16 x .60)
        = .0317 + .0960
        = .1277 = 12.77%

E. Capital Budgeting

Capital budgeting is the process companies use to evaluate alternative long-term investment projects. It uses methods such as net present value calculations and weighs other non-quantitative factors such as the company's core strategy and where it believes its competitive strengths lie. A company may compare the net present values of various projects using the WACC as the discount rate.

A company operating in several industries may use a higher assumed WACC and discount rate for its riskier businesses and a lower WACC for its less risky businesses. It may also evaluate projects by comparing their Internal Rates of Return (IRR). The IRR is the discount rate at which the net present value is equal to zero.

III. LIQUIDITY AND WORKING CAPITAL MEASURES AND RATIOS

Liquidity is the ability to turn assets into cash quickly without incurring loss. Ensuring corporate liquidity on a day-to-day basis is the responsibility of the cash manager. This ongoing task necessitates careful measurement and continual monitoring of net working capital, so that the company has sufficient financial resources to pay upcoming bills and take advantage of investment opportunities that may present themselves unexpectedly.

A. Why Liquidity is Needed

There are three primary reasons a company needs to manage liquidity. These are:

1. **Transactions Requirement** - Because a company's cash flows are unsynchronized, it must hold in reserve cash and near-cash resources to meet financial requirements.

2. **Precautionary Requirement** - Since a company's cash inflows and outflows are unpredictable, it must maintain cash or near-cash balances to meet its expenses.

3. **Speculative Requirement** - Surplus liquid resources allow a company to take advantage of investment opportunities which may arise.

B. Sources of Liquidity

A company's liquidity arises from:

1. Cash flow from operations

2. Available cash and readily marketable short-term investments

3. Unused short-term borrowing capacity

C. Determining the Appropriate Level of Liquidity

Both surplus and insufficient liquidity can affect a company negatively.

1. **Insufficient Liquidity** - The costs associated with not having sufficient liquidity include:

   - **Costs of Delayed Payments** - These include damage to the company's credit standing, foregone cash discounts, and interest charges.

   - **Cost of Lost Opportunities** - This is the opportunity cost of foregoing purchases or investments under advantageous terms and conditions.

   - **Additional Interest Costs** - These are the costs that arise from unanticipated borrowing. They may be significant if interest rates are generally rising, or if the company must pay higher rates due to increased risk or weakened financial condition.

   - **Transaction Costs** - Companies can incur unnecessary brokerage and administrative costs when securities are sold or a line of credit is used to replenish a company's cash balances.

   A company with inadequate liquidity may become insolvent and be forced to seek court protection by filing for bankruptcy. The liquidation that can result is expensive, and the legal fees can be significant. Even if a company is allowed to continue operations, its image may be tarnished to the extent that it loses customers, creditors and shareholder confidence. It will incur higher capital costs as a result. The company will become less able to take advantage of business opportunities.

2. **Excess Liquidity** - Too much liquidity also has disadvantages. The opportunity cost of holding excess cash arises from the loss of earnings because the funds were not invested more profitably.

3. **Proper Levels of Liquidity** - The dollar volume of cash inflows and outflows is a major determinant of the level of liquidity a company needs. Even slight timing differences between cash inflows and outflows can cause a large drain on cash resources. This is particularly true if individual receivables are significant in size. Only a few days' delay in a customer's payment can cause substantial problems. Also, the company's sales may fluctuate from month to month while it incurs expenses at a steady rate. These factors require a company to maintain adequate cash reserves and make it imperative for the cash manager to continually measure, monitor, and forecast liquidity.

D. Working Capital Measures and Ratios

Liquidity is measured using working capital ratios and related calculations. These standardized and widely used formulas allow a company's management to determine adequate liquidity levels, establish liquidity policy and guidelines, and continually monitor liquidity. Banks, other creditors, investors, analysts and ratings agencies use the same working capital and liquidity measures to assess a company's creditworthiness and its short-term financial health. The principal methods of measuring corporate liquidity include the calculations which follow. (The example data in the calculations refer to Exhibits 2.1 and 2.2. All dollar amounts are in thousands.)

1. **Current Ratio** - The current ratio is defined as total current assets divided by total current liabilities. This ratio measures a company's ability to meet its current obligations, or the degree to which current obligations are covered by current assets.

$$\text{Current Ratio} = \frac{\text{Total Current Assets}}{\text{Total Current Liabilities}} = \frac{\$8,000}{\$3,400} = 2.4$$

2. **Quick Ratio** - The quick ratio is defined as cash plus short-term investments and accounts receivable divided by total current liabilities. It is also known as the "acid test" ratio and is considered a more conservative measure of liquidity than the current ratio. The quick ratio measures the degree to which a company's current liabilities are covered by its most liquid current assets. (Note that inventory and prepaid expenses are not included in this ratio because they are the least liquid of the current assets.)

$$\text{Quick Ratio} = \frac{\text{Cash} + \text{S/T Investments} + \text{Acct. Rec.}}{\text{Total Current Liabilities}}$$

$$= \frac{\$1,500 + \$1,300 + \$1,700}{\$3,400} = 1.3$$

3. **Cash Flow to Total Debt Ratio** - Cash flow to total debt is defined as net income plus depreciation divided by total long-term and short-term debt. Short-term debt consists of short-term notes, debentures, commercial paper, or other short-term debt obligations. A relatively low ratio indicates an inability to repay debt. Studies of failed companies have found this ratio to be accurate in predicting financial failure.

$$\text{Cash Flow to Total Debt Ratio} = \frac{\text{Net Income} + \text{Depreciation}}{\text{Short-Term Debt} + \text{Long-Term Debt}}$$

$$= \frac{\$850 + \$200}{\$1,800 + \$3,900} = \frac{\$1,050}{\$5,700} = .18$$

4. **Cash Conversion Cycle** - The cash conversion cycle measures liquidity from another perspective. It calculates the time required for a company to convert cash outflows necessary to produce goods into cash inflows through collection of accounts receivable. By adding the average age of the inventory (measured by days of inventory), and average days of accounts receivable (measured by days of receivables), and subtracting the average age of the accounts payable (measured by days of payables), it measures how efficiently a company is using its current assets and liabilities.

$$\text{Days' Inventory} = \frac{\text{Inventory}}{\text{Cost of Goods Sold}} \times 365 = \frac{\$2,600}{\$9,200} \times 365 = 103.2 \text{ Days}$$

$$\text{Days' Receivables} = \frac{\text{Accounts Receivable}}{\text{Annual Sales}} \times 365 = \frac{\$1,700}{\$15,000} \times 365 = 41.4 \text{ Days}$$

$$\text{Days' Payables} = \frac{\text{Account Payable}}{\text{Cost of Goods Sold}} \times 365 = \frac{\$1,600}{\$9,200} \times 365 = 63.5 \text{ Days}$$

Cash Conversion Cycle = Days' Inventory + Days' Receivables - Days' Payables

= 103.2 Days + 41.4 Days - 63.5 Days = 81.1 Days

In this example, the company has cash invested in its operating cycle an average of 81.1 days.

5. **Cash Turnover** - Cash turnover is the number of cash conversion cycles through which a company goes in a year.

$$\text{Cash Turnover} = \frac{365}{\text{Cash Conversion Cycle}} = \frac{365}{81.1} = 4.5 \text{ Times}$$

The cash conversion cycle and cash turnover are measures of efficiency that can be used to compare companies in the same or similar industries.

IV. DEBT MANAGEMENT AND COVERAGE RATIOS

Apart from liquidity ratios, there are other standard and widely-used financial ratios that are used to determine a company's creditworthiness and debt coverage. No single ratio provides a complete picture of a company's financial soundness or operational efficiency, but groups of ratios considered together can reveal a great deal. Analysis of key ratios is also an integral part of the evaluation of a company by rating agencies, such as Standard and Poor's, or Moody's. Rating agencies may use their own unique calculations to measure the ability of a company to meet interest payments and the overall efficiency with which it uses debt. However, most of the formulas they use are variants of the following calculations.

A. Times Interest Earned (TIE)

This is a coverage ratio which indicates how many times a company's earnings before interest and taxes (EBIT) exceed its interest obligations. The higher this ratio, the greater the ability of the company to pay off debt.

$$\text{TIE} = \frac{\text{Operating Profit}}{\text{Interest Expense}} = \frac{\$1,600}{\$300} = 5.3 \text{ Times}$$

B. Long-Term Debt to Capital

This ratio measures the percentage of long-term debt relative to all of the long-term capital used in the company's capital structure. Long-term debt includes long-term notes and bonds, term loans, and capitalized lease obligations. Equity capital includes all preferred and common equity accounts. The higher this ratio, the greater the proportion of debt a company is using in its long-term capital structure, and the greater the extent to which it is leveraged.

$$\text{LT Debt to Capital} = \frac{\text{Long-Term Debt}}{\text{Long-Term Debt + Equity}} = \frac{\$3,900}{\$3,900 + \$8,200} = 32.2\%$$

C. Debt to Tangible Net Worth

This ratio measures a company's debt as a percentage of its tangible net worth, its total equity minus intangibles such as goodwill, patents, trademarks, etc.

$$\text{Debt to Tangible Net Worth} = \frac{\text{Total Debt}}{(\text{Total Equity} - \text{Intangible Assets})}$$

$$\frac{\$1,800 + \$3,900}{\$8,200 - \$0} = 69.5\%$$

D. Total Liabilities to Total Assets

This ratio measures the percentage of all liabilities relative to the total asset base of the company. The higher this ratio, the more liabilities (as opposed to equity) the company uses to finance its asset base.

$$\text{Total Liabilities to Total Assets} = \frac{\text{Total Liabilities}}{\text{Total Assets}} = \frac{\$7,300}{\$15,500} = 47.1\%$$

V. PERFORMANCE MEASUREMENTS

These ratios measure the ability of a company to generate profits on sales or returns on assets and capital. Income statement amounts are annualized in the calculation of these ratios.

A. Return on Common Equity

This ratio measures the earnings available to common shareholders (net income less any preferred stock dividends or amortization), expressed as a percentage of the common equity. In this example, where the company has no preferred stock, the earnings available to common shareholders is equal to net income. The higher this ratio, the greater the return to the common shareholders of the company.

$$\text{Return on Equity} = \frac{\text{Earnings Available to Common Shareholders}}{\text{Common Equity}}$$

$$= \frac{\$850}{\$8,200} = 10.4\%$$

B. Return on Sales

This ratio measures the net income of a company as a percentage of its sales. The higher this ratio, the more after-tax profits the company generates on a given sales level.

$$\text{Return on Sales} = \frac{\text{Net Income}}{\text{Revenues}} = \frac{\$850}{\$15,000} = 5.7\%$$

C. Return on Total Assets

This ratio measures the net income of a company as a percentage of its total assets. The higher this ratio, the more after-tax profits the company is generating from its asset base.

$$\text{Return on Total Assets} = \frac{\text{Net Income}}{\text{Total Assets}} = \frac{\$850}{\$15,500} = 5.5\%$$

D. Other Financial and Performance Measurement Concepts

Other financial and performance measurement concepts include:

1. **Economic Value Added** - This is a measure of the incremental value that a company's investments add in terms of their impact on market capitalization. Put simply, it is after-tax operating profit minus an appropriate charge for the opportunity cost of all capital.

    EVA = Operating Profit x (1-Tax Rate) - (WACC x Total Capital)
    EVA = $1,600 x (1-0.35) - (0.1277 x $12,100) = ($505)

2. **Cash Conversion Efficiency** - This calculation measures the efficiency with which a company converts sales into cash. It is calculated by dividing cash flow from operations by sales.

    Cash Conversion Efficiency = Cash Flow From Operations/Sales

    $$\text{Cash Conversion Efficiency} = \frac{\$550}{\$15,000} = 0.037 = 3.7\%$$

3. **Working Capital Turnover** - This ratio measures how many times per year a company converts its working capital into sales. It establishes a relationship for the amount of working capital used to support a given level of sales.

    $$\text{Working Capital Turnover} = \frac{\text{Sales}}{\text{Net Working Capital}} = \frac{\$15,000}{\$8,000 - \$3,400} = 3.3 \text{ Times}$$

While financial ratios and performance measurement calculations reveal a great deal about a company's financial and operating condition, they do have certain limitations. The following table summarizes their advantages and disadvantages.

USE OF FINANCIAL RATIOS AND PERFORMANCE MEASUREMENTS

ADVANTAGES	DISADVANTAGES
Easily computed	Summarize accounting information and do not reflect economic value
Widely-used	Express static not dynamic relationships
Information easily obtained	Cannot reflect qualitative value (managerial talent, intangibles)
Allow assessment of historical performance	Often miss variability of cash flows and are not necessarily indicative of future performance
Allow for comparison between companies	Use of different accounting methods can distort calculations and comparisons

Questions

These chapter questions are to test and review the information in the text and are not examples of CCM examination questions, nor are they in the examination format.

Answers can be found at the back of the book on pgs. 362-363.

1. What is GAAP?

2. What methods can a company use in its reporting of a negative cash balance?

3. What are the three basic financial statements?

4. What is the present value of $1,500 two years from now if the opportunity cost is 5 percent?

5. What are the primary incentives for a company to finance its capital structure with debt?

6. What are the three primary reasons a company needs liquidity?

7. What are the common ratios used to measure working capital?

8. What is the cash conversion cycle?

9. What are the disadvantages of using financial ratios?

10. What is the difference between cash and accrual accounting?

11. What are four types of opinions that an auditor can render for financial statements?

12. What is the impact of leverage on financial results?

CHAPTER 3

The U.S. Financial Environment

OVERVIEW

This chapter describes the role of the various types of financial institutions in the U.S., the agencies that supervise them, and the legislation and regulations that impact the treasury function.

LEARNING OBJECTIVES

Upon completion of this chapter and the related study questions, the reader should understand:

1. The principal functions of commercial banks, investment banking firms, thrifts, and other institutions

2. The functions and structure of the following regulatory agencies: the Federal Reserve System, the Office of the Comptroller of the Currency, the Office of Thrift Supervision, the Federal Deposit Insurance Corporation, the Federal Financial Institutions Examination Council, the Securities and Exchange Commission, the Department of Justice, and state banking boards and commissions

3. How the banking system evolved through significant legislative, regulatory, legal, and market developments

4. How key Federal Reserve regulations affect a cash manager

5. How the Uniform Commercial Code affects a cash manager

KEY CONCEPTS

1. Structure and Dynamics of the U.S. Financial System

2. Regulatory Institutional Framework

3. Role of the Federal Reserve

4. Evolution of the U.S. Financial System

OUTLINE

I. INTRODUCTION

To protect against a concentration of economic and political power, U.S. regulators have historically made it difficult for banks and financial institutions to consolidate and/or acquire major equity positions in industrial enterprises. The legal and regulatory framework has encouraged institutional segmentation. As a result, different entities tend to serve different functions: commercial lending and deposit taking, mortgage provision, insurance sales, and securities underwriting. This makes the U.S. financial system distinct from its counterparts in other developed countries, where financial institutions are less segmented and in many cases may own equity in industrial enterprises.

The current regulatory environment is fostering a liberalization of these restrictions and the continued consolidation of the financial services industry.

II. FINANCIAL INSTITUTIONS: FUNCTIONS AND SERVICES

This section discusses the functions of commercial banks and other types of financial institutions as well as the services they offer.

A. Commercial Banks

Defined by law as a financial institution that accepts deposits and makes business loans, a commercial bank offers a wide range of products and services. The term commercial bank is used to describe everything from small, single facility community banks with a few million dollars in assets to large, global institutions with numerous locations and billions in assets.

Most large banks are owned by bank holding companies, which may also own limited purpose non-banking subsidiaries. Commercial banks, their holding companies, and non-bank subsidiaries provide a wide range of products and services as detailed below.

1. **Deposit Accounts** - An important function of a commercial bank is to serve as a depository for cash. There are two basic types of depository accounts, – demand deposit accounts and time deposit accounts. There are also interest-bearing accounts that combine the features of demand and time deposits.

    • **Demand Deposit Accounts (DDAs)** - Commonly referred to as checking accounts, DDAs are a method by which an account holder uses a financial institution to transfer funds to a third party. The method of payment can be by check, wire transfer, or Automated Clearing House (ACH) transfer. Present law prohibits payment of interest on demand deposits held by businesses. The three exceptions to this regulation are sole proprietorships, government entities, and not-for-profit organizations. This regulation is currently under review. Balances are held in DDAs for the following purposes:

      ♦ **Transaction Balances** - Deposits held by companies as part of collection and disbursement activity.
      ♦ **Compensating Balances** - Deposits held by companies in the form of collected balances which are used to pay for bank services.
      ♦ **Correspondent Balances** - Balances from other banks held to facilitate check clearing, securities settlement, negotiation of letters of credit, and other transactions.

- **Time Deposits** - Time deposits must be held at a bank, thrift, or credit union for a specified period. Examples of time deposits include:

  - **Certificates of Deposit (CDs)** - CDs are negotiable or non-negotiable obligations of a bank offered at either fixed or variable interest rates. Jumbo CDs are deposits of $100,000 or more; they are sold to individuals and companies. Maturities may range from seven days to several years.

  - **Negotiable CDs** - Generally sold in $1 million blocks to companies, money market funds, and other large investors. Being negotiable, they can be sold to another investor prior to maturity. Maturities generally range from 14 days to five years, but most have maturities of 12 months or less.

  - **Retail CDs** - Non-negotiable CDs sold to individual investors in amounts that vary from institution to institution. Maturities generally range from three months to five years.

  - **Savings Accounts or Passbook Savings Accounts** - Accounts that pay interest on balances. They are mainly held by individuals and not-for-profit institutions, but companies may also hold them.

- **Other Interest-Bearing Accounts** - Accounts that have some of the features of both demand and time deposits. Among examples are the following:

  - **Money Market Deposit Accounts** - Accounts that pay an unregulated rate of interest determined by the bank and allow limited check-writing and electronic withdrawals. They are available to all types of businesses and individuals.

  - **Negotiable Order of Withdrawal (NOW) Accounts** - Accounts that offer unrestricted check writing and pay unregulated rates of interest. NOW accounts are limited to individuals, sole proprietorships, not-for-profit organizations, and governmental entities.

2. **Credit Services** - Banks provide loans to companies of all sizes, to not-for profit organizations, and to individuals. The following are examples of credit services:

- **Short-Term Loans** - Loans designed primarily for working capital purposes such as temporary or seasonal increases in inventory or accounts receivable. Short-term loans are expected to be repaid from conversion of the current assets they finance. Short-term borrowing is often under a line of credit which allows a company to borrow up to a specified amount, repay, and borrow again at any time. (See Chapter 13, Borrowing.)

- **Long-Term Loans** - Loans designed primarily for capital improvements such as plant and equipment. The source of repayment is generally expected to be earnings from the project being financed.

- **Leasing** - Leases provide an alternative to long-term loans for financing capital equipment. (See Chapter 13, Borrowing.)

- **Mortgages** - Commercial banks provide mortgage financing for commercial and residential real estate.

3. **Investment Banking Services** - Investment banking services offered by commercial banks include the following:

   • **Commercial Paper (CP)** - Commercial paper consists of unsecured, short-term promissory notes issued by companies. Banks act as agents to place the commercial paper of their customers with investors. Commercial bank holding companies also issue commercial paper. (See Chapter 12, Short-Term Investments, and Chapter 13, Borrowing.)

   • **Loan Sales** - Banks structure lending facilities so that short-term loans can be sold to other banks and investors.

   • **Private Placements** - Banks work with their customers to place long-term loans with institutional investors such as insurance companies.

   • **Corporate Bonds and Equities** - Some banks underwrite corporate bonds and equities through investment and brokerage subsidiaries.

4. **Payment and Collection Services** - Banks assist companies by acting as clearing agents for checks, and by originating and receiving wire transfers and ACH transactions. (See Chapter 4, The Payments System, and Chapter 6, Collections.)

5. **Trade Services** - Banks provide the following services to facilitate payment of trade obligations, particularly with foreign trading partners (see Chapter 15, International Cash Management):

   • **Trade or Commercial Letters of Credit (L/Cs)** - L/Cs are documents issued by a bank, guaranteeing the payment of a customer's draft up to a stated amount for a specified period provided certain conditions are met. In effect, the issuing bank substitutes its name and credit on behalf of its customer.

   • **Letters of Credit Confirmations** - L/C confirmations are issued by a bank at the request of a customer when that customer is unsure of the status of the original issuing bank. In such instances, another bank may confirm (guarantee) performance under the original L/C. In the event of default, the confirming bank is responsible for the payment.

   • **Documentary Collections** - A documentary collection is a payment method that processes the collection of a draft and accompanying shipping documents through international correspondent banks. Instructions regarding the specifics of the transaction are contained in a collection letter or form that accompanies the documentation. It is the responsibility of the seller (exporter) to determine the specific instructions to be used in the collection letter.

   • **Banker's Acceptances (BAs)** - A BA is a negotiable short-term instrument used primarily to finance the import, export, or domestic shipment of goods, or the storage of readily marketable staples.

6. **Credit Enhancement or Payment Guaranty** - Banks may issue standby L/Cs on behalf of their customers to ensure payment of the customers' obligations to third parties.

7. **Agent or Fiduciary Services** - An agent is a bank or trust institution that manages assets whose title remains with the owner. A fiduciary is an individual or institution to whom certain property is given to hold in trust according to a trust agreement. Among examples of agent or fiduciary services are the following:

   - **Trust Services** - Banks invest, manage, and distribute monies as instructed in wills, trusts, and estates.

   - **Investment Management** - Banks manage portfolios of investments for their customers.

   - **Corporate Pension Plans** - Banks act as agents for corporations in establishing and managing employee pension programs.

   - **Qualified Employee Benefit Plans** - Banks act as agents for qualified employee benefit plans.

   - **Corporate Trustee** - Banks, as trustees for a corporate bond or preferred stock issues, monitor compliance with indenture agreements. These are formal agreements between an issuer of bonds and a bondholder.

   - **Transfer Agent** - Banks serve as transfer agents by keeping records of the sale and purchase of stocks and bonds, and maintaining records of the shareholders of a corporation by name, address, and number of shares.

   - **Registrar** - Banks serve as registrars by maintaining lists of current stockholders and bondholders for the purpose of remitting dividend and interest payments.

   - **Paying Agent** - Banks receive funds from an issuer of stocks or bonds to pay dividends to stockholders and principal and interest to bondholders.

   - **Custody Services** - Banks provide safekeeping for securities. Under a custody agreement, a bank buys, sells, receives, and delivers securities at the customer's request.

8. **Consulting Services** - Banks provide consulting services for corporate customers in areas such as cash management, mergers and acquisitions, and corporate financial structure.

9. **Risk Management Services** - Fluctuations in exchange rates, interest rates, or prices of commodities can adversely impact a company's financial performance. For example, currency movements against the U.S. dollar can impact the profitability of a company that operates in international markets. To limit these risks, banks and other financial institutions offer a variety of products such as swaps, forwards, futures, and options. These instruments are known as derivatives because their value is derived from, or based on, underlying assets. (See Chapter 14, Financial Risk Management.)

10. **Broker/Dealer Services** - Banks act as brokers and dealers for certain permissible investment securities and foreign currencies, and trade for their own account as an extension of that role.

B. Investment Banking and Brokerage Firms

Investment banking and brokerage firms provide a wide range of services. Not every firm is a full service provider. Certain firms specialize more in investment banking, others more in brokerage; certain firms deal principally with institutional customers, others with retail customers.

1. **Stock and Bond Underwriting** - Underwriting is the principal function of investment banking. When an investment banking firm underwrites a stock or bond offering, it assures the issuer of a definite sum of money for the issue at a definite time. In purchasing the entire issue from the issuer, the underwriter assumes the risk of price and marketability. The investment banker's intermediation function is often described as having two components – origination and distribution. Underwriting is the origination function, and selling the securities to investors is the distribution function.

2. **Commercial Paper** - Investment bankers have traditionally acted as underwriters and dealers for commercial paper.

3. **Institutional and Retail Brokerage** - Brokerage services involve the sale of securities to institutional and retail customers. It is the distribution side of the investment banker's intermediation function.

4. **Investment Research** - Investment banking firms have research analysts who are industry specialists and who give advice to large institutions as well as individual investors.

5. **Investment Advisory and Portfolio Management** - Similar to commercial banks, investment banking firms provide investment advice and manage investment portfolios for large institutions and individuals.

6. **Risk Management** - Investment banking firms offer derivative products such as interest rate and currency swaps, forwards, options, and futures. They also offer foreign exchange services.

C. Thrift Institutions

Thrift institutions have traditionally been depositories that accept consumer deposits and lend money, primarily in the form of home mortgage loans. The Depository Institutions Deregulation and Monetary Control Act of 1980 (DIDMCA) provided for a phase-out of interest rate ceilings for thrift institutions and commercial banks, and allowed savings institutions to make commercial as well as consumer loans. There are two types of thrift institutions:

1. **Savings and Loan Associations** - Savings and Loans (S&Ls) are federally or state chartered and owned by either shareholders or depositors. Their deposits are federally insured by the Federal Deposit Insurance Corporation (FDIC), a regulatory agency described in detail in Section III.

2. **Savings Banks or Mutual Savings Banks** - Historically, savings banks and mutual savings banks have been state chartered and owned by depositors, but the Garn-St. Germain Depository Institutions Act of 1982 allowed them to switch to a federal charter and to convert to stock ownership.

D. Credit Unions

Credit unions are not-for-profit financial corporations chartered by federal or state agencies. Membership in a credit union is restricted to people with a common bond such as an employer, association, or community organization. Credit unions can provide retail financial services similar to those offered by other types of financial institutions. Members/owners often enjoy higher savings and lower lending rates. Deposits in most credit unions are insured by the National Credit Union Share Insurance Fund (NCUSIF).

E. Mutual Funds

Mutual fund providers sell shares to investors, offering these investors diversification and professional portfolio management. These providers include brokerage firms, banks, and investment companies. Shares may be redeemed through the provider which insures liquidity. Share values fluctuate with the performance of the fund, and mutual fund shares are not insured against losses as deposits are. Money market mutual funds invest in short-term securities such as Treasury bills, certificates of deposit, and commercial paper.

F. Other Financial Institutions

A variety of other financial institutions specialize in certain types of lending:

1. **Industrial Credit and Capital Companies** - Subsidiaries of large industrial corporations raise funds in the commercial paper market and lend to companies and individuals. A captive finance company typically finances the purchase of its own company's products.

2. **Factors** - Factors provide short-term financing to companies by purchasing their accounts receivable at a discount. They may assume the responsibility and the risk for collecting them. (See Chapter 5, Credit and Accounts Receivable Management.)

3. **Insurance Companies** - Insurance companies are primarily long-term lenders to companies. Insurance companies have started to compete with banks for short-term and medium-term loans. They also provide leasing services, guaranteed investment contracts, and universal life insurance policies with long-term savings features.

4. **Consumer Finance Companies** - Consumer finance companies extend credit to individuals and businesses.

III. REGULATORY AGENCIES

The United States has a dual banking system of federally and state chartered banks. At the federal level, bank supervision is shared primarily by three agencies: the Board of Governors of the Federal Reserve System, the FDIC, and the Office of the Comptroller of the Currency (OCC). The Securities and Exchange Commission (SEC), and the Department of Justice have regulatory roles as well. At the state level, banks are regulated by state banking boards and commissions.

A. Federal Reserve System (Fed)

The Fed is an independent agency of the U.S. government. The following is a description of the roles and structure of the Fed:

1. **Organization** - The Fed has three components: the Board of Governors, the Federal Open Market Committee, and the 12 Federal Reserve banks and their branches.

   - **Board of Governors** - Each of the seven members is appointed to a 14-year term by the President of the United States and confirmed by the Senate. Primary functions include formulation of credit and monetary policy, as well as supervision of the Federal Reserve banks, state-chartered member banks, and bank holding companies. The President appoints one governor as chairman and another as vice chairman; each serves a four-year term and may be reappointed.

     The Board is advised by the following committees:

     - **Federal Advisory Council** - Consists of 12 members, one member – traditionally a commercial banker – from each Federal Reserve District.

     - **Consumer Advisory Council** - Members represent the interests of consumers.

     - **Thrift Institutions Advisory Council** - Members represent the interests of savings and loan associations, mutual savings banks, and credit unions.

   - **Federal Open Market Committee (FOMC)** - The FOMC implements monetary policy, principally by conducting open market operations. There are 12 committee members, including seven members of the Board of Governors, the president of the Federal Reserve Bank of New York, and presidents of four other Federal Reserve banks. They serve on a rotating basis.

   - **Federal Reserve District Banks** - There are 12 Federal Reserve districts with one Federal Reserve bank serving each district. The 12 reserve banks have 25 branches. Additionally, there are Regional Check Processing Centers (RCPCs). Commercial banks in the region hold the stock of the Federal Reserve banks and are represented on their boards, but do not maintain control the way stockholders normally do. The Board of Governors appoints some members of each Reserve Bank's board as well as its chairman. A map illustrating the Fed is shown in Exhibit 3.1.

EXHIBIT 3.1
Federal Reserve Check Processing Regions

Courtesy of the Federal Reserve

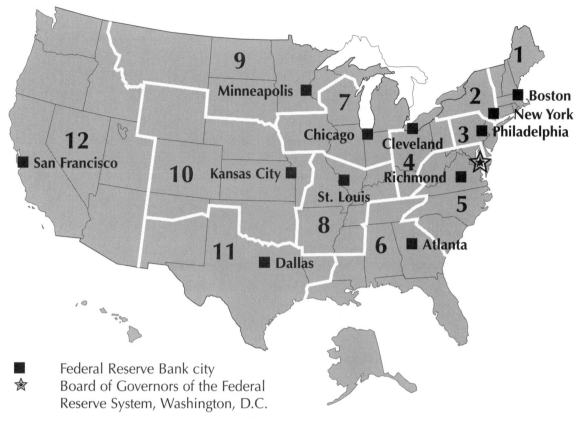

■ Federal Reserve Bank city
☆ Board of Governors of the Federal Reserve System, Washington, D.C.

2. **Roles** - The Fed has five principal roles: It acts as a supervisor and regulator of certain financial institutions, as the manager of U.S. monetary policy, as a wholesaler of banking services, as the fiscal agent of the U.S. Treasury, and as a consumer protection agency for financial services.

- **Supervision and Regulation** - The Fed has primary responsibility for supervising and regulating several types of banking organizations:

  ◆ All bank holding companies, their non-bank subsidiaries, and their foreign subsidiaries

  ◆ State-chartered banks that are members of the Federal Reserve System (state member banks) and their foreign branches and subsidiaries

  ◆ Edge Act and agreement corporations, through which U.S. banking organizations conduct operations abroad

- **Monetary Policy** - The Federal Reserve Act directs the Fed to conduct monetary policy in such a way as to maximize employment, promote price stability, and maintain moderate long-term interest rates. The Federal Reserve's monetary policies influence the demand for or supply of reserves at banks and other depository institutions. The effects of monetary policy are transmitted to the rest of the economy through the reserves market. The Board implements monetary policy primarily through open market activities. The FOMC oversees open market operations to influence money market conditions and the growth of money and credit.

- **Banking Services** - For a commercial bank, the Fed is both a regulator and a provider of services. It also oversees the payments system in the following ways:

  - ◆ **Check Clearing** - The Fed receives check deposits from depository institutions and then clears checks back to the drawee banks.

  - ◆ **Wire Transfers** - The Fed operates Fedwire, the domestic large-dollar, same-day electronic transfer system.

  - ◆ **Automated Clearing House (ACH) System** - The Fed is the main operator of the ACH, which processes and settles electronic payments in a batch mode.

- **Fiscal Agency** - The Reserve Banks and their branches function as the banker for the federal government. They maintain the Treasury Department's checking accounts, clear Treasury checks drawn against them, accept payments for federal taxes on behalf of the Internal Revenue Service (IRS), and act as fiscal agent for the Treasury Department to issue, redeem, and transfer ownership of government securities.

- **Consumer Protection Agency** - The Fed also issues regulations to carry out major federal laws governing consumer credit protection, such as Truth in Lending, Equal Credit Opportunity, and Home Mortgage Disclosure. Many of these regulations also apply to various lenders outside the banking industry.

B. Office of the Comptroller of the Currency (OCC)

The OCC grants charters to, regulates, supervises, and examines national banks. It monitors bank performance and issues supervisory agreements.

C. The Office of Thrift Supervision (OTS)

The OTS serves the same functions for S&Ls as the OCC does for national banks.

D. Federal Deposit Insurance Corporation (FDIC)

The primary role of the FDIC is to protect depositors from losses caused by bank insolvency.

1. **Deposit Insurance** - The FDIC insures deposits up to $100,000 per personal or corporate depositor per institution in all federally chartered banks and most state banks. The deposit insurance premium rate charged banks is set by the FDIC on the basis of a bank's risk profile.

2. **Supervision** - The FDIC supervises, examines, and regulates insured state-chartered banks that are not Federal Reserve members.

3. **Role in Bank Failures** - One of the FDIC's most important roles is in determining the course of action in the event of bank failure. The FDIC is usually appointed receiver of failed insured institutions. The agency is charged with finding a merger partner or liquidating the bank's remaining assets and paying insured depositors.

E. The Federal Financial Institution Examination Council (FFIEC)

The FFIEC coordinates the activities of the Fed, the OCC, the FDIC, and the OTS to assure consistency in the implementation of regulatory policy.

F. Securities and Exchange Commission (SEC)

The SEC is a federal agency which regulates and supervises the sale of securities to maintain a fair and orderly market for investors. Among its responsibilities are the following:

- Registering public offerings of debt or equity securities by banks or bank holding companies as well as all other corporations

- Setting financial disclosure standards for corporations that sell securities to the public

- Requiring filing of quarterly and annual financial statements by companies with publicly owned securities

- Regulating mutual funds and investment advisors

G. Department of Justice

The Department of Justice, as well as the Fed, reviews and approves proposed bank mergers and holding company acquisitions to determine their effect on competition as part of overall antitrust supervisory responsibility.

H. State Banking Boards and Commissions

Under the dual nature of the U.S. banking system, each state has its own banking board and commission. Among the responsibilities of these state agencies are the following:

- Issuing charters for new state banks

- Supervising and examining all state-chartered banks

- Reserving the right to approve all applications of banks operating within state borders to form holding companies, to acquire affiliates or subsidiaries, or to establish branch offices

- Reserving the right to impose liquidity requirements and minimum equity capital requirements on state-chartered banks

IV. FEDERAL LEGISLATION

The following is a summary of the key provisions of selected bank legislation that demonstrates how the U.S. banking system evolved into its current form:

A. Federal Reserve Act (1913)

- Provided the foundation for the current banking system

- Granted the Fed supervisory power over member banks (chartered national banks were required to become members and to comply with reserve requirements)

- Empowered the Fed to create a check collection and settlement system through member banks

B. Edge Act (1918)

- Permitted U.S. banks to invest in corporations that engage in international banking and finance

- Permitted the establishment of subsidiaries to conduct international banking business such as import and export financing, foreign exchange, letters of credit, and documentary collections in other cities in the U.S. and overseas

C. McFadden Act (1927)

- Established the state boundary as the primary limit for bank expansion by prohibiting banks from accepting deposits across state lines

- Prohibited branching across state lines unless approved by state governments, thereby relegating to the states the power to decide the extent of bank branching within and outside state borders

The following are two more recent legislative actions that have modified the McFadden Act:

- The Douglas Amendment (1956) - Allowed banks to merge across state lines if each state permitted it, but did not allow bank holding companies to acquire banks across state lines. (Legislation enacted by individual states has allowed bank holding companies to acquire banks and bank holding companies in states both within and outside their regions.)

- The Interstate Banking and Branching Efficiency Act (1994) - Phased out, over a three year period, the state barriers against branching established by the McFadden Act. (Full interstate branching was achieved in June 1997, except for Texas and Montana.)

D. The Glass-Steagall Act (also known as the Banking Act of 1933)

- Prohibited commercial banks from securities underwriting except for government issues

- Prohibited securities firms from engaging in bank-like activities such as deposit gathering

- Required the Fed to establish interest-rate ceilings on all types of accounts and prohibited the payment of interest on demand deposits. Provisions of this Act are incorporated in Federal Reserve Regulation Q.

- Created the FDIC to guarantee deposits up to a stipulated maximum amount

E. The Securities Laws of 1933, 1934 and 1940

- These laws established the SEC and govern the issuance of securities.

F. Electronic Funds Transfer Act (EFTA) (1978)

- Defined the rights and responsibilities of individuals using EFT services except for wire transfers

- Limited customer liability for unauthorized banking transactions involving automated teller machines (ATMs) and point of sale (POS) terminals, provided the customer promptly notifies the bank or other institution that issued the card

- Provisions of this act are incorporated in Federal Reserve Regulation E

G. Depository Institutions Deregulation and Monetary Control Act (DIDMCA) (1980)

- Required all deposit-taking institutions to maintain reserves at the Fed

- Made Fed services such as the discount window and check clearing available to all deposit-taking institutions

- Mandated the Fed to reduce and/or price payment system float

- Priced previously free Fed services according to the standards of a tax-paying vendor

- Provided for phasing out of Regulation Q interest rate ceilings

- Permitted banks to offer NOW accounts, check writing accounts with an unregulated interest rate for individuals, not-for-profit organizations, and government entities

H. Garn-St. Germain Depository Institutions Act (1982)

- Extended the legal lending limit of banks to 15 percent of capital and surplus for unsecured loans and 25 percent for secured loans

- Allowed the FDIC to arrange mergers of banks across state lines when suitable intrastate partners could not be found

- Allowed banks to offer accounts to compete with money market mutual funds

I. Expedited Funds Availability Act (1988)

- Defined funds withdrawal time periods for deposited checks and payable through drafts

- Established return procedures for payable through drafts and checks

- Provisions of this act are incorporated in Federal Reserve Regulation CC

J. Financial Institutions Reform, Recovery and Enforcement Act (FIRREA) (1989)

- Consolidated the Federal Savings and Loan Insurance Corporation (FSLIC) resources under the FDIC

- Dismantled the Federal Home Loan Bank Board (FHLBB) and established the Office of Thrift Supervision (OTS) to assume the FHLBB's supervisory responsibilities

- Established the Resolution Trust Corporation (RTC) to make timely disposal of assets of failed S&Ls. (The RTC is no longer in existence.)

- Gave the FDIC increased flexibility to raise deposit insurance premiums charged to banks and savings and loan associations

K. Federal Deposit Insurance Corporation Improvement Act (FDICIA) (1991)

- Established numerous higher standards for financial institution safety and soundness in the wake of several bank failures during the late 1980s

- Mandated the FDIC to declare insolvent any bank or thrift that failed to maintain equity capital equal to two percent of its assets

- Required the FDIC to change its deposit insurance premiums from a flat fee basis to a risk-adjusted basis

L. Interstate Banking and Branching Efficiency Act (IBBEA) (1994)

- Permitted bank holding companies to acquire a bank located in any state effective September 1995

- Allowed banks in one state to merge with banks in another state beginning June 1997, so long as neither state took legislative action to prohibit interstate mergers between the date of enactment and May 1997

- Allowed banks to establish new branches in states where they do not maintain a branch if the host state passes a law expressly permitting such branches

V. FEDERAL RESERVE REGULATIONS

After banking legislation is passed by Congress, the law is implemented through rules and regulations imposed by the regulatory agencies. The following are examples of banking regulations affecting cash managers which are promulgated by the Federal Reserve:

A. Regulation D

Imposes uniform reserve requirements on all depository institutions with different levels of reserves for different types of deposits. The Fed can use this regulation in controlling the supply of money.

B. Regulation E

Establishes the rights, liabilities, and responsibilities of parties to consumer-related electronic funds transfers (EFT) and protects consumers using EFT systems, such as those involved in ATM, ACH, and credit card transactions. Reg E also establishes the guidelines for documentation of electronic transfers.

C. Regulation J

Establishes procedures, duties, and responsibilities for check collection and settlement through the Federal Reserve System.

D. Regulation Q

Prohibits depository institutions from paying interest on corporate demand deposit accounts. Prior interest rate ceilings on all other deposit accounts were phased out in 1986 by the DIDMCA.

E. Regulation CC

* Establishes rules designed to speed the collection and return of checks and imposes a responsibility on banks to return unpaid checks expeditiously.

* Establishes endorsement standards for banks and companies to follow in depositing and clearing checks.

* Imposes the same return procedures that apply to checks to payable-through-drafts.

VI. THE UNIFORM COMMERCIAL CODE (UCC)

The UCC is a uniform set of laws governing commercial transactions enacted separately and sometimes in different forms by each state. The UCC defines the rights and duties of the parties in a commercial transaction and provides a statutory definition of commonly used business practices. The four articles most relevant to a cash manager are as follows:

A. Article 3 - Negotiable Instruments

Among the provisions of Article 3 are the following:

1. **Negotiable Instruments** - Article 3 defines a negotiable instrument and the forms it may take, including a draft, a check, a certificate of deposit, and a note.

2. **Accord and Satisfaction** - Originally, this section was drafted to permit a check to constitute a payment made in full (accord and satisfaction) when a message to that effect was written on the face of the check and the check was deposited. However, this allowed for the possibility of inadvertent accord and satisfaction when the

customer wrote "paid in full" on a check for a disputed claim--especially if the check was collected through a lockbox. The revised section permits avoidance of inadvertent accord and satisfaction if the payee discovers the error and returns the payment to the payor within 90 days.

3.   **Unauthorized Signatures** - A bank's failure to examine a forged drawer's signature is not failure to exercise ordinary care to the extent that such failure does not violate the bank's procedures and that these procedures do not unreasonably vary from general banking practices. At the same time, a bank can only charge a customer's account for checks which are properly payable, and an unauthorized signature does not pass this test. However, a company may be held liable if it does not exercise ordinary care related to check issuance and does not notify the bank of multiple forgeries by the same wrongdoer in a timely manner.

B. Article 4 - Bank Deposits and Collections

Among the provisions of Article 4 are the following:

1.   **Bank Parties** - Article 4 defines the various bank parties to the deposit and collection process and their respective rights and duties.

2.   **Relationship Between Payor Bank and Customer** - Article 4 defines the following:

   • When a bank may charge a customer's account.

   • Bank's liability to a customer for failing to honor a good check.

   • Customer's right to stop payment.

   • Bank's option not to pay an item more than six months old (stale date).

   • Customer's duty to report an unauthorized signature or alteration.

3.   **Company Obligations** - A company has the duty to examine bank statements within a reasonable time, not to exceed 30 days after the statement has been sent, and to report to the bank any unauthorized signatures or alterations. This, coupled with the Ordinary Care provision of UCC3, makes it imperative that companies reconcile their accounts on a timely basis.

C. Article 4A - Funds Transfers

Article 4A provides a legal framework that outlines the risks, rights, and obligations of parties in connection with funds transfers through Fedwire, the Clearing House Interbank Payments System (CHIPS), and the ACH. Among the provisions of Article 4A are the following:

1.   **Security Procedures** - The bank must make security procedures for verifying payment orders available to the customer, and the bank and the customer must agree that those procedures are commercially reasonable. Some common security measures include the use of Personal Identification Numbers (PINs), callbacks, encryption, and message authentication.

2. **Consequential Damages** - Banks are not responsible for consequential damages, which are losses resulting from the action or error made by the bank beyond the simple loss of funds. A bank incorrectly executing a payment order remains liable for interest losses or incidental expenses. The bank is liable for consequential damages only if it agrees to assume this liability in a written agreement with the customer.

D. Article 5 - Letters of Credit

Article 5 covers commercial letters of credit requiring documentary drafts or documentary demands for payment. It does not cover standby letters of credit. Among the provisions of Article 5 are the following:

- Defines a letter of credit, a documentary draft, or documentary demand for payment.

- Defines the roles of the issuer of the letter of credit, the applicant for whom the credit is issued, the beneficiary of the credit, the advising bank, and the confirming bank.

- Defines the issuer's obligation to the applicant, including the duty to examine documents to see that they comply with the terms of the credit and to honor a demand for payment that complies with the terms of the credit.

QUESTIONS

These chapter questions are to test and review the information in the text and are not examples of CCM examination questions, nor are they in the examination format.

Answers can be found at the back of the book on pgs. 364-365.

1. What are the major products and services offered by commercial banks?

2. What is the principal function of an investment banking firm?

3. Who charters savings banks and mutual savings banks?

4. In what ways are credit unions different from banks?

5. What are the five major roles of the Federal Reserve?

6. Who grants charters to national banks?

7. Who is the primary regulator of national S&Ls?

8. What legislation permits U.S. banks to invest in corporations engaged in international banking and finance?

9. What legislation originally prohibited banks from accepting deposits across state lines, and what is the current status of legislation in this area?

10. What legislation separates commercial from investment banking?

11. What legislation mandated the Federal Reserve to reduce and/or price float?

12. What legislation consolidated the two financial institution insurance funds under the FDIC?

13. What are the primary provisions of the Interstate Banking and Branching Efficiency Act of 1994?

14. What Federal Reserve regulation prohibits the payment of interest on corporate demand deposits?

15. What Federal Reserve regulation established rules for handling return of checks and payable-through-drafts?

16. What article of the Uniform Commercial Code (UCC) permits avoidance of inadvertent accord and satisfaction?

17. Under UCC Article 4A, is a bank responsible for consequential damages?

CHAPTER 4

Payments System

OVERVIEW

This chapter deals with the basic structure of the U.S. payments system, which processes paper-based and electronic payments. It covers the mechanics of each of its major components and instruments, the regulatory and institutional framework in which it operates, and the key implications for cash management.

LEARNING OBJECTIVES

Upon completion of this chapter and the related study questions, the reader should understand:

1. The mechanics and applications of the following principal paper instruments: checks, payable through drafts, preauthorized drafts, and depository transfer checks

2. The mechanics and applications of the following principal electronic payment instruments: ACH, Fedwire, and CHIPS

3. How the Federal Reserve System and the banking industry define and measure payment system risk and the actions they take to reduce it

KEY CONCEPTS

1. Paper-Based Payment Methods

2. Electronic Payment Methods

3. Check Clearing

4. Funds Availability, Balances, and Float

5. Payment System Risk

OUTLINE

I. OVERVIEW OF PAYMENT METHODS

Checks are the most widely used method of payment in the United States today. However, while the majority of transactions are by check, the greatest volume of dollars is transferred through three electronic payment networks: the Automated Clearing House (ACH), Fedwire, and the Clearing House for Interbank Payment System (CHIPS).

II. PAPER-BASED PAYMENTS

A. Domestic Check System Terminology

A check is a demand instrument used to transfer funds from the payor to the payee. It is important for a cash manager to know the terminology associated with checks; this includes:

1.   **Payor** - The party who issues the check

2.   **Payee** - The party to whom the check is made payable

3.   **Drawee Bank** - The bank on which the check is drawn, the payor's bank

4.   **Depository Bank** - The bank which accepts an item for deposit for credit to a customer's account

5.   **Provisional Credit** - The payee receives ledger credit when the check is deposited. The credit is provisional, subject to final clearing of the check.

6.   **Return Item** - A check the drawee bank rejects and returns to the depository bank

B. Components of a Check

All checks are similarly configured and generally contain the following elements:

1. **Signature** - A check requires the authorization, most typically the signature, of the payor. Sometimes more than one signature is required. Some companies use either mechanically generated or computer-printed facsimile signatures.

2. **Magnetic Ink Character Recognition (MICR) Line** - The information necessary to process checks by machine is contained in the MICR line, which is printed with special characters on the lower portion of the check. These characters can be read by magnetic or optical scanning equipment. The information contained in the MICR line of a business check is illustrated in Exhibit 4.1.

3. **Transit Routing Number** - The MICR line on a check contains the transit routing number, which the depository bank uses to route the check back to the drawee bank.

4. **Encoded Amount of the Check** - Is the part of the MICR line that provides, in machine readable form, the dollar amount of the check. A company may pre-encode checks prior to depositing them or the depository bank encodes them.

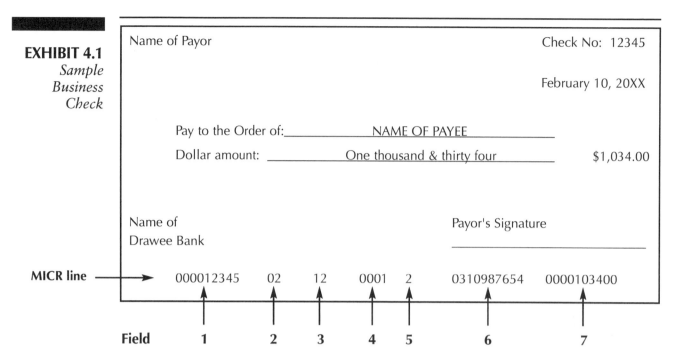

EXHIBIT 4.1
*Sample
Business
Check*

Name of Payor   Check No: 12345

                                                                  February 10, 20XX

            Pay to the Order of:_____NAME OF PAYEE_____

            Dollar amount: _____One thousand & thirty four_____ $1,034.00

Name of   Payor's Signature
Drawee Bank   _____

MICR line ———→   000012345   02   12   0001   2   0310987654   0000103400

Field   1   2   3   4   5   6   7

The MICR line contains information in a fixed format that allows the depository bank to route the check back to the drawee bank and the drawee bank to identify the account and amount to debit. Fields 2-5 are called the Transit Routing (TR) Number.

1. **Serial Number** - Also called the auxiliary on-us field on a business check.
    - This number is frequently the check number.
    - It assists the drawee bank in providing a variety of account reconcilement services such as sorting the cleared checks before returning them to the payor.
    - It may also be used for identification codes of divisions or subsidiaries.
    - It is a key to providing stop payment and positive pay services.

2. **Federal Reserve Bank Code** - Two digits (01 to 12) identify the drawee bank's Federal Reserve district. Numbers greater than 12 identify a non-bank depository institution such as a thrift.

3. **Federal Reserve Office** - The first digit identifies the Fed branch responsible for handling the drawee bank. The second digit is the availability classification.

4. **Bank Identification Number** - Four digits make up the bank's ABA identification number. That number designates the bank and location to which the item must be delivered. A number of banks have more than one identification number, which facilitates the handling of certain types of checks.

5. **Check Digit** - This digit, when combined with the other numbers, enables the computer to verify the accuracy of the routing number for the benefit of the automated routing process.

6. **Payor's Account Number** - This number is assigned to the payor by the drawee bank.

7. **Encoded Amount of Check** - This number should agree with the amount placed on the check by the payor. The amount is typically encoded on the check by the depository bank.

C. The Check Clearing Process

To effect final settlement, a check must be presented to and accepted by the drawee bank, the institution on which it is drawn. The key event in the check clearing process is presentment – the delivery of a check to the payor's bank. At the time of presentment, value is subtracted from the bank's account with a Federal Reserve bank (the Fed), a correspondent bank, or some other clearing institution. Normally, the amount is also subtracted from the payor's account on the same business day. The steps are illustrated in Exhibit 4.2.

EXHIBIT 4.2
Steps in Check Clearing System

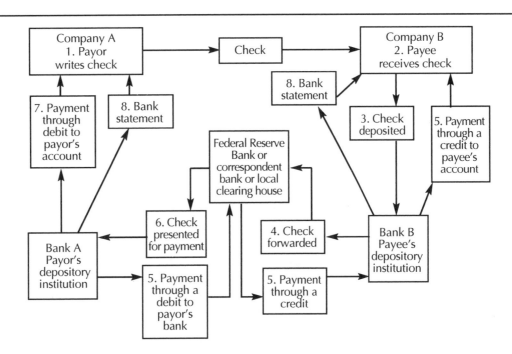

STEPS IN THE CHECK-CLEARING SYSTEM

Step 1:   Company A prepares and mails a check to Company B.

Step 2:   Company B receives and processes the check.

Step 3:   Company B deposits the check in its account at Bank B.

Step 4:   Bank B processes the check and transports it to a clearing system.

Step 5:   The clearing system gives value to Bank B in the amount of the check and subtracts value from Bank A for the same amount. The clearing agent (if any) can be the Federal Reserve System, a correspondent bank, or a local clearing house.

Step 6:   The check is physically presented by the clearing agent to Bank A where the amount is deducted from Company A's account. This step may occur simultaneously with Step 5.

Step 7:   This step does not occur at a predetermined time in the cycle, but on the day of posting. Company A must have funds available in Bank A to cover the amount of the check.

Step 8:   Both banks provide reports to their respective companies in the form of periodic bank statements.

1. **Role of the Depository Bank** - The depository bank receives checks for credit to its customers' accounts. The bank's processing operation encodes the check amount on the MICR line. The checks are processed in batches by a reader-sorter machine, which captures and stores the information carried on each check and sorts the checks based on their transit routing numbers. The checks are then transported to the check clearing system.

2. **Role of the Drawee Bank** - In the check clearing process, the drawee bank is responsible for inspecting the check for proper signature, alterations, appropriate dating, stop payments, and positive pay instructions. Generally, banks do not check dates and will honor post-dated and stale-dated checks. Drawee banks also review accounts for active status, adequate funds, and holds.

    The drawee bank has until midnight local time on the banking day following presentment to conduct a review of the check and authorize final payment. If the bank returns a check that exceeds $2,500, it must notify the depository bank of the return by 4:00 p.m. on the second banking day following presentment. When the returned checks are received by the depository bank they may be redeposited or charged back to the depositor's account.

D. The Check Clearing System

Banks present checks into the clearing system in **cash letters**, bundles of checks accompanied by lists of individual items and other control documents.

1. **Clearing Channels** - Banks use a number of channels for check clearing. Selection of a channel is a function of deposit bank processing time, geographic location, and the availability schedules of clearing agents. Availability (the release of deposited funds for use) is granted to the depository bank if the check reaches the endpoint (the drawee bank or location established by the clearing agent) prior to a prearranged deposit deadline. Availability schedules define the number of days after deposit before funds become available for use.

    - **On-Us Check Clearing** - This channel involves a single bank and is used when the payee deposits the check in an account at the same bank on which it is drawn. The bank simultaneously debits the payor's account and credits the payee's account.

    - **Clearing Houses** - These are either formal or informal associations formed by banks in a geographic area to permit the exchange of items drawn on the other participants. Representatives from the member banks meet daily to present checks to each other. The net value is transferred by debiting and crediting correspondent accounts or through reserve accounts each bank maintains with the local Fed. Nationwide clearing houses are being established to facilitate check clearing.

    - **Federal Reserve Bank** - The Federal Reserve Bank also acts as a check clearing agent. A bank deposits checks it has received into its account at a Federal Reserve bank, and the Fed credits the bank's account for the amount of the checks. The Fed then transports the checks to the drawee bank. Upon presentation at the drawee bank, the Fed subtracts the amount of the checks from the drawee bank's Fed account.

- **Correspondent Bank** - The sending bank, or depository bank, maintains a deposit account with another bank, called a correspondent bank, to which it sends checks. The correspondent bank collects the items through its local clearing house and credits the account of the sending bank with the proceeds of the checks.

2. **Direct Send** - As an alternative to using the clearing channels above, banks may make arrangements to send cash letters directly to the paying banks or to a non-local Federal Reserve bank. These arrangements enable banks to meet various deposit deadlines and achieve faster clearing times. The sending bank maintains a deposit account with the paying bank or non-local Fed, which credits the account of the sending bank with the proceeds of the checks.

3. **Drawee Endpoints** - An endpoint is the location of the drawee bank where final settlement is effected. Four general classifications of drawee endpoints are:

   - **City Items** - Checks drawn on banks located in Federal Reserve cities.

   - **RCPC Items** - Checks drawn on banks serviced by a Federal Reserve regional check processing center (RCPC).

   - **Country Items** - Checks drawn on banks located outside the area served by a Federal Reserve city or RCPC.

   - **High-Dollar Group Sort (HDGS) Items** - HDGS is a method the Fed uses to expedite the processing of high-dollar checks through the system. When a bank has more than $10 million of checks presented daily from outside its Fed district, the Fed automatically makes a second presentment .

4. **Other Check Clearing Factors**

   - **Deposit Deadlines** - Each transit routing number has a specific deposit deadline that must be met if the clearing bank is to receive the designated availability.

   - **Same-Day Settlement** - A Federal Reserve rule requires that if a check is presented to a drawee bank by 8:00 a.m. local time, the drawee bank must settle in same day funds by the close of Fedwire. No presentment fee can be charged. This rule is intended to expedite check collection services.

   - **Electronic Check Presentment (ECP)** - With ECP, the data captured by the reader/sorter, not the physical check, is electronically transmitted to the drawee bank. The drawee bank uses this information to debit the funds from the payor's demand deposit account. The actual check may be sent to the drawee bank for subsequent handling or the check or an image of the check may be retained by the depository bank. ECP accelerates the clearing of checks and thus the notification of checks being returned by the drawee bank.

     Banks, with the support of organizations such as the Electronic Check Clearing House Organization (ECCHO), are developing programs for the electronic exchange of check information. Electronic exchange of information enables verification of funds availability prior to physical presentment of the check to the drawee bank, affording expedited return of non-sufficient-funds (NSF) checks.

E. Funds Availability

When funds from a check become available for use depends on several factors: the time and day the check is deposited, the drawee endpoint, and the bank of deposit's ledger cutoff time and availability schedule.

1. **Ledger Cutoff Time** - A bank's ledger cutoff is the time of day when a deposit must be received to be posted to the depositor's account. Items deposited after the ledger cutoff time are considered to have been received by the bank on the next banking day. For example, if a bank has a published ledger cutoff time of 3:00 p.m. a deposit made at 2:00 p.m. on a Friday will be credited to the ledger balance on Friday. However, a deposit made to the same bank at 4:00 p.m. that day will not be credited to the ledger balance until Monday.

2. **Deposit Deadline** - A deposit deadline is the time of day, based on an item's drawee endpoint, by which an item must be at the depository bank's processing center ready for transit in order to qualify for the availability stated on that bank's availability schedule. Ledger credit must be granted prior to the deposit deadline. If a check comes into the bank processing center after the deposit deadline, the next day's deposit deadline becomes effective.

    For example, if a bank's ledger cutoff time is 3:00 p.m., the Wednesday banking day starts at 3:01 p.m. on Tuesday and ends at 3:00 p.m. on Wednesday. A Wednesday deposit deadline of 10:00 p.m. means the item must have been received at the processing center prior to 10:00 p.m. on Tuesday in order to receive the availability specified on the bank's availability schedule. If an item is deposited at 8:00 a.m. Wednesday, it has missed Wednesday's deposit deadline (10:00 p.m. Tuesday) and availability will be determined based on Thursday's deposit deadline, but ledger credit will still be granted on Wednesday. In effect, the deposit deadline specified on an availability schedule must fall between the time of deposit and the ledger cutoff time for the availability on the schedule to be granted.

3. **Availability Schedules** - Availability schedules specify, for each drawee endpoint, when a bank grants credit for deposited checks to the depositor's available or collected balance. The assignment of availability can be in whole or fractional banking days. Checks are generally assigned between zero and two days' availability. The Fed has availability schedules for banks, correspondent banks have availability schedules for other banks, and banks have availability schedules for their customers. Many banks have multiple availability schedules. The schedule a bank offers to a particular customer is a pricing decision.

Exhibit 4.3 illustrates a sample availability schedule.

	TR No.	Endpoint Location	Endpoint Description	Deposit Deadline	Availability
EXHIBIT 4.3 *Sample of Availability Schedule*	0641-xxxx	Nashville, TN	RCPC	2:30 P.M.	1
	0650-xxxx	New Orleans, LA	City	1:00 A.M.	0
	0740-xxxx	Indianapolis, IN	City	9:30 P.M.	0
	0810-xxxx	St. Louis, MO	City	1:00 A.M.	0
	1021-xxxx	Denver, CO	Country	2:30 P.M.	1
	1130-xxxx	Houston, TX	City	1:00 P.M.	0

4. Balances and Float

- **Ledger Balances** - Ledger balances are bank balances that reflect all entries to a bank account, regardless of whether or not the deposited items have been collected and are available for withdrawal. Ledger balances are important for accounting purposes but not for funds availability or bank compensation purposes. If the ledger balance is negative, there is a ledger overdraft. There is a service charge and/or an interest charge for such an overdraft.

- **Deposit Float** - Deposit float has two meanings:

  - Deposit float is the sum of the deposited items that are in the process of collection.

  - Deposit float is also used to refer to the interval between the time an item is deposited and the time the funds are collected. For example, cash managers often refer to an average float of a certain number of days, meaning the average length of time they must wait for deposited funds to become available.

- **Collected Balances** - Collected balances reflect the balance in an account for which the bank of deposit has received settlement. Collected balances are the difference between ledger balances and the deposit float.

  For example, suppose a $1,000 check deposited on Tuesday into an account with a zero balance is granted one-day availability. This means that the bank grants the customer use of the funds after a wait of one banking day. While the ledger balance increases by $1,000 on Tuesday, the collected balance does not increase until Wednesday. On Tuesday, the deposit float is equal to $1,000 and the collected balance is equal to the ledger balance of $1,000 minus the deposit float of $1,000, or $0.

- **Available Balances** - Available balances are the amount of funds available for withdrawal from an account. They are equal to the sum of: (1) the collected balances, (2) the balances that are scheduled to be collected by the end of the banking day, and (3) those additional amounts for which availability must be granted under Federal Reserve Regulation CC.

Assuming a ledger cutoff time of 5:00 P.M. and the availability schedule in Exhibit 4.3, a company would receive ledger and collected balances as shown in Exhibit 4.4 if its deposits were made on Monday at the times specified.

EXHIBIT 4.4
*Sample of
Availability
Schedule*

Assuming a ledger cut-off time of 3:00 P.M. and the availability schedule shown in Figure 4.3, a company would receive ledger and collected balances as follows if its deposits were made on Monday at 8:00 A.M. or 8:00 P.M.

	8:00 A.M. Deposit Time		8:00 P.M. Deposit Time	
Endpoint	Ledger Balance	Collected Balance	Ledger Balance	Collected Balance
Nashville	Monday	Tuesday	Tuesday	Wednesday
New Orleans	Monday	Tuesday	Tuesday	Tuesday
Indianapolis	Monday	Tuesday	Tuesday	Tuesday
St. Louis	Monday	Tuesday	Tuesday	Tuesday
Denver	Monday	Tuesday	Tuesday	Wednesday
Houston	Monday	Monday	Tuesday	Tuesday

5. **How Banks Assign Availability**

Most banks assign availability using the proof of deposit (POD) method. Under the POD method, availability is assigned to each check as it passes through the automated check processing equipment. Availability is assigned based on the time and day of deposit and the check's endpoint. Some banks may negotiate special availability for selected high volume customers.

6. **Other Factors Determining Availability**

- **Drawee Location** - Checks drawn on banks in geographically distant or isolated locations generally have longer availability times than those drawn on nearby banks.

- **Time of Deposit** - Checks must reach the processing center and be ready for transit by a certain time of day in order to receive the designated availability.

- **Day of Deposit** - Special availability considerations may apply to items deposited immediately preceding a weekend or bank holiday.

- **Pre-Encoding** - If a customer MICR encodes the dollar amount on the checks it deposits, the customer may receive faster availability, a later cutoff time, and/or reduced service charges.

- **Reject Items** - Checks that are rejected by a bank's automated check processing equipment are likely to miss critical deposit deadlines, resulting in longer availability and additional processing fees.

- **As-of Adjustments** - An as-of adjustment changes the date of a transaction, for the purpose of calculating collected balances, to a different date from the one on which the transaction actually occurred. For example, if a bank originally granted one-day availability but actually cleared the check in two days, it would add one more day of float in calculating collected balances.

- **Fractional Availability** - As an alternative to as-of adjustments, a bank may grant what is known as fractional availability. For example, under normal circumstances a bank may experience an average collection interval of one day, but may miss availability deadlines five percent of the time. Rather than make as-of adjustments, it could assign fractional availability of 1.05 days to its customers.

F. Federal Reserve Float

In the process of clearing checks, banks sometimes receive availability from the Fed before the Fed can generate the offsetting debit. The difference in timing between the availability granted a clearing bank and the actual presentment of the item to the drawee bank is called Fed float. Fed float represents interest-free loans to banks and, indirectly, to companies. The 1980 Depository Institutions Deregulation and Monetary Control Act (DIDMCA) mandated both the reduction and pricing of this benefit.

The amount of Fed float has been significantly reduced since then. A fee for the remaining Fed float is charged to banks through as-of adjustments, clearing balance requirements, and interest charges at the Fed funds rate. Some banks pass this charge on to their customers through as-of collected balance adjustments, explicit interest charges, or by granting fractional availability.

G. Additional Paper Payment Instruments

A number of other payment instruments have check-like attributes and clear through the same channels as checks. The following are examples of these instruments:

1. **Payable Through Draft (PTD)** - A PTD is a payment instrument resembling a check that is drawn against the payor and not the bank. A draft is handled like a check through the clearing system, but the responsibility for paying the draft lies with the drawee. The primary reason companies use PTDs is to preserve the right to review the items prior to final payment. Insurance companies often use PTDs for claim reimbursement because the PTD gives them an opportunity to verify the signature and endorsements before honoring it. Some state and local governments use a form of PTD called a government warrant.

2. **Pre-Authorized Draft/Check** - The payor authorizes the payee to draw a draft/check against the payor's account. The payee, rather than the payor, initiates the transaction. Mortgage, insurance, and other recurring payments may be made this way.

3. **Money Order** - A money order is a prepaid instrument issued by parties such as companies, banks, or the Post Office. The purchaser is the instrument's payor, and the money order is the obligation of the issuer.

4. **Travelers Checks** - Such instruments are prepaid and similar to money orders. Two signatures typically are required by the purchaser: one at issuance and one at the time the check is used.

5.   **Depository Transfer Checks (DTC)** - DTCs are checks used in moving funds from one account to another account held by the same company, usually in cash concentration systems. No signature is required, but for security there is often a payee restriction. Normally the payee can only be an account at the concentration bank. Electronic transfers have largely replaced paper DTCs.

6.   **Sight Draft** - A sight draft is payable on demand and is usually presented in combination with other documents showing that the terms of the transaction have been met. Sight drafts are primarily used to support international trade.

7.   **Time Draft** - This payment mechanism is like a sight draft but is not payable until a specified future date. Time drafts are used in international trade transactions that by contract call for delayed payments.

8.   **Cashier's Check/Certified Check** - A cashier's check is a check drawn by a bank on its own funds and signed by a bank officer. A certified check is drawn by a depositor on his checking account; it carries the signature of a bank officer certifying the check to be genuine and guaranteeing its payment.

III. ELECTRONIC PAYMENTS

There are three electronic funds clearing systems.

A. The Automated Clearing House System (ACH)

The ACH system was developed by the financial industry in the early 1970s as an electronic alternative to checks. In an ACH transaction, payment information is processed and settled electronically, thereby increasing reliability, efficiency, and cost-effectiveness. In addition, an ACH transaction is capable of transferring more information about a payment than is possible on a check.

1.   **Structure** - The ACH is a network of regional associations, inter-bank associations, and private-sector processors. These ACH associations and processors are called ACH operators. Many regional ACHs are operated by the Fed. The majority of financial institutions are members of an ACH association.

The National Automated Clearing House Association (NACHA) is a membership organization that provides marketing and educational assistance and establishes the rules, standards, and procedures that enable financial institutions to exchange ACH payments on a national basis.

2.   **Processing** - The ACH system currently is a batch-process, store-and-forward system. Transactions received by the bank during the day are stored and processed later in batches. They are then forwarded in batches to the bank's ACH operator.

3.   **Participants** - Exhibit 4.5 shows the parties in an ACH transaction.

EXHIBIT 4.5
ACH Transaction Participants

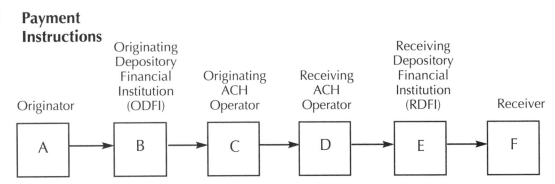

4. **How ACH Transactions Differ from Checks** - The terminology and mechanics of the ACH system differ from those of the check clearing system.

   ACH transactions differ in four significant ways from checks:

   - A check is paper-based; an ACH transaction is electronic.

   - A check is limited to payment instructions; an ACH transaction can also transmit additional payment-related information.

   - The parties to a check are referred to as the payor and the payee; the parties to an ACH transaction are the originator and receiver.

   - A check can only debit a payor's account and credit a payee's account; an ACH can be either a debit or a credit transaction. ACH credit transactions move funds from the originator's account to the receiver's account; ACH debit transactions move funds from the receiver's account to the originator's account.

Exhibit 4.6 shows the steps in a typical ACH credit transaction in which Company A (the originator) uses direct deposit to initate payroll payments to its employees (the receivers).

EXHIBIT 4.6
*An ACH Credit
Transaction
(Direct Deposit
of Payroll)*

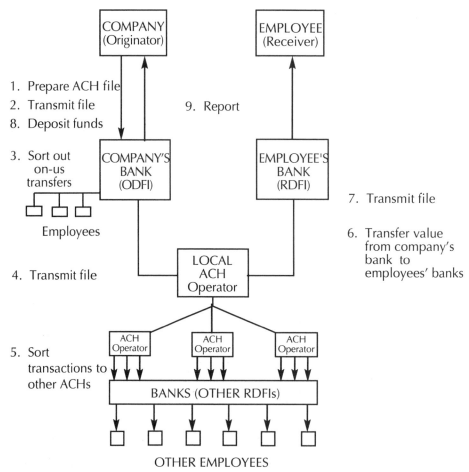

Step 1: A company prepares a file that may contain hundreds of payroll transactions. The file contains each employee's account number, the transit routing number of the employee's bank, the amount of the transfer, the transit routing number of the company's bank, the company's account number, and other pertinent information.

Step 2: The company transmits the file to its bank, the originating depository financial institution (ODFI).

Step 3: The company's bank sorts out on-us transactions for employees who have accounts with the bank and credits their accounts on settlement date.

Step 4: The company's bank merges the company's transactions involving other financial institutions with transactions from other firms. A combined file is transmitted to the ACH operator servicing the originating institution.

Step 5: The local ACH operator sorts out those transactions which involve banks in its area and sends the remaining transactions to other ACH operators.

Step 6: Settlement, or transfer of value, occurs when specified in the file. For payroll this is normally after two days.

Step 7: The ACH operator presents a file to the employee's bank containing all transactions pertaining to that bank. The amount the employee receives is credited to the employee's account.

Step 8: This step does not come at a predetermined time in the cycle. On or before the day the ODFI's account is debited, the company must have funds available in the bank to cover the transactions.

Step 9: Both banks provide reports in the form of periodic bank statements, and possible daily deposit and withdrawal reports.

An ACH debit transaction is identical to the credit transaction outlined in the exhibit, except that the file contains a code indicating that the account at the Receiving Depository Financial Institution (RDFI) is to be debited instead of credited and value is transferred from the receiver to the originator.

5. **ACH Risk Issues** - The increasing volume of funds being moved through the ACH system has caused regulators and system participants to become more aware of the associated risks.

   - **Credit Risk** - An Originating Depository Financial Institution (ODFI) has credit exposure to the originator of an ACH transaction. In the case of a credit origination, exposure exists from the time the ODFI releases an ACH file to the ACH operator until settlement occurs. Once a file is released to the ACH operator it may not be recalled or reversed (reversing entries may be submitted only for correction of errors). If the originator's account has insufficient funds at the time of settlement, an overdraft occurs. If the originator filed for bankruptcy prior to settlement, the ODFI cannot settle against the originator's account. For a debit origination, the risk is that return items will be received and the funds remaining in the originator's account will not be sufficient to cover them. NACHA rules require ODFIs to establish and monitor exposure limits for all ACH originators.

     In addition, the Federal Reserve Payments System Risk Policy recommends that an ODFI:

     - Perform credit assessments on originators generating large dollar volume ACH files
     - Establish interday credit limits for originators
     - React to minimize risk if an originator's financial condition is deteriorating

     As a result, more ODFIs now require financial information, credit approval and limit monitoring, or prefunding for ACH originations.

   - **Large-Value Payment Risk** - Because ACH transactions are significantly less expensive than wire transfers, some originators have migrated large dollar transfers to the ACH system. ACH system controls are not as extensive as wire transfer controls, and credit risk to ODFIs increases with large payments. As a result, ACH system participants, regulators, and ODFIs are starting to limit the maximum dollar amount of a single entry or, alternatively, to price large transactions to compensate for the risk, thereby eliminating the financial incentive to move such transfers into the ACH system.

6. **ACH Payment Formats** - There are ACH formats for both consumer and corporate payments. All ACH payment formats move funds in essentially the same manner. The most appropriate format for a particular payment is determined by the relationship between the parties, the information exchanged, and the types of ACH payment services offered by the participating banks.

   The format of an ACH payment message is identified by a three-letter standard entry class in the header of the message. The most commonly used formats are as follows:

   - **Prearranged Payment or Deposit (PPD)** - The PPD format is the payment application by which consumers may authorize credits or debits to their accounts by a company or financial institution. These are normally recurring payments in fixed amounts.

- ◆ **PPD Credits** - Examples of consumer credits are payroll, expense reimbursement, dividends, social security, retirement benefits, and tax refunds.

- ◆ **PPD Debits** - Examples of consumer debits are rent and mortgage payments, subscriptions, dues and memberships, insurance premiums, installment debt payments, and utility payments.

- **Cash Concentration or Disbursement (CCD)** - CCD is an electronic payment format used for concentration and disbursement of funds within or between companies. A single 94-character record contains the standard entry class indicating the type of transaction, transit routing numbers for the originating and receiving financial institutions, and the originator and receiver account numbers. CCD is the only corporate ACH format that does not have space for an additional addenda record, but it does contain space for a reference number.

- **Cash Concentration or Disbursement Plus Addendum (CCD+)** - CCD+ is one of the formats used for the U.S. Treasury Vendor Express program and for corporate-to-corporate payments. It is useful when only a limited amount of information must be transmitted. This format is identical to CCD but with an addenda record. The addenda record is a free-form space for up to 80 characters of descriptive data. The CCD+ addenda record is also used to report federal and state tax payment information. The data conforms to the Tax Payment (TXP) banking conventions.

- **Corporate Trade Exchange (CTX)** - The CTX format is designed for corporate-to-corporate trade payments. It consists of a standard ACH payment transaction and a variable-length message addendum designed to convey remittance information in the Accredited Standards Committee (ASC) X12 data standard. The addendum can accommodate 9,999 records of 80 characters each. CTX is useful for payments related to multiple invoices and those with substantial invoice detail.

The NACHA operating rules require all financial institutions participating in the ACH to accept all types of ACH entries and post the dollar amounts to the proper accounts; however, some institutions may not have the capability to process addenda records. Addenda records contain remittance details that follow the standard payment information in ACH payment messages.

7. **Settlement** - ACH transactions carry settlement dates that determine the availability of funds. Transactions are settled one or two business days after the file is released to the ACH Operator. Both the receiver and the originator are settled on the same day, so that the float associated with checks does not exist in the ACH system. Among the conventions governing settlement are the following:

- Credit originations are usually entered into the system two banking days prior to settlement.

- Debit originations are usually entered into the system on the banking day prior to settlement.

- Cutoff times for receipt of ACH files vary by ODFI; some ODFIs may accept files over the weekend for Monday settlement.

- Memo posting is posting of an ACH credit or debit on a memo basis early in the day when the actual credit or debit will not settle until later that day.

8. **Prenotification** - Prenotifications (prenotes) are optional zero-dollar entries that are sent through the ACH system prior to live entries. Prenotes provide a verification function at the receiving bank before entries for settlement are processed. For example, when a company adds a new employee to its direct deposit of payroll program, it may use prenotification to ensure that the bank's transit routing number and the employee's personal bank account number(s) are correct. Prenotes are optional, but are useful to ensure that all records are correct prior to transaction, especially in consumer applications.

9. **Authorization** - Companies originating ACH transactions should obtain prior consent from the receiver authorizing the ACH transaction. For debits to consumer accounts, this consent must be in writing.

10. **Advantages of Using ACH** - The ACH system provides numerous advantages compared to paper-based systems. These include:

    - **Reduced Banking Costs** - An ACH transfer is less expensive than a check and much less expensive than a wire transfer.

    - **Reduced Reconciliation and Cash Application Costs** - Because payments are automated, reconciliation time is reduced. Cash application costs are generally reduced compared to paper-based systems.

    - **Faster Inflows** - The use of ACH debits accelerates cash inflow by reducing delays caused by invoicing, the mail, internal processing, and bank clearing channels.

    - **Control of Payment Timing** - The use of ACH debits and credits increases control of payment initiation and funds availability.

    - **More Accurate Forecasting** - The control of payment timing increases the accuracy of cash flow forecasts.

    - **Increased Reliability** - ACH transactions reach their destination in a timely and predictable manner.

    - **Enhanced Service** - Customers and employees benefit from enhanced service such as automatic bill paying and direct deposit of payroll.

    - **Reduced Fraud** - ACH is less susceptible to fraud compared to the use of checks.

11. **Disadvantages of Using ACH** - The following are considered disadvantages of the ACH system:

- **Reduction in Disbursement Float** - The payor may lose float benefits accruing from invoicing, mail, processing, and check clearing delays. However, before switching to electronic payments, some corporate trading partners renegotiate payment terms.

- **Loss of Control with Direct Debits** - Payors have security and liability concerns regarding direct debits. However, some banks have systems designed to prevent unauthorized debit and credit activity or amounts in excess of preapproved limits. Companies must notify the bank within one working day if an unauthorized ACH transaction is discovered.

- **System Start-up Costs** - There can be significant development costs including computer software and hardware investments, training of employees, and education of customers.

B. Fedwire

The Fedwire is the Federal Reserve funds transfer system. It is a real-time method of transferring immediate funds and supporting information between two financial institutions, using their respective Federal Reserve accounts. The system is reliable and secure but, compared to checks and ACH transactions, relatively expensive to use.

1. **Communications and Settlement** - The Fedwire is both a communications and a settlement system. Except for delays that might result from either a customer or bank temporarily reaching an overdraft limit, funds are moved almost instantaneously once a request has been received and validated by the originating bank. The transaction is final once it has been sent by the originating bank and receipt is confirmed by the Fed.

2. **Hours of Operation and Deadlines** - Fedwire hours are 12:30 a.m. to 6:30 p.m., ET. Banks establish earlier cutoff times for customers and other internal departments to allow time for processing.

3. **Mechanics of a Wire Transfer** - Exhibit 4.7 shows the steps in a typical wire transfer. The entire process generally takes only minutes.

EXHIBIT 4.7
Mechanics of a Wire Transfer

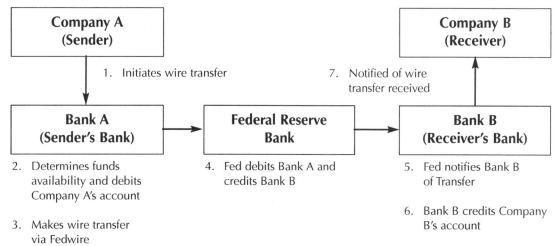

Step 1: Company A initiates a request to transfer funds to Company B. This is typically done through a PC or by a telephone call. Security procedures may include the use of Personal Identification Numbers (PINs), test key calculations or message authentication algorithms, dual authorization of the transfer, or callbacks to verify instructions. Most telephone calls are recorded for security purposes and to resolve disputes.

Step 2: Bank A checks to see if Company A has sufficient funds in its account. If it does, Bank A debits Company A's account. If not, appropriate credit approval must be obtained or the transfer must wait until sufficient funds are available.

Step 3: Bank A uses the Fedwire to transfer funds to Company B through the Federal Reserve System.

Step 4: The Federal Reserve (Fed) debits Bank A's reserve account and credits Bank B's reserve account.

Step 5: The Fed notifies Bank B of the transfer, including account information for Company B. If Bank B is in a different Fed district from Bank A, the information is routed through the Fed's communication network to the appropriate receiving Federal Reserve Bank.

Step 6: Bank B credits Company B's Account.

Step 7: Bank notifies Company B of receipt of wire transfer.

4. **Payment Finality** - In the event the sending bank fails to settle, the Federal Reserve guarantees the transferred funds to the receiving bank.

5. **Fedwire Format** - The Fedwire format has been expanded to interface with the Clearing House Interbank Payments System (CHIPS) and the Society for Worldwide Interbank Financial Telecommunications (S.W.I.F.T.) system. The expanded format includes information required by federal authorities to combat illegal money laundering activity.

6.   **Types of Fedwire Funds Transfers** - Among the different classifications of Fedwire transfers are the following:

- **Repetitive** - Repetitive transfers are used when a company makes a transfer frequently between the same debit and credit parties. The bank has a record of the debit and credit parties and receives electronic and telephonic instructions to make the transfer. A unique identifier is assigned to each instruction template. Only the date and dollar amount may be changed.

- **Semi-Repetitive** - With semi-repetitive transfers, the debit and credit parties remain the same but the description may be changed along with the date and dollar amount. Semi-repetitive transfers allow some of the control of repetitive transfers and some of the flexibility of non-repetitive transfers.

- **Non-Repetitive (Free Form)** - With non-repetitive transfers, the debit and credit parties are different each time. Additional security steps may be required.

- **Drawdown** - A drawdown is a request sent by a company to a bank to initiate a wire transfer from its own or another party's account. The party being debited must preauthorize the transfer. Drawdowns are most frequently used as part of a company's concentration system.

7.   **Wire Transfer Security** - Security in wire transfer is critical. Commercially reasonable security procedures are necessary in order to comply with Uniform Commercial Code Article 4A (UCC4A). Security procedures are generally outlined in a bank's wire transfer agreement. Among the types of security procedures that are commonly used are the following:

- Physical security and limited access at both the company and the bank

- Passwords and Personal Identification Numbers (PINs) to identify authorized users

- Test keys or codes to validate wire transfers

- Repetitive wires to limit where and to whom funds can be transferred

- Dual approval (one person enters the wire and another reviews and releases it)

- Electronic security methods such as encryption (the scrambling of a message by the sender and the unscrambling of the message by the receiver) and message authentication (a digital signature which prevents an unauthorized person from changing a wire)

- Security tokens or keys to guard against misuse or fraud

8.   **Pricing** - The total price to a user of a wire transfer varies significantly. Both the sending institution and the receiving institution may impose a charge.

C. Clearing House Interbank Payments System (CHIPS)

CHIPS is an independent large-dollar funds transfer network operated by the New York Automated Clearing House. It was established in 1970 to substitute electronic payments for paper checks used in international dollar transactions between foreign and American banks. It is also used for payments under letters of credit and documentary collections and for third-party transfers. Institutions outside New York City use their New York Edge Act subsidiaries as agents or gain access to CHIPS through correspondent banks.

1. **Operation** - Transfers between member banks are received and authenticated during the day. Transfers are batched, and at the end of the day net amounts due to or from each of the settling participants are settled using the clearing banks or the Fed. Non-settling participants settle via correspondent banks. Transfers are executed on a same-day basis and may be unwound (reversed) only if a member bank cannot honor its net debit position.

2. **Finality** - The receiving bank that credits a customer and allows use of the funds bears the risk that the sending bank will not settle. A fund consisting of collateral posted by all members has been established to insure against the failure of a participant.

D. Society for Worldwide Interbank Financial Telecommunications (S.W.I.F.T.)

S.W.I.F.T. is the major international interbank telecommunications network that transmits international payment instructions as well as other financial messages. It is not a funds transfer network. Messages are transferred requesting debits and credits to correspondent accounts (in addition to other types of messages). Settlement occurs through Fedwire, CHIPS, correspondent accounts, or other means. The formats and uses of the S.W.I.F.T. network are being enhanced to include functions such as balance reporting.

E. Payments System Risk

The growth of payment volume in recent decades and several large bank failures during the 1970s have prompted greater attention by the Federal Reserve System to reducing payments system risk.

1. **Types of Risk** - Today's payment system creates four kinds of risk for banks:

    • **Systemic Risk** - The risk that the failure of one major bank could cause other banks to fail and cause a collapse of the payments system.

    • **Credit Risk** - The risk that the party funding a transaction will default on its settlement obligation.

    • **Operational Risk** - The risk of processing mistakes, or system disruptions.

    • **Fraud Risk** - The risk that someone might alter a transaction or enter a false item which could cause a loss for the disbursing party.

2. **Daylight Overdrafts** - A daylight overdraft is an intra-day exposure occurring when an account is in an overdraft position during the business day. Banks may have daylight overdrafts in their Federal Reserve bank accounts, and companies may have daylight overdrafts in their accounts at commercial banks.

Examples of transactions that often create daylight overdrafts include the following:

- A bank may repay Fed funds borrowed for the previous night but not receive the proceeds of new borrowings until later that day.

- A bank customer that issues commercial paper may repay funds to investors in the morning but not receive funds from investors in a replacement issue until the afternoon.

Controlling daylight overdrafts has been one of the primary objectives of recent Federal Reserve measures to control risk among the large-dollar payment networks. The Fed has mandated that all banks using the large-dollar payment systems must have in place a sender net debit cap limiting the intra-day overdraft that the bank may incur over all the large-dollar systems. The caps are determined by a Fed schedule based on the bank's self-evaluation of its overall creditworthiness as an institution, its credit policies, and operational controls. The self-evaluation must be approved by a bank's board of directors. The Fed uses pricing as the primary method of controlling the level of daylight overdrafts. In effect, this is a market solution rather than a regulatory solution. It measures daylight overdrafts on a minute-by-minute basis and charges fees based on the magnitude and duration of the overdraft.

Daylight overdraft limits have not been a major obstacle to corporate money transfers, although there are occasional delays when companies or banks reach their limits.

In addition, the Fed has mandated that all banks must establish bilateral net credit limits that define the maximum amount of net payments the bank may receive from another bank over private networks such as CHIPS. The reason for the net credit limits is that payments on CHIPS are not settled until the end of the day. A higher amount of payments received and credited to beneficiaries means a higher exposure to the sending bank's failure to settle at the end of the day.

IV. Future of The Payments System

Electronic methods for moving funds have evolved rapidly in recent years, and the trend away from paper-based systems is continuing. New methods for accessing and communicating via the payments system are also evolving rapidly. Recent innovations include Financial Electronic Data Interchange (FEDI), home banking, PC-based financial transactions, and the use of the Internet for initiating payment instructions. Technological developments are expected to continue influencing payment methods into the foreseeable future.

Questions

These chapter questions are to test and review the information in the text and are not examples of CCM examination questions, nor are they in the examination format.

Answers can be found at the back of the book on pgs. 365-367.

1. With a check, what is the difference between the payor and the payee?

2. What is the purpose of the Magnetic Ink Character Recognition (MICR) line?

3. What are the various methods used to clear checks?

4. What is a cash letter?

5. What is a direct send?

6. What is an on-us item?

7. What are High Dollar Group Sort (HDGS) items?

8. What is the difference between a ledger balance and a collected balance?

9. What is deposit float?

10. What factors determine availability?

11. What is Federal Reserve float?

12. Why is a payable through draft (PTD) not a check?

13. What differentiates a time draft from a sight draft?

14. What are the most commonly used ACH formats?

15. When does settlement occur in an ACH transaction?

16. How does settlement through Fedwire differ from settlement through the ACH?

17. How does a repetitive wire transfer differ from a non-repetitive transfer?

18. What is the major difference between CHIPS and S.W.I.F.T.?

19. Why is the Federal Reserve concerned about daylight overdrafts and what action has it taken to address this concern?

20. What are the various security procedures used to provide commercially reasonable security for wire transfers?

CHAPTER **5**

Credit and Accounts Receivable Management

OVERVIEW

This chapter describes how and why companies extend credit, how they manage accounts receivable and forecast income, and how cash managers are involved in these and related activities.

LEARNING OBJECTIVES

Upon completion of this chapter and the related study questions, the reader should understand:

1.   The objectives of corporate credit and accounts receivable management

2.   How credit and accounts receivable management fit into corporate finance and treasury operations

3.   The forms of credit extension

4.   How companies make customer credit decisions

5.   The commonly used terms of sale, including credit terms

6.   How companies measure and monitor accounts receivable

7.   How companies develop credit policies

8.   How companies calculate the costs and benefits of credit policies

9.   How companies finance accounts receivable

10.   How the cash application process works

11.   Legislation that affects credit and collection

KEY CONCEPTS

1. Rationale for Credit Sales

2. Credit Management

3. Accounts Receivable Monitoring and Control

4. Aging of Receivables - Days' Sales Outstanding (DSO)

5. Collection Management

6. Accounts Receivable Forecasting

OUTLINE

I. **Objectives of Trade Credit and Accounts Receivable Management**

II. **Organization of the Credit and Accounts Receivable Management Function**
    A. Responsibility
    B. Role of the Cash Manager

III. **Credit Policies**
    A. Reasons for Offering Trade Credit
    B. Credit Policy Constraints
    C. Financing Implications
    D. Income and Costs

IV. **Credit Standards**
    A. Considerations in Credit Extension Decision Making
    B. Information Sources
    C. The Five Cs of Credit
    D. Quantitative Credit Analysis
    E. Billing and Collection Methods

V. **Forms of Credit Extension**
    A. Open Account
    B. Installment Credit
    C. Revolving Credit
    D. Letter of Credit (L/C)

VI. **Considerations Pertaining to Terms of Sale**
    A. Common Terms of Sale
    B. Common Credit Practices
    C. Cost of Trade Credit

VII. **Accounts Receivable Monitoring and Control**
    A. Purpose
    B. Days' Sales Outstanding (DSO)
    C. Aging Schedule
    D. Accounts Receivables Balance Pattern

VIII. **Financing Accounts Receivable**
    A.   Unsecured Borrowing
    B.   Secured Borrowing
    C.   Securitization
    D.   Captive Finance Subsidiary
    E.   Third-Party Financing
    F.   Credit Cards
    G.   Factoring
    H.   Private Label Financing

IX. **Cash Application**
    A.   Open Item
    B.   Balance Forward
    C.   Electronic Data Interchange (EDI)

X. **Legislation Affecting Credit and Collections**
    A.   Pricing and Interest Charge Restrictions
    B.   Consumer and Commercial Credit Legislation
    C.   Uniform Commercial Code (UCC)
    D.   Bankruptcy and Reorganization

I. OBJECTIVES OF TRADE CREDIT AND ACCOUNTS RECEIVABLE MANAGEMENT

Accounts receivable result from a company's decision to sell goods and services on a credit basis. Accounts receivable are an asset of the company evidencing the extension of trade credit. Sales, accounting, and finance personnel all become involved in credit and accounts receivable management activity. Effective credit and accounts receivable management entails the following:

- Establishing and communicating a company's credit policies

- Establishing terms of sale consistent with overall company objectives

- Evaluating customer creditworthiness and setting customer credit lines

- Ensuring prompt and accurate customer billing in conjunction with customer service or billing departments

- Creating, preserving, and collecting accounts receivable

- Maintaining up-to-date records of accounts receivable

- Following up on overdue accounts and initiating collection procedures when necessary

II. ORGANIZATION OF THE CREDIT AND ACCOUNTS RECEIVABLE MANAGEMENT FUNCTION

Typically, companies break down credit and accounts receivable management along the following lines:

A. Responsibility

1. **Credit Management** - Credit managers administer credit policies that include:

   - Establishing credit-granting standards

   - Establishing terms of credit extension

   - Approving customers for credit sales

   - Setting individual and aggregate credit limits

2. **Accounts Receivable Management** - Administration of a company's accounts receivable is generally the responsibility of the credit manager, although other finance personnel may also be directly involved. Either way, receivable management entails:

   - Billing and processing payments

   - Monitoring payment patterns

   - Collecting delinquent accounts

3. **Sales and Customer Service** - Sales and customer service departments work closely with credit managers to develop credit policies because credit is principally a sales tool used to attract customers.

4. **Outsourcing Credit and Accounts Receivable Management** - Captive finance companies, or factors, may in some cases assume full or partial responsibility for credit and accounts receivable management.

B. Role of the Cash Manager

Working relationships with other departments and employees involved in credit management are important for a cash manager.

1. **Organizational Relationship** - Credit policy and collection of accounts receivable have a significant impact on timing of cash inflows. Typically, credit and/or accounts receivables managers, but not cash managers, are responsible for such matters.

2. **Information Links** - Credit and cash managers need strong information links and cooperative working relationships with employees in a company's other areas, such as sales, billing, and accounting in order to:

- **Track Customer Payments** - A cash manager is responsible for establishing and maintaining the banking network. The credit management function needs to have input to and receive feedback from this network regarding customer payments when a financial institution collects accounts receivables through a lockbox or asset-based borrowing arrangement.

- **Forecast Accurately** - The credit department provides important information used in cash forecasting. Credit policies affect the accuracy, nature, and timing of cash flows.

- **Process Collections and Apply Payments** - The cash manager may also oversee collections processing. This includes applying payments to customer accounts and generating information required for posting to the accounts receivable ledger.

III. CREDIT POLICIES

Company credit policies delineate credit standards, credit terms, and collection policies. If a company is to offer credit, it must address the following matters:

- **Credit Standards** - Granting credit has two stages, determining who will be granted credit and determining a customer's credit limit.

- **Credit Terms** - The contract must clearly specify the terms of sale to different customers.

- **Collection Policy** - A company must establish policies and procedures to collect payment should a credit customer fail to pay according to the specified terms.

To ensure consistent application and fairness, it is important for a company to have written credit policies and procedures. After a company has established its basic credit policies, it must develop procedures and information systems necessary to monitor accounts receivable for compliance with credit terms and to detect changes in customer payment patterns.

A. Reasons for Offering Trade Credit

Credit is a sales tool. Companies consider the following factors when extending credit:

1. **Market Share** - The portion of the market they are targeting

2. **Competition** - The credit terms competitors offer

3. **Promotional Efforts** - Credit terms necessary to attract new customers

4. **Sales Facilitation** - The needs of potential customers without access to other sources of credit

5. **Convenience** - The ease with which customers and potential customers can make credit purchases on an open account basis

6. **Profit** - The potential profitability of charging for credit through interest income

B. Credit Policy Constraints

The following factors influence a company's credit policies:

1. **Industry Practice and Company Strategy** - The credit terms customarily offered in many industries may not change for extended periods. It may be difficult for a seller to change from customary practices unless a buyer is offered some form of incentive, such as a discount, in return.

2. **Contractual Obligations** - Changes in receivable balances can affect working capital ratios, which must be kept in compliance with any debt covenants.

3. **Legal Issues** - The Robinson-Patman Act prohibits various forms of price discrimination. State commerce and usury laws may also limit certain credit practices or forbid them outright.

C. Financing Implications

Companies offering trade credit generate accounts receivable that convert to cash when the customers pay bills in the normal course of business. A company's credit terms, together with its sales and collection patterns, determine the levels of its accounts receivable and impact a company's financing needs.

1. **Use of Funds** - Receivables are assets that must be financed. A company's ability to extend credit is directly related to its ability to finance receivables. Mismanagement of receivables can cause liquidity problems such as delayed customer payment.

2. **Source of Liquidity Collateral** - Existing accounts receivable can be used as collateral for loans. Alternatively, they can be sold for cash to third parties called factors.

D. Income and Costs

Trade credit can increase a company's income, but there are also associated costs.

1. Income

    *   **Increased Sales** - Offering credit terms may attract additional sales volume and may result in increased profitability.

    *   **Interest Income** - Interest on installment payment arrangements can be a significant source of profit.

2. Expense

    The expenses involved in trade credit include:

    *   **Accounts Receivable Carrying Costs** - Like any other asset on a company's balance sheet, accounts receivable have carrying costs. Typically, a company determines this cost by using its marginal cost of short-term borrowings or its weighted average cost of capital.

- **Credit Department Costs** - These may include personnel costs, data and payments processing, and other costs required to sustain a department responsible for a company's trade credit operation.

- **Credit Evaluation** - This includes the costs of obtaining and analyzing credit information.

- **Discounted Payments** - When customers take advantage of an offered discount, but sales volumes do not increase, total net revenue is reduced. This loss of revenue may be fully or partially offset by a reduction in accounts receivable carrying costs.

- **Selling, Production, and Administration Costs** - A liberalized credit policy can increase sales, but also often increases administration and production costs of handling the increased volume.

- **Collection Expenses** - The cost of collecting delinquent accounts can be significant.

- **Bad Debt Expense** - Accounts receivable that are determined to be uncollectible must be charged off. Most companies estimate their level of losses and create a reserve account through periodic charges to bad debt expense. The timing and volume of bad debt expense and charge-offs are important aspects of credit policy.

- **Insurance** - Companies can reduce the impact of bad debts by purchasing various types of insurance designed to cover sales losses. Companies must include insurance premiums into the cost/benefit analysis when they assess the potential profitability of credit sales. (See Chapter 14, Financial Risk Management and Chapter 15, International Cash Management.)

- **Discrepancies in Payments** - The cost of monitoring, investigating, and resolving discrepancies between invoices and payments customers make can be high. Personnel must research discrepancies, ascertain the legitimacy of shortfalls and deductions, and handle all related bookkeeping, invoicing, and payment adjustment matters.

IV. CREDIT STANDARDS

It is important for a company to set and maintain its credit standards, which apply both to credit extension and billing and collection policies.

A. Considerations in Credit Extension Decision Making

Companies wish to avoid two circumstances in extending trade credit:

1. **Rejection of Acceptable Credit Risks** - If a company rejects a customer who is a good risk, the company loses potential sales.

2. **Acceptance of Substandard Risks** - If a company accepts a customer who does not pay according to the specified terms, the company incurs monitoring, collection, and/or bad debt costs.

Making credit standards more stringent will generally reduce risks but will also increase the frequency of rejecting acceptable risks. In practice, the costs of these two types of considerations are difficult to quantify. However, credit is a sales tool, and a zero default rate probably means that a company's credit terms are too strict.

B. Information Sources

A company must consider the type, quantity, and cost of information when establishing its method of analyzing credit requests. It can gather credit information in stages from internal and external sources, at each stage weighing costs against the expected benefits.

1. **Internal Sources** - The most important sources of internally generated credit information include the following:

    -   A credit application and agreement form completed by the applicant

    -   The company's own records regarding actual payment history of the applicant

2. **External Sources** - A company can use a wide variety of external sources to assist in determining the creditworthiness of a credit applicant.

    -   **Financial Statements** - Both audited and unaudited financial statements provide important information on corporate credit applicants.

    -   **Trade References** - Other companies are contacted to obtain their actual payment experiences regarding credit terms extended to the applicant.

    -   **Banks or Other Creditors** - The customer's bank or other financial creditors (commercial finance or leasing companies) can also provide valuable information about the customer's financial condition and available credit. Though banks or financial creditors may be reluctant to discuss their detailed experience with trade creditors, they will typically provide standardized credit information.

    -   **Agencies** - Various local and nationwide agencies collect, evaluate, and report information on the credit history of most companies. Their credit reports include information such as payment history, financial information, maximum outstanding credit amounts, length of time credit has been available, and any actions that have been necessary to achieve collection.

C. The Five Cs of Credit

Credit analyses depend upon the type of information available and the trade-off between costs and the benefits. The traditional factors companies consider are known as the five Cs of credit. These are:

1. **Character** - The perceived honesty or integrity of an individual applicant, or of the officers of a corporate applicant. These are seen as an indication of intent or willingness to pay, as evidenced by personal or corporate payment history.

2.   **Capacity** - The current and future financial resources a company or individual can commit to pay obligations when due. This is often assessed using financial liquidity ratios and cash flow forecasts.

3.   **Capital** - A customer's short- and long-term financial resources that could be called upon if the immediate cash flow is insufficient to meet payment obligations.

4.   **Collateral** - The assets or guarantees available to secure an obligation in the event payment is not made as agreed.

5.   **Conditions** - The general economic environment and economic conditions existing for the customer and the seller that affect the ability of the customer to pay and the willingness of the company to grant the credit.

D. Quantitative Credit Analysis

Quantitative methods for both corporate and consumer credit analysis include:

1.   **Business Credit Analysis** - Quantitative analysis of credit information begins with an examination of a credit applicant's financial statements, frequently through ratio analysis, which assesses a customer's financial condition. The measures used most often include liquidity and working capital ratios (current, quick, and cash flow-to-debt ratios), debt management and coverage ratios (times interest earned, long-term debt-to-capital, debt-to-total assets, and total liabilities to total assets ratios), and performance measures (return on equity, return on sales, and return on total assets). Ratios can provide valuable insight when evaluated in relation to industry standards published by credit rating agencies and other associations. Some commercial credit analysis can involve credit scoring, which is described below. (See Chapter 2, Accounting and Financial Concepts, for more information on ratio analysis.)

2.   **Consumer Credit Analysis** - Major issuers of retail credit, such as department stores, use quantitative credit scoring models and often develop a different model for each billing region. These quantitative approaches are cost effective and can aid in complying with consumer credit legislation that is discussed later in the chapter. Formal statistical analysis is often used to identify the factors that distinguish paying customers from non-paying customers. Credit bureaus also assess creditworthiness based on proprietary models.

3.   **Credit Scoring** - One technique companies use to estimate the creditworthiness of applicants is known as credit scoring. It involves a four step process:

  • Differentiating standard and high-risk accounts based on such data as monthly income, outstanding obligations, and the employment history of the applicant

  • Weighing the characteristics of those who fit into each category to establish creditworthiness

  • Setting cutoff scores for credit approval and denial

  • Applying further analysis to applicants whose scores fall in between the cutoff points

E. Billing and Collection Methods

The major objective of a collection policy is to speed the conversion of accounts receivable into cash while minimizing collection expense and bad-debt losses. The type of credit a company offers impacts significantly the collection methods it uses.

1. **Invoicing** - The first step in collecting an account is to send prompt and correct invoices with the terms of payment clearly stated. Effective cash management involves reducing invoice float, the interval between the time goods and services are purchased and the time the customer receives an invoice. Delays in invoice preparation or errors on the invoice can extend the entire payment process by days or even weeks.

2. **Statements** - Sometimes companies send summary statements of outstanding invoices as a reminder to customers that payment is due. Retail consumer billing typically involves sending statements listing goods or services purchased over a month's period.

3. **Delayed Payments** - When payment is not received by the due date, a company has a variety of options:

    - Sending a duplicate invoice

    - Mailing a form letter or series of form letters

    - Making telephone calls, which will also determine if there is a perceived dispute or need for a duplicate invoice

    - Visiting the customer in person

    - Suspending further sales until past due items are paid

    - Negotiating with the customer for payment of past due amounts

    - Claiming or realizing proceeds of any pledged collateral

    - Attempting to negotiate additional corporate or personal guarantees or trying to obtain a lien on specific assets

    - Initiating direct legal action or turning delinquent accounts over to a collection agency

V. FORMS OF CREDIT EXTENSION

Trade credit can be extended to a customer in the following ways:

A. Open Account

This method, sometimes called open book credit, is the most common type of commercial trade credit in the U.S.; it works as follows:

- A seller issues an invoice, which is formal evidence of the obligation, and records the sale as an account receivable.

- The customer is billed for each transaction by an invoice and/or by a monthly statement covering all invoices generated during the billing period.

- Full payment of invoiced amounts is expected within the specified credit terms unless certain discounts or deductions are made available to the customer.

- A buyer's creditworthiness is reviewed periodically, but the buyer does not need to apply for credit each time an order is placed.

- Companies usually charge fees for late payment.

B. Installment Credit

In this form of credit, a company requires a customer to make equal monthly payments, each of which contains a principal and an interest component. Installment credit is used frequently for the purchase of high-value consumer durables such as automobiles. Frequently the seller requires the buyer to sign a contract, which specifies the terms of the obligation, explains credit terms in full, and discloses rates of interest and other costs.

C. Revolving Credit

Under revolving credit terms, a company grants credit without requiring specific approval of each transaction as long as the account is current. The account is usually considered current if the credit outstanding is below an established credit limit and minimum payments have been made on time. If the account is not paid in full by the monthly payment due date, an interest charge is calculated based on the average amount outstanding over the entire period. (Revolving credit also refers to a type of bank loan which is described in Chapter 13, Borrowing.)

D. Letter of Credit (L/C)

An L/C is a device used to effect a payment in which a bank guarantees a seller that the bank, not the buyer, will pay for the agreed upon purchase when the seller presents documents conforming to specified conditions pertaining to the sale and delivery of goods or services. Typically, it is the buyer who pays for opening an L/C. L/Cs are commonly used in import/export transactions.

A variant of a commercial L/C is a Standby L/C, which serves as a guarantee to secure credit sales to a specific buyer. A Standby L/C is only drawn upon if payment in the transaction it supports is not made. (See Chapter 15, International Cash Management.)

VI. CONSIDERATIONS PERTAINING TO TERMS OF SALE

Buyers and sellers have a variety of standard terms of sale that they can choose from to conclude transactions. They are often specified in sales agreements, invoices, or other legal or commercial documents.

A. Common Terms of Sale

Standard sale terms stipulate the form and timing of payment and receipt of goods or services; many involve credit. The most common credit terms include:

1. **Cash Before Delivery (CBD)** - CBD terms require the buyer to make full and final payment before shipment or receipt of goods. It is often used when the seller does not know the buyer or when the seller considers the buyer a greater credit risk than he is willing to accept.

2. **Cash on Delivery (COD)** - The seller ships the goods and the buyer pays upon receipt. If the buyer refuses payment, the goods are returned, and the seller must pay the shipping cost.

3. **Cash Terms** - The buyer generally has a week to 10 days to make payment. This method is frequently used in sales of highly perishable items.

4. **Net Terms** - The seller specifies a net due date by which the buyer must pay in full. For example, terms of Net 30 require the buyer to pay within 30 days from the date of invoice, date of delivery, or some other specified date.

5. **Discount Terms** - In addition to specifying a net due date, the seller may also offer a discount if payment is made prior to that date. Terms of 2/10 Net 30 mean that the total amount is due within 30 days of the invoice date, but the buyer can take a two percent discount if payment is made within 10 days.

6. **Monthly Billing** - The seller issues a monthly statement covering all invoices prior to a cutoff date, typically the 25th of each month. The buyer must pay by a specified date the following month. The seller may allow the buyer to take a discount for prompt payment. For example, if the terms are 1/10, Prox Net 30, the buyer may take a discount of one percent if payment is made by the 10th day of the following month. The total due must be paid by the 30th day of the month.

7. **Draft/Bill of Lading** - This collection method is also known as a documentary collection. The seller collects payments through banking channels. Having shipped goods to the buyer, the seller sends shipping and title documents to the bank, which then transmits them to the buyer's bank. The buyer gains possession of the documents upon paying the bank or upon signing a draft agreeing to pay at a future date. Upon collection, the buyer's bank remits payment to the seller's bank. This method is more common to international trade than it is to domestic trade.

8. **Seasonal Dating** - The seller agrees to accept payment at the end of the buyer's selling season, when the buyer has cash. This allows manufacturers to provide short-term financing for a buyer's purchases and reduces the manufacturer's inventory costs. It is common in industries with distinct seasonality of sales such as toys, greeting cards, garden supplies, sporting goods, or textbooks. The seller may offer scaled discounts to encourage the buyer to pay early.

9. **Consignment** - Under a consignment agreement, the seller ships the goods to the buyer with no obligation to pay until the goods have been sold or used. The title to the goods remains with the seller until that date.

B. Common Credit Practices

Considerations regarding credit terms are as follows:

1. **Penalty Fees** - In addition to offering credit terms, companies often assess a penalty fee for payments received after the due date. This fee is usually a percentage of the past due amount. The fee should be clearly stated at the time of the sale and shown on the invoice.

2. **Credit Limits** - In addition to the terms of each sale, companies' credit managers must also determine the aggregate amount of credit they should grant each customer. Companies usually grant new customers credit at the lowest limit. After a period of satisfactory payment performance, they raise the credit limit to the next level. Companies review credit levels periodically to determine relevance and adjust them as necessary.

3. **Eligibility for Discount** - Companies determine a benchmark date for eligibility for discounts. This can be the postmark date of the payment remittance or the date funds are received.

C. Offering Discounts

The seller, when offering cash discounts, must evaluate the cost of doing so versus the benefits to be gained from receiving payment early. Exhibit 5.1 shows how the annualized cost of credit is calculated.

Standard practice provides the following alternative methods of accounting for sales discounting:

1. **Gross Method** - Gross sales revenues are recorded on the income statement and discounts are taken as an expense on the income statement.

2. **Net Method** - Amounts are entered into the receivables and revenue accounts net of the discounts. Any discounts not taken are then shown as income.

EXHIBIT 5.1 *Annualized* *Cost of Trade* *Credit*	$$\text{Annualized Cost of Trade Credit} = \frac{\text{Early Pmt. Discount}}{(1 - \text{Early Pmt. Discount})} \times \frac{365}{(\text{Net Pmt. Period} - \text{Discount Pmt. Period})}$$

Example

Given terms of 2/10, Net 30, the cost of not taking the discount (i.e., paying the net amount on day 30 rather than the discounted amount on day 10) can be calculated as:

$$\text{Cost of Trade Credit} = \frac{.02}{(1-.02)} \times \frac{365}{(30 - 10)} = 37.24\%$$

If a buyer were able to borrow funds at a rate of less than 37.24%, then he should do so and take the discount for early payment. If borrowed funds cost more than 37.24% or if they are not available, then the buyer should delay payment until the net due date.

A company with excess cash reserves must compare this annualized cost to investment rates. If alternative investment rates available to the company exceed the annualized cost of trade credit, then the discount should not be taken and payment should be delayed until the net due date.

VII. ACCOUNTS RECEIVABLE MONITORING AND CONTROL

Monitoring and controling a company's accounts receivable are important aspects of the overall credit policy. They are often the responsibility of the cash manager.

A. Purpose

Monitoring of accounts receivable should be performed at both an individual account and an aggregate level. A customer aging schedule is a useful method for tracking individual receivables, and a report of days sales outstanding is a useful measure of total accounts receivable.

1. **Monitoring Individual Accounts** - Companies should monitor individual accounts for the following reasons:

    • There may be errors or delays in the invoicing or payment process.

    • Some customers may intentionally delay payment until follow-up is initiated.

    • A change in financial condition may alter the ability of a customer to make timely payments and may require a curtailment of future credit sales.

2. **Monitoring Aggregate Accounts Receivable** - Companies should monitor aggregate accounts receivable for the following reasons:

- Changes in accounts receivables may impact liquidity and prompt the need for additional financing.

- A significant change in the level of overall accounts receivable may be a symptom of a change in business that could affect a company's financing needs. Management should analyze these changes to determine underlying causes and any corrective actions that need to be taken. Developments that could prompt significant changes include:

  - Variations in sales volume

  - Modifications of credit standards policy

  - Fluctuating economic conditions

  - Responding to competitors' actions

- Accounts receivable serve as a basis for forecasting the amount and timing of future cash receipts.

B. Days' Sales Outstanding (DSO)

Another method of measuring accounts receivable is Days' Sales Outstanding (DSO), which companies calculate by dividing accounts receivable outstanding at the end of a time interval by the average daily credit sales of the period. DSO gives a single number that can be compared to stated credit terms or to an historic trend to provide an indication of a company's overall collection efficiency. It may, however, be distorted by changing trends in sales volume, payment pattern, or by a strong seasonality in sales.

Exhibit 5.2 describes a basic method for calculating DSO. The average daily sales of $3,444.44 is computed without considering the pattern of sales for the period.

EXHIBIT 5.2

*Days' Sales
Outstanding
(DSO)
Calculation*

Assume

Outstanding Receivables of $285,000 at the end of Month 3
Credit Terms of Net 60
DSO Averaging Period of 3 months (90 days)
Credit Sales History:
  Month 1 = $ 90,000.00
  Month 2 = $ 105,000.00
  Month 3 = $ 115,000.00

DSO Calculation

$$\text{Average Daily Credit Sales} = \frac{(\$90,000.00 + \$105,000.00 + \$115,000.00)}{90} = \$3,444.44$$

$$\text{Days' Sales Outstanding (DSO)} = \frac{\text{Outstanding Accounts Receivable}}{\text{Average Daily Credit Sales}} = \frac{\$285,000.00}{\$3,444.44} = 82.74 \text{ Days}$$

Average Past Due Calculation

$$\text{Average Past Due} = \text{DSO} - \text{Average Days of Credit Terms}$$

$$= 82.74 \text{ Days} - 60 \text{ Days} = 22.74 \text{ Days}$$

C. Aging Schedule

An aging schedule divides accounts receivable into those that are current and those that are past due in 30-day increments. Companies can analyze the aging of receivables on an aggregate or customer-by-customer basis. An aging analysis identifies past-due accounts, which become less collectable as their age increases.

An example of an aging schedule is shown in Exhibit 5.3. With credit terms of Net 30, this aggregate aging schedule shows that 30 percent of the accounts receivable are past due. The aging schedule can be a more informative breakdown than DSO because it provides information on the distribution, not just a single average. However, an aging schedule can send the same potentially misleading signals as DSO when sales vary significantly from month to month.

Age of Accounts	Accounts Receivable	% of Accounts Receivable
0-30 days	$1,750,000	70%
31-60 days	375,000	15%
61-90 days	250,000	10%
91+ days	125,000	5%
Total	$2,500,000	100%

EXHIBIT 5.3
Example of an Aging Schedule

D. Accounts Receivable Balance Patterns

Aging schedules are used to establish receivables balance patterns, which are useful cash forecasting tools. They specify the percentage of credit sales in a time period, usually a month, that remains outstanding in the company's accounts receivable at the end of that and each subsequent time period.

Exhibit 5.4 gives an example of a company whose sales are collected as follows:

    5% of sales collected in the current month after sale
40% of sales collected in the next month after sale
35% of sales collected two months after sale
20% of sales collected three months after sale

At the end of March, there will still be $50,000 of accounts receivable outstanding (uncollected) from January's sales. This can be forecast as follows:

January Sales			=	$ 250,000.00
Collected in: January	=	(.05 x $250,000)	=	$ 12,500.00
Collected in: February	=	(.40 x $250,000)	=	$ 100,000.00
Collected in: March	=	(.35 x $250,000)	=	$ 87,500.00
Total Collections			=	$ 200,000.00

Total Outstanding Receivables from January Sales = $ 250,000 - $ 200,000 = $50,000

EXHIBIT 5.4
Example of a Receivables Balance Pattern

Month Sales	Sales	Remaining Accounts Receivable from Month Sales at the End of March	Remaining Accounts Receivable as a % of Month Sales
January	$250,000	$50,000	20%
February	$300,000	$165,000	55%
March	$400,000	$380,000	95%
April	$500,000		

The total outstanding accounts receivable balance at the end of March is:
$595,000 = ($50,000 + $165,000 + $380,000)

The estimate of cash inflows for April = 5% of April sales + 40% of March sales + 35% of February sales + 20% of January sales:

$$\text{Estimated April Inflows} = \begin{array}{l} (.05 \times \$500,000) \\ + (.40 \times \$400,000) \\ + (.35 \times \$300,000) \\ + (.20 \times \$250,000) \\ = \quad \$340,000 \end{array}$$

A company's collection history determines its normal balance pattern. Management can evaluate any shifts by comparing current patterns with historical norms. Furthermore, variations in sales patterns do not affect balance patterns nor do they send misleading signals regarding future cash inflows. Companies can use balance patterns to project accounts receivable levels, collections, and forecast future cash inflows.

VIII. FINANCING ACCOUNTS RECEIVABLE

Accounts receivable, which are a major component of current assets, can be financed in a variety of ways.

A. Unsecured Borrowing

A company that offers trade credit can borrow unsecured funds from a financial institution to support accounts receivable if it has sufficient available credit capacity.

B. Secured Borrowing

If a company cannot finance its accounts receivable with unsecured borrowings, it may be able to pledge its accounts receivable as collateral and borrow on a secured basis. A bank will select those accounts receivable it accepts as collateral and extend the company a loan. The company will remit the funds owed to the bank upon collection of the receivables.

C. Securitization

Large companies, particularly those with finance subsidiaries such as automobile and credit card companies, bundle their receivables and issue securities backed by them. Consumers' installment payments are used to pay off the instruments' principal and interest. Securitization allows a company to free up capital and enhances its creditworthiness. (See Chapter 12, Short-Term Investment and Chapter 13, Borrowing.)

D. Captive Finance Subsidiary

A company may be able to create a wholly owned subsidiary to perform credit operations and obtain accounts receivable financing for the sale of its products. Since the finance company is a subsidiary of the parent company, the advantages and disadvantages specified earlier in this chapter apply. In addition, because many companies' receivables represent a significant proportion of their assets, operating a captive finance subsidiary enhances the parent's liquidity significantly and allows it to obtain capital at a lower cost than it otherwise could.

E. Third-Party Financing

A company collects the information necessary to complete a credit application from its customer and forwards it to a financial institution, which decides whether or not to grant credit. Because of the administrative costs this entails, the companies that do this tend to manufacture and market big-ticket items such as production machinery.

Although third-party financing through an institution can free up capital, companies that use it relinquish control over the type of customer they want to attract and may miss marketing opportunities. Furthermore, a company may have to discount the price of the goods sold in order to compensate the third party, and thus forgo potential income.

F. Credit Cards

A third party, usually a bank or another financial institution, may offer a credit card that a merchant accepts as payment. The agreement between the seller and the financial institution specifies that the seller receives payment electronically on the day following the transaction.

1. **Advantages** - Credit cards offer the following advantages:

   - The seller bears none of the direct costs of running a credit department.

   - Depending upon the agreement, the seller has few or no funds tied up in financing accounts receivable.

   - The third party usually absorbs bad-debt losses.

2. **Disadvantages** - The disadvantages in using credit cards for customer financing are as follows:

   - The seller loses control over the determination of acceptable credit customers.

- The seller loses the promotional aspects of having its own list of credit customers.

- Major direct costs include fees associated with the transaction, which depend upon the average size of the sale, the total volume, and the type of business or organization.

G. Factoring

Factoring usually involves the outright sale of receivables to a factor. In most factoring arrangements the buyer of the receivables has no recourse to the seller. In other words, the factor must absorb the loss if the customer fails to pay. However, in some cases, the factoring arrangement stipulates the factor does have recourse, in which case the seller is still liable if the factor cannot collect.

Most factoring is performed on a notification basis. The company notifies the customer that the account has been sold, and the payment is remitted directly to the factor.

1. **Advantages of Factoring** - Factoring has the following advantages:

    - It reduces or eliminates the cost of maintaining a credit department.

    - It reduces uncertainty in the timing of payments.

    - It extends the range of customers to whom a company can grant credit. Because the factor can share the risk, together they may be able to extend credit to customers that the company otherwise could not.

    - It may improve the credit-extension process. The factor may have access to information that enables it to extend more credit with fewer delinquencies. Department stores and retail chains often rely on this type of financing.

2. **Disadvantages of Factoring** - Disadvantages of factoring include the following:

    - Factors may charge high fees, particularly in non-recourse agreements.

    - The seller loses control over who is granted credit and may require its own credit operation to assess those customers rejected by the factor.

    - Some companies believe that having their receivables factored conveys a sign of financial weakness; although in certain industries factoring is a standard practice.

H. Private Label Financing

With private label financing, a third party operates the credit function in the name of the seller rather than the seller administering its own credit program. Private label financing allows the seller to retain many of the promotional aspects of conducting its own credit function while incurring none of the costs of maintaining a credit operation or financing accounts receivable. At the same time, the seller does not receive the full face value of the sale and may lose the authority to decide which customers should receive credit. From the customer's perspective, the credit appears to be arranged through the seller.

IX. CASH APPLICATION

Cash application is the process of applying a customer's payment against outstanding invoices. There are two basic ways to accomplish this:

A. Open Item

An open item system is most commonly used in business-to-business sales. Each invoice sent to a customer is recorded in the accounts receivable file. When a payment is received, it is matched with the specific invoices being paid and any payment discrepancies (discounts, allowances, adjustments, etc.) are noted. Remittance information, which typically accompanies payments, usually details which invoices are being paid, as well as any adjustments to the payment. This application process may be manual or automated or a combination of the two.

Many companies have automated cash application programs that take the payment and remittance information and, through a series of algorithms, apply the payments by matching them to specific invoices. A high rate of successful automated applications greatly reduces the amount of manual effort required to complete the application process.

Lockbox processors may provide payment and remittance data to a company to facilitate the cash application process. One common service is to capture the data in the MICR line of the check. Elements captured include the drawee bank's transit routing number, the payor's bank account number, and the check amount. The transit routing number and bank account number can be used to identify the customer (using an internal database) and additional information gathered from remittance materials. The capture of this remittance data by the lockbox processor may be automated (using pre-encoded payment stubs) or manual. The additional remittance data may include such items as:

- Invoice numbers

- Amounts paid

- Customer account numbers

- Remitter's name

- Discounts and adjustments taken

- Dates

- Other pertinent information

Some lockbox processors access a company's accounts receivable system information during lockbox processing in order to look up such things as account numbers and other pertinent information. Others match payments and invoices – to the extent possible – prior to data transmission to the company using information provided by the company or on encoded payment stubs returned with the payments. These services are designed to increase a company's automated payment application rate, thereby increasing the overall efficiency of the process.

B. Balance Forward

Balance forward systems are used most often by companies selling goods and services to individual consumers. In a balance forward system, a credit limit is established for each individual, and as purchases are made or services are provided, the accounts receivable outstanding increases. When payments are made, the accounts receivable balance is reduced by the amount of the payment.

C. Electronic Data Interchange (EDI)

Given the increased use of EDI, a company's accounts receivable system must be able to process electronic payments and remittance information in order to use this information to properly apply payments. Because of the increased remittance information accompanying the payment in an EDI environment, the cash application rate may be increased through automation of the process. (See Chapter 9, Electronic Commerce.)

X. LEGISLATION AFFECTING CREDIT AND COLLECTIONS

Many laws and regulations affect the area of credit and collections.

A. Pricing and Interest Charge Restrictions

Because the extension of credit is a benefit to the buyer, credit terms can be considered a part of the price of the product or service being sold.

1. **Robinson-Patman Act (1936)** - The Robinson-Patman Act specifically prohibits price discrimination among customers where a cost basis cannot be demonstrated as the reason for price differences. Different credit terms are acceptable if they are industry practice or in cases in which cost differences can be substantiated.

2. **Usury Laws** - Usury laws, which vary significantly from state to state, restrict the interest rates or penalty fees that companies can charge on installment credit.

B. Consumer and Commercial Credit Legislation

A number of laws regulate the statement of terms, the credit analysis and approval process, and the collection practices that can be employed when selling on a credit basis to consumers. Some of the more important federal legislation and regulations are:

1. **Truth in Lending Act (1969)** - This act requires lenders to disclose the true annual interest rate and the total dollar cost on most types of loans.

2. **Fair Credit Reporting Act (1971)** - This law enables consumers to access the information in their credit files at little or no cost.

3. **Fair Credit Billing Act (1975)** - This act is an amendment to the Truth in Lending Act and protects charge account customers from billing errors by permitting them to use the same legal defenses against banks or other third-party credit card companies that they could previously use against merchants.

4. **Equal Credit Opportunity Act (1975)** - This act prohibits creditors from discriminating against credit applicants on the basis of sex, marital status, race, color, religion, national origin, age, or receipt of public assistance.

5. **Fair Debt Collection Practices Act (1978)** - This act is designed to eliminate abusive and unfair debt collection practices such as threats of financial ruin, loss of job or reputation, or harassing telephone calls.

C. Uniform Commercial Code (UCC)

In general, revolving credit, installment credit, and sales finance transactions are covered by provisions of the UCC, which is the model for many state laws pertaining to commerce.

D. Bankruptcy and Reorganization

Under the Federal Bankruptcy Reform Act of 1978, a company may file for liquidation under Chapter 7 or reorganization under Chapter 11. Individuals typically file for reorganization under Chapter 13. Reorganization allows a company to pay off debts gradually and operate under a court-supervised plan for returning to financial soundness. Filing of a petition protects the debtor from a list of actions by creditors. The law established a federal bankruptcy court system with exclusive jurisdiction over bankruptcy cases.

Questions

These chapter questions are to test and review the information in the text and are not examples of CCM examination questions, nor are they in the examination format.

Answers can be found at the back of the book on pgs. 367-368.

1.   What are the major objectives of credit management?

2.   What are the three elements of a credit policy?

3.   What is the effective cost of not taking a discount under terms of 3/20 Net 60?

4.   What are the five C's of credit?

5.   What is credit scoring?

6.   What are revolving credit terms?

7.   What is seasonal dating?

8.   A firm has outstanding receivables of $125,000. Its credit terms are Net 30. If during the past three months sales are $75,000, $100,000 and $90,000, how many days' sales are outstanding?

9.   What is factoring?

10.   What federal legislation prohibits price discrimination?

11.   What federal legislation requires disclosure of the true cost of a loan?

CHAPTER 6

Collections

OVERVIEW

This chapter discusses the objectives of a collection system, the principal methods that companies and other organizations use to collect payments, and the role of the commercial banking system in the collection process.

LEARNING OBJECTIVES

Upon completion of this chapter and related study questions, the reader should know:

1. The objectives of a corporate collection system

2. The components of collection float

3. How companies select processing systems

4. The differences among over-the-counter, mail, and electronic collection methods

5. The service features of lockbox providers

6. The differences between wholesale and retail lockboxes

7. How to conduct a collection study

8. How to calculate the cost of float and the dollar savings from a lockbox

9. The functions and applications of electronic and other collection systems

KEY CONCEPTS

1. Collection System Purposes

2. Components of Collection System Float

3. Differences Among Collection Methods

4. Different Types of Lockboxes

5. Collection Studies

6. Lockbox Costs and Benefits

7. Other Electronic Collection Systems

OUTLINE

I. Objectives of a Collection System

II. Collection Float
    A. Components
    B. Measurement

III. Collection System Considerations
    A. Payment Practices
    B. Payments System
    C. Nature of the Business
    D. Payment Instrument Characteristics
    E   Float/Administrative Cost Tradeoff

IV. Collection Methods and Products
    A   Over-the-Counter/Field Deposit Systems
    B. Mail Processing Systems
    C. Electronic Systems

V. Types of Lockboxes
    A   Wholesale Lockbox
    B. Retail Lockbox
    C. Hybrid Lockbox

VI. Issues Pertaining to Lockbox Selection
    A. Lockbox Cost/Benefit Analysis
    B. Collection Studies
    C. How Lockbox Service Features Vary
    D. Lockbox Networks
    E. Customized Services

VII. Image Technology

VIII. Electronic Collection Systems
    A. Wire Transfers
    B. Automated Clearing House (ACH) Corporate-to-Corporate Payments
    C. Preauthorized Payments

IX. Other Collection Systems
    A. Net Settlement Systems
    B. Retail Collection Systems

I. OBJECTIVES OF A COLLECTION SYSTEM

A collection system is a set of arrangements and management procedures used to gather and process customer payments. The major objectives of a corporate collection system include:

- **Mobility of Funds** - Move funds from a customer's (payor) account into a company's (payee's) account within the banking system as quickly and cost effectively as possible. To do this, a company must integrate its collection system with its cash concentration system.

- **Accessing Information** - Provide accurate and timely information on cash flows, levels of bank balances, and availability of funds in a manner that interfaces easily with other components of a company's treasury information management system.

- **Updating Accounts Receivable** - Update accounts receivable records promptly and accurately and, through linkages, also update credit and treasury management systems. Mistakes or failures to update customer files can jeopardize potential sales because of credit limitations thereby damaging customer relationships.

- **Providing Audit Trails** - Provide audit trails for the company's internal and external auditors.

II. COLLECTION FLOAT

Collection float is the interval between the time the payor mails the check and the time the payee receives available funds at its financial institution. Converting accounts receivable into collected funds requires minimizing collection float.

A. Components

Collection float has three components: mail, processing, and availability. Each represents a collection interval along the cash flow timeline.

- **Mail Float** - Mail float is the interval between the time a check is mailed and the date it is received by the payee or at the processing site. It usually ranges from one to five calendar days or more.

- **Processing Float** - Processing float is the interval between the time the payee or the processing site receives the check and the time the check is deposited at a financial institution. It can range from less than one day to three calendar days or more.

- **Availability Float** - Availability float is the interval between the time a check is deposited and the time a company's account is credited with collected funds. It typically ranges from zero to two business days and is determined by the depository institution's availability schedule. (This is the same as deposit float discussed in Chapter 4.)

The components of collection float are illustrated in Exhibit 6.1.

EXHIBIT 6.1

Components of Collection Float

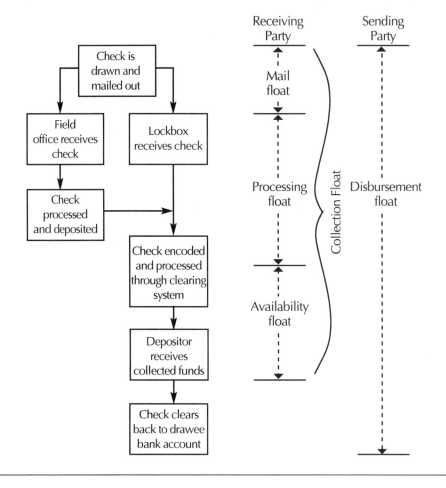

B. Measurement

Collection float is usually measured in dollar-days and is a function of the transaction's dollar amount and the number of days' delay. The dollar-days of float on an individual check are calculated by multiplying the dollar amount of the check by the number of days between mailing and crediting.

Batch	Dollar Amount	Calendar Days of Float	Dollar-Days of Float
1	$1,500,000	x 4 =	$ 6,000,000
2	4,500,000	x 2 =	9,000,000
3	3,000,000	x 6 =	18,000,000
	$9,000,000		$33,000,000

EXHIBIT 6.2

Example of Float Measurement

Note: In this example there are 30 calendar days in the month and the opportunity cost of funds is 9%.

$$\text{Average daily float} = \frac{\text{Total Dollar-Days of Float}}{\text{Total Calendar Days in Period}}$$

$$\text{Average daily receipts} = \frac{\text{Total Dollar Amount}}{\text{Total Calendar Days in Period}}$$

$$\text{Average delay} = \frac{\text{Total Dollar-Days of Float}}{\text{Total Dollar Amount}}$$

$$\text{Annual cost of float} = \text{Average Daily Float} \times \text{Opportunity Cost of Funds}$$

$$\text{Average daily float} = \frac{\$33,000,000}{30} = \$1,100,000$$

$$\text{Average daily receipts} = \frac{\$9,000,000}{30} = \$300,000$$

$$\text{Average delay} = \frac{33,000,000}{9,000,000} = 3.67 \text{ days}$$

$$\text{Annual cost of float} = \$1,100,000 \times .09 = \$99,000$$

Exhibit 6.2 provides a step-by-step analysis of float measurement as follows:

1. Each of the three batches of checks has a different number of calendar days of float.

2. The dollar-days of float are calculated for each batch and then totaled.

3. The average daily float is calculated by dividing the total dollar-days of float by the number of calendar days in the period.

4. The average delay, or the average number of days of float, is calculated by dividing the total dollar-days of float by the total dollar amount.

5. The annual cost of float is calculated using a company's incremental opportunity cost of funds.

III. COLLECTION SYSTEM CONSIDERATIONS

In designing a collection system, a company must take into account the following issues:

- Commonly accepted payment practices

- The structure of the payments system

- The nature of its business (wholesale versus retail)

- Characteristics of the payment instrument used

- The cost of float and system administration

A discussion of each of these considerations follows.

A. Payment Practices

In the U.S., checks are the most frequently used payment instrument for both corporate and consumer bill paying, although the dollar volumes of electronic payments are vastly greater and the use of electronic payments is increasing. Electronic payments offer the potential for substantial cost savings for corporate payors and receivers. This is especially true if electronic payments become the predominant method of payment and are used as an integral part of electronic data interchange (EDI) systems. However, in the U.S., checks provide the payor with disbursement float and are an established way of doing business acceptable to most trading partners.

B. Payments System

All collection systems must be designed in light of the particular strengths and limitations of a country's payments system. Three features that distinguish the U.S. payments system from that of most other countries are:

- Checks are used in most payments. Large cash transactions are rare.

- There is a relatively large number of banks and financial institutions. The U.S. financial system is both highly evolved and very competitive.

- The extent of nationwide branch banking is relatively limited. Although legal barriers to national branch banking have fallen, the U.S. system remains fragmented.

C. Nature of the Business

The nature of a company's business impacts the collection system it uses.

- Typically, high transaction volume retail operations like a fast food store receive virtually all of their payments in cash.

- A time-critical transaction such as a securities settlement or a real estate closing, or simply a very large dollar amount, may require a wire transfer with same-day value.

• A supplier usually sends an invoice to its customer and receives a check as payment. The check is generally accompanied by remittance information about invoices paid, partial payments, discounts, and deductions.

D. Payment Instrument Characteristics

Each payment instrument has different characteristics and uses. Often the instrument used is a matter of negotiation between the seller and the buyer. The most preferred method for the one may not be best for the other.

1. **Cash** - Cash is the principal means of payment in many retail businesses. Cash provides the seller with immediate funds.

2. **Check** - A check is used for most corporate and consumer bill payments. Depending on when and how it is deposited and cleared, a check usually provides the seller with zero- to two-day availability from the day it is deposited.

3. **Payment Cards**

    • **Credit Cards** - The acceptance of credit cards by retailers is widespread. Increasingly, credit cards also are becoming a preferred method of payment among wholesalers.

    • **Debit Cards** - Consumer use of debit cards as a method of payment is growing in acceptance. Debit cards replace cash and check transactions. The seller/merchant is provided with zero- to two-day availability.

    • **Purchasing Cards** - Purchasing or procurement cards can be used to pay for supplies, inventory, equipment, or services. Organizations using these cards have been able to reduce the costs of purchasing and maintain or increase control.

    • **Smart Cards** - Smart cards have silicon chips embedded within them. They are capable of storing important data which can be updated. The cards can be used as stored value devices enabling cardholders to make fewer cash transactions. From the standpoint of collections, smart cards are similar to credit or debit card transactions.

4. **Automated Clearing House (ACH)** - Consumer and corporate use of the ACH as a method of payment is growing in acceptance, as is the use of ACH by companies to pay trading partners. Settlement usually occurs one or two days after origination.

5. **Wire Transfer** - Wire transfer as a method of payment is primarily used by companies for large dollar transactions. The payee is provided with immediate funds.

E. Float/Administrative Cost Tradeoff

An optimal collection system minimizes the sum of float, processing, and administrative costs. For example, if a company chooses to use a lockbox system (a cash collection system in which a company's customers mail payments to a post office box near the company's bank), it must determine the number and location of lockbox sites. Additionally, if more than one is used, each customer must be assigned to a specific lockbox. While adding more collection points generally reduces float, it increases administrative and processing costs.

IV. COLLECTION METHODS AND PRODUCTS

Companies collect payments from their customers over-the-counter, through the mail, and through electronic networks. Exhibit 6.3 provides an overview of these three systems.

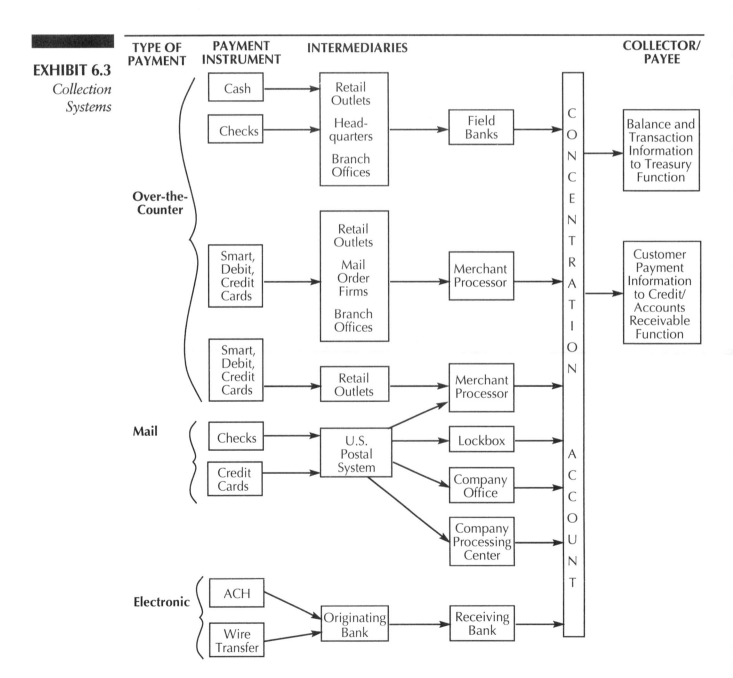

EXHIBIT 6.3
Collection Systems

A. Over-the-Counter/Field Deposit Systems

Various businesses may collect receipts over-the-counter at field locations. Field units include local offices and retail stores. Methods used by retail establishments to collect at the point of sale include cash, checks, credit cards, debit cards, and smart cards. A wholesale customer or its agent may deliver checks or cash to a vendor's office. Alternatively, a payee or its agent may pick up checks or cash from the customer when making a delivery. Companies must carefully consider various attributes when selecting deposit or collection banks, including:

1. **Location** - A deposit bank whose branches are close to the field units offers convenience and increased cash handling security for local managers.

2. **Branch Banking** - Where statewide, regional, or interstate branching is available, collections may be simplified by using branches of the same bank or banks. This reduces the company's administrative and cash concentration costs. The company may, however, lose some flexibility in selecting convenient deposit bank locations and incur a risk by relying on only one bank.

3. **Compensation** - The compensation of field banks can be by fees, balances, or both.

4. **Deposit Reconciliation Services** - A bank with multiple branches may offer deposit reconciliation services, also called branch consolidation services. These services enable deposits from multiple locations to be credited to a single corporate bank account. The use of magnetic ink character recognition (MICR) encoded deposit tickets allows banks to identify each company deposit location and produce reports on a daily, weekly, or monthly basis.

5. **Pre-Encoded Check Deposits** - Companies that pre-encode checks to be deposited can get lower fees and/or faster availability.

6. **Cash Processing** - A company that accepts cash has two options for making cash deposits:

   • **Branch Deposits** - An employee of the company can take cash to a nearby bank or bank branch for deposit. However, because of the security risk involved, banks may refuse to accept large cash deposits at certain locations or withhold granting credit until final verification of the deposit.

   • **Centralized Cash Processing** - Centralized cash processing involves sending armored couriers to pick up cash from a company's location and deliver it to a processing site. This method is commonly used for transporting large amounts of cash because it reduces security risks. Companies can reduce fees by prepackaging cash and coins and by putting each denomination of coin in standard rolls, or by filling standard bags with loose coins of a particular denomination. If a company delivers cash in mixed denominations, the bank may charge extra for counting and verification. Banks may charge for these services in different ways, such as the amount of time required to verify the deposit, the dollar amount of the deposit, or the number of bills and deposits processed.

B. Mail Processing Systems

Companies receive checks from consumers and from other companies in the mail directly or through lockboxes. For payments received in the mail, a company may use either its own processing center or a lockbox. Deciding which method to use depends primarily on the volume of checks processed and the dollar amounts of the checks.

1. **Company Processing Center** - With a company processing center, a company does its own processing and deposit preparation. It is typically used by a company with a large volume of relatively small-dollar payments.

    Advantages - The advantages of company processing centers over lockboxes include:

    *   **Control** - A company maintains total control over the operation.

    *   **Flexibility** - It is easier to make changes in an internal system than it is in a lockbox processor's system.

    *   **Customization** - Processing is customized to meet a company's needs rather than standardized to meet the needs of a lockbox processor.

    *   **Facilitation of Updating** - Updating payor information may be faster.

    *   **Reduced Cost** - With large volume and small dollars, a company may find internal processing less expensive than paying a third party for the same amount of work because a company can realize the same economies of scale as a lockbox processor.

    *   **Capability Assurance** - A company is assured of future processing capability, as opposed to relying on a lockbox processor that may eliminate the service.

    Disadvantages - The disadvantages of processing centers over lockboxes include:

    *   **Reduced Cost Effectiveness** - A company must staff and equip the processing center. Check volume must be sufficient for a company to have a cost-efficient operation and peak volume must be accommodated.

    *   **Lack of Contingency Sites** - A company may lack a contingency site to prevent an interruption in payment processing.

    *   **Reduced Processing and Efficiency** - There may be a greater time lag between processing the items and depositing the checks.

    *   **Slower Delivery** - A company processing center may not receive mail through a unique ZIP code or be located where the company has operations resulting in greater mail float.

2. **Lockbox** - A lockbox is a collection system in which a third party receives payments at a specified lockbox address, processes the remittances, and deposits them in the payee's account. Lockboxes can be electronic, paper-based, or a combination of the two. They are one of the most widely used cash management methods.

    Advantages - Lockboxes have the following advantages over a company processing center:

    *   **Reduced Float** - A lockbox reduces the three components of collection float as follows:

        *   **Mail Float** - Mail float is usually reduced because a lockbox processor uses its own unique ZIP code to speed mail delivery. Also, a lockbox processor makes frequent mail pickups from a postal facility instead of waiting for the mail to be delivered. A lockbox may also be located close to a payor.

        *   **Processing Float** - Processing float is usually reduced because remittances are mailed directly to the lockbox processor, eliminating a company's intermediary role in receiving, processing and delivering checks to the bank. Further, many lockbox processors operate 24 hours a day, seven days per week, with emphasis on peak periods.

        *   **Availability Float** - Availability float is usually reduced because lockbox processors schedule work to meet critical availability deadlines. These are deadlines by which checks must reach the bank's proof and transit area.

    *   **Efficient Processing** - A lockbox provides efficient processing through economies of scale. In addition, trained personel process the work for a particular account, and others are trained to back up these specialists.

    *   **Greater Control and Enhanced Record Keeping Capability** - A lockbox establishes an external audit trail for payments received and segregates check processing from other accounts receivable functions. A lockbox may be required by company auditors even when it is not economically justified based on float reduction.

    *   **Uninterrupted Service** - Lockboxes are less vulnerable to service interruptions and are more easily re-started following disasters.

    Disadvantages - Lockboxes have the following disadvantages relative to company processing centers:

    *   **Reduced Operational Control** - A company has less control over the operation than with a company processing center.

    *   **Greater Costs** - A company with very high transaction volume may be able to run its own processing center at a cost that is lower than that of a lockbox.

C. Electronic Systems

Modern telecommunications and data transmission systems linked to personal computers (PCs), along with the Internet, have transformed the way payments are remitted, transfers made, and financial information disseminated. (See Chapter 9, Electronic Commerce.)

- **Home Banking** - Home Banking Services are available from financial institutions or brokerage houses or can be part of software systems connecting users to third-party providers. Generally, these are PC-based services with a broad array of capabilities which may include bank or brokerage account inquiry, account transfer and transaction and bill paying services. As their use becomes more widespread, companies must adapt collection systems to accept and process payments received through these systems.

- **Telephone Initiation** - Telephones can be used to transfer funds and make payments from accounts at financial institutions. Sometimes these transactions involve credit and other types of payment cards.

- **Personal Computers** - When linked to the Internet and telecommunications systems, PCs can be used in a variety of financial, data transmission, and analytical applications.

- **Internet** - Organizations can use the Internet to transfer funds, receive and make payments, and disseminate and acquire financial data. Web sites can be configured to provide fee-based services both related to and independent of the Internet. These utilize credit card numbers for payment.

V. TYPES OF LOCKBOXES

There are three different types of lockboxes as follows:

A. Wholesale Lockbox

Wholesale lockboxes are configured to process corporate-to-corporate payments, which, unlike consumer payments are, usually for large amounts and can be matched to specific invoices. Often several invoices are paid with one check. Detailed information usually is required about the invoices paid, discounts taken, returns, and allowances. Wholesale collection systems emphasize float reduction and timely handling of information related to the invoices being paid. These lockbox systems:

- Process small-to-moderate numbers of large-dollar remittances for each customer

- Minimize collection float

- Provide accurate and timely information on payments received

- Typically process remittances manually

- Process partially paid invoices or one payment for several invoices

- Adjust for discounts, returns, and allowances

• Process remittance information accompanying the payment that does not conform to a standard format or formats

While lockbox processes vary, the typical steps in a wholesale lockbox operation are described below and illustrated in Exhibit 6.4.

EXHIBIT 6.4
Example of Wholesale Lockbox Processing

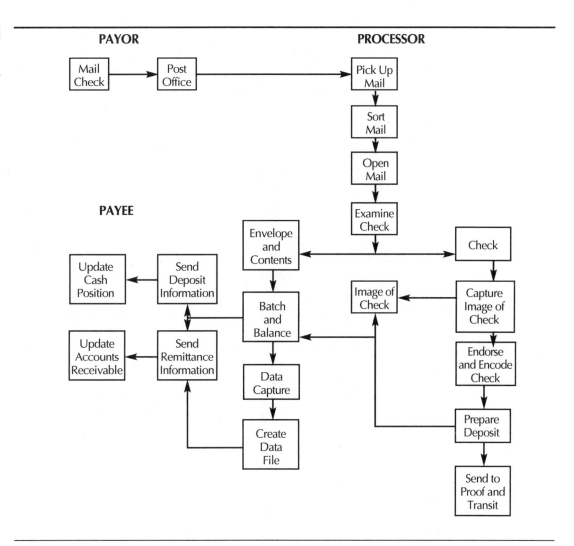

Step 1:   **Mail Check** - The payor is instructed by a company to mail checks to a lockbox address.

Step 2:   **Pick Up Mail** - Mail is picked up from a postal facility according to a predetermined schedule.

Step 3:   **Sort Mail** - The processor sorts mail by lockbox number.

Step 4:   **Open Mail** - The mail is opened.

Step 5: **Examine Checks** - Checks may be examined for postdating, restrictive legends, agreement between written and numeric amounts, as agreed upon by the bank and the customer.

Step 6: **Separate Checks and Advices** - Checks are separated from remittance advices and other contents.

Step 7: **Capture Image of Checks** - If required, the checks are copied by means of photocopier or imaging technology.

Step 8: **Endorse and Encode Checks** - Checks are encoded with a dollar amount and endorsed.

Step 9: **Prepare Deposit** - Check amounts are added, balanced, and deposit tickets are prepared.

Step 10: **Clear Checks** - Checks are sent to the proof and transit department for clearing.

Step 11: **Send Deposit and Remittance Data** - The processor provides both deposit information (such as the amount of the deposit and its availability) and remittance information (such as invoices paid and deductions or discounts taken). This information is transmitted daily to the company or to its concentration bank.

The lockbox processor may also capture remittance data either electronically or manually from the check or remittance advice and transmit it to the company. Detailed remittance data may be captured on paper or CD-ROM and sent by courier, mail, or electronically.

B. Retail Lockbox

In retail lockbox systems, payors are generally consumers. Payments are often small-dollar amounts and frequently involve installments or recurring payments and scannable remittance documents. Because of the large number of items to be handled, processing cost is a more critical consideration than float reduction. Retail lockboxes are configured for:

- Processing large volumes of retail small-dollar remittances, usually from consumers

- Minimizing processing costs rather than reducing collection float

- Processing scannable, standardized remittance advice, sometimes contained on return documents, which usually accompany checks

- Using automated processes and specialized equipment which:

  ◆ Opens envelopes

  ◆ Reads scan lines on checks and return documents that contain information such as the payor's account number, the total amount due, the minimum amount due, and the due date, using optical character recognition (OCR) and magnetic ink character recognition (MICR) techniques

◆ Electronically transmits data captured to update accounts receivable

◆ Automatically encodes the dollar amount of the check during the scanning process

C. Hybrid Lockbox

Hybrid lockboxes (sometimes referred to as whole-tail lockboxes) combine features of both wholesale and retail lockboxes. They are configured, often on a customized basis, to process both company-to-company and retail payments. They are used by companies, such as utilities, whose consumer customers usually return standardized (scannable) remittance documents that can be processed automatically, and whose business customers usually remit documents that require manual handling. The processor aggregates remittance data and transmits it to the company.

VI. ISSUES PERTAINING TO LOCKBOX SELECTION

Assessing the suitability of using a lockbox system or systems requires comparing the costs of paying fees to lockbox processors to internal processing costs and assessing the savings from reducing collection float.

A. Lockbox Cost/Benefit Analysis

The economic benefit of using a lockbox is comprised of the following elements:

1. **Float Savings** - Using a lockbox can result in float savings by reducing mail, processing, and availability delay.

2. **Costs** - Lockboxes have both fixed and variable cost components. The company should compare both the fixed and the variable cost differences between a lockbox and a company processing center. Lockbox providers have many ways of charging, but the following are some basic concepts:

   • **Fixed** - Fixed monthly costs may include fees for preparing deposits, renting the post office box, sending remittance data to the company, balance reporting, and account maintenance. Often several of those costs are bundled into a lockbox maintenance charge. There also may be a charge for transferring funds to a con-centration bank.

   • **Variable** - Variable costs may include per-item deposit and processing charges and the charges for transmitting remittance data, photocopying, imaging and micro-filming. These and other custom processing charges are often on a per-item basis. For example, some costs, such as those for deposit preparation, may be considered either fixed or variable depending on the lockbox processor.

3. **Calculation of Net Benefit** - The net benefit from a lockbox is equal to the reduction in float opportunity costs plus the reduction in internal processing costs minus lockbox processing costs. Float opportunity cost is a function of the dollar amount of the collected items, the total collection time for items, and a company's current investment or borrowing rate.

Exhibit 6.5 is an example of a lockbox cost/benefit analysis including the tradeoff between the savings from float reduction and the cost of a lockbox.

EXHIBIT 6.5
*Example of
Lockbox
Cost/Benefit
Analysis*

This exhibit shows the lockbox savings and associated costs for a company with $108,000,000 annual sales ($9,000,000 per month). Each of the items is assumed to be a batch of checks with average size of $9,000; the annual volume of checks is 12,000. The company's annual opportunity cost is 9%. The company's internal check processing cost assuming no lockbox is $.25 per item. The lockbox processor charges $10,000 per year plus a processing cost of $.50 per item.

WITHOUT LOCKBOX

Batch	Dollar Amount	Calendar Days of Collection Float Without Lockbox	Total Dollar-Days
1	$1,500,000	x 4 =	$ 6,000,000
2	4,500,000	x 2 =	9,000,000
3	3,000,000	x 6 =	18,000,000
Total Deposits	$9,000,000	Total Float without Lockbox	$33,000,000

Divided by 30 calendar days = Average Daily Float		$ 1,100,000
Times Opportunity Cost/Investment Rate = Annual Cost of Float (9%)		$ 99,000

WITH LOCKBOX

Batch	Dollar Amount	Calendar Days of Collection Float With Lockbox	Total Dollar-Days
1	$1,500,000	X 3 =	$ 4,500,000
2	4,500,000	X 1 =	4,500,000
3	3,000,000	X 5 =	15,000,000
Total Deposits	$9,000,000	Total Float with Lockbox	$ 24,000,000

Divided by 30 calendar days = Average Daily Float		$ 800,000
Times Opportunity Cost/Investment Rate = Annual Cost of Float (9%)		$ 72,000

Annual Cost of Float Without Lockbox		$ 99,000
Annual Cost of Float With Lockbox		($ 72,000)
Lockbox Float Savings		$ 27,000
Fixed Lockbox Cost		($ 10,000)
Variable Lockbox Cost: 12,000 checks x $0.50		($ 6,000)
Saving of Internal Lockbox Processing Cost: 12,000 x .25		$ 3,000
Net Dollar Benefit of Lockbox		$ 14,000

B. Collection Studies

The objective of a collection study is to minimize the cost of processing and collection float. These studies use remittance data (consumer remittance envelopes, photocopies of checks, and bank statements) to provide information for analysis such as:

- Location and geographic concentration of remitting customers

- Location of customers with largest payments

- Intercity mail times

- Bank availability schedules

- Difference between company and bank processing costs

- Administrative costs associated with using lockboxes

1. **Mail Time Studies** - Cash management banks and treasury consulting companies do periodic studies to compare mail times for various combinations of cities. These services generally report mail times between central city post offices for a uniform distribution of mailings throughout the week. If necessary, adjustments can be made for non-surveyed mail points and day-of-the-week mail experience.

   The results of mail time studies are combined with information from banks' availability schedules to compare both city-average and banks' availability statistics. Banks or consultants use this data in conjunction with an analysis of a company's actual remittances to determine which cities or combinations of cities are the most effective collection sites.

   Computer analysis is performed to produce an optimal solution. This can be attractive for a company with many banking relationships that is willing to consider many different combinations of cities.

2. **Processing Cost** - A collection study should take into account not only collection float but the difference in processing costs between a company processing center and a lockbox, and the price differences among lockbox processors.

3. **Site Selection** - In doing a study, a company will usually select a number of potential sites based on the following criteria:

   - **Availability** - A lockbox in a Federal Reserve city or Regional Check Processing Center (RCPC) generally gets faster availability than one in a Federal Reserve country point.

   - **Mail Center** - A lockbox is usually best located in a city with a major airport and a major postal processing center.

   - **Customer Base** - A lockbox is usually best located near high concentrations of customers.

- **Service Quality** - Processors may be pre-screened for service quality before they are included in a study. The overall quality of service and responsiveness to a company's inquiries is as important as mail time and availability performance. A number of processors have dedicated customer service representatives and guaranteed response times for answering inquiries. A company must evaluate the ability of a processor to serve its particular needs.

4. **Lockbox Processor Selection** - There are a number of considerations in selecting a lockbox processor:

    - **Processor Characteristics** - Among the characteristics to consider are the following:

        - Hours and days of operation
        - Payment processing capabilities
        - Check processing procedures
        - Availability schedules
        - Data transmission capabilities
        - Deposit and balance reporting capabilities
        - Postal facility's mail processing capabilities
        - Discount and processing fees for credit cards
        - Return item handling capabilities
        - Costs
        - Disaster recovery capabilities
        - Imaging capabilities

    - **City and Processor Selection** - A company may first select lockbox cities based on a lockbox study and then select processors within those cities, but there are other factors to consider that could modify the decision. Some processors may try to demonstrate features such as processing time and availability schedules that are better than the average for their cities and win customers from cities with marginally better mail times.

    - **Relationship Banks** - Using lockbox services at a bank where a company has an existing relationship may allow the company to strengthen that relationship by protecting access to credit facilities and making better use of operating balances for bank compensation benefits.

C. How Lockbox Service Features Vary

In selecting a lockbox processor, a cash manager should determine how the lockbox operation meets the company's particular needs. This is a more important characteristic than the technology used. The company should consider the following service features in evaluating each processor:

1. **Mail Time Performance** - Mail delivery time often varies considerably among cities. Among the reasons for this are: total mail volume, post office proximity to the

airport and the lockbox processor, post office processing capabilities, and airline schedules. Desirable sites have post offices that process mail 24 hours per day, sort bar-coded envelopes automatically, read non-bar-coded envelopes with OCR equipment, and make a unique ZIP code available to a lockbox processor.

2. **Unique ZIP Codes** - Most processors offering lockbox services have a unique ZIP code for lockbox remittances. Depending on their capabilities for fine sorting, this feature may speed processing of incoming mail and save several hours of mail and processing float daily.

3. **Deposit Deadlines** - Lockbox systems should process remittances expeditiously in order to ensure meeting deposit deadlines and achieve optimal availability. Frequent mail pick-ups and varying staffing levels to ensure efficient peak-time processing can help with meeting critical check clearing deadlines. As deposit deadlines approach, an effective lockbox operation should identify and process large-dollar items first. The number of deposits the bank makes each day from a lockbox to a customer's account can vary according to agreed upon terms. Each company must weigh the cost of frequent deposits versus the benefit of improving availability.

4. **Availability** - Banks may offer several availability schedules. A company should know which availability schedule is applicable. A better availability schedule may be offered for a higher price or when merited by the overall profitability of the relationship.

   Some banks assign availability in their lockbox departments rather than in check processing. Either way, a company may receive fractional availability or bear the risk of adjustments if the bank incurs a float loss in clearing a check.

5. **End-Point Analysis** - An end-point analysis, in which all checks drawn on banks in selected cities are broken down by days of float, is an effective way to measure and compare different banks' availability schedules.

6. **Ledger Cutoff Time** - In evaluating a lockbox system, it is important to consider total collection time, not just availability. The bank's cutoff time for giving ledger credit on the same day can vary and must be considered in conjunction with its availability schedule. A check with one-day availability before the ledger cutoff may have two-day availability if it is processed after the ledger cutoff.

7. **Payment Media** - Some lockboxes can handle both paper and electronic payments and can capture associated remittance data.

D. Lockbox Networks

Lockbox networks may involve several processors in different cities or a single processor with multiple locations. A network permits a company to have a number of collection points and get consolidated remittance data. Funds concentration is simplified and a company may deal with fewer processors.

E. Customized Services

Lockbox providers are beginning to include additional services such as:

• Payor address change updates

- Conversion of remittance data and payments to ACH format

- Receivables management

VII. IMAGE TECHNOLOGY

Image technology is used to facilitate processing of both wholesale and retail lockbox payments. This technology allows paper documents to be scanned, converted to a digital image, and stored for subsequent handling and processing. The data capture process is enhanced through the use of intelligent character recognition (ICR), which reads handwritten or typed information, and OCR, which reads pre-printed information. The documents scanned can be both checks and remittance advices. Potential benefits of applying image technology to the remittance processing function include reduced overall processing costs, increased productivity, improved accuracy, and the ability to capture data for automated posting to accounts receivable.

With respect to the second benefit, the degree of data capture automation achievable with image technology is generally higher with retail than with wholesale payments because of the presence of a scannable return document. This facilitates posting of retail remittances.

Wholesale payments often do not contain the seller's original invoice or OCR advice. Instead, a buyer may enclose its own payment document, a check stub with limited information, or nothing at all. As a result, any machine-readable data is often supplemented with manual entry data for wholesale remittances.

Imaging services allow companies to identify potential unauthorized check activity and obtain copies in a more timely fashion, allowing companies to respond quickly to customer, employee, and vendor inquiries. In addition to the actual processing of items, it can be applied to the delivery and storage of remittance data output. A lockbox provider can transmit to a company images of its deposit and detailed payment information or supply this data on a CD-ROM. Companies that can benefit from this feature are those that must research payment information to respond to a high volume of customer service inquiries.

VIII. ELECTRONIC COLLECTION SYSTEMS

A company can receive a payment via wire transfer or ACH.

A. Wire Transfers

Wire transfers are used for large-dollar payments when speed and finality are important.

B. ACH Corporate-to-Corporate Payments

Electronic payments through the ACH are less expensive than wire transfers, but payment instructions must be submitted to the bank one or two days prior to settlement. Vendors may issue ACH debits against customer accounts or customers may issue ACH credits to vendor accounts. Companies generally consult with their trading partners in advance to determine which payment formats are appropriate, as well as to negotiate the timing of ACH payments.

1. **Applications** - Though most bills are paid by check, companies may collect a portion of their payments by ACH. A number of companies have initiated comprehensive programs to originate payments through the ACH. Examples of applications include:

   • **Manufacturer's Suppliers** - Many suppliers to manufacturing companies are receiving payments through the ACH as part of a more comprehensive EDI program that includes electronic issuance of purchase orders and invoices.

   • **Dealers with Floor Plans** - A floor plan is a loan to a dealer to finance inventory which is paid back when the financed item is sold. Automobile, truck, and farm equipment suppliers that provide floor plan financing have utilized the ACH network extensively to debit their dealers.

   • **Debit Programs** - Companies can also collect funds by debiting their customer's bank accounts. This is typically done in one of two ways. A supplier may notify a customer in advance of the data and the exact amount of the debit. Or a buyer can notify the supplier of the desire to make a payment. The supplier then originates an ACH debit. The latter option offers the customer greater control.

   • **Purchasing Cards** - As discussed in Section III of this chapter, purchasing or procurement cards can be used to pay for supplies, inventory, equipment, or services.

2. **Advantages** - Potential benefits of ACH corporate-to-corporate payments for the payee include:

   • **Reduced Float** - Reduction of collection float

   • **Lowered Cost** - Reduction of receivables processing cost; lower overall cost compared to either a check payment or wire transfers

   • **Improved Forecasting** - Improved cash flow forecasting

3. **Disadvantages** - Despite possible cost saving opportunities in the long run, there are many potential deterrents to the use of ACH corporate payments. The disadvantages include:

   • **Need for Trading Partner Negotiation** - The payor (buyer) and the payee (seller) must agree to make the switch.

   • **Adjusting Float** - When a company starts to receive payments electronically, there must be agreement on when the effective use of funds is being transferred under the existing system and what the settlement date of the ACH transaction should be.

     The payor and the payee may negotiate a settlement time for an ACH transaction that puts each party in approximately the same economic position as when checks were used to settle invoices.

   • **Set-Up Costs** - Preparation to receive ACH corporate-to-corporate payments may require an additional investment in processing software and communications equipment.

- **Reluctance** - In the case of remittance information accompanying ACH debits a company may be reluctant to give someone outside the company the authority to debit its bank account.

4. **Preparation** - A company preparing to receive ACH corporate-to-corporate payments for the first time should take the following steps:

   - **ACH Formats** - Since many ACH payment formats are available, the format to use should be discussed and agreed upon with the payor.

   - **Bank Capabilities** - ACH receiving and translating capabilities should be discussed and agreed upon with the bank where payments will be received.

   - **Payment-Related Information** - The company should determine how to receive payment-related information. Compare the capabilities and costs of banks and value-added networks (VANs) to transmit full details related to the payment. VANs are computer-based systems that facilitate invoicing and payment between organizations and vendors. They ensure that the systems are compatible. A company may want to consider buying translation software to enable automated receipt of ACH remittance information to update its accounts receivable system.

     There is still debate about the preferable alternative. Some favor sending the payment and payment information together through a bank, while others favor sending the payment through a bank and the payment information through a VAN.

C. Preauthorized Payments

Preauthorized debits are a payment method in which the payor approves in advance the transfer of funds from the payor's bank account to the payee's bank account. These payments are often for the same dollar amount and at the same time each month, but variable dollar amounts and schedules are possible. Where there is payment variability, written notice of the withdrawal must be provided to the customer ten days prior to the transfer of funds.

Preauthorized payments are for the most part made through the ACH. Consumer payments are governed by Federal Reserve Regulation E and National Automated Clearing House Association (NACHA) rules; electronic corporate-to-corporate payments are governed by Article 4A of the Uniform Commercial Code and NACHA rules.

1. **Applications** - Preauthorized payments are used by both consumers and corporations. Corporate payments are made to pay suppliers and trading partners. Consumer payments are commonly made for applications such as:

   - Insurance payments

   - Utility payments

   - Mortgage payments

   - Association or club dues

2.   **Advantages** - The advantages of preauthorized payments include:

   - Possible elimination of invoicing

   - Reduction of processing float because deposits do not need to be prepared

   - Elimination of availability float because of immediate availability on settlement day

   - Fewer delinquent payments

   - Reduction of the incentive for the customer to switch vendors

   - Reduction of cash application costs

   - More timely notification of account closing

3.   **Disadvantages** - The disadvantages of preauthorized payments include:

   - Additional costs and time needed to educate customers

   - Customer resistance to having their bank accounts debited by another party

   - Cost and time involved in preparing and sending billing statements to meet regulatory requirements or customer service considerations

   - Initial time and effort needed to set up each customer's standard monthly payment instructions, including the correct bank transit routing number and customer account number

   - Cost and time involved in handling returned transactions resulting when a customer changes banks without prior notification

IX. OTHER COLLECTION SYSTEMS

A. Net Settlement Systems

In some industries, companies make exchanges and buy and sell from each other. For example, Airline A accepts a ticket from Airline B in exchange for a passenger making a change in reservations. Through a clearing system, it returns the ticket and is reimbursed by the airline that originally wrote the ticket. These clearing systems process transaction information and allow participants to make periodic net settlements with each other.

B. Retail Collection Systems

There are a number of alternative retail collections systems that may have benefits such as improving cash flow, reducing paperwork, reducing per item transaction costs, and increasing the accuracy and timeliness of accounts receivable updating. These systems include the following:

1. **Credit Cards** - Credit cards are a frequently used payment method. They are accepted both electronically and manually.

   - **Electronic Acceptance** - Using a stand-alone credit card authorization/draft capture terminal or a magnetic stripe reader integrated into the merchant's cash register system, the merchant swipes the presented card through the reader so that the magnetic stripe on the back of the card is read. This stripe contains, among other things, the cardholder's account number and name. Once the dollar value of the sale is entered into the terminal, the transaction is routed via telephone lines to the merchant's bank/processor for authorization. If approved, a receipt is printed for the customer to sign. The terminal accumulates transaction information throughout the day, and, at settlement time, transmits the accumulated transaction information to the merchant's bank/processor. Within two business days, the merchant's bank/processor credits the merchant's checking account for the total dollar amount of the accumulated transactions. Electronic acceptance has become the predominant method of processing credit card transactions.

   - **Manual Acceptance** - Using a paper sales draft and a telephone, the merchant records the sales transaction information on the draft and obtains an authorization from a voice operator or an audio response unit. If approved, the merchant obtains the cardholder's signature on the draft. The merchant can mail or deliver the drafts to its bank/processor. The bank may treat these deposits as various availability items, usually one, two, or three days.

   - **Charges** - At the end of the month the merchant bank/processor typically deducts a fee (discount) and other charges from the merchant's checking account. Alternatively, these charges may be invoiced to the merchant. Availability and discount amounts are pricing decisions negotiated between the bank/processor and the merchant. Other charges may include terminal rental, authorizations, and supplies.

   - **Authorizations and Chargebacks** - A credit card payment is not guaranteed, even when authorized. An authorization indicates that the cardholder has available credit but it does not indicate that the right person is using the card. A merchant may receive a chargeback (i.e., a returned transaction) for as long as six months after funds have been received. When fraud occurs, the time may be even longer. Signature verification is necessary to determine if the authorized person is using the card.

2. **Debit Cards** - Debit cards work like credit cards except that the transactions post to bank deposit accounts as withdrawals rather than to credit card accounts as future amounts owed.

   Upon settlement of a transaction, money has been transferred from the purchaser's account to the merchant's account. Debit cards settle in one of the following ways:

   - **On-Line** - A personal identification number (PIN) is required to initiate the transaction. Positive authorization is received from the cardholder's bank. The merchant receives zero to two days' availability.

   - **Off-Line** - There are two types of off-line programs:

- **National Association (VISA or MasterCard) Debit Cards** - The purchaser's bank deposit account is automatically debited. Availability is usually two days.

- **Proprietary Cards** - Settlement for proprietary cards is through the ACH. Availability is usually one day.

3. **Automated Teller Machine (ATM) Networks** - Vendors that deal with a large number of retail customers may be able to make arrangements with banks for bills to be paid at ATMs. The payment is transferred manually or electronically from the customer's account to the vendor's account at the time of sale, or when the customer initiates payment through the ATM.

4. **Telephone Banking** - Vendors can make arrangements with financial institutions that offer telephone banking services to have consumers authorize the debiting of their accounts by phone. The call may be to an operator, a touchtone telephone, or a voice response system. Smart or screen telephones with added capabilities are increasingly used to facilitate this process.

5. **Bill Paying Services** - Individuals usually use these services to make payments to companies, primarily utilities and retailers. Methods for initiating bill paying services include ATMs, phones, and personal computers.

6. **Home Banking** - Home banking services are offered by financial institutions or can be part of a personal financial software system that connects the user to a third-party provider. Generally, these services are PC-based products with a broad array of capabilities that may include bank account inquiry, account transfers, and bill paying services. As more of these services are used by consumers, companies must adapt their collection systems to receive and process these types of payments.

7. **The Internet** - The Internet can be used to make remittances and to transfer payments and financial data. Web sites on the Internet can be configured to receive payments, either for Internet related activity or to purchase other goods and services. Such transactions involve credit card payments. The use of the Internet for financial transactions and data transfer is evolving.

8. **Agents** - Retailers and financial institutions may act as agents for collecting monthly payments related to service providers such as cable and utility companies.

9. **Smart Cards** - Smart cards are plastic cards that have computer chips embedded within them. Ths is an emerging technology that is capable of storing important data, including monetary value that can be electronically replenished. The cards can be used as stored value devices that enable cardholders to make fewer cash transactions. From a collections standpoint, smart cards operate in a manner similar to credit or debit card electronic transactions.

Questions

These chapter questions are to test and review the information in the text and are not examples of CCM examination questions, nor are they in the examination format.

Answers can be found at the back of the book on pgs. 368-370.

1. What are the major objectives in establishing a collection system?

2. What are the three major collection methods?

3. What are some key considerations in designing a collection system?

4. What elements compose collection float?

5. What determines availability float?

6. A company has provided the following information:

Batch	Dollar Amount	Calendar Days of Float	Dollar-Day of Float
1	$100,000	3	$ 300,000
2	$350,000	4	$ 1,400,000
3	$210,000	2	$ 420,000
			$ 2,120,000

If the company's opportunity cost is 7% and there are 30 calendar days in the month, what is the annual cost of float?

7. What determines the selection of a mail payment processing system?

8. What are the major advantages of a lockbox?

9. What is the difference between a wholesale and a retail lockbox?

10. The company in Question 6 is considering using a lockbox, which would reduce float as follows:

Batch	Dollar Amt.	Calendar Days of Float	Dollar Days of Float
1	$100,000	1	$ 100,000
2	$350,000	2	$ 700,000
3	$210,000	1	$ 210,000
			$ 1,010,000

The lockbox processor will charge $1,000 per year and a processing cost of $.30 per item. The current internal processing cost is $.20 per item. The annual volume of checks is 6,000. If the annual float cost without the use of a lockbox is $4,947 (see Question 6), is a lockbox appropriate for this company?

11. What is an over-the-counter/field deposit collection system?

12. What is a pre-authorized debit?

13. What system would benefit companies in the same industry that buy and sell from each other on a regular basis?

14. What impact will image technology have on collection systems?

15. What are the major types of retail collection systems?

CHAPTER **7**

Cash Concentration

OVERVIEW

This chapter discusses why companies concentrate cash, the objectives of a cash concentration system, the principal funds concentration mechanisms, and how to minimize cash concentration system costs.

LEARNING OBJECTIVES

Upon completion of this chapter and related study questions, the reader should understand:

1. The objectives of a cash concentration system

2. Factors impacting cash concentration system configuration

3. The advantages and disadvantages of the principal funds transfer mechanisms used in cash concentration systems

4. The cost components of a cash concentration system and how to minimize them

5. How to reduce risk and increase control in a cash concentration system

KEY CONCEPTS

1. Cash concentration system objectives

2. Cash concentration system design determinants

3. Funds transfer mechanism alternatives

4. Cash concentration system cost components

5. Risk and control considerations as applicable to cash concentration systems

OUTLINE

I. OBJECTIVES OF A CASH CONCENTRATION SYSTEM

Cash concentration is the transfer of funds from outlying depository locations to a central bank account, commonly referred to as a concentration account, where they can be managed more efficiently. A cash concentration system should be designed to accomplish the following:

- **Minimize Bank Balances** - Fewer accounts with balances means fewer excess balances and more efficient cash use. Concentrating cash enables a company to reduce excess bank balances.

- **Pool Funds** - Concentrating cash enables a company to buy larger blocks of short-term securities, thus saving on commissions and possibly boosting portfolio yield. It may also allow a company to reduce debt or take greater advantage of supplier discounts.

- **Simplify Cash Management** - The account consolidation made possible by a cash concentration system enables cash managers to manage a company's daily liquidity more easily.

- **Improve Control** - Separation of deposit gathering from other cash management functions, such as disbursement control, tracking, and forecasting, enables cash managers to control a company's funds more easily. Cash concentration also provides a clearer audit trail for incoming deposits.

- **Reduce Transfer Costs** - Account consolidation concentrates cash and reduces total transfer costs.

II. CONCENTRATION SYSTEM CONFIGURATION

The configuration of a company's concentration system depends on the size and geographic dispersion of its collection and disbursement system, the funds transfer alternatives available to it, and the capabilities of the banking network it uses.

A. Collection System

The collection system a company uses has a major impact on its cash concentration system. The two major types of collection systems are:

1. **Over-the-Counter/Field Banking Systems** - Companies with regional sales offices or widely dispersed retail outlets deposit over-the-counter cash and checks in various accessible outlying depository banks. Such systems are characterized by:

    - **Multiple Collection Points** - A company with many locations needs a local depository convenient to each location.

    - **Multiple Banks** - A field banking system may use various local banks if their locations are proximate to field offices.

    - **Limited Provision of Cash Management Services** - Because sales and deposit information is often sent directly to company headquarters or a concentration bank by the company's field units, headquarters may require fewer deposit and balance reporting services from field banks. Generally, field offices do not use cash management services extensively, even if the field banks can provide them.

    - **Deposit Availability** - Deposits consist mainly of coin, currency, and local checks. Coin and currency are usually given immediate availability. Local checks may take one day to clear; on-us items may clear faster.

2. **Lockbox Systems** - These allow a company to collect payments at one or more lockbox sites that will transfer available funds to a concentration bank. A company may use several lockbox sites to optimize collection float and may also use separate lockboxes for different subsidiaries.

    Though lockbox cash concentration systems vary, most have the following characteristics:

    - **Limited Collection Points** - Most companies try to consolidate their lockbox systems at one or more lockbox sites.

    - **Use of Regional and Money Center Banks and Third-Party Processors** - A lockbox system often uses regional or money center banks and third-party processors.

    - **Provision of Corporate Services** - Lockbox systems typically offer the following capabilities and services:

        ◆ Daily reporting of transaction details and ledger and collected balances

        ◆ Movement of funds through wire transfer or the automated clearing house (ACH)

        ◆ Other treasury management services

- **Deposit Availability** - Because a large percentage of the checks a lockbox processes are drawn on non-local endpoints, a portion of a company's daily deposit may not be available for one or two banking days from the day of deposit.

A typical concentration system incorporating both a field banking system and a lockbox system is illustrated in Exhibit 7.1

EXHIBIT 7.1
*Example of
a Cash
Concentration
System*

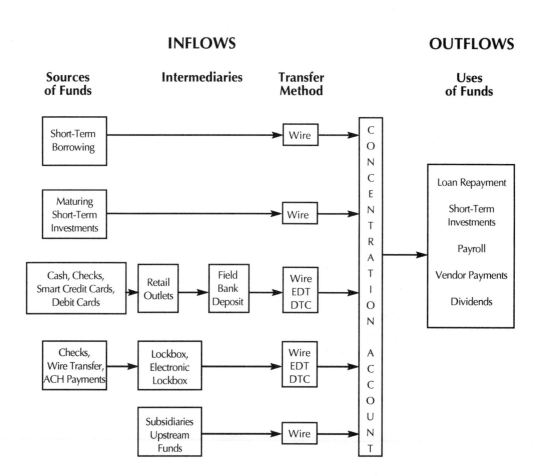

- **Electronic Lockbox** - Growing use of electronic data interchange (EDI) transactions reduces but does not eliminate the need for multiple lockbox sites.

B. Disbursement System

The degree to which a company's disbursement system is centralized also helps determine its cash concentration system configuration. The differences, which are examined in detail in Chapter 8, Accounts Payable and Disbursements, include:

1. **Centralized Check Issuance** - In this type of system, headquarters controls disbursement accounts and is responsible for check writing and account reconciliation.

2. **Decentralized Check Issuance** - In this type of system, checks are written on local disbursement banks and account reconciliation is performed at the local level.

Decentralized systems require closer monitoring of disbursement accounts by a company's headquarters.

C. Funds Transfer Alternatives

The most frequently used mechanisms for concentration are Electronic Depository Transfers (EDTs) and wire transfers.

1. **Electronic Depository Transfers (EDT)** - An EDT, which is an ACH transaction that concentrates cash, is the most common method of depository transfer in use today. It has virtually replaced depository transfer checks (DTCs), which are paper instruments formerly used by companies to transfer funds from outlying depository locations to their concentration account.

   Field offices, field banks, headquarters offices, lockbox banks, and concentration banks can originate EDTs. A field office can initiate a credit transfer from the field account to the concentration account, notifying headquarters of the transfer amount. Alternatively, the field office may notify either headquarters or the concentration bank of the deposit amount, and the headquarters or concentration bank then initiates a debit transfer from the field account to the concentration account.

   Some large retail networks transmit information on cash receipts from point-of-sale (POS) terminals to headquarters. Headquarters then transmits ACH debit instructions to a concentration bank.

   - **Notifying the Concentration Bank** - A field unit or lockbox provider can send deposit information to the concentration bank by voice, telephone, or personal computer. This information can be transferred in the following ways:

     - **Through a Third-Party Vendor** - Several third-party providers specialize in gathering deposit information from field units. Deposit data may be transmitted to both a concentration bank for EDT preparation and company headquarters for follow-up of non-reporting units. In some cases, deposit data is sent to headquarters, which then notifies the concentration bank as to the amounts to be transferred.

     - **Through Headquarters** - Some field managers may call headquarters directly or convey deposit data electronically. Headquarters then relays deposit data to a concentration bank.

     - **Through the Concentration Bank Directly** - Some banks are able to receive deposit reports directly from field units or lockbox providers.

   - **Cost** - EDTs are the least expensive method for transferring funds. In many cases the cost of an EDT includes both a charge for the transaction and a charge for the amount of transmission time.

   - **Settlement** - One-day settlement is the industry norm.

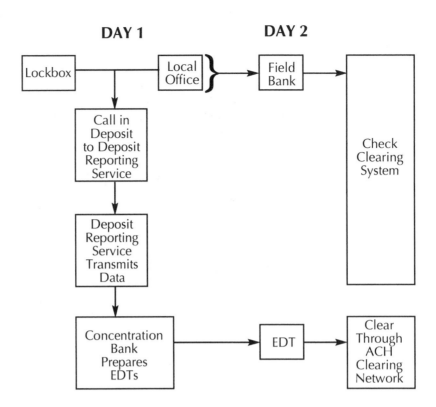

EXHIBIT 7.2
*Example of
EDT Clearing*

2. **Wire Transfers** - Wire transfers are an alternative method for concentrating large dollar amounts where same-day value and finality are critical.

Funds can be transferred using the following methods:

*   Either the local manager or the headquarters staff may initiate a request to a depository bank to wire funds to a concentration bank.

*   A field or lockbox bank may have standing instructions to transfer funds that exceed a specified balance on a periodic basis. Standing instructions specify the amount, frequency, and destination of the transfer.

*   Headquarters may send transfer instructions to a concentration bank to wire funds from a field or lockbox bank. This is known as a drawdown transaction. A company gives standing instructions to a lockbox or field bank authorizing a concentration bank to initiate the wire transfers.

Deposit information that is related to the wire transfer can be sent to headquarters through deposit reports, telephone, or electronic data transmission.

Wire transfers provide immediate funds and help reduce excess balances at deposit banks. They are typically used when large amounts of immediately available funds are deposited in a lockbox or a field bank.

Wire transfers are the most expensive funds transfer mechanism.

D. Banking Network

The number of banking relationships a company has will impact the transfer and administrative costs of its concentration system. If branches of a single bank can be used, the number and costs of concentration transfers can be reduced. In addition, administrative tasks like account reconciliation are simplified. The growth in statewide and interstate branch banking will benefit companies by reducing concentration costs.

III. CASH CONCENTRATION COST COMPONENTS

The costs of cash concentration include the opportunity costs of maintaining excess balances, transfer charges, and administration.

A. Excess Bank Balances

An account has an excess balance when its average collected balance is greater than either the amount that a bank requires for compensation or the target level that a company has chosen to maintain.

1. **Determining Required Balances** - Determining required balances in concentration system accounts involves the following:

    - **Account Analysis** - Most banks provide an account analysis statement showing the price of each service used, the volume of activity, and the compensation required. Banks may charge clients by requiring maintenance of certain balance levels or by fees.

    - **Estimates for Field Banks** - Some field banks may not provide account analyses. In the absence of an account analysis, a company and its bank may have to decide jointly on a fair compensating balance.

2. **How Excess Balances Arise** - Excess balances arise for the following reasons:

    - **Deposit Reporting Delays** - Deposit reports by field units may be delayed by local management or the deposit information gathering system resulting in delayed concentration transfers and excess balances.

    - **Clearing Delays** - Concentration using EDTs can cause one or more days of delay between transfer initiation and clearing or settlement. Excess balances may be created when immediately available funds are deposited, or when checks deposited in field or lockbox banks clear before the concentration transfers clear back to the deposit account.

    - **Transfer Initiation Delays** - A company or its concentration bank may fail to prepare transfers on time. Failure to originate an EDT in time to meet the bank's deadline delays settlement an extra day.

B. Transfer Charges

Collection systems involve various transfer and service reporting costs. Typically these include:

1. **Bank Charges** - Deposit and concentration banks may charge for: deposits, outgoing wires, EDT clearings, deposit reports, overdrafts, and account maintenance.

2. **Third-Party Vendor Charges** - A company may use vendors to assist in concentration. Vendors charge for collecting deposit information from field units or lockbox providers and for transmitting data to a concentration bank and/or company.

C. Administrative Costs

The administrative costs of operating a concentration system include the following:

1. **Managing Deposit Reporting** - Receiving and monitoring daily deposit reports from local managers, lockbox providers, and concentration banks are major administrative responsibilities.

2. **Scheduling Cash Transfer** - Cash transfer scheduling involves deciding when and what amounts to transfer. These are routine decisions if a company's policy is to transfer the entire amount of the daily deposit. Otherwise, there is a cost associated with deposit monitoring and decision making.

3. **Incurring Overdrafts** - Occasionally, accounts in concentration systems are overdrawn due to misdirected transfers, missed deposit deadlines, or returned items. When a check deposited at a field or lockbox bank is returned after it was included in the concentration transfer, a field office may reimburse a field bank for it directly or reduce the next transfer by the amount of the check.

4. **Missing Deposit Deadlines** - Ensuring that deposits are made in field banks in time to receive same-day ledger credit accelerates the availability of funds and reduces expenses related to overdrafts.

IV. TECHNIQUES TO REDUCE CONCENTRATION SYSTEM COSTS

Companies can improve concentration system efficiency (and reduce overall costs) by improving transfer timing and reducing transfer costs. To do this, they must factor the value of accelerated funds into the calculations they use in comparing various concentration system alternatives.

A. Improving Transfer Timing

Companies can reduce excess balances by removing information delays, anticipating availability, or by using a faster transfer mechanism.

1. **Removing Information Delays** - Delays in informing a concentration bank of required transfers can extend the float interval thereby delaying availability. The process can be expedited by:

    • **Establishing Cutoff Times** - Cutoff times can be set so that transfer reports meet a concentration bank's schedule.

    • **Requiring Timely Reports** - Monitoring both non-reporting and reporting locations enables companies to eliminate information delays.

2. **Anticipating Availability** - Anticipation involves initiation of a transfer before cash becomes available at the deposit bank. The bank initiates the transfer on the basis of projected deposit availability. Because the ledger balance is certain, there exists little risk of ledger overdraft. However, this method risks drawing on uncollected funds since potential delays in the clearing system or returned items can cause collected balances to be unpredictable.

3. **Using Faster Payment Mechanisms** - Wire transfers make funds available immediately, whereas EDTs become available after one day.

B. Reducing Transfer Costs

Companies can reduce the costs of operating cash concentration systems by transferring funds less frequently and by using less expensive transfer mechanisms.

1. **Transfer Timing** - Transfer costs can be reduced by altering policies and procedures governing timing of transfers as follows:

   - **End Daily Transfers** - While daily transfers are often the norm, many companies transfer less frequently if the deposit amounts do not justify the expense, particularly if daily deposits are smaller than target balances. Transferring funds once a week or less may be sufficient.

   - **Match Timing of Receipt With Timing of Transfer** - Companies that deposit receipts on certain days of the week can increase efficiency by making transfers only on those days.

   - **Balance Averaging** - Companies can time transfers to keep account balances positive and offset service charges. Banks average collected balances monthly, and some days' positive balances may offset other days' negative balances for calculating earnings credit.

2. **Transfer Mechanisms** - Companies can change the transfer mechanisms they use.

   - **EDT versus Wire Transfer** - For companies whose deposits are mostly checks with delayed availability, it is advantageous to transfer funds using an EDT on the day of deposit rather than to initiate a wire transfer on the day funds become available.

   - **Repetitive Wire Transfers** - Repetitive wire transfers are usually less expensive than non-repetitive transfers.

3. **Target and Threshold Concentration** - Target and threshold concentration are two methods of limiting balances. Many bank concentration systems offer headquarters the flexibility to change amounts reported by field units, thereby adjusting the amount transferred.

   - **Target Concentration** - With target concentration, a target balance is set and all funds above that balance level are transferred to the concentration bank. This system maintains balances at the desired level. It could involve transfers as frequently as daily.

- **Threshold Concentration** - Threshold concentration minimizes the number of transfers. With threshold concentration, a company allows account balances to build to a predetermined level before transferring funds to the concentration bank. A cash manager can monitor average balances and adjust them as necessary over time.

4. **Deposit Reconciliation Services** - By using deposit reconciliation, a company may deposit funds from multiple locations to its regional or central concentration account. MICR-encoded deposit tickets identify each location and enable a bank to produce daily, weekly, or monthly deposit reports by location. This service reduces the number of bank accounts that must be maintained, and thus the number of transfers, possibly decreasing concentration system costs. Deposit reconciliation is becoming more prevalent as statewide branch banking and interstate banking become more widespread.

C. Comparing Transfer Costs

In determining whether to use an EDT or a wire transfer to concentrate funds, it is important to establish the value of funds acceleration. By comparing this value to the costs of the alternative transfer methods, the appropriate transfer mechanism can be selected.

For example, assume the following:

1. Total costs for an EDT are $1.00.
2. Total costs for a wire transfer are $20.00.
3. Transfer amount is $100,000.
4. The opportunity costs of funds is 10%.
5. A wire transfer accelerates funds one day faster than an EDT.

$$\text{Funds Value} = \text{Transfer Amount} \times \text{Days Accelerated} \times \text{Opportunity Cost}$$

$$= \$100,000 \times 1 \times \left(\frac{.10}{365}\right)$$

$$= \$27.40$$

Because the funds value, $27.40, exceeds the incremental cost of a wire transfer ($20.00 - $1.00 = $19.00), it is advantageous for the company to use a wire transfer rather than an EDT.

An approach for determining the minimum wire transfer amount required to break even is as follows:

$$\text{Minimum Transfer} \quad = \quad \frac{\text{Wire Cost} - \text{EDT Cost}}{\text{Days Accelerated} \quad \text{x} \quad \left(\dfrac{\text{Opportunity Cost}}{365 \text{ Days}}\right)}$$

$$= \quad \frac{\$20.00 \quad - \quad \$1.00}{1 \text{ Day} \quad \text{x} \quad \left(\dfrac{.10}{365 \text{ Days}}\right)}$$

$$= \quad \$69,350$$

As long as the wire transfer amount is larger than $69,350, the additional cost of the wire transfer is justified.

V. RISKS AND CONTROLS

The operation of cash concentration systems involves a number of issues including:

A. Timely Processing

The primary operational risk of a concentration system is the failure to make deposit calls and/or report deposits accurately by a concentration bank's clearing deadline. Many banks offer services that allow companies to monitor deposit reporting.

B. Fraud

A potential for fraud exists when an employee does not deposit the amount reported, or does not deposit or report the amount received. This type of fraud may go undetected for a period of time. Preventive measures include the following:

- Requiring more than one type of report from field offices such as a sales report that allows a comparison with deposits

- Requiring these different reports to be prepared and reviewed by different staff members daily

- Conducting unscheduled audits of field offices

- Instructing field banks to return any items that can result in overdrafts and to notify headquarters of these actions

- Promptly reconciling bank accounts

C. Bank Overdraft

The potential for overdraft exists at concentration banks. Failure to make a transfer from a deposit bank to a concentration bank can cause account overdrafts at the concentration bank. Conversely, making too large a transfer or an unanticipated return item can cause an overdraft at the deposit bank.

D. Bank Failure

Field deposit systems typically have many banks, and a company may be at risk if one fails. Timely concentration limits this risk. To reduce this risk further, a cash manager needs to monitor the creditworthiness of each bank in a company's concentration system.

E. Disaster Recovery Plans

All companies are vulnerable to the collapse of their concentration systems. Should a company's system or any of its components go down, it can take a long time and great expense for the company to recover. To minimize the impact of a disaster, companies should draw up comprehensive disaster recovery plans.

Questions

These chapter questions are to test and review the information in the text and are not examples of CCM examination questions, nor are they in the examination format.

Answers can be found at the back of the book on pgs. 370-371.

1.   What are the objectives of a cash concentration system?

2.   What is EDT?

3.   What other electronic alternative is available for concentration other than an EDT, and when is it generally used?

4.   What are the major cost components of a cash concentration system?

5.   What can cause excess balances?

6.   What is anticipation?

7.   What is threshold concentration?

8.   A company provides the following information:

   • EDT costs total $1.00
   • Wire transfer costs are $22.00
   • A wire accelerates availability one day
   • Opportunity cost of funds is 8%

   What is the minimum wire transfer required to break even?

9.   What are some ways fraud may be prevented in a concentration system?

10.   Why is the pooling of funds a valuable objective of cash concentration?

11.   What are some of the key considerations in designing a cash concentration system?

CHAPTER 8

Accounts Payable and Disbursements

OVERVIEW

This chapter discusses the objectives of accounts payable and disbursements, and the principal methods and products used for disbursements.

LEARNING OBJECTIVES

Upon completion of this chapter and the related study questions, the reader should understand:

1. The objectives of accounts payable and disbursement systems

2. The components of disbursement float

3. How companies organize disbursement activities

4. Disbursement products and their applications

5. The accounts payable function

6. Check reconciliation and supporting services

7. Technological developments in accounts payable

KEY CONCEPTS

1. Accounts Payable and Disbursements

2. Disbursement Float

3. Check Reconciliation and Supporting Services

OUTLINE

I. ACCOUNTS PAYABLE AND DISBURSEMENT SYSTEM OBJECTIVES

The basic goal of managing an accounts payable and disbursement system is to disburse funds to vendors, suppliers, employees, and other payees in a timely, accurate, and cost-effective manner. Specifically, the objectives of an accounts payable and disbursement system include:

A. Cost Reduction

A company's net cost of making payments includes:

1. **Opportunity Costs**

    - The cost of excess borrowing or lost investment income when idle balances exist in disbursement accounts

    - The cost of missed or early payments, which include:

        ◆ The costs of paying bills late, such as lost discounts, late fees, and ill will

        ◆ The opportunity costs of paying bills early, such as interest income lost or extra interest expense incurred

2. **Disbursement Account Costs**

    - Fixed costs, such as account maintenance and balance reporting

    - Variable costs, including checks paid, account reconciliation, stop payments, and zero balance transfers

    - Overdraft costs, including the monetary costs of overdrawing disbursement accounts and the cost of possible damage to the banking relationship

B. Disbursement Float Management

Disbursement float results from the delay between the time a payor mails a check and the time funds are debited from the payor's account. This form of float is analogous to collection float, except that it is viewed from the payor's perspective. Disbursement float has the following components:

1. **Mail Float** - Mail float is the delay between the time a check is mailed and the date the check is received by the payee or at a designated processing site.

2. **Processing Float** - Processing float is the delay between the time the payee or processing site receives the check and the time the check is deposited.

3. **Clearing Float** - Clearing float is the delay between the time a check is deposited by the payee and the time the payor's account is debited. Generally, the payee's account is credited with collected funds at the same time the payor's account is debited.

The components of disbursement float are illustrated in Exhibit 8.1.

EXHIBIT 8.1

Components of Disbursement Float

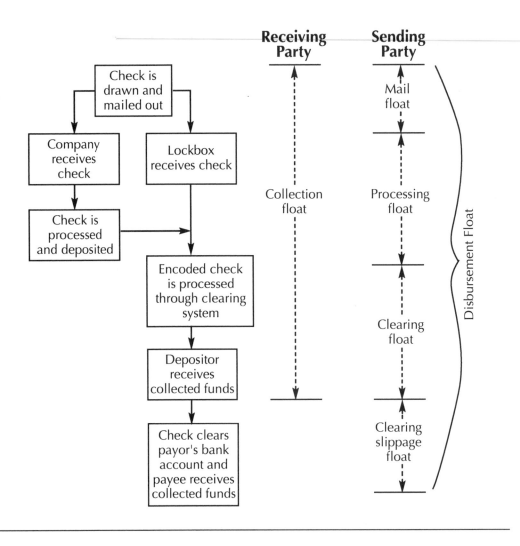

C. Information Access

Obtaining timely and accurate information about the status of disbursement accounts and disbursement clearings enables a company to manage its cash position effectively.

D. Fraud Prevention

Funds should be protected from unauthorized use through written policies and internal controls, as well as the use of quality check stock and banking services such as positive pay.

E. Relationship Maintenance

It is important for companies to maintain good relationships with payees such as employees, vendors, suppliers, tax agencies, and shareholders and/or bondholders.

II. DISBURSEMENT SYSTEM CONSIDERATIONS

There are several considerations in planning and managing a disbursement system.

A. Centralization versus Decentralization

Disbursement systems may be centralized, decentralized, or a combination of both. Each system has advantages and disadvantages.

1. **Centralized Check Issuance** - In this type of system, headquarters issues checks and funds and reconciles accounts.

The advantages of centralized check issuance include:

- Concentrated excess cash, which can be used for loan repayment or investment

- Improved access to cash position information

- Improved coordination of cash inflows and outflows

- Restricted access to the system, thus improving overall control

- Reduced cost

The disadvantages of a centralized check issuance may include:

- Potential increase of disbursement float, which can damage relations with payees

- Delayed payments to suppliers resulting in loss of discounts

- Need for coordination between headquarters and field offices to resolve problems

2. **Decentralized Check Issuance** - With this type of system, a company issues and reconciles accounts at the local level. Typically, checks are drawn on a local bank.

The advantages of decentralized check issuance may include:

- Improved relationships with vendors and other payees, since disputes may be resolved more directly

- Greater autonomy for local managers

The disadvantages of decentralized check issuance include:

- Increased possibility of excess balances at the local level

- Increased difficulty of obtaining information about a company's day-to-day cash position

- Reduced disbursement float, if disbursement bank and payees are local

- Increased likelihood of unauthorized disbursements because of greater access to the system

- Increased transfer, reconciliation, and administrative costs

3. **Checks Written at Local Level on a Centralized Disbursement Bank** - In this system, check issuance and check reconciliation (in some cases) are performed at the local level, but checks clear on a centralized disbursement bank. Headquarters is responsible for choosing disbursement banks and funding disbursement accounts.

The advantages of checks written locally on a centralized disbursement bank may include:

- Reduced excess balances in field locations

- Improved access to information about a company's cash position

- Reduced number of banking relationships

- Decentralized control, which facilitates proper payment timing

- Increased opportunity for volume discounts on disbursement bank services

The disadvantages of checks written locally on a centralized disbursement bank may include:

- Reduced control by headquarters over check issuance

- Increased administrative costs due to dual nature of system

- Increased difficulty of problem resolution since a non-local bank is used for checks sent to local vendors

B. Control and Fraud Prevention

Disbursement fraud is a significant problem. Technological advances have increased the frequency, sophistication, and ease of creating fraudulent checks. These advances include color copiers, high-resolution laser printers, and document scanners designed for use with a personal computer. As a result, control and fraud prevention are an important responsibility of accounts payable and treasury operations. Control and fraud prevention measures include the following:

1. Developing and implementing written policies and procedures for the creation and distribution of disbursement checks

2. Separating functional authority for collection and disbursement of funds

3. Separating expense approval, check-signing authority, and account reconciliation responsibilities

4. Using safety paper and watermarks that are difficult to reproduce on check stock

5. Using reputable printing companies

6. Storing check stock and signature plates in separate secured areas with controlled access

7. Securing canceled checks or switching to check safekeeping with CD-ROM output

8. Using printing processes that do not require preprinted check stock (such as laser printing of checks and MICR lines)

9. Using positive pay, a service that matches check serial numbers and dollar amounts against the company's issue file to determine the checks to be paid

10. Setting a maximum dollar amount limit on checks issued from each type of account (checks issued above this limit are returned to the depositor as unauthorized)

11. Increasing the use of electronic payment methods, utilizing appropriate security features

12. Using an electronic payment authorization service (similar to positive pay for checks) to protect against fraudulent ACH debits

C. Disbursement Networks

Disbursement networks are systems that establish check mailing locations and drawee banks based on disbursement studies. They are designed to optimize disbursement float and are not widely used. The cost and control benefits of making disbursements from just one or two banks often outweigh the float benefits of using a greater number of banks.

D. Compliance with Trade Terms

An accounts payable manager needs to monitor compliance with trade payment terms; for example, compliance with having paid a bill by a postmark date in order to take advantage of a trade discount opportunity or avoid late payment charges or interest penalties.

E. Funding Disbursement Accounts

A cash manager must ensure that disbursement accounts are adequately, but not excessively, funded.

F. Special Payment Types

1. **Freight Payments** - Some banks and third parties offer a payment service in which freight payment specialists pay all of a shipper's freight bills, audit bills for possible overcharges and duplicate payments, and provide reports that help a company compare costs for different routes and carriers.

2. **Tax Payments**

- **Federal Tax Deposits** - The Electronic Federal Tax Payment System is the primary method for collecting and accounting for taxes withheld by employers from individuals' salaries and wages, as well as corporate business and excise taxes. In recent years, most companies have been mandated to make these deposits electronically. The primary mechanism for making electronic tax payments is the ACH. Either debits or credits may be used. Wire transfers also are allowed.

- **State Tax Payments** - Many states require companies with tax payments above certain amounts to remit taxes electronically. This may be done with an ACH credit or debit, with some states permitting the use of a wire transfer as well. The standard payment convention for state tax payments via the ACH is known as TXP, but usage and specific formats vary from state to state.

3. **Electronic Benefit Transfers** - Most states have implemented or are in the process of developing electronic benefit transfer systems for food stamps. These systems allow recipients of government transfer payments to receive benefit payments through automated teller machines (ATMs) and point of sale (POS) terminals.

III. DISBURSEMENT PRODUCTS AND METHODS

There are several disbursement products or methods that cash managers can utilize to manage the disbursement process.

A. Zero Balance Accounts (ZBAs)

ZBAs are used by many companies to help manage their disbursement processes.

1. **Description of a ZBA** - A ZBA is a disbursement account on which a company writes checks, even though the balance in the account is maintained at zero. Checks debited against a ZBA for payment are covered by a transfer of funds from a master account located in the same bank. Funding of the ZBA is automatic and involves only an accounting entry by the bank. A ZBA can also be a depository account from which funds are debited and transferred into a master account at the end of each day. Some ZBAs are used for both collections and disbursements.

2. **How ZBAs Work** - Credits and debits to be posted are netted at the close of each business day. If there is a debit balance in the ZBA, the ZBA will be credited and a debit made to the master account. This brings the balance in the ZBA back to zero.

3. **ZBAs in Multi-Division Companies** - Multi-tiered ZBAs may be used to allow companies with multiple divisions or subsidiaries to write checks on separate accounts or to segregate different types of payments such as payrolls, dividends, and accounts payable. The cash manager can control the balances and funding of a master account and its associated ZBAs as if they were all one large account. This reduces excess balances and the need for multiple manual transfers.

B. Controlled Disbursement

Another method used to minimize balances in disbursement accounts is controlled disbursement.

1. **Description**

    - Controlled disbursement is a bank service that provides notification of the dollar amount of checks that will clear against the controlled disbursement account that day. This information is usually available by early or mid-morning. The disbursement bank must receive its final cash letter of the day from the local Federal Reserve bank (Fed) early in the morning so that the checks can be sorted and the company notified of its funding requirement.

    - One of the principal advantages of a controlled disbursement account is that it allows a company to calculate its daily cash position early enough to take advantage of better market rates for investing or borrowing.

    - Under the Fed's High Dollar Group Sort (HDGS) program, the local Fed automatically makes a second presentment to drawee banks with more than $10 million in daily presentments from banks outside their Fed district. This presentment delays the communication of final clearing totals until mid-morning.

2. **Payor Bank Services**

    - Payor Bank Services is an information service of the Fed which electronically notifies controlled disbursement banks early in the morning of all checks that will be physically presented later that day. There are typically two notifications: the first between 5:30 and 7:30 a.m. local Fed time, and the second between 9:30 and 10:30 a.m. local Fed time. Banks process the Fed data and notify customers of their funding requirements.

3. **Discrepancies After Notification**

    There are several instances where discrepancies arise between the reported disbursement clearings and the actual amount of checks presented for payment.

    - Controlled disbursement accounts must deal with same-day presentment items. These are checks drawn on the disbursement bank, which are directly presented from another bank by 8:00 a.m. According to Fed regulations, these checks must be paid the same day they are presented. These same-day presentment items may need to be handled by a different processing method than the rest of the controlled disbursement checks. Banks also have the option of designating the local Fed as the clearing point for same-day presentment items, thereby eliminating the challenge of combining presentment totals.

    - There is risk of presentment after the morning notification. A check missed by the Fed in the Payor Bank Services notification but discovered the same morning will be presented that day.

    - Checks may also be presented for payment at the disbursement bank by the payee. These checks, commonly known as over-the-counter items, may also cause discrepancies in clearing totals.

Some banks offer options to prevent problems caused by late presentments. The bank guarantees that the final presentment amount will be equal to the morning notification, and makes necessary adjustments to the account the next day.

4. **Funding Controlled Disbursement Accounts**

   • A controlled disbursement account is normally funded from a company's concentration account. Either the company or the bank can fund the account. The transfer is usually on a same-day basis.

   • If concentration and controlled disbursement accounts are in unrelated banks, a wire transfer or the ACH can be used for funding. Credit approval may be required for ACH funding and the company may have to maintain a balance equal to one day's average clearings in the disbursement account.

5. **Credit Risk** - The fact that controlled disbursement poses credit risk for a bank has important implications for companies. There are two situations in which a bank has credit exposure:

   • With ACH funding, there is risk that an ACH funding debit may be returned by the bank on which the debit is drawn. By the time the returned ACH debit reaches the disbursement bank, it may be too late to return any disbursement checks. The disbursement bank is owed funds and becomes a creditor of the company.

   • With the use of an affiliated bank for disbursing, with funding through the parent bank, there is no problem if the affiliate bank is funded directly on a same-day basis by a wire transfer. However, if the parent bank automatically funds the affiliate with immediate funds before the parent bank receives good funds from the company, there is an intraday overdraft and a potential overdraft problem at the parent bank. Since the affiliate bank does not have an overdrawn account, it cannot legally refuse to pay the checks even though there may be an overdraft at the parent bank, unless this option is provided for in the service agreement.

   Such risks make it very likely that a bank will undertake a credit review of a company that wants to use its controlled disbursement service. In some cases, a formal credit facility may be required.

6. **How to Select a Controlled Disbursement Bank** - In addition to overall relationship considerations, companies should consider several other factors when selecting a controlled disbursement bank. While disbursement float remains important for some companies, other considerations have become more important. They include:

   • **Timeliness of Reporting of Disbursement Totals** - This is important because a company wants to make investing or borrowing decisions as early as possible to take advantage of better market rates.

   • **Processing Accuracy** - Processing errors can result in overfunding or underfunding of the disbursement account.

   • **Volume Capacity** - Check processing capacity should be sufficient, so that reporting deadlines can be met.

- **Reporting Detail and Reconciliation Services** - Reports should contain adequate detail and be timely enough to meet a company's information needs.

- **Price** - Service pricing should reflect fair and reasonable compensation.

- **Customer Service Support** - Bank customer service staff should provide prompt and knowledgeable responses to a company's requests.

C. Payable Through Drafts (PTDs)

A PTD is a payment instrument resembling a check that is drawn against the payor, not the bank, and for which the payor has a period of time to honor or refuse payment. Some important aspects of PTDs and their use include:

- The deadline under Federal Reserve Regulation CC for approval or rejection of a PTD is the same as for a check.

- PTDs are frequently used for insurance claims and other field office disbursements that have multiple signers and require final headquarters' approval. They give a company time to ensure that all terms have been met or expenditures authorized.

- Electronic payable through drafts are ACH debits to a company's account in which the company is notified in time to pay or reject each item.

D. Multiple Drawee Checks

Multiple drawee checks, also known as payable-if-desired (PID) checks, are checks that can be presented for payment at a bank other than the drawee bank. Both bank names appear on the check.

- **Applications** - Examples include payroll in states that require employees to be paid by checks payable in the state, payroll for employees on assignments away from the company office, and dividend checks.

- **Banking Arrangements** - Companies maintain balances and/or pay a fee at an alternate payment bank to compensate it for cashing multiple drawee checks. The alternate bank will require indemnity from the paying company for any loss, including fraud, relating to those checks. Some banks are unwilling to provide this service.

E. Imprest Accounts

An imprest account is an account maintained at a prescribed level for a particular purpose or activity, and periodically replenished to the prescribed level. For example, a field office may have an imprest account for local disbursements with a balance sufficient for one or two months' expenses. Based on an established time frame or level of imprest account balances, the office submits expenses to headquarters for approval, and headquarters reimburses the imprest account.

F. Electronic Disbursement Methods

Electronic disbursements via the Fedwire and ACH are used for payments from corporations to individuals, from individuals to corporations, and from corporations to corporations. (See Chapter 4, Payments System.) The item volume of such payments is low compared to checks, but continues to increase as the value of float declines, and the emphasis on expense control increases. The increasing use of electronic commerce will also stimulate the growth of these forms of electronic disbursements. (See Chapter 9, Electronic Commerce.)

IV. ACCOUNT RECONCILIATION AND SUPPORTING SERVICES

Banks provide account reconciliation services to meet companies' information and control requirements. The following services are available:

A. Sort Only

In a sort only service, a bank sorts the checks by check serial number for a company.

B. Partial Reconciliation

In a partial reconciliation service, a bank lists all checks paid in numerical order by check serial number, or in chronological order by date paid. For each item, the paid report generally shows the check serial number, dollar amount, and date paid. The listing is available as a paper report, on CD-ROM, and/or via electronic transmission.

C. Full Reconciliation

With a full reconciliation service, a company supplies an electronic file of checks issued to its bank and the bank matches checks paid against the file. The bank supplies a listing, either as a paper report and/or in electronic format, of checks paid and outstanding in check serial number order.

D. Positive Pay

Positive pay, also known as match pay, is used to combat check fraud. With this service, the company transmits a file of issued check information to the bank soon after issuance. The bank matches check serial numbers and dollar amounts of checks presented for payment against the issue file and pays only those checks that match. Exceptions are conveyed to the company for disposition. Some positive pay services match against the payee field as well as the serial number and amount in an effort to detect altered payees.

A similar service, known as reverse positive pay, occurs when the bank transmits a file of the checks presented for payment to the company on a daily basis. The company matches this file to its list of checks issued and notifies the bank of any items it wishes to have returned. This service does not prevent fraudulent checks from being cashed at the payor bank teller line since the bank does not have access to the issue file.

E. Inquiries and Stop Payments

Stop payments can be initiated by a company by voice, electronically, or in writing. Written confirmation may be required by the bank for telephone instructions. Stop payments are usually good only for six months and must be renewed, if necessary.

Many banks offer information reporting systems which allow customers to electronically inquire whether a check has been paid, to place a stop payment, and/or to request a copy of the paid item. (See Chapter 10, Information and Technology Management.)

F. Check Retention (Check Safekeeping)

In a check retention service, a bank retains paid checks for periods that typically range from one to six months. Microfilm or image records are maintained by the bank for seven years. Companies can receive images of the checks on microfilm, microfiche or CD-ROM. Some banks offer on-line retrieval of images.

G. High-Order Prefix (Divisional Sort)

The high-order prefix sorting service allows a single account to be used by a company with multiple units. Codes identifying the various units are included in the check serial number field. Reports are available showing unit subtotals.

V. ACCOUNTS PAYABLE DEVELOPMENTS

There are several relatively new services that have an important impact on the operation and management of the accounts payable area.

A. Integrated or Comprehensive Accounts Payable

An integrated or comprehensive accounts payable service allows a company to outsource all or part of the company's accounts payable and/or disbursements functions. Two common approaches to managing an integrated or comprehensive accounts payable service are:

- A company sends a single data file to a third-party service provider containing a list of all payments to be made. The file contains information on when to issue a disbursement and to whom, as well as instructions on the payment method to be used (check, wire, or ACH).

- Alternatively, the third-party service provider maintains a database of a company's payees that includes detailed information such as preferred payment methods, specific remittance information, and receiving financial institutions. The database is periodically updated as new payees are added or an existing payee's remittance profile changes (for example, if a payee switches to ACH instead of check for its standard payment type). In such cases, as a company makes a disbursement, it sends to the third-party provider only limited payment information.

With either approach, the third party issues the payments immediately or warehouses them until a future date as instructed by the data file. A company using these types of services is outsourcing much of its disbursements function and potentially reducing the overall costs of its accounts payable operations.

B. Purchasing/Procurement Cards

Many companies are implementing the use of purchasing (or procurement) cards for the small dollar purchase of supplies, inventory, equipment, and service contracts. Though companies have long used credit cards for travel and entertainment expenses, the use of credit cards for routine procurement is growing. Cards are issued to designated employees, with spending limits and types of purchases pre-specified for each employee. The advantages of a purchasing card include:

- Cost savings by eliminating the processing of high-volume, low-dollar purchasing orders and payments

- Improved control over expenditures by applying spending parameters before purchases are made rather than through the expense reimbursement process

- Better vendor relations through earlier payments

- Improved reporting on spending with specific vendors, which may aid in the negotiation of more favorable discounts

C. Imaging Services

Imaging technology is a major component of many disbursement services. Both the front and the back of a check may be captured and converted into digital information using optical scanning. Check images (all of them or selected ones) may be transmitted to a company's computer and stored there or sent to a fax machine. The check images may also be stored in a bank database, which a company can access to view or retrieve the images. Any of these methods allows a company faster access to check information.

Imaging services are particularly useful in conjunction with positive pay services. They help a company identify potential unauthorized check activity and make critical pay/no-pay decisions on checks in a timely manner. Images of checks can be obtained in a more timely fashion than photocopies, allowing companies to respond quickly to inquiries from customers, employees, and vendors.

Some financial institutions are capturing check images on CD-ROM as a substitute for microfilm or microfiche.

Questions

These chapter questions are to test and review the information in the text and are not examples of CCM examination questions, nor are they in the examination format.

Answers can be found at the back of the book on pgs. 371-374.

1.   What are the five major objectives of a disbursement system?

2.   How may disbursement systems be organized?

3.   What are the three components of disbursement float?

4.   What are the various ways of preventing check fraud?

5.   What is controlled disbursement?

6.   What is a zero balance account (ZBA)?

7.   What is the Electronic Federal Tax Payment System (EFTPS)?

8.   Who provides Payor Bank Services?

9.   What factors should be examined in the selection of a controlled disbursement bank?

10.   What is positive pay?

11.   What is the difference between a partial and full reconciliation?

12.   How does controlled disbursement cause credit risk for a bank?

13.   What are the two common approaches to managing an integrated or comprehensive accounts payable service?

14.   What are purchasing cards and what is their benefit to a company?

15.   How are imaging services used in disbursements?

CHAPTER **9**

Electronic Commerce

OVERVIEW

This chapter describes Electronic Commerce (EC) and its relationship to Electronic Data Interchange (EDI) and electronic payments systems. It discusses the costs, benefits, and barriers to EC, as well as the standards for sending and receiving electronic messages. It also discusses the roles of the various software and service providers and the impact of EC on a company.

LEARNING OBJECTIVES

Upon completion of this chapter and the related study questions, the reader should understand:

1. EC and how it relates to EDI and electronic payments

2. How companies implement EDI

3. The benefits and costs of EC, as well as barriers to its implementation

4. How EC standards and software are used

5. The role of Value-Added Networks (VANs) and Value-Added Banks (VABs) in EC

6. How EC affects a company

7. How the Internet can facilitate EC

KEY CONCEPTS

1. The Implementation, Costs, and Benefits of EDI

2. EC Standards and Software

3. The Role of Value-Added Networks (VANs) and Value-Added Banks (VABs)

4. The Impact of EC on Company Operations

5. Use of the Internet for EC

OUTLINE

I. BASICS OF ELECTRONIC COMMERCE (EC)

The majority of business documents and payments exchanged among companies in North America are paper-based and move through the check clearing and postal systems. EC is an alternative to this paper-based system, and companies are implementing it in various forms. EC is enabling companies to form closer ties and become strategic partners with their vendors and customers.

A. Definitions

There are several important definitions related to EC:

1. **Electronic Commerce** - EC is the exchange of business information from one organization to another in an electronic format. It usually entails the electronic connection of any entity, application, or computer to another using a mutually agreed upon standard.

    The range of electronic commerce is shown in Exhibit 9.1. At one end of the continuum are totally unstructured messages, such as facsimile (fax) transmissions and electronic mail (e-mail). At the other end are highly structured messages, such as EDI. Enabled e-mail represents a middle ground between unstructured e-mail and more structured EDI messages. This format is created by agreements among e-mail users to maintain specific standards for transmission of business data via e-mail messages.

EXHIBIT 9.1

Electronic
Commerce

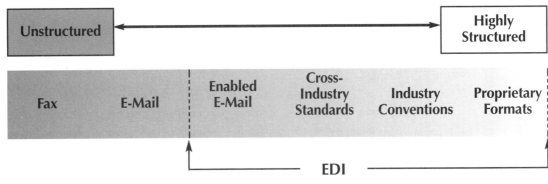

2. **Electronic Data Interchange (EDI)** - EDI provides a vehicle for the electronic movement of business data in a standard format from one company's application system (such as an order entry system, purchasing system, or billing system) to another company's application system. It allows senders to generate EDI messages directly from their applications, and it allows receivers to bring data into their applications without the need to re-enter any of the information.

This definition of EDI generally excludes fax and e-mail, which are unstructured in nature. However, certain forms of these transmissions meet the definition of EDI. They utilize standard formats to provide for the communication of data among business application systems.

Several electronic networks are used for EDI:

- **Local Area Network (LAN)** - A LAN connects computers within the same organization and usually within the same physical vicinity. A LAN typically is used within one company or one department of a company.

- **Wide Area Network (WAN)** - A WAN connects computers and LANs in several locations. Typically, a WAN belongs to one company and links the headquarters office with subsidiaries.

- **Intranet** - An intranet is a LAN or a WAN that uses the open standards of the Internet rather than proprietary software for communication among computers. This allows users to access information via commonly available browsers rather than proprietary user interfaces. (A browser is software that enables access to remote data.)

- **Extranet** - An extranet is a WAN in which two or more organizations share information using Internet protocols. Access is restricted to the participants.

- **Internet** - The Internet is an unrestricted, worldwide WAN to which everyone with the appropriate hardware and software has access. Communication on the Internet is made possible by open communication standards and protocols among users operating over an Internet service connection.

Specific EDI standards may be used in multiple industries, a single industry, or among selected trading partners as detailed below:

- **Cross-Industry EDI** - Cross-industry EDI is a format standard that addresses the needs of many different users in many industries. If a company sends a cross-industry EDI purchase order to another company that conforms to the same standard, the receiving company can capture the purchase order data directly without re-entering data.

- **Industry Convention EDI** - Industry convention EDI is a specific format standard or a subset of the more generic cross-industry EDI standards used within a particular industry. Examples of industries that utilize these types of EDI standards include grocery, retail, automotive, electrical manufacturing, and chemical production and distribution.

- **Proprietary EDI** - Proprietary EDI is developed by one company for exclusive use with its trading partners. Many companies using proprietary formats are shifting to the use of cross-industry or industry convention standards.

3. **Electronic Funds Transfer (EFT) and Financial EDI (FEDI)** - These are subsets of EDI. The distinguishing feature that characterizes EFT is the exchange of value, which requires the involvement of financial intermediaries, such as banks to send and receive electronic payments. Examples of EFT include wire transfers and automated clearing house (ACH) payments.

   FEDI is the electronic transmission of payments and payment-related information in standard formats between company trading partners and/or their banks. FEDI includes electronic format for invoices, payment initiation, lockbox deposit reports, and remittance information sent either directly to a trading partner or processed through a financial institution or communications intermediary.

B. Types of EFT Systems

Several types of EFT systems are available in the U.S. (These are covered in full detail in Chapter 4, The Payments System.)

1. **Fedwire Transfers** - In an EC application, wire transfers can be initiated by payors by using a bank's standard EDI transmission system or its information reporting system. The recipient of a wire transfer can receive electronic notification of the incoming funds from a bank, either through a standard EDI transaction set or through a bank's information reporting system.

2. **ACH Transfers** - In an EC application, the ACH system is an electronic-based payments systems that enables exchange of debits and credits. It offers several types of standardized formats for the transmission of payment and remittance information.

C. Relationship Between EDI, FEDI, and EFT

Exhibit 9.2 shows an example of the relationship between companies and their financial and communications intermediaries engaging in non-financial EDI, FEDI, and EFT. A supplier (seller) may send an EDI invoice to a customer. The customer (buyer) sends a FEDI payment instruction to its bank. The customer's bank sends an electronic payment and associated information to the supplier's bank through the ACH system. The supplier's bank notifies the supplier of the received payment through an electronic deposit report. The payment-related information transmission is an example of FEDI.

Exhibit 9.2 also shows two independent parties or service providers, such as Value-Added Networks (VANs) or Value-Added Banks (VABs), that assist companies in the transmission of EDI messages. (The role of these providers is discussed in Section III of this chapter.)

EXHIBIT 9.2
Relationship Between EDI, FEDI, and EFT

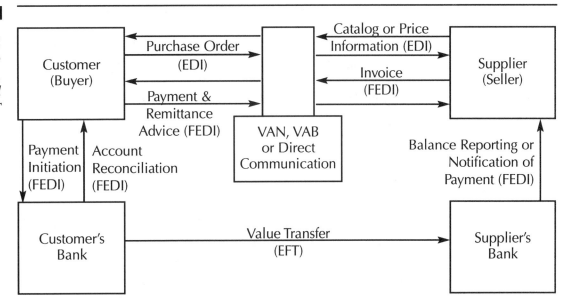

EDI, FEDI, and EFT - Parties and Applications

Mode	EDI Electronic Data Interchange	FEDI Financial EDI	EFT Electronic Funds Transfer
Parties Involved	Company-to-Company Company-to-VAN/VAB VAN/VAB-to-VAN/VAB VAN/VAB-to-Company	Company-to-Company Company-to-Bank Bank-to-Bank Bank-to-Company	Bank-to-Bank (Value Transfer)
Applications	Catalog Price Information Request for Quote Purchase Order PO Acknowledgement Production Schedule Shipping Information	Invoice Payment & Remittance Advice Payment Initiation Lockbox Information Balance Information Account Information Reconcilement Info. Account Analysis	ACH Debits ACH Credits Wire Transfers CHIPS

D. Factors Influencing the Use of EDI

The structures of companies' EDI systems vary widely, depending on the number of trading partners, the volume and type of EDI transactions used, and whether the company is an originator or receiver of EDI transactions. Companies implement EDI for many reasons, including:

1. **Reaction to a Request from Customer or Supplier** - Some companies implement EDI at the request (sometimes at the mandate) of key customers. These companies are generally suppliers to a company, which is already a heavy EDI user. This type of EDI implementation is often done on a small scale initially, using a PC and off-the-shelf software. Over time, the use of EDI at these companies may grow, but in the early stages, they are implementing EDI only with one or more major customers, and they are referred to as EDI spokes.

2. **Cost Saving and Greater Efficiency** - Other companies implement EDI to reduce costs. They usually implement EDI after analyzing the benefits and costs, as well as surveying potential trading partners. EDI also facilitates the outsourcing of financial functions to a third-party provider.

3. **As Part of a Redesign or Re-Engineering Process** - Some companies implement EDI on a large scale to maintain, or possibly increase, their competitive edge. Historically, these companies have been large manufacturers and retailers, who stand to benefit from the cost reductions, improved productivity, or decreased order lead times from EDI. Companies that encourage many of their suppliers to implement EDI are referred to as EDI hubs. Though these hubs often start as EDI originators, sending EDI purchase orders to their suppliers, they tend to become EDI recipients also as their trading partners begin to send EDI invoices in response to purchase orders. One of the major challenges for a large EDI hub is to provide the necessary support and training for the many EDI spokes with which it deals.

II. BENEFITS AND COSTS OF EC AND EDI

The major benefits and costs involved in the implementation of EC and EDI include:

A. Benefits

1. **Improved Productivity** - Once data is entered at the beginning of a transaction, the same data can be moved from one application to another without manual intervention. EC and EDI eliminate manual processes such as filing, matching, sorting, and retrieving material as well as envelope stuffing, stamping, and mailing.

2. **Reduced Cycle Time** - EDI transactions have no mail-time delays and involve minimal processing time. EDI facilitates just-in-time (JIT) inventory management in many companies, lowering inventory levels.

3. **Lower Error Rates** - Since EC makes data re-entry unnecessary, it reduces error rates and enables faster data processing. For example, using EDI for receiving remittance information may allow for greater accuracy in the posting of payments to the accounts receivable ledger.

4. **Improved Cash Forecasting** - EC eliminates mail time, thereby reducing or eliminating uncertainty in cash flow timing, enabling more accurate cash flow forecasting, and improving management of working capital.

5. **Improved Communication Capabilities** - With EDI, it is possible to be notified that a message has been received by the other party. Acknowledgment that a customer has received an invoice (which is not available in a mail-based system) can help to resolve issues of payment timing between buyer and seller.

B. Costs

Among the costs that need to be considered in the implementation of EC and EDI are the following:

1. **Software** - EDI or other electronic data must be integrated with data from existing applications. This usually requires modification of current business software applications. In addition, data must be translated from the company's current format into a recognized EDI format. Commercially available software packages are capable of performing translation processes for standard EDI formats.

2. **Hardware** - EDI may require major investments in computer equipment. A company may choose to use hardware on hand, or to install new systems for EDI implementation. Computer security hardware such as key locks, equipment utilized for encryption and authentication, or removable data storage are necessary for data protection.

3. **Communications** - EDI data must be sent from one party to another. This communication may be done either directly (usually over telephone lines) or through a VAB or VAN. Regardless of how data is transmitted, costs must be determined. The company needs to include costs of communications software and hardware (modems, communications interfaces, etc.) in this process.

4. **The Internet** - EDI is transmitted over the Internet via intranet and extranet systems. Costs vary, but they usually require a monthly payment to the provider of the Internet connections.

5. **Encryption and Message Authentication** - Encryption and message authentication are additional security measures used in EC. They require additional hardware and software. (See Chapter 10, Information and Technology Management.)

6. **Education and Training** - EDI often requires that a company train both its internal personnel and its trading partners. For a company adding EDI to a major application, this can be a significant expense.

7. **Trading Partner Selling and Support** - Benefits of EDI depend on economies of scale and accrue only when a significant number of transactions are involved. Implementation often requires the company to seek trading partners, who are willing to send and receive EDI messages.

8. **Negotiating with Trading Partners** - Implementing EDI may affect the timing of payments and require the renegotiation of credit terms. Negotiation can be costly and protracted, particularly if it involves legal or audit matters.

C. Additional Barriers

In addition to the readily identifiable costs of implementing EDI systems, there are other barriers and drawbacks to EDI implementation, including:

1. **Convenience of Paper-Based Systems** - The U.S. Postal Service delivers to all addresses in the U.S. for a uniform postage fee and provides low cost delivery of paper-based correspondence and payments. Virtually all companies and individuals have access to the postal delivery system, as well as a bank or other financial intermediary, to handle the payment part of the cycle.

2. **Tradition of Paper-Based System** - Legal, audit, and processing structures surrounding paper-based systems in the U.S. are highly evolved. Almost all of the Uniform Commercial Code and most accounting and legal standards are based on paper-based contracts and business conventions that require signatures for reporting and control purposes. Attempts to address the regulatory, legal, and audit issues involved with EC are still evolving.

3. **Dual Systems May Be Required Initially** - Many companies implementing EDI and/or electronic payments find they must continue to use dual systems (both paper and EDI) after EDI implementation.

4. **EDI Capabilities of Banks** - Banks and other financial intermediaries have only recently been required to pass remittance information from the receiving bank to the receiving company. Companies trying to make electronic payments to suppliers may find that some of their suppliers' banks are not yet capable of fully complying with this mandate.

III. EDI INFRASTRUCTURE

Further growth in the use of EDI systems depends on extending its infrastructure. There are four primary infrastructure components:

- EDI standard formats

- EDI software

- Communication networks and standards (VANs and VABs)

- Computer hardware

A. EDI Standard Formats

To send information electronically, companies must agree on a specific format and structure for electronic messages and the data they contain. In the early days of EDI, some companies designed proprietary formats and communication interfaces and either encouraged or mandated trading partner participation. Proprietary data formats and technical requirements are adequate when a company deals with a small number of partners. When a company has many EDI partners, however, a common standard becomes necessary.

1. **Development of EDI Standards** - EDI standards have evolved from proprietary standards to the current cross-industry and international standards.

    - **ASC X12 Standards** - The Accredited Standards Committee (ASC) of the American National Standards Institute (ANSI) is the coordinating body, which develops cross-industry EDI standards in North America. The development of the current U.S. standards for EDI began in 1968 with efforts of the transportation industry to establish standards for communications between and within railroads, ocean carriers, air carriers, and motor carriers. Based on this early work, the grocery and retail industries also developed EDI standards. In 1979, ASC X12 was formed to develop general EDI standards that could be used in a variety of industries.

    - **Industry Modification of ASC X12 Standards** - Several industries – such as the automotive, chemical, communications, and health care industries – have adopted ASC X12 standards. Others have adopted subsets of X12 standards. This practice is expected to continue in other industries with common requirements.

    - **UN/EDIFACT Standards** - Many countries have become involved in developing EDI standards. This has led to the development of United Nations EDI for Administration, Commerce, and Transportation (UN/EDIFACT) rules, a set of internationally agreed-upon standards, directories, and guidelines for the electronic interchange of structured data that relates to trade in goods and services between independent computerized information systems. UN/EDIFACT standards are widely used in Europe and some Asian countries.

2. **ASC X12 Structure** - The ASC X12 format standard consists of rules governing the translation of one or more business documents into electronic messages.

    - **Transaction Set** - A transaction set is the electronic equivalent of a paper business document or form. Specific rules govern formats for standard business documents. Examples of typical business documents that are converted to EDI transaction sets are purchase orders, shipping documents, invoices, and remittance advices.

    - **Data Segments** - Related information elements, such as the line item in the purchase order, are known as data segments. Most transaction sets contain at least three data segments and usually many more.

    - **Data Element** - Data segments consist of data elements, such as price, unit of measure, and quantity. Data elements are defined in a data dictionary.

3. **ASC X12 Financial Transaction Sets** - By convention, numbers, and names are used to identify ASC X12 transaction sets. Some of the common EDI transaction sets used in the finance area include:

    - **810 Invoice** - This allows the user to convey invoice data, such as unit price, quantities purchased, and terms of sale, from a seller to a buyer.

- **820 Payment Order/Remittance Advice** - This transaction set has two purposes. It initiates a money transfer to a payee and/or provides the payee with information describing the purpose of the associated payment. The 820, which allows multiple invoices to be paid in a single payment, also includes the amount of discounts and other payment adjustments.

- **821 Financial Information Reporting** - This transaction set facilitates bank-to-corporate account reporting. It provides for the reporting of multiple levels of financial information, including balances, transaction summaries, and individual transactions. It can be used for balance and transaction reporting, account reconciliation, and bank account statements.

- **822 Customer Account Analysis** - This transaction set allows banks to transmit account analysis information (balances, services, volumes, service charges, etc.) to their corporate customers. Treasury Management Association (TMA) service codes are used in the 822 transaction set to identify bank balances, services, and associated charges.

- **823 Lockbox Information** - This transaction set conveys lockbox check data including remittance detail (such as payors, invoices, and amounts being paid), deposit totals, and available funds.

- **824 Application Advice** - This transaction set accommodates acceptance, acceptance with change, or rejection of data received from another transaction set. It can be used to notify a payor of changes in information received in an 820 Payment Order/Remittance Advice.

- **828 Debit Authorization** - A company can use this transaction set to provide information to a financial institution regarding electronic debits that the company has authorized against its accounts by another company. It allows the payor (buyer) greater control; it can specify certain payees (sellers), certain time periods, dollar limits, and even specific debit transactions. This transaction set can also be used to convey check issue files for positive pay or reconciliation applications.

- **835 Health Care Claim Payment/Advice** - The health care industry uses this transaction set to transmit medical claim payment and remittance information.

- **997 Functional Acknowledgment** - A recipient uses this transaction set to confirm to an originator that the transmitted sets were received, and that they were in compliance with ASC X12 standards.

4. **NACHA Standard Formats for ACH Payments** - ACH transactions use various standardized formats. The most commonly used include:

    - **Prearranged Payments and Deposits (PPD)** - Companies use this format to effect a transfer of funds to or from a consumer account. Applications using PPD formats include direct deposit of payroll and consumer payments.

- **Cash Concentration or Disbursement (CCD)** - This format is used to effect transfer of funds between companies or between one company's accounts. Applications include cash concentration and corporate-to-corporate payments. In an EDI environment, a company may use its treasury information system to generate a list of required concentration transfers for electronic transmission to its financial institution. This format contains only limited space for ancillary payment information and thus has limited use for corporate-to-corporate trade payment information exchange.

- **CCD Plus Addenda (CCD+)** - The CCD+ format combines the widely used CCD record with an 80-character addenda record, which can be used to specify the invoice being paid or give other reference information necessary for application of the payment. The federal government's Vendor Express program uses the CCD+ format and has been recently expanded to use the CTX (Corporate Trade Exchange) format.

- **Tax Payment Format (TXP)** - This format is a modification of the CCD+ format designed for the electronic payment of taxes to state and federal governments.

- **Corporate Trade Exchange (CTX)** - The CTX format combines the record structure and enveloping required by the ACH system with the flexible length standards of ASC X12. A CTX transfer is essentially an ASC X12 820 (Payment Order/Remittance Advice), 813 (Electronic Filing of Tax Return Data), or 835 (Health Care Claim Payment/Advice) using ACH communications protocols. It allows the remittance information contained in the ASC X12 820, 813, or 835 to move through the ACH network rather than having to be separated from the payment and sent using a third-party network or through direct communication.

5. **Changing Standards and Recent Developments** - As information needs change and companies gain experience in EDI, the standards themselves evolve. Each year, most standards bodies publish revisions. While this process is necessary to adapt the standards to changing needs, it poses some problems for EDI users. A company's trading partners may be using different versions of the standard, and an EDI user must often support multiple versions of the EDI standards. EDI software, VANs, and VABs help to rectify these problems.

B. EDI Software

EDI systems rely on specialized software, which converts data into standard formats and transmits it between trading partners.

1. **Functions Performed by EDI Software** - EDI software assembles information into transaction sets for electronic transmission. Transaction sets can be created by a company itself or provided by a third party. They can be provided by a single integrated software package or by several software programs exchanging information with each other. The process, which is illustrated in exhibit 9.3, is for an outgoing EDI message. It is reversed for an incoming message.

- **File-Conversion** - The first step is to convert paper-based information from the company's records into an electronic file that is readable by the formatting component of the EDI software.

- **Translation** - This stage, also known as formatting, takes the input data from the file conversion step and translates it into the desired EDI standard format. Most software is capable of formatting data into any accepted cross-industry standard or industry convention. In essence, this step creates EDI transaction sets according to required formats and protocols. Some banks perform EDI translation services for their customers.

- **Communication** - This software application establishes communications either directly with the trading partner or with a VAN or VAB. It sends (or receives) the EDI formatted data to (or from) another party using mutually acceptable communication protocols.

EXHIBIT 9.3
*Steps
Performed
by EDI
Software*

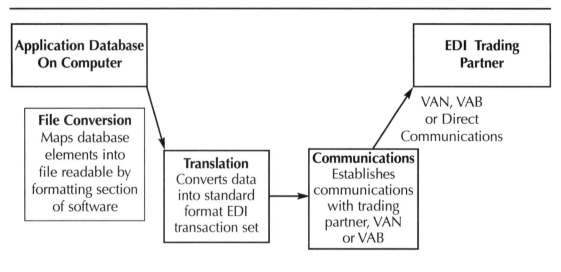

2. **Availability of EDI Software** - EDI software packages with mapping utilities are available for most computer platforms and operating systems. In addition, most EDI software is table-driven, meaning that all of the requirements and formats for EDI transaction sets are stored in easy-to change tables. By changing them, the software can produce any desired transaction set and can be easily updated as standards evolve.

C. Value-Added Networks (VANs)

A VAN is a communications intermediary which provides various services to the users of EC. VANs resolve interface problems between two companies that have different computer systems, different format needs, and different protocols. Thus, VANs make it easier for companies to implement EDI and to add new EDI trading partners. VANs offer many services to their customers, including the following:

- **Communications Capacity** - VANs maintain large numbers of communications lines with many different transmission speeds and communications protocols. Companies using VANs are assured of sufficient communications capacity to meet their EDI needs.

- **Mailboxing** - This enables one trading partner to send transaction sets to the other's mailbox for storage. When the other trading partner is ready, it retrieves the transaction sets. This solves the problem of finding a time when both partners can communicate.

- **Protocol Conversion** - This enables one partner to use a communication package with one transmission protocol to communicate with a partner that uses another protocol.

- **Standards Conversion** - Some VANs offer the ability to receive a document in one format and translate it into another format before sending the information to the customer.

- **Line Speed Conversion** - This is provided so that messages may be received and sent at whatever line speed the parties require.

- **Gateway to Other VANs or VABs** - Gateways to other VANs or VABs enable companies to communicate with any of their trading partners, who use different VANs or VABs.

- **Implementation Assistance** - This is frequently offered in the form of consulting, software, and training of trading partners.

D. Value-Added Banks (VABs)

Some banks (VABs) provide VAN services for information related to payments. They make possible the translation of electronic payment and remittance information between trading partners that use different communication protocols. Some VABs may also provide EDI services that are not directly related to payments or FEDI.

1. **VAB Payment Services** - VABs can provide integrated payables (see Chapter 8, Disbursements) in two different ways:

    - One approach is to have a company send a single data file to the VAB containing a listing of all payments to be made. The file contains information on when to issue a payment and to whom, as well as instructions on the payment method to be used (i.e., check, wire, or ACH). These instructions may be in a proprietary format or in an ASC X12 820 transaction set (Payment Order/Remittance Advice).

    - Alternatively, the VAB maintains a database of a company's payees that includes detailed information, such as preferred payment methods, specific remittance information, and receiving financial institutions. The database is periodically updated as new payees are added or an existing payee's remittance profile changes (i.e., payee switches to ACH instead of check for its standard payment type). In such cases, a company making payments sends only limited information to the third party.

    With either approach, the VAB either issues the payments immediately or warehouses them until a future date as instructed by the data file. A company utilizing these types of services is outsourcing much of its disbursement functions and potentially reducing the overall costs of its accounts payables operations.

2. **VAB Collection Services** - Some banks offer collection services that record the receipt of incoming payments (such as checks, ACHs, and wires), reformat the data, and transmit the data to the company. This service is generally referred to as an electronic lockbox and provides the information to a company in a proprietary format, a BAI lockbox format, or an ASC X12 format.

3. **Electronic Clearing House Services** - There are several national and regional electronic clearing house services operated by third parties or member banks that specialize in providing various types of EDI services to their members and/or customers. These clearing houses allow member banks to offer a wider range of EDI services than they could provide on their own.

E. Computer Hardware

A variety of computer systems, ranging from single-user PCs to large mainframes, can accommodate EDI. Some companies, particularly those new to EDI, may initially choose a PC, because of low cost and ease of implementation. As EDI transaction volumes increase, companies may choose to implement EDI on their mainframes or in a client-server environment.

IV. CREDIT TERMS AND EDI TRANSACTIONS

Most credit terms used today assume a paper-based system involving mailed invoices and checks.

A. Impact of EDI and EFT

EDI enables companies to complete processing more rapidly. EFT also removes much of the payment float due to mail, processing, and availability delays. Therefore, many companies are re-examining conventional credit terms. Other things being equal, faster payments are a disadvantage to buyers and an advantage to sellers. To compensate for changes in the cash flow timeline, companies are beginning to negotiate new EDI-based credit terms.

B. Negotiating Shared Benefits

EDI can bring significant cost savings to both parties. EDI makes it possible to shift the timing and/or amount of cash flows so that both buyer and seller realize significant savings. Buyers and sellers can transfer value by changing the terms of transactions. It is important to note that some companies will negotiate terms separately with each of their trading partners, while other companies may decide to unilaterally adjust terms for all of their trading partners. Two common approaches are:

1. **Price Changes (Discount)** - The seller offers the buyer a cash discount to compensate for earlier payment. For example, a seller offers a 1.5% discount if a customer allows its account to be electronically debited on the day the product or service is delivered. This may compare to normal payment under the paper system of 30 days or more.

2. **Payment Timing Changes** - The buyer delays payment to take advantage of the shorter intervals of electronic payment, compared with the time required for paper checks. For example, a customer initiates an ACH payment to its supplier three days later than a check payment would have been mailed out. This offsets or mitigates the loss of float resulting from the switch to EFT.

The amount of the discount required to renegotiate credit terms successfully in an EDI environment depends on the present value impact of changing the payment timing and any transaction cost savings resulting from electronic versus paper-based payments. Companies using a discount approach will set the discount for electronic payment approximately equal to the benefits or cost reduction derived from the earlier payment.

Companies that change the timing of the payment will often determine a "float-neutral" solution to payment timing, which simply makes the electronic payment date equal to the paper payment date, plus the normal collection float. Regardless of the approach, a successful solution will be one that provides benefits to both the buyer and the seller.

V. EC INFLUENCE OF PROCESS REDESIGN

EC plays an integral part in the redesign of finance functions or processes. Two primary examples of such re-engineering are the implementation of Evaluated Receipts Settlement and Paid-on-Production.

A. Evaluated Receipts Settlement

ERS is a payment method designed to eliminate the need for a supplier to provide an invoice to the customer. The dollar amount for ERS payments is based not on an invoice, but on a calculation of the quantity actually received by the customer multiplied by the price on the purchase order. The supplier does not send an invoice, but is simply paid by the customer on an agreed date after receipt of the shipment. The use of ERS allows the customer to automate its payables process and the supplier to automate the receivables and payment application process.

B. Paid-on-Production

Paid-on-production is the process by which a payment record is created for goods and/or services when they are used rather than when they are shipped or delivered. It is similar to consignment sales in retail, but is based on usage within a manufacturing environment. Typically there is only one supplier, and title to the product transfers when the product is used in the manufacturing process rather than at the receiving dock as in ERS. Because of legal concerns relating to liability, potential bankruptcy, and use of inventory assets for supporting loans, it is important to determine exactly when and where title to the inventory transfers from the supplier to the manufacturer.

VI. The Internet

Increasingly, companies are using the Internet as a payment and financial information channel. Because the Internet is open to access by virtually anyone with a PC almost anywhere in the world, it is attractive to many businesses as a means to reach more customers and to make it easier for customers to do business with them. However, the very openness and extent of the Internet make security a major concern for financial uses. Many, if not most, Internet-based systems are proprietary intranets that have sophisticated security systems in place to ensure confidentiality of information, protect company networks and databases from unauthorized access, and prevent fraud. Properly secured systems, such as these, can handle company-to-company transmissions, consumer-to-company transactions, or both.

Questions

These chapter questions are to test and review the information in the text and are not examples of CCM examination questions, nor are they in the examination format.

Answers can be found at the back of the book on pgs. 374-376.

1.   What are the primary benefits of EC?

2.   What are the three basic types of EDI?

3.   What electronic networks are used for EDI?

4.   What is the difference between EDI, FEDI, and EFT?

5.   What are the costs that must be considered in an EC or EDI implementation?

6.   What are the major barriers to EDI implementation?

7.   What is UN/EDIFACT?

8.   What are the primary ASC X12 financial transaction sets?

9.   What are the primary NACHA formats for ACH payments?

10.   What are the basic steps performed by EDI software?

11.   What are the services offered by VANs to their customers?

12.   What are the services offered by VABs to their customers?

13.   How are credit terms affected by EDI?

14.   What is ERS?

CHAPTER 10

Information and Technology Management

OVERVIEW

This chapter introduces information technology as it is used by cash managers to perform a variety of daily tasks. It covers the objectives of daily information management, the different types of internal and external data sources and their applications, the different kinds of Treasury Management Information Systems (TMIS) available, and the security, database management, and disaster recovery issues involved with their use.

LEARNING OBJECTIVES

Upon completion of this chapter and the related study questions, the reader should know:

1. The objectives of daily information management

2. TMIS processing tasks and timeframes

3. The different sources and uses of both internal and external TMIS data

4. The basic levels of TMIS technology

5. Examples of advanced TMIS technology and capabilities

6. Benefits and costs of TMIS technology

7. Database management, security, and disaster recovery issues involved with information management

KEY CONCEPTS

1. Cash Position

2. TMIS: Tasks, Technologies, and Capabilities

3. Database Management

4. Systems Security

5. Disaster Recovery

OUTLINE

I. OBJECTIVES OF DAILY INFORMATION MANAGEMENT

Information management is an integral part of cash management. One of the key responsibilities of a cash manager is to prepare a company's daily cash position or statement. This task requires access to timely and accurate information on the following:

- Bank balances (ledger, collected, available)

- Cash inflows (collections and concentration)

- Cash outflows (disbursements)

- Maturity status of short-term investments

- Maturity status of short-term debt

The objectives of daily information management are as follows:

- **Determining Cash Requirements** - A daily cash position assists a cash manager in determining a company's cash needs. If additional cash is required to meet short-term obligations, it may be necessary to access lines of credit or sell marketable securities. If excess cash is available, it may be invested.

- **Tracking Activity** - As part of preparing a daily cash position, a cash manager obtains information about a wide variety of individual transactions such as incoming and outgoing wire transfers, the collection of accounts receivable, the clearing of disbursement items, and automated clearing house (ACH) credits and debits. This information is often used to identify exception items, resolve problems, and identify potential fraud.

- **Identifying Opportunities** - Knowing a daily cash position enables a cash manager to take advantage of investment, trade payment, and debt repayment opportunities.

- **Updating Forecasts** - A daily cash position facilitates comparison of forecasted cash flows with actual cash flows. Variances are used to update forecasts, if necessary. As part of this process, a cash manager may also adjust target or compensating balances at financial institutions.

- **Updating Management Information** - The daily cash position is compared to financial data compiled from a wide range of sources. The cash manager and others within the company use the information to update performance measurements, long-term forecasting, and budget analyses. While management information is gathered daily, it is usually reported weekly, monthly, or quarterly, depending on the size and needs of the company.

Although the treasury function's use of information and technology involves more than just the preparation of a cash position, this daily compilation has been the driving force behind the development of Treasury Management Information Systems (TMIS).

II. TMIS PROCESSING: TASKS AND TIMEFRAMES

A. Processing Tasks and Responsibilities

Treasury acts as a clearing house for financial information. The cash manager is responsible for:

- Compiling information from a wide range of internal and external sources

- Sorting, storing, and analyzing this information

- Reporting information to management

On a daily basis, the cash manager is responsible for the following:

- Obtaining account balances and transaction detail from external sources

- Obtaining internal information that affects the cash flow timeline

- Consolidating the external and internal information into the cash position worksheet

- Integrating data on current-day activities

- Determining the cash position

- Initiating funds transfers

- Executing investment and/or borrowing decisions

- Updating the cash position worksheet and the short-term cash forecast

While compiling internal financial information, a cash manager must communicate with other areas of the company such as sales, purchasing, credit and accounts receivable, accounts payable, payroll, and accounting. External sources of data include financial institutions and third-party information providers. Increasingly, treasury departments use electronic systems to store, edit, share, and retrieve information using compatible computer systems connected through either a local area network (LAN) or a wide area network (WAN).

B. Processing Timeframes

The timeframes for treasury reporting vary depending on the industry, the type and size of the company, and the degree to which management relies on financial information for decision-making. The following are examples of different timeframes and reports:

- Daily - Cash position

- Weekly - Short-term cash forecast

- Monthly - Account analysis summary

- Quarterly - Investment and debt maturity schedule

- Annually - Funding and investment plan

III. TMIS INTERNAL DATA: TYPES AND USES

Examples of internal information that is exchanged between treasury and other areas of the company are listed below:

INTERNAL DATA	
Types	**Uses**
Sales Summary Reports Information on actual and projected weekly or monthly sales	**Preparation of a Cash Journal** The recording of individual debits and credits affecting the cash account
Purchasing Summary Reports Information on actual and projected weekly or monthly purchases	**Updating General Ledger** The posting of transactions to their proper general ledger accounts
Cash Receipts and Disbursements Information on actual and anticipated collections and disbursements	**Cash Forecasting** The preparation of short-term forecasts
Aging Schedules Information on the aggregate status of accounts receivable, as well as information on large individual collection items which are outstanding	**Funds Flows Between Operating Units** The tracking of cash flows between different operating units of a company or between different subsidiaries of a parent company
Investment Schedules Information on the sale, purchase, and maturity of short-term investments	**Monthly Budget Analysis** The comparison of budget to actual financial performance, and the investigation of variances
Debt Repayment Schedules Information on the issuance and repayment of short-term borrowings along with related interest payments	

IV. TMIS EXTERNAL DATA: SOURCES AND USES

A. External Sources of TMIS Data

On a day-to-day basis, a cash manager needs information from external as well as internal sources. The primary external sources are the company's financial institutions.

B. Types of External Data

Information gathered from external sources falls into one of two categories as follows:

EXTERNAL DATA

Prior Day	Current Day
Balance and Transaction Activity Information on current ledger and collected balances, one- and two-day float, debit and credit detail, and adjustment items, average balances, and balance history	**Lockbox Deposits and Remittance Detail** Information on lockbox deposits and the float breakdown of the deposits
Target Balance Activity Information on the status of actual balances compared to target balances	**Controlled Disbursement** Information on the amount of check clearings that need to be funded
Investment and Borrowing Activity Information on investment purchases and sales, as well as loan drawdowns and repayments	**Cash Concentration Reports** Electronic Depository Transfer (EDT) activity and exception reports, such as those identifying sending locations that have not reported daily deposits (may also be available on prior-day reports)
International Transaction Activity Information on international wire transfers, drafts, letters of credit, and foreign exchange transactions	**Wire Transfers** Information on both incoming and outgoing wire transfers
Custody Activity Information on securities safekeeping and approaching maturities	**ACH Transactions** Information on ACH debits and credits
Check Inquiry Information on the clearing status of individual items that have been issued	**Investments** Information on maturing investments
Stop Payment Activity Information on the status of stop payment requests	**Money Market and Foreign Exchange Rates** Information on same-day market activity for purposes of investment, borrowing, and foreign currency exchange
Account Analysis Information on account charges and services	**Return Items** Checks deposited into the company's account that have been returned unpaid
	Positive Pay Exception Items Checks presented for payment for which a matching issue has not been provided by the company

C. Multi-Bank Reporting

Companies that have two or more banks may establish an arrangement in which one of the company's financial institutions or a third-party reporting service gathers and consolidates the account balances and transaction activity from each of the company's financial institutions. This arrangement is commonly referred to as data exchange.

D. Uses of External Data

A company uses external data for various purposes. Examples of different uses for the same data are shown in Exhibit 10.1.

	Type of Information Accessed	Primary Use	Other Uses
EXHIBIT 10.1 *Uses of External Data*	Lockbox Detail	Update Accounts Receivable	Research Customer Inquiries
	Concentration Bank Deposits	Initiate Transfers	Update Cash Scheduling
	Controlled Disbursement	Fund Accounts	Manage Disbursement Float
	Transaction Detail	Track Individual Debits and Credits	Detect Internal or External Fraud
	Short-Term Investments	Access Daily Market Information	Review Investment Strategy
	Short-Term Borrowing	Initiate Line of Credit Drawdown	Update Cash Forecasting
	Account Analysis	Monitor Target Balances	Monitor Bank Pricing

E. External Information Formats

The two standardized formats for transmission of external data are the Bank Administration Institute (BAI) format and the Accredited Standards Committee (ASC) X12 821 Financial Information Reporting transaction set. The BAI format is the more established and more commonly used. However, there is a migration toward ASC X12 821, which is an Electronic Data Interchange (EDI) transaction set. (See Chapter 9, Electronic Commerce.)

V. REPORTING MECHANISMS

The five most common types of reporting channels are:

1. **Personal Computer (PC)** - PCs are used to gather prior- and current-day information from both external and internal sources. Some systems have interactive capabilities which enable users to initiate transactions. The software that enables PC access and reporting can reside either on a financial institution's computer or a company's PC, depending on the application.

2. **Direct High-Speed Connection** - Large amounts of data can be transmitted directly between computers via telecommunication lines.

3. **Telephone** - Telephone reporting is often used to gather prior-day information such as ledger and collected balances, and transaction totals, as well as current-day information such as lockbox deposits, controlled disbursement clearings, and cash concentration detail. It may involve gathering information manually via person-to-person contact or accessing an automated voice response unit.

4. **Facsimile (FAX)** - As with telephone reporting, FAX transmissions can report prior- and current-day information.

5. **Internet** - Companies can also communicate information over the Internet via e-mail or file transmission.

Use of any one of these mechanisms does not exclude use of the others. In many cases, a cash manager compiles information on a daily basis using a combination of these methods.

VI. INFORMATION REPORTING SYSTEMS

Financial institutions and third-party vendors offer access to account activity and transaction initiation through various systems – some are modular in design, but others are single-purpose systems. For instance, a bank can have one system with different modules for information such as account balances, concentration, and ACH initiation, and distinctly separate systems for initiating wire transfers, initiating stop payments, and positive pay data. Bringing them all together into one system with one point of access gives clients an electronic window through which they can see their cash management information. Exhibit 10.2 shows more examples of information reporting modules.

EXHIBIT 10.2
Information Reporting Systems

Prior-Day Information Modules	Current-Day Information Modules
Account Balances and Float Information	Lockbox Deposits
Debits/Credits	Controlled Disbursement Totals
Loans/Investments	ACH Debits and Credits
International Transactions	Wire Transfers
	Money Market Interest Rates
	Cash Concentration Totals and Detail
	Foreign Exchange Rates

VII. TREASURY WORKSTATIONS

A treasury workstation is typically a PC which has software that gathers information from both internal and external sources, then compiles the data for purposes of analysis and decision making. A treasury workstation can either be stand-alone or part of a LAN or WAN. In addition to automating a number of manual tasks, treasury workstations enable cash managers to prepare and distribute financial information in a variety of customized spreadsheets and management reports. Treasury workstation software can either be purchased from a vendor or developed in-house.

A. Capabilities

Treasury workstations have three primary attributes:

1. **Modularity** - Treasury workstation software is modular in design. Among the basic modules included in many programs are balance reporting, cash forecasting, investment portfolio management, and debt scheduling. Additional modules offer the

user choices such as general ledger interface, word processing, e-mail, foreign exchange management, and letters of credit information and initiation capabilities.

2. **Data Integration** - A treasury workstation is capable of integrating a wide range of information from both internal and external sources. The data may be downloaded into the computer and organized in a spreadsheet.

3. **Database Management** - Treasury workstations also provide the user with database management capabilities. This allows the user to determine how to store, retrieve, and organize information. It also allows the user to customize spreadsheets for financial reporting.

B. Modules

Treasury workstations enable cash managers to measure, monitor, and manage information more efficiently and extensively than is possible using manual or non-integrated procedures. Exhibit 10.3 shows examples of treasury applications facilitated by the use of a treasury workstation.

EXHIBIT 10.3
Treasury Workstation Modules

Treasury Workstation Module	Treasury Application
Account Balance Report	Monitor Ledger and Collected Balances
Target Balance Report	Manage Compensating Balances
Cash Position Worksheet	Manage Cash Position
Transaction Detail Report	Monitor Individual Debits and Credits
Investment Portfolio Management	Manage Short-Term Investments
Debt Scheduling	Monitor Debt Repayment
Letters of Credit	Issue Letters of Credit

VIII. TRANSACTION INITIATION

Increasingly, cash managers are using more automated methods for initiating transactions once they have compiled and analyzed data and completed the daily decision-making process.

A. Types of Transactions

Examples of the types of transactions that cash managers can initiate include:

• Wire transfers

• ACH debits and credits

• Stop payments

- Letters of credit

- Investment purchases and sales

- Loan drawdowns and repayments

- Foreign exchange transactions

B. Mechanisms

As with data gathering, several mechanisms can be used to initiate transactions. The most common include:

- PC

- Direct High-Speed Connection

- Telephone

- Internet

- FAX

IX. TMIS BENEFITS AND COSTS

A. Benefits

The benefits of using TMIS technology may include:

- Improved productivity

- Expedited data gathering, compilation, and analysis

- Increased forecasting accuracy

- Reduced borrowing expenses

- Improved short-term investment returns

- Improved management reporting

B. Costs

The costs of using TMIS technology include:

- Hardware and software selection, purchase, and installation

- Start-up and personnel training expenses

- Administration, maintenance, and overhead

- Telecommunications charges

- Transaction service charges

- System security expenses

X. TMIS SECURITY

A. Database Management Issues

Treasury data files contain information that, if improperly disseminated or misused, can leave companies vulnerable to defalcations and breaches of confidentiality. Consequently, controlling access to treasury information is vital. Proper internal control requires separation of duties pertaining to data access and use. For example, the same individual should not create, approve, and send a wire transfer. Determining who should have access to information entails not only consideration of technical competency but also of appropriate designation of responsibilities within the company.

A user must have a working knowledge of how to:

- Set up a database correctly

- Enter, edit, and update data accurately

- Protect the database's security, confidentiality, and integrity at all times

B. Security Risks

The three most common types of risks TMIS involves are:

1. **Data Loss** - This can be precipitated by a number of factors including:

    - Power surges or failures

    - Computer failure

    - Telecommunications system failure

    - Software defects

    - Intentional tampering with data

    - User error

    - Misplaced or lost storage devices, such as disks, CDs, tapes

The degree of data loss risk depends on the nature of the information that is lost and the amount of time involved in restoring it--if it can be restored at all.

2. **Unauthorized User Access** - There are two different types of unauthorized user access:

    • Unauthorized individuals within the company are able to access information by logging on to a computer in the treasury area or by means of a company's LAN.

    • Unauthorized users outside the company access information either accidentally or intentionally.

    The risks in both cases are that the unauthorized user has access to confidential information, can intentionally alter or destroy data, and/or may initiate unauthorized or fraudulent transactions.

3. **Computer Viruses** - A computer virus is a software program that is designed to corrupt or destroy data. Some viruses are relatively harmless and may affect only a small portion of a software program. Other viruses can sabotage an entire information system. Readily available anti-virus protection programs should be employed but are not always fail-safe.

C. Security Safeguards

Companies need to take steps to prevent either authorized or unauthorized users from executing fraudulent transactions. Companies can safeguard the security of TMIS by:

1. **Creating a Security Officer/System Administrator Position** - Assigning specific responsibility for TMIS security to a designated individual is a basic safeguard. This individual should be responsible for developing, monitoring, and enforcing information security policies and procedures.

2. **Developing Written Policies and Procedures** - Companies should establish formal policies that spell out all procedures for approval of access levels and protection of passwords. As with all such written policies, they are only effective if they are implemented, enforced, and periodically updated.

3. **Establishing Physical Security** - Physical security includes protection of both hardware and software. Actions range from simply storing computer systems and software in a secure place to restricting physical access to certain areas. The degree of physical security, as with all safeguards, depends upon many factors, including the risks involved, the costs, personnel constraints, and the practicality of imposing such controls.

4. **Instituting Basic Access Requirements** - Access requirements should include the following:

    • Requiring user identification and authorization such as a password and personal identification number (PIN)

    • Monitoring event log-on activity (maintaining a record of who accesses the system and what activities they perform)

- Limiting sign-on attempts

- Activating automatic log-off procedures when the system is not in use

- Enforcing periodic password changes

5. **Establishing Different Levels of User Access** - An additional safeguard is to establish different levels of access:

   - **First level** - At the first level, employees are allowed access to inquiry functions only. Inquiry functions permit authorized users to view information, but prevent them from inputting or editing data.

   - **Second level** - At the second level, authorized users can view, input, and edit information, but are not allowed to initiate transactions.

   - **Third level** - At the third level, authorized users have the authority to view, input, edit, and initiate.

Limiting access supports control through segregation of duties. For example, a transaction should not be transmitted by a person who entered or edited it.

6. **Requiring Backup Storage** - Backup storage can be accomplished in different ways depending on the system. Data can be backed up through the use of:

   - Diskettes

   - Tapes

   - CD-ROM or optical disks

   - Removable hard drives

   - Transmission via a LAN or a WAN to another computer system

   - Transmission to a mainframe

7. **Instituting Computer Virus Protection Methods** - Virus protection methods include:

   - Using virus protection programs

   - Prohibiting downloads from outside sources

   - Establishing an approved software program policy

   - Buying software from reputable dealers

   - Prohibiting installation of copied or pirated software

8. **Using Electronic Security** - Two of the most common methods of electronic security are the following:

- **Encryption** - Encryption is a process which electronically scrambles a message so that only persons who have compatible decryption hardware and/or software can interpret the message.

- **Message Integrity** - Message integrity is accomplished by using a digital signature to protect the integrity of a message from tampering. The sender of the message calculates a message authentication code (MAC) using a previously agreed-upon algorithm, encrypts the MAC, and transmits it with the message. The receiver independently calculates the MAC, decrypts the orignal MAC, and compares the two. A match indicates, with a very high probability, that the message has not been changed in transit.

D. Disaster Recovery

All TMIS and other electronic communications systems are vulnerable to disasters such as earthquakes, fires, and power outages. Banks and corporate treasuries should have disaster recovery plans that include:

- Identifying internal and external threats

- Assessing business risks

- Determining what is needed to perform critical tasks

- Developing backup or alternative systems and sites

- Obtaining management approval

- Testing at least every six months

- Keeping the plan current

XI. Current Issues

A. Year 2000

Many computer hardware and software systems are unable to distinguish between dates in the 20th century and dates in the 21st century. This shortcoming threatens the viability of many financial computing systems currently in use, such as those for billing, calculating loan payments, payrolls, and employee benefits. Various software programs and hardware components have been developed to modify computing systems to fix this problem, but the cost to companies and governments of correcting this deficiency has been estimated to be many billions of dollars.

B. Treasury's Organization-Wide Role

Technological developments have dramatically increased access to financial information. Technology now enables greater numbers of people to access and analyze unprecedented amounts of financial information. As a result, financial personnel are increasingly involved in all aspects of corporate activity and their expertise is used throughout the corporate organization. The role of the financial function is expected to continue to grow in importance.

Questions

These chapter questions are to test and review the information in the text and are not examples of CCM examination questions, nor are they in the examination format.

Answers can be found at the back of the book on pgs. 376-378.

1.   What are the objectives of information management?

2.   What are the typical tasks a cash manager performs on a daily basis?

3.   What are the types of internal data exchanged between the treasury area and other areas of the company?

4.   What are the sources of current-day information for the cash manager?

5.   What is multi-bank reporting?

6.   What are the five most common types of reporting mechanisms?

7.   What is a treasury workstation?

8.   What modules are often found in treasury workstation systems?

9.   What types of transactions can be initiated through a treasury workstation?

10.   What are the primary benefits and costs associated with TMIS technology?

11.   What are the most common security risks with TMIS?

12.   What are the basic types of security safeguards for TMIS?

13.   What steps should be included in a disaster recovery plan?

CHAPTER **11**

Forecasting Cash Flows

OVERVIEW

This chapter describes the objectives of forecasting. It explains forecast horizons and the principal techniques used for forecasting.

LEARNING OBJECTIVES

Upon completion of this chapter and the related study questions, the reader should know:

1. The objectives of cash forecasting

2. The distinction between short-, medium-, and long-term forecasting

3. The steps in the forecasting process: data selection, source selection, forecast method selection, and forecast validation and implementation

4. The various forecasting methods and how to apply them to forecasting cash flows

KEY CONCEPTS

1. Short-, Medium-, and Long-Term Forecasting

2. Steps in the Forecasting Process

3. Forecasting Methods

OUTLINE

I. Objectives of Cash Forecasting

II. The Forecasting Process
   A. Forecasting Horizons
   B. The Operating and Cash Flow Cycles
   C. Cash Flow Components
   D. Degree of Certainty
   E. Data Identification and Organization
   F. Forecast Method Selection and Validation

III. Forecasting Methods
   A. Receipts and Disbursements Forecast
   B. Distribution Forecast
   C. Pro Forma Financial Statements
   D. Statistical Forecasting

I. OBJECTIVES OF CASH FORECASTING

Forecasting cash flows is one of the more important tasks of cash management. The objectives of predicting cash flows include:

- **Liquidity Management** - Forecasting a company's net cash position at different intervals is essential for scheduling investment maturities and anticipating borrowing requirements.

- **Financial Control** - Using variance analysis to compare actual cash flows with projected cash flows can help identify problems such as unanticipated inventory changes, delays in accounts receivable collection, and mistiming of payments. Early identification allows a company to initiate corrective measures.

- **Meeting Strategic Objectives** - Cash flow forecasts are used to project future funding requirements and to support a company's strategic objectives.

- **Capital Budgeting** - Forecasts of revenues, expenditures, and funding are required for evaluating potential projects and capital budgeting.

- **Managing Costs** - Cash forecasts can help management optimize cash usage by minimizing borrowing costs and excess bank balances and enhancing short-term investment income.

- **Managing Currency Exposure** - Companies conducting business internationally can use various forecasting techniques to determine foreign cash flows and to assess their degree of foreign currency exposure.

II. THE FORECASTING PROCESS

Development of a particular forecast depends on many factors such as the forecast horizon, the company's size and its industry, structure, sources of information, and forecasting tools.

A. Forecasting Horizons

The time interval over which information is to be forecast is an important consideration. Cash flow forecast horizons can range from one day to several years. The forecast horizon can be thought of as a continuum, with distinctions made between short-, medium-, and long-term intervals.

1. **Short-Term Forecasting** - Short-term forecasts predict cash receipts and disbursements and the resulting balances on a daily, weekly, or monthly basis. Short-term forecasts aid in scheduling cash concentration transfers for field and lockbox accounts, funding disbursement accounts, and making short-term investing and borrowing decisions. Short-term forecasting is also important in establishing and managing target balances for purposes of bank compensation.

2. **Medium-Term Forecasting** - Cash flow forecasts from one to 12 months are an integral part of cash budgeting and are referred to as medium-term forecasts. They project the inflows (collections from sales and other sources of funds), and outflows (expenses and other uses of funds) on a monthly basis. They are used to determine the company's need for short-term credit or the availability of funds for short-term investments. They can also serve as a benchmark for performance by comparing actual cash flows to projected cash flows from the cash budget.

3. **Long-Term Forecasting** - Long-term forecasts cover any period beyond one year. They take into consideration projections of long-term sales and expenditures as well as market factors. Such forecasts are of strategic importance because they relate to long-term financial planning for the company. They are also used by financial institutions and rating agencies for credit analysis and evaluation.

B. The Operating and Cash Flow Cycles

The business operating cycle determines the basic configuration of day-to-day cash flows. A company's credit, inventory, and payables policies (and those of its suppliers) have an impact on cash flows as shown by the cash flow timeline. The business operating cycle and the cash flow timeline are discussed in Chapter 1, The Role of Cash Management in Corporate Finance.

C. Cash Flow Components

Proper forecasting of cash flows necessitates dividing them into their components. One approach is to divide cash flows into categories of operating, investing, and financing activities. These categories can be further segregated into outflows and inflows. For example, operating cash inflows might be segregated by product line, type of customer, or region, while operating cash outflows can be segregated into large-dollar vendor payments, small-dollar vendor payments, and payroll.

D. Degree of Certainty

Proper forecasting of cash flow also necessitates assigning degrees of certainty to each component.

1. **Certain Flows** - For many companies, the timing and amounts of a significant number of cash flows are known in advance. Typical examples of certain cash flows include interest, royalties, and tax payments.

2. **Predictable Flows** - Cash collections from credit sales are an example of a cash flow component that can be predicted with reasonable accuracy. The cash flow on a given day depends on factors such as the recent history of credit sales. A prediction of future cash flows can then be made on the basis of past observations. Disbursements such as payroll are also predictable, based as they are on records of hours worked and projected float on payroll checks. Similarly, patterns of clearings of vendor checks can also be determined on the basis of past clearing times.

3. **Less Predictable Cash Flows** - Some cash flows, such as those related to sales of a new product, unexpected repairs pending settlement of insurance claims, or the cost of settling a strike, are difficult to forecast. The experience and judgment of the forecaster are important in these instances.

E. Data Identification and Organization

The identification of suitable data to be used in the forecast is an important element of the forecasting process. Cash managers should consider the following factors:

1. **Sources** - Information should be gathered from external and internal sources, including the company's banks, field managers, sales managers, and the accounts payable and accounts receivable departments.

2. **Identification** - The identification of sources is affected by the degree of centralization or decentralization in the company's structure. In a decentralized company, field managers usually have the most current financial data related to their operations. A centralized company is less dependent on numerous field sources.

3. **Account Structure** - The bank account structure used by the company is also important. For example, using a single master account to collect all cash inflows and disperse all cash outflows via Zero Balance Accounts (ZBAs) helps facilitate cash flow forecasting compared to a system of multiple stand-alone accounts.

4. **Reporting Requirements** - In order to ensure the usefulness of the data selected, it is essential that the data be precisely defined and accurately reported in a timely manner.

5. **Historical Data** - Prior-period data can be useful in determining the timing and amount of future cash flows related to sales—for example, previous credit sales experience and individual customer payment histories.

F. Forecast Method Selection and Validation

The process of selecting a method of forecasting involves:

1. **Establishing Data Relationships** - Cash managers should ascertain the statistical relationship between the available data and the cash flow components to be forecast before selecting the appropriate forecasting method. This determination can come from forecaster intuition, past experience, graphical views of the data, or more sophisticated quantitative statistical techniques. For example, cash disbursements can be modeled as a function of invoices received for payment, and cash collections can be based on prior-period credit sales.

2. **Selecting a Method** - A forecasting method is selected after the relationship is determined between the input data and the cash flow to be forecast. Forecasting models should be cost-effective. Any forecasting system or model must be maintained along with the data required to produce the forecast. Sophisticated computer-based models may require systems support and personnel to provide data input. The cost of more detailed analyses must be weighed against the expected improvement in the accuracy of forecasts.

3. **Testing and Validating Relationships** - The degree of explanatory power can be assessed in the course of model development; the higher the correlation between expected (predicted) values and actual values on which the model is based, the better it is.

    A model can be refined and validated using the following methods:

    *   **In-Sample Validation** - In-sample validation tests how well the model works using the historical data from which the model was developed. Using randomly chosen data within the sample, the forecast model's predicted results are compared with actual values.

    *   **Out-of-Sample Validation** - Out-of-sample validation tests the accuracy of the forecasting models using data not involved in the model's estimation. For example, if three years (36 months) of monthly data are available, the model is estimated using the first 30 months of data. The model can then be validated by comparing the model's predictions to actual values over the remaining six months of data.

    *   **Ongoing Validation** - Continuing feedback from projected versus actual comparisons allows continuous evaluation and refinement of the model.

III. FORECASTING METHODS

The method a company uses for a given forecast depends greatly on the forecasting horizon. Many companies use short-term forecasts based on information relating to receipts and disbursements that will occur in the near future. There are a number of methods which incorporate individual cash flow details to develop accurate short-term cash projections. Two of the more important methods for short-term forecasting include receipts and disbursements forecasts and distribution forecasts. Medium- and long-term forecasting methods include generating pro forma financial statements. Statistical analytical techniques may be applied across all time horizons.

A. Receipts and Disbursements Forecast

Projecting receipts and disbursements is fundamental to short-term cash forecasting. This begins with the creation of separate schedules of cash receipts and disbursements. Both schedules are prepared on a cash basis rather than an accrual basis. This method tends to forecast cash accurately in the short term and near medium term, especially when accounts receivable and accounts payable data are incorporated.

- **Receipts Schedule** - A receipts schedule consists of a projection of collections from customers (cash sales or payments on accounts receivable) and other cash inflows such as interest or dividends received from investments. A receipts schedule should also include non-recurring cash inflows such as the proceeds from asset sales.

- **Disbursements Schedule** - A disbursements schedule involves forecasting the cash disbursements for purchases and other cash outflows, such as payroll, taxes, interest, dividends, rent, and debt repayments.

- **Completed Forecast** - Completing the forecast involves combining the receipts and disbursements schedules and comparing the results to a desired minimum cash balance.

In Exhibit 11.1, a company has determined its minimum cash requirements to be $50,000 to cushion it against unexpected expenses or to allow it to take advantage of unanticipated opportunities. The beginning cash balance is the ending cash balance from the prior week. The final two lines of the forecast represent the forecasted surplus or deficit cash position each week. With this information, a company can better manage its borrowing and investing activity.

EXHIBIT 11.1
Receipts and Disbursements Forecast

$ Amounts in $1,000	Week 1	Week 2	Week 3
Cash Receipts	$1,000	$1,100	$ 950
Cash Disbursements	(870)	(1,450)	(1,000)
Net Cash Flow	130	(350)	(50)
Beginning Cash Balance	100	230	(120)
Ending Cash Balance	230	(120)	(170)
Minimum Cash Req. (Target Balance)	(50)	(50)	(50)
Financing Needed (Deficit)		$170	$220
Investable Funds (Surplus)	$180		

B. Distribution Forecast

A distribution forecast provides estimates of cash flows on a daily basis over a specified interval based on historical patterns. It is particularly appropriate for short-term forecasts. The distribution percentages may be calculated two ways:

1. **Simple Average** - Distribution percentages can be estimated by averaging past daily cash flows related to a particular category of disbursements. For example, the cash manager may sample past clearings of payroll checks and discover that on average 40 percent of a certain category of payroll checks cleared on the day checks were issued, 50 percent the day after, and 10 percent two days after check issuance. The problem with taking a simple average is that more factors than just the number of days after check issuance may affect the check clearing delay.

2. **Regression Analysis** - It is very likely that the day of the week the check was distributed, the day of the month of check issuance, and/or the proximity of holidays may affect the distribution of check clearings. If more than one factor affects the proportion of a period's cash flow that one day represents, the method requires application of a statistical estimation technique such as regression analysis. This distribution method allows seasonality and other trends to be incorporated into forecasts. However, it requires large amounts of data and may need to be revised as business conditions change.

Exhibit 11.2 is an example of forecasting using the distribution method.

EXHIBIT 11.2
Forecasting Using the Distribution Method

A company has used regression analysis based on historical data to estimate the proportion of dollars that will clear on a given business day. It has determined that this proportion depends on the number of business days since the checks were distributed. The estimated proportions are given below.

Business Days Since Distribution	Percentage of Dollars Expected to Clear
1	13%
2	38%
3	28%
4	13%
5	8%
Total	**100%**

Therefore, if $100,000 in checks are distributed on Wednesday, May 1, the checks are estimated to clear according to the schedule below.

Date	Business Days After Distribution	Day of the Week	Percentage of Dollars Clearing	Forecasted Dollars Clearing
May 2	1	Thursday	13%	$13,000
May 3	2	Friday	38%	$38,000
May 6	3	Monday	28%	$28,000
May 7	4	Tuesday	13%	$13,000
May 8	5	Wednesday	8%	$ 8,000
			TOTAL **100%**	**$100,000**

C. Pro Forma Financial Statements

Projected income statements and balance sheets can be used to forecast cash flows over a longer time horizon. One of the simplest procedures for constructing pro forma financial statements is based on the percentage-of-sales method, as illustrated in Exhibit 11.3.

Percentage-of-Sales - The percentage-of-sales method involves projecting financial statements based on sales forecasts and the historical relationship between sales and certain balance sheet items such as cash, accounts receivable, inventory, and accounts payable.

The percentage-of-sales method is accomplished by:

• Forecasting the income statement and balance sheet based on the relationships mentioned above

• Calculating the projected ending cash balance by determining the impact on cash of the forecasted income statement and balance sheet changes

• Comparing the projected ending cash balance with the company's target cash balance and adjusting the pro forma statements to fund any shortfall or apply any surplus cash

EXHIBIT 11.3

Forecasting with Pro Forma Financial Statements (Percentage-of-Sales Method)

Assume the following income statement and balance sheet (in thousands) represent a company's actual position as of December 31, 1999.

Income Statement

Sales	$ 2,000	
Cost of Goods Sold	(1,500)	[75% of Sales]
Selling & Admin. Exp.	(200)	[10% of Sales]
Depreciation	(100)	
Interest Expense	(38)	
Income Before Taxes	162	
Taxes	(55)	[34% Tax Rate]
Net Income	$ 107	

Balance Sheet

Cash	$ 100	Payables	$ 50
Receivables	300	Notes (at 12%)	150
Inventory	200	Bonds (at 10%)	200
Net Fixed Assets	400	Common Equity	600
Total Assets	$1,000	Total Liab. & Equity	$1,000

To generate the percentage-of-sales forecast, the following assumptions are made (all numbers are in thousands):

- Sales will increase by 10% to $2,200 in the year 2000
- Cost of goods sold, selling and administrative expenses, payables, and operating current assets and liabilities (receivables, inventory, and payables) are a constant percentage of sales
- Cash balance is derived from the cash flow statement
- Additional fixed assets in the amount of $100 will be purchased
- Depreciation will be $50
- Notes will be reduced to $100 at the beginning of the year
- Dividends will be $24

(Continued)

EXHIBIT 11.3

Forecasting with Pro Forma Financial Statements

Projected Income Statement (in thousands) - Year Ending December 31, 2000

Sales	$ 2,200	
Cost of Goods Sold	(1,650)	[75% of Sales]
Selling & Admin. Expense	(220)	[10% of Sales]
Depreciation	(50)	
Interest Expense	(32)	[.12 x 100 + .10 x 200]
Income Before Taxes	248	
Taxes	(84)	[34% Tax Rate]
Net Income	$ 164	
Dividends	(24)	
Retained Earnings	$ 140	

Projected Balance Sheet (in thousands) Year Ending December 31, 2000

Cash (From Cash Flow Statement)	$ 95	Payables (2.5% of Sales)	$	55
Receivables (15% of Sales)	330	Notes		100
Inventory (10% of Sales)	220	Bonds		200
Net Fixed Assets (NFA) (Prior NFA + New Fixed Assets – Depreciation) ($400 + $100 – $50)	450	Common Equity (Prior Common Equity + Retained Earnings) ($600 + $140)		740
Total Assets	$ 1,095	Total Liab. & Equity	$	1,095

All of the projected account balances except cash are calculated based upon the given assumptions. The ending cash balance is determined by evaluating the impact on cash of the income statement activity and balance sheet changes and adjusting the beginning cash balance accordingly. (This procedure is described in Chapter 2, Section I, D, 3: "Statement of Cash Flows.")

(Continued)

EXHIBIT 11.3

Forecasting with Pro Forma Financial Statements

Projected Statement of Cash Flows (in thousands)		
Beginning Cash		$100
Cash Flows from Operating Activities		
Net Income	$164	
Adjustments to reconcile net income to cash		
Depreciation	50	
Increase in Accounts Receivable	(30)	
Increase in Inventory	(20)	
Increase in Accounts Payable	5	
Net Cash Provided (Used) in Operating Activities		169
Cash Flows from Investing Activities -		
Purchase of Fixed Assets		(100)
Cash Flows from Financing Activities		
Net Repayment on Debt	(50)	
Dividends Paid	(24)	
Net Cash Provided (Used) by Financing Activities		(74)
Ending Cash Balance		95

If the projected ending cash balance is less than the company's established target balance, the shortfall must be funded through taking on additional debt, issuing equity, or selling assets. Conversely, if the projected cash balance exceeds the target, the surplus may be invested in additional assets, used to reduce debt, and/or distributed to shareholders. In the above example, if the target cash balance were $110, then $15 in additional cash would need to be raised. If this were accomplished through an increase in notes payable, then the December 31, 2000, balance sheet would appear as before, except that cash would be $110 and notes payable would be $115.

D. Statistical Forecasting

Statistical forecasts project cash flows in two ways:

• Through extrapolation, or

• By determining the relationship (correlation) between a predicted cash flow or cash flow component (dependent variable) and other known cash flow components (independent variables or determinants).

Statistical forecasting is particularly applicable to projections requiring analysis of extensive data, and it is useful for identifying and analyzing trends.

Two of the more common techniques of statistical analysis are:

1. **Time Series Forecasting** - A time series model seeks to forecast a variable based on past observations of that variable. The primary types of time series forecasting applicable to cash forecasting are discussed below.

   • **Simple Moving Average** - Simple moving averages base a forecast on a rolling or moving average of past historical values. A forecast prepared using a simple moving average will always lag any trend in the actual cash flow. Also, the longer the time period over which the moving average is calculated, the greater the smoothing of individual data point variances; the shorter the time period, the less the smoothing of individual data point variances. Exhibit 11.4 shows how to calculate a five-day moving average.

EXHIBIT 11.4

Forecast with Simple Moving Averages and Exponential Smoothing

Day	Actual Cash Flow (X_t)	Moving Average Forecast Forecast (N=5)	Error	Forecast with Exponential Smoothing Forecast (α = .4)	Error
1	$110,000				
2	120,000				
3	115,000				
4	122,000				
5	126,000				
6	124,000	$118,600	$5,400	$118,600	$5,400
7	129,000	121,400	7,600	120,760	8,240
8	133,000	123,200	9,800	124,056	8,944
9	132,000	126,800	5,200	127,634	4,366

Moving Average Forecast
Moving Average Forecast for day 6 is:
($110,000 + 120,000 + 115,000 + 122,000 + 126,000)/5 = $118,600
Which results in a forecast error of $124,000 − $118,600 = $5,400

Exponential Smoothing Forecast
The exponential smoothing forecast begins with the day 6 forecast of
$118,600 based on the moving average forecast.
Then, the day 7 forecast using exponential smoothing is:
.4 [$124,000] + (1 − 0.4) [$118,000] = $120,760
This results in a forecast error of $8,240 ($129,000 − $120,760 = $8,240).

- **Exponential Smoothing** - Exponential smoothing is a variation of a simple moving average. The exponential smoothing technique uses the previous forecast value, the most recent actual value, and a user-determined value known as the smoothing constant. This smoothing constant is typically designated as "α" (referred to as alpha) and may range between 0 and 1. Setting α closer to 1 will result in more weight being placed on the most recent actual value and correspondingly less weight on the previous forecast value, resulting in less smoothing of the series. The forecaster must determine how much smoothing is required and choose the smoothing constant, α, accordingly. Note, a value of α can be estimated statistically from historical data. Exhibit 11.4 provides an example of exponential smoothing based on the relationships developed below:

Next Period Forecast = α [Current Period Actual] + (1 – α) [Current Period Forecast]

This formula can be expressed more formally as:

$$F_{t+1} = \alpha X_t + (1 - \alpha) F_t$$

Where:

F_{t+1}	= Cash flow forecast for the next period (t+1)
F_t	= Cash flow forecast for the current period (t)
α	= Smoothing constant ($0 \leq \alpha \leq 1$)
X_t	= Actual cash flow for the current period (t)

As in the simple moving average forecast, a simple exponential smoothing forecast will lag trends in the data. To correct for this, and to allow for seasonality in the forecast, more complex extensions of exponential smoothing allow the user to incorporate these factors.

2. **Regression Analysis** - Regression analysis is a statistical technique that systematically identifies the relationship between the variable being predicted (the dependent variable) and selected or appropriate explanatory or independent variables. Though there are many forms of regression analysis, the most basic is that of a simple linear regression model. This approach essentially determines a line that best represents the relationship between a single dependent variable and a single explanatory variable. Regression analyses (especially the more complex types) are most often done using a computer program that determines the relationship between the variables in question through a series of mathematical algorithms and which can also display the relationship in a graphic format.

Questions

These chapter questions are to test and review the information in the text and are not examples of CCM examination questions, nor are they in the examination format.

Answers can be found at the back of the book on pgs. 378-379.

1. What are the objectives of cash forecasting?

2. What are the major steps involved in the forecasting process?

3. What are the two major short-term forecasting methods?

4. One long-term forecasting method is the use of pro-forma statements. What is the technique that is used to prepare a pro-forma statement?

5. What are the primary types of time series forecasting?

6. The following cash flow information is provided:

Day	Cash Flow
1	100
2	150
3	250
4	210

   What is the four-day moving average forecast for day 5?

7. How does exponential smoothing differ from the simple moving average forecast?

8. What are the steps in selecting a forecasting method?

9. What are the three types of forecast validation?

10. What is regression analysis?

CHAPTER 12

Short-Term Investments

OVERVIEW

This chapter explains why companies hold short-term investments and how they determine and carry out investment policies. It presents the characteristics of various short-term financial instruments – the returns they offer, their risks, and the fundamentals of different short-term investment strategies.

A financial instrument or security evidences a transaction between two parties. To one party it represents an investment, to the other, an obligation. This chapter discusses financial instruments from the investor's point of view (as assets). Chapter 13, Borrowing, discusses financial instruments from the borrower's perspective (as liabilities).

LEARNING OBJECTIVES

Upon completion of this chapter and the related study questions, the reader should know:

1. Why companies hold short-term investments

2. How companies assign authority and responsibility for short-term investments

3. How companies typically determine investment policies

4. Factors influencing short-term investment yields

5. The most frequently issued short-term government, agency, municipal, bank, and corporate short-term investment instruments

6. How prices are quoted for short-term investment instruments, and how yields are calculated according to money market, bond-equivalent, and effective annual yield quoting conventions

7. The basic term structure of interest rates, and how yield curves can change under different market environments

8. The differences between active and passive short-term investment strategies, and specific strategies such as matching, riding the yield curve, and dividend capture

KEY CONCEPTS

1. Short-Term and Long-Term Investments

2. Liquidity and Marketability

3. Money and Capital Markets

4. Yield

5. Term Structure of Interest Rates

6. Short-Term Investment Strategy

OUTLINE

I. Introduction

II. Why Companies Hold Short-Term Investments
   A. Liquidity Provision
   B. Temporary Surplus Funds
   C. Income Generation

III. Short-Term Investment Issues and Corporate Policies
   A. Short-Term Investment Objectives
   B. Responsibilities for Short-Term Investment Policies
   C. Factors that Influence Short-Term Investment Policies
   D. Instrument and Portfolio Characteristics and Attributes
   E. Investment Management
   F. Performance Measurement

IV. Markets for Financial Instruments
   A. Money Market (Short-Term Financial Instruments)
   B. Capital Market (Long-Term Financial Instruments)

V. Financial Instruments
   A. U.S. Treasury Securities
   B. Agency Securities
   C. Municipal Obligations
   D. Bank Financial Instruments
   E. Repurchase Agreements (Repos)
   F. Corporate Obligations
   G. Money Market Mutual Funds
   H. Asset-Backed Securities
   I. Collateralized Mortgage Obligations (CMOs)

VI. Yield
   A. Factors that Influence Yields
   B. Basic Yield Definitions
   C. Yield Quoting Conventions
   D. Yield Calculations
   E. Duration
   F. The Yield Curve

I. INTRODUCTION

Ensuring corporate liquidity, meaning the ease with which assets can be converted into cash without material loss, is a key objective of successful cash management.

Companies need cash to meet their ongoing obligations in a timely manner. However, the opportunity cost of holding cash in checking accounts can be significant. In order to minimize foregone interest income, companies invest actively in readily marketable, interest-earning securities that have a stable market value.

A company will quickly become insolvent if it is not liquid, i.e., if it does not have sufficient resources to meet its day-to-day obligations. A company's short-term investment strategy should facilitate reducing the cost of maintaining ample liquidity while increasing interest income.

II. WHY COMPANIES HOLD SHORT-TERM INVESTMENTS

Companies generally hold short-term investments, which are defined as those that mature in a year or less, for three main reasons:

A. Liquidity Provision

Reserve liquidity is the primary reason companies invest in short-term securities. Companies cannot always depend on sufficient cash inflows during a period to cover that period's financial obligations. A portfolio of short-term investments can help adjust working capital imbalances, and it may be used in conjunction with short-term borrowing.

B. Temporary Surplus Funds

From time to time, a company may receive cash for which it has no immediate use. This can come from a variety of sources, including:

1.   **Ongoing Operations** - A company may gradually accumulate excess cash from positive operating cash flow.

2.   **Seasonal Performance** - A company, such as a retail outlet during the holiday season, may generate a large proportion of its cash in one period of time. It will need those funds to finance its operations over the rest of the year.

3.   **Asset Sales** - A company may sell assets and have no immediate use for the proceeds.

4.   **Securities Issuance** - The amount and timing of equity and debt offerings are often determined by economic factors other than a company's short-to-medium-term financial requirement. The timing of such issues is determined not only by corporate need, but also by financial market conditions. When interest rates are low, it is advantageous for companies to issue debt instruments. When equity prices are considered to be high, companies are more likely to sell stock. Proceeds from securities offerings often exceed a company's immediate cash needs and may be invested in short-term securities.

C. Income Generation

Companies also invest in short-term financial instruments to generate income. A variety of instruments offer both safety and yield. Companies should manage their short-term investments prudently, and in a manner consistent with their policies governing risks and expected investment returns.

III. SHORT-TERM INVESTMENT ISSUES AND CORPORATE POLICIES

A company failing to manage cash properly can incur high costs for working capital and forego the potential revenues that short-term securities can yield. It can lose significant amounts through making poor investment choices, assuming unnecessary risks, assigning investment responsibilities to unqualified personnel, or failing to implement effective cash management practices.

To address these issues, and to meet its overall short-term investment objectives, a company should implement a clearly defined and written investment policy. Such a document should not only put forth criteria for instrument suitability and portfolio configuration, but also delineate specific individual responsibilities for making policy, implementing it on a day-to-day basis, and reviewing and auditing investment performance. The policy statement should also provide for its own periodic review.

A company's short-term investment policy is indicative of its tolerance for risk. An investment policy must address several key issues, including the following:

- Requirements governing security selection and portfolio configuration

- Management responsibilities and authority vis-a-vis short term investment activity

- Financial controls

- Performance measurement

A. Short-Term Investment Objectives

A company conducts its short-term investment activity to meet several objectives:

1.   **Preservation of Principal** - This is the guiding principle most companies follow in choosing among short-term investment alternatives. Some degree of risk is inherent

in all investments. Those that offer higher returns usually carry greater risks. Ensuring against loss involves controlling risk, as follows:

- Identifying risks to which various investment alternatives are subject

- Determining the relationships between security risks and the financial returns they offer

- Choosing instruments that offer both income and safety of principal

2. **Liquidity Management** - Holding a portfolio of short-term instruments is one way companies enhance liquidity. Unused borrowing capacity is another.

3. **Investment Return and Risk** - Companies seek to maximize returns from short-term investments, but the risks and returns different companies consider acceptable can vary depending on factors such as risk tolerance, earnings predictability, investment size, industry practice, and resources available for selecting and monitoring their short-term investments. While longer-term investments often carry higher returns, they are likely to be more volatile than short-term financial instruments.

B. Responsibilities for Short-Term Investment Policies

Delineating responsibilities for short-term investment involves the following:

1. **Setting Policy** - A company's short-term investment policy should identify those who are ultimately responsible for such matters. In most companies, the board of directors or a designated committee of the board determines and monitors overall investment policy.

2. **Implementation** - The treasurer, cash manager, their staffs, or an internal or external specialized investment manager, or managers, may all be involved in implementing a company's investment policy. The responsibilities of each individual or group of individuals involved must be clearly delineated.

C. Factors that Influence Short-Term Investment Policies

Companies' short-term investment policies and decisions regarding them are influenced by factors such as:

1. **Purpose** - Different companies emphasize somewhat different objectives for short-term investments. Some stress liquidity preservation others stress income generation.

2. **Maturity and Segmentation** - A portion of a company's short-term investment portfolio may be required at all times as a liquidity reserve, while other portions may be designated for less immediate use. The maturity profile should reflect capital spending plans and cash flow forecasts.

3. **Tax Status** - A company must consider the tax implications of its investment decisions. Its effective tax rate determines the after-tax return from taxable investments, and the advantage offered by tax-exempt alternatives.

4. **Staffing** - Carrying out an active internally-managed short-term investment program requires resources, including staff and systems. Alternatively, a company may find it more cost effective to use an outside investment management company.

5. **Investment Restrictions** - Laws, industry guidelines, internal corporate policies, and covenants to loans or debt instruments can restrict short-term investment choices.

6. **Reporting Requirements** - Financial Accounting Standard (FAS) 65 requires that securities maturing within 90 days be listed as Cash & Equivalents on corporate balance sheets. Those investments that have maturities greater than 90 days are listed as Marketable Investments.

    A company may report additional information on certain types of short-term investments on its balance sheet to satisfy the requirements of shareholders, creditors, or industry regulators.

D. Instrument and Portfolio Characteristics and Attributes

A comprehensive investment policy must also address the types of securities or financial instruments a company considers appropriate, any limits to their use or proportion in the portfolio, and requirements for the portfolio's overall configuration.

1. **Acceptable Instruments** - Typically, a company will specify the types of securities that are acceptable investments in terms of their characteristics.

    • **Maturity** - Most financial instruments have a maturity date on which the obligation they represent is settled. Original maturities vary from overnight to many years in the future. Interest rate movements affect the prices of all securities, and the prices of fixed-income securities move inversely to changes in interest rates. The longer a security's term to maturity, the greater its price variation as interest rates change.

    • **Quality** - The credit quality of many instruments can be determined by ratings assigned by credit rating agencies. There are rating systems for corporate bonds, bank issues, banks, municipal obligations, commercial paper, certain types of preferred stock, and money market funds.

        ◆ With some securities, such as unrated commercial paper or loan participations, the investor must analyze and evaluate the credit quality of the borrower.

        ◆ If a financial intermediary provides support or credit enhancement by issuing an instrument such as a standby letter of credit to guarantee the obligation of the borrower, the obligation then assumes the credit rating of the institution providing the credit enhancement.

Exhibit 12.1 contains the different ratings that various rating agencies assign to short-term financial instruments.

	Moody's	Standard & Poor's	Duff & Phelps	Fitch
EXHIBIT 12.1 *Short-Term Credit Ratings* Taxable	Prime 1 (P1)	A1+	1+	F1+
		A1	1	F1
	Prime 2 (P2)	A2	2	F2
	Prime 3 (P3)	A3	3	F3
Tax-exempt	MIG 1	SP1+	1+	F1+
		SP1	1	F1
	MIG 2	SP2	2	F2
	MIG 3	SP3	3	F3

- **Marketability** - Securities that can be sold in large volumes quickly and without substantial price concessions are a primary source of corporate liquidity. A large, active secondary market for a security ensures its marketability. Securities for which secondary markets are not active are less liquid. To compensate investors, instruments with less liquidity often carry higher yields.

2. **Diversification** - The risk inherent in a portfolio differs from the average risk of the securities that make up the portfolio. Diversification reduces portfolio risk.

   Investment policies can set minimum requirements for, or limits on, various types and categories of securities. Requirements can be stated in terms of maturities or other instrument characteristics, such as issuance by a particular entity (for example, the U.S. Treasury) or by rating classification. An investment policy may express limits in dollar amounts or in terms of portfolio proportion. For example, a company's policy might limit investment in any one money market fund to $10 million and stipulate that 25 percent of its short-term investment portfolio consist of U.S. Treasury obligations maturing in three months or less.

3. **Acceptable Dealers and/or Issuers** - Accredited securities dealers such as those belonging to the National Association of Securities Dealers (NASD) or accredited banks and other financial institutions are typically less likely to buy or sell securities of questionable or indeterminant value.

4. **Investment Authority** - A policy should clearly state the size and types of transactions in which company officials can engage.

5. **Custody Requirements** - Physical securities purchased by a company are typically delivered against payment in accounts at financial institutions where the securities were purchased or other institutions selected for that purpose. The policy should specify an authorized custodian.

E. Investment Management

A company has alternatives for managing short-term investments. Whether to handle short-term investments internally or externally depends on the size of the company's investment portfolio, investment objectives, and policies.

1. **Internal** - A company can manage its short-term investments using its own staff exclusively.

2. **External** - A company can hire an investment management company, a bank, or a financial advisory service to manage or assist in managing its short-term investments.

F. Performance Measurement

Portfolio performance should be measured using an appropriate benchmark or basis of comparison that allows for equitable and meaningful assessment. Typically, short-term investment portfolios are measured in comparison with the return of U.S. Treasury instruments, the Fed funds rate (the rate the Fed sets for overnight bank borrowing), an index rate for commercial paper, or the London InterBank Offered Rate (LIBOR). In any case, a portfolio's performance is typically stated in basis points (a basis point is 1/100th of one percent or .0001) over or under the benchmark for the interval of time being measured. For example, a portfolio of short-term investments might return 20 basis points under high-grade corporate commercial paper or five basis points above three-month U.S. Treasuries over a specified time period.

IV. MARKETS FOR FINANCIAL INVESTMENTS

The market for debt and equity instruments has two major components: the money market on which short-term fixed-income or debt securities trade, and the capital market, which is where longer-term instruments, stocks, and bonds trade. Generally, cash managers concern themselves with the money market.

A. Money Market (Short-Term Financial Instruments)

Rather than a single integrated entity or a particular exchange, the money market is a group of markets on which debt instruments that mature in a year or less are traded. Money market securities include: Treasury bills, federal agency securities, municipal obligations, commercial paper, banker's acceptances, negotiable certificates of deposit, loans to securities dealers, and repurchase agreements (repos).

The major direct participants in the money market are U.S. and foreign government securities dealers (some of which are large diversified financial institutions), commercial paper dealers, banker's acceptance dealers, and money market brokers specializing in various short-term instruments.

B. Capital Market (Long-Term Financial Instruments)

The term capital market refers to the exchanges where long-term debt and equity instruments are bought and sold, and the dealers involved. There are two types of long-term debt instruments: notes, which mature in less than 10 years, and bonds, which mature in 10 years or more. Equity instruments are stocks, the most conventional of which are common and preferred issues. The major U.S. exchanges are the New York Stock Exchange, the American Stock Exchange, and Nasdaq.

While companies in many industries do not invest extensively in long-term securities, cash managers should concern themselves with the capital market for the following reasons:

1. Capital market developments affect the money market.

2. Even though companies do not often invest in long-term securities, bonds maturing within a year or preferred stock may be suitable for some companies' short-term portfolios.

3. Evaluation of a company's long-term securities can help ascertain the creditworthiness of that company and the overall risk profile for all the securities it issues, including its short-term instruments.

V. FINANCIAL INSTRUMENTS

Short-term securities in which companies typically invest reflect widely differing credit quality, yields, maturities, and marketability.

Almost all short-term securities are issued in registered form; they are typically placed in the name of the investor or held in the street name (the name of the broker/dealer through which they were purchased). Only the owner or his legal agent can collect interest and principal payments or sell the securities. (Historically, short-term instruments have also been issued in bearer form. In this case, the name of the investor is not recorded upon issuance, and the holder of the security is entitled to interest and/or principal payments or to sell the instrument. Bearer instruments are increasingly rare.)

A. U.S. Treasury Securities

U.S. Treasury securities are instruments the U.S. government issues to finance its activities. The U.S. government's need for funds is enormous, and its debt securities appeal to a broad spectrum of investors. The market for U.S. Treasury securities is the largest and most actively traded in the world.

U.S. Treasury securities are considered risk-free with respect to default. They are virtually the only securities issued in the U.S. to enjoy that reputation, and they serve as a benchmark for other financial instruments. The interest rates as determined by the market for U.S. Treasury instruments are used as a reference point and market indicator. Many other securities (and loans) have yields established as a spread over a similar-term Treasury instrument.

Typically, U.S. Treasuries account for the safest portion of a company's portfolio of short-term financial instruments.

1. **Characteristics** - Characteristics of U.S. Treasuries and the markets on which they trade are known to all participants in financial markets worldwide. They include:

   • **Issuance Through Auctions** - Virtually all primary Treasury offerings are sold at a type of auction known as a Dutch auction. A Dutch auction is a process whereby the price of a security is lowered until it prompts a responsive bid, whereupon the security is sold. When a Treasury instrument is to be offered, the Treasury officially invites bids. Eligible banks, broker/dealers, and other private and governmental entities tender bids for specific amounts of securities at specific yields. The securities go to the bidders offering the highest prices (i.e., lowest yield/interest cost to the Treasury).

- **Registered Form of Issue** - Treasury securities are registered and issued in book entry form. Securities certificates do not physically move when they are traded. Book entries are made when ownership changes.

- **Marketability and Liquidity** - The secondary market for U.S. Treasury securities is enormous and has low transaction costs. Participants can readily and efficiently buy and sell significant volumes with negligible if any impact on market prices.

- **Value Retention** - U.S. Treasuries are backed by the full faith and credit of the U.S. Government. Because of this, they are considered to be free from credit risk.

- **Partial Tax Exemption** - Interest income on Treasuries is exempt from state income tax. Many states do however charge corporations a franchise tax from which U.S. Treasury securities are not exempt.

- **Widely Regarded Yields** - Yields on U.S. Treasury securities are generally the standard against which rates and prices in the other fixed income securities markets are compared. Other investment alternatives generally trade at yields above those of government securities, reflecting their perceived relative default risk.

2. **Types of U.S. Treasury Securities** - In its financing operations, the U.S. Treasury issues the following types of securities:

- **Treasury Bills (T-bills)** - T-bills are the most liquid securities in the money market because of the volumes issued, their credit quality, and their short maturities. They are issued each week on a discount basis in maturities of 13, 26, and 52 weeks. T-bills are available in a minimum denomination of $10,000 and in multiples of $1,000 thereafter. They are usually traded in round lots of $1,000,000. The discount rate on T-bills is quoted in annualized terms.

- **Treasury Notes (T-notes)** - T-notes are issued with original maturities of two, five, seven, and 10 years. The minimum denomination for new issues of two year notes is $5,000, while longer maturities have a $1,000 minimum. All notes are available in $1,000 increments above their minimum amounts. As in the case of T-bills, T-notes are usually traded in round lots of $1,000,000. T-notes are interest-bearing securities on which interest is paid semi-annually. Interest is calculated on the actual number of elapsed days using a 365-day year.

- **Treasury Bonds (T-bonds)** - T-bonds are similar to T-notes, but with maturities ranging from 10 to 30 years.

3. **Money Market Treasury Funds** - These money market funds carry the same credit quality given to obligations of the U.S. government because they are made up exclusively or principally of U.S. government securities.

B. Agency Securities

Another type of investment instrument (commonly referred to as agency issues) has some degree of federal government backing although few are issued by federal government agencies. In a few cases, such as securities issued by the Government National Mortgage Association (Ginnie Mae) and the Department of Veterans Affairs (VA), the securities are, in effect, backed by the full faith and credit of the U.S. government. In most cases, such as the mortgage-backed securities (MBS) issued by the Federal National Mortgage Association (Fannie Mae) and Freddie Mac (formerly the Federal Home Loan Mortgage Corporation), the securities are backed by the strength of the corporation, though there is a strong implication that in a crisis the federal government would intervene to help repay investors.

1.   **Characteristics**

- **Liquidity and Yield** - Although the amount of outstanding agency issues is smaller than Treasuries, the liquidity of most agencies compares favorably with other money market instruments. Agencies usually trade at higher yields than Treasuries of the same maturity.

- **Low Credit Risk** - While credit risk exists, the market tends to view it as minimal.

- **Limited Tax Exposure** - Interest income on many agency issues is exempt from state and local income taxes but not state franchise taxes.

2.   **Issuers**

- **Housing-Related Organizations** - Fannie Mae and Freddie Mac were originally government agencies but now are private, shareholder-owned companies often referred to as government-sponsored enterprises (GSEs). Both can borrow from the U.S. Treasury. They purchase mortgages from lenders and package them into MBS. Ginnie Mae is part of the Department of Housing and Urban Development. It creates MBS and other securities which it guarantees for timely payment of principal and interest with the full faith and credit of the U.S. government. The Department of Veterans Affairs securitizes certain real estate loans, the "Vinnie Macs," which are backed by the full faith and credit of the federal government.

  The Federal Home Loan Bank (FHLB) System, a GSE, is the largest issuer of private debt in the world. It funds its activities through a variety of debt products called consolidated obligations (COs), which are typically AAA rated by Standard & Poor's and Moody's.

  The other federal housing corporations are the Financial Assistance Corporation and the Resolution Funds Corporation.

- **Agricultural Corporations** - There are four agricultural GSEs which issue high quality debt. The cooperatively-owned Federal Farm Credit Banks Funding Corporation raises capital for the 225 lending institutions in the Farm Credit System through the sale of System-wide bonds and notes. These are insured by the Farm Credit System Insurance Corporation. The federal Farm Credit Administration is the regulator of the banks, the Funding Corporation, and the Insurance Corporation.

The CoBank and district Banks for Cooperatives issue debt to make funds available to agricultural cooperatives. The Federal Agricultural Mortgage Corporation (Farmer Mac) provides a secondary market for agricultural loans and rural real estate and home mortgages.

- **Sallie Mae** - Founded as a federally-chartered, shareholder-owned company, Sallie Mae was reorganized in 1997 as SLM Holding Corporation (SLMHC), a private Delaware corporation. SLMHC is not considered a GSE. However, it still conducts most of its student loan financing activities through the Student Loan Marketing Association, a wholly owned subsidiary, which is a GSE. The GSE funds its operations through issuance of debt securities, which are considered agency securities. Sallie Mae uses the proceeds to purchase college loans which are insured by guaranty agencies and reinsured by the federal government.

- **Other Government Corporations** - There are more than 20 other government corporations, including the Tennessee Valley Authority and the Rural Telephone Bank, which issue highly rated debt obligations.

C. Municipal Obligations

Municipal obligations are debt instruments issued by state and local governments or their agencies. State and local government agencies include school districts, housing authorities, sewer districts, municipally-owned utilities, and authorities running toll roads, bridges, and other transportation facilities.

1. **Bonds and Notes** - Municipalities generally issue bonds or notes, many of which are exempt from various state and local income taxes as well as federal income tax.

   - **Bonds** - Most municipal obligations are long-term bonds. State and local governments generally sell long-term bonds to finance the construction of schools, housing, pollution-control facilities, roads, bridges, and other capital projects. A secondary market for municipal bonds exists but is not as active as the market for newly issued bonds.

   - **Notes** - Municipal notes, also known as anticipation notes, are municipal debt instruments with an original maturity of two years or less. These notes are usually issued to help overcome a temporary cash shortage in anticipation of forthcoming revenues.

2. **Types of Securities** - Municipal securities fall into three broad categories. These are:

   - **General Obligation Securities** - General obligation securities have the full faith, credit, and taxing power of the issuing entity securing the payment of principal and interest. This usually means that the securities are backed by all of the issuer's resources and its authority to levy taxes.

   - **Certificates of Participation (COPs)** - COPs are securities used by municipal issuers to finance certain equipment purchases and capital projects.

- **Revenue Securities** - Payments of interest and principal on revenue securities are made from specific sources such as tolls, user fees, or rents paid by those who use the facilities financed by the proceeds of the security issue. Sometimes they are enhanced by letters of credit or other guarantees.

D. Bank Financial Instruments

Domestic and foreign banks issue short-term certificates of deposit (CDs), time deposits, and banker's acceptances (BAs). Typically they all offer higher yields than Treasuries.

1. **Certificates of Deposit**

    - **Retail CDs** - Retail CDs are interest-bearing deposits that financial institutions in the U.S. offer, with original maturities ranging from seven days to several years. These are also referred to as domestic CDs and generally have maturities of less than one year. They require a minimum investment of $100,000, but are usually traded in $1,000,000 units. Since most retail CDs that companies hold are negotiable, there is a secondary market for these instruments. There is a wide variety in types of CDs. The basic ones are:

        - **Fixed-Rate CDs** - The interest rate is established at the time of issue. Interest is paid periodically over the term or at maturity.

        - **Floating (Variable) Rate CDs** - Interest is adjusted periodically as rates change. For example, on six-month CDs, interest is paid and the rate is reset every 30 days. CDs with maturities of one year or longer may pay interest and reset rates every three months. The rate is expressed as a spread (percentage and/or basis points) over a widely-used index rate such as the 90-day T-bill, Fed funds, or LIBOR.

    - **Yankee CDs** - Yankee CDs are U.S. dollar-denominated CDs issued by foreign banks through their branches in the U.S. market.

    - **Eurodollar CDs** - Eurodollar CDs are U.S. dollar denominated CDs issued by banks outside the U.S. Although the primary issuers are European banks, Eurodollar CDs may be issued by any bank located outside of the U.S., including foreign branches of U.S. banks. Original maturities are usually less than two years, although most have maturities of six months or less. Eurodollar CDs are negotiable, and there is a large secondary market. Eurodollar CDs offer marginally higher yields than domestic CDs because they are slightly less liquid and entail higher risk. The risk derives from the fact that they are not subject to U.S. banking regulations.

2. **Eurodollar Time Deposits** - Eurodollar time deposits are non-negotiable, fixed-rate time deposits issued by banks outside the U. S., with maturities ranging from overnight to several years. Most have maturities in six months or less. Because they are subject to foreign risk, they offer higher yields than comparable domestic time deposits.

3.   **Banker's Acceptance (BA)** - A BA is a negotiable short-term instrument used primarily to finance the import, export, or domestic shipment of goods or the storage of readily marketable commodities. The debt obligation on the part of the bank is evidenced by a time draft drawn by the borrower that is then accepted by the bank on which it is drawn. By accepting the draft, the bank becomes directly obligated for payment of the draft on the maturity date. By substituting its own credit for that of the borrower, the bank creates a readily marketable instrument that can be discounted in the money market. (See Chapter 13, Borrowing, and Chapter 15, International Cash Management.)

4.   **Bank Notes** - Bank notes represent unsecured or subordinated debt of the bank. Corporate cash investors buy them because they may offer yields competitive with similarly rated commercial paper, but they offer the additional advantage of being direct obligations of the bank, rather than of a bank holding company. However, they do not carry federal deposit insurance.

E. Repurchase Agreements (Repos)

A repurchase agreement or repo is a type of collateralized transaction between a securities dealer and an investor. For an investor, a repo involves the purchase of a security with an agreement to sell it back to the initial seller at a future date. Most repos are negotiated with U.S. Treasury or agency securities, or mortgage-backed pass-through securities and CMOs issued or guaranteed by Ginnie Mae, Fannie Mae, or Freddie Mac. Repos reflect direct negotiation between the buyer and seller, with terms based on the needs of the counterparties. Interest is calculated on an actual/360-day basis. The seller of a security under a repo agreement continues to receive all interest and principal payments on the security. The purchaser receives a fixed rate of interest on a short-term investment.

Repos can be viewed as relatively safe. However, investors have incurred significant losses on repo investments because they did not exercise proper care in controlling and valuing their collateral. Repos may become unsecured transactions if the purchaser does not take the appropriate steps to perfect an interest in the collateral.

The repo market has grown because it is a relatively attractive money market instrument for investors and a comparatively inexpensive financing alternative for security owners. Repo yields are determined by the supply and demand of other money market instruments. They also depend on the type of collateral used (highest quality, most liquid collateral results in repos with the lowest yield). Since repos are negotiated directly between buyer and seller, terms are flexible. Maturities can range from overnight to over one year. Often, transactions involve an "open repo," which is an overnight repo that rolls over automatically until terminated.

1.   **Structure** - Typically, a securities dealer will sell a repo to an investor who agrees to sell it back at a specific time, either overnight or for a specific number of days or on open contract, at a price that will result in a predetermined yield. The securities dealer collateralizes the repo with bonds. The investor is providing the dealer short-term funds, while the dealer is providing the investor short-term collateralized investments.

The Public Securities Association repurchase agreement is considered the industry standard. In addition to repos backed by U.S. Treasuries, there are also agency-backed, corporate-backed, money-market, and whole loan collateral repos.

2. **Purpose** - Repos help securities dealers finance their inventory of securities, typically Treasuries. (A similar type of transaction known as a reverse repo helps dealers borrow inventory and make deliveries.)

3. **Risk** - The market for repos is not as liquid as the market for many other instruments. In a repo transaction, the investor takes collateral but is still exposed to the creditworthiness and business practices of the dealer. Also, the investor must continually monitor the value of the collateral to make sure it does not drop below the value of the repo. If a dealer breaches the agreement, the investor, under its terms, has the right to the collateral.

Investors may take collateral in the following ways in decreasing order of safety:

- In delivery versus payment (DVP), the investor pays the custodial agent who maintains an account for the investor.

- In a tri-party arrangement, the dealer's custodial agent maintains a custodial account for the investor. The dealer pays the fee.

- Under hold-in-custody, the dealer maintains a custodial account and monitors the collateral.

F. Corporate Obligations

Several types of corporate debt and equity obligations are suitable for short-term investment portfolios.

1. **Commercial Paper** - Commercial paper (CP) is an unsecured promissory note issued by a corporation for a specific amount to mature in 270 days or less.

- CP may be interest-bearing or discounted; it is usually discounted.

- Issuers sell CP directly to investors or through dealers. Dealers include securities companies and commercial banks.

- The issuer's obligation may be backed by a standby letter of credit, which is similar to a guarantee from a bank, or a bond is issued by an insurance company with a high credit rating.

- CP is rated by credit rating agencies based on attributes such as liquidity, cash flow potential, earning trends, position in the industry, quality of management, and backup credit facilities.

- Some dealers also sell unrated CP. These unrated issues carry substantially higher yields to compensate investors for the greater credit risk they incur.

2. **Preferred Stock** - Preferred stock is a type of equity instrument that has preference over common stock in its claim to a company's earnings and assets. Preferred dividends are paid before common stock dividends can be paid and, like common stock, offer a tax advantage to corporate investors. Currently, a corporate investor may exclude 70 percent of stock dividends received from current income as long as the stock is held at risk (cannot be hedged) for more than 45 days. This is called the intercorporate dividend deduction.

Generally, preferred stock is considered a long-term investment, but there are several types of preferred stock that are designed to be suitable for short-term investors. They usually feature some type of adjustment to the stated dividend amount which is expressed as a percentage and is tied to an interest rate index in order to provide a stable price. Typically, the types of preferred stocks suitable for short-term investments are as follows:

- **Adjustable-Rate Preferred** - Adjustable-rate preferred stock has a dividend rate that is adjusted quarterly based on current Treasury yields.

- **Dutch Auction Preferred** - Also known as money market preferred stock, auction-rate preferred is characterized by a dividend rate that adjusts every 49 days, which is beyond the minimum holding period for the inter-corporate dividend deduction. The dividend rate adjustment is based on bids from investors. Its benchmark is the 60-day, AA-rated, commercial paper composite. Securities dealers are invited by the issuer to bid in a Dutch auction every seven weeks. Typically, they act as agents for their clients. Existing holders may retain their shares and receive dividends at the new rate.

G. Money Market Mutual Funds

Money market mutual funds are commingled funds of highly liquid, diversified short-term money market instruments in which investors have an ownership interest. They are an increasingly important component of corporate short-term investment portfolios and offer an acceptable alternative to other securities, particularly under changing interest rate conditions. For example, when interest rates are falling, fund managers can extend their maturities to lock in yield. Investors in the fund thus get the greater return of longer-term instruments while enjoying the liquidity and stability of a principal comparable to investments with shorter maturities.

Money market mutual funds are configured to report a net asset value of $1.00/share. They generate different yields and have slightly different risk thresholds. Money market mutual funds can provide a company with a professionally-managed marketable securities portfolio at a low management cost. These funds can also be useful in providing a benchmark for assessing short-term investment portfolio performance. Money market mutual funds charge management fees or service charges based on the investor's balance, level of activity, and services provided.

H. Asset-Backed Securities

Asset-backed securities are debt obligations that companies issue that are secured by specific assets. These can include receivables, such as the obligations that credit card holders have to credit card companies, or the installment payments that consumers pay finance subsidiaries, major retailers, and automobile companies. Asset-backed securities can even be backed by inventories. Rating agencies rate many issues of asset-backed securities just as they do other types of financial instruments. Asset-backed securities enable issuing companies to free up capital the same way that they do through factoring receivables.

I. Collateralized Mortgage Obligations (CMOs)

A CMO refers to a type of mortgage-backed security created and backed by federal agencies such as Fannie Mae and Freddie Mac. These securities are formed from pools of mortgages divided into different instruments (tranches), each of which contains a specified portion of the principal and interest payment streams emanating from the aggregated mortgages to separate CMO securities.

CMOs are sometimes enhanced with options and/or futures. Different CMOs have varying performance characteristics. Although many types of mortgage-backed securities are safe and generally stable investments, some may be highly volatile should interest rates change.

VI. YIELD

Yield is a measure of the gain an investor derives from a financial instrument. Typically, it is stated as an annual rate of return, expressed as a percentage.

A. Factors that Influence Yields

There are four interrelated factors that determine the investment suitability of a short-term financial instrument:

1. **Marketability** - The marketability of securities affects their yield because investors require a higher return for holding securities that are more difficult to sell.

2. **Default Risk** - Investors typically require a higher yield to compensate for the risk that the principal will not be paid under the original terms. The greater the likelihood of default, the higher the risk premium, and the higher the expected yield. A risk premium is the extra yield above the yield of a risk-free security that investors require as compensation for assuming the additional risk. U.S. government securities are considered to have no default risk, and other short-term securities are evaluated in comparison to them. Credit rating services attempt to quantify relative default risk through evaluation and assignment of credit ratings.

3. **Price Risk** - Price risk is the uncertainty over the price at which a security can be sold prior to maturity and is a function of interest rates. An increase in rates will cause the price of fixed income securities to fall. A decrease in interest rates will cause the price of fixed income securities to rise. Generally, securities with longer maturities are subject to more price risk than similar securities with shorter maturities.

4. **Tax Status** - The tax status of an investment has an impact on its yield. Tax-exempt securities provide a lower pre-tax yield than taxable securities of similar maturity and default risk. When comparing taxable and tax-exempt instruments, the tax-exempt yield is usually converted to a taxable equivalent yield as follows:

$$\text{Taxable Equivalent Yield} = \frac{\text{Tax-Exempt Yield}}{(1 - \text{Marginal Tax Rate of Investor})}$$

This taxable equivalent yield can then be used to compare the tax-exempt instrument with other taxable investments. An example of a calculation of taxable equivalent yield is shown in Exhibit 12.2.

EXHIBIT 12.2

Example of Taxable Equivalent Yield Calculation

Assuming a corporate investor's marginal tax rate of 34 percent, the taxable equivalent yield for an investment with a tax-exempt yield of 6 percent is determined as follows.

$$\text{Taxable Equivalent Yield} = \frac{\text{Tax-Exempt Yield}}{1 - \text{Marginal Tax Rate of Investor}}$$

$$\text{Taxable Equivalent Yield} = \frac{.06}{1 - .34} = 9.09\%$$

The interest income from obligations of the U.S. government is exempt from state income taxes (though not from state franchise taxes) while the income from obligations of state and local governments is generally exempt from Federal income taxes. Securities issued by a given state are often exempt from income taxes in that state but may not be exempt from taxes in other states.

B. Basic Yield Definitions

Yield can be calculated in two different ways:

1. **Current Yield** - This is an instrument's annual interest payment divided by its price. It indicates what the instrument will return in terms of interest on an annual basis.

    For example, if a five percent note with a face, or par, value of $1,000 is bought at a market price of $900, the annual interest payment from the note is $50, but since only $900 was paid for it, the current yield is $50 divided by $900, or 5.56 percent.

2. **Yield to Maturity (YTM)** - This is a calculation of a debt instrument's total yield from a specific date to maturity. It takes into account the discount or premium on an instrument in addition to its coupon or interest payments. (When an instrument is purchased at a premium to face value, the calculation assumes an amortization to par, and when it is purchased at a discount the calculation assumes an accretion to par.)

    Algebraically, the relationship among these factors can be expressed as:

$$P_0 = \frac{C_1}{(1+YTM)} + \frac{C_2}{(1+YTM)^2} + \ldots + \frac{C_n}{(1+YTM)^n} + \frac{FV}{(1+YTM)^n}$$

Where:

P_0	=	Current market price
n	=	Number of periods until maturity
$C_{1, 2, \ldots n}$	=	Dollar amount of the coupon payment in periods 1, 2, ... n
FV	=	Face value of the instrument
YTM	=	Yield to maturity

For example, if a bond with a face value of $1,000 maturing in one year has a coupon of five percent and a price in the market of $950, its yield to maturity is 10.53 percent. The numerator is the coupon (five percent or $50) added to the principal ($1,000). The denominator is 1 + the yield to maturity, raised to the first power. That expression is equal to the current price ($950). Solving for yield to maturity results in 10.53%:

$$950 = (\$1,000 + \$50) \div (1+YTM)^1.$$

If n (the number of periods) is greater than 1, complex algorithms are necessary to solve for YTM.

C. Yield-Quoting Conventions

Not all rates quoted in the markets are easily comparable. Rates for various financial instruments are quoted and priced differently, and interest payments are timed differently.

1. **Interest-Bearing Instruments** - Some instruments, for example certificates of deposit (CDs) and Eurodollar deposits, pay interest in arrears at maturity or at periodic intervals and are thus called interest-bearing instruments.

2. **Discount Instruments** - Other instruments, such as Treasury bills and banker's acceptances, are discounted; the investor pays the face value of the instrument minus the interest (the discount) and receives the face value at maturity. The discount is the face value multiplied by the discount rate, times the number of days to maturity divided by the year basis (360 or 365).

3. **Year Basis** - Most short term instruments, commercial paper, and Treasury bills, for example, pay interest calculated on a 360-day basis. Treasury bonds and Treasury notes pay interest on a 365-day basis.

4. **Nominal Yield** - The quoted yield on an annual basis for most investments is a simple annual rate, called a nominal yield, and does not reflect compounding.

5. **Money Market Yield** - Money market yield (MMY) is the nominal yield quoted on a 360-day basis.

6. **Bond Equivalent Yield** - Bond equivalent yield (BEY) is the nominal yield quoted on a 365-day basis.

7. **Effective Annual Yield** - The most reliable way to compare all of these instruments is to calculate their effective annual yields. Effective annual yields assume compounding and are calculated on a 365-day basis. Because of compounding, an effective annual yield assumes that the investor always has the opportunity to reinvest funds at the same rate. For example, assume a company receives $500 in interest on an investment of $10,000, and the investment matures in 150 days. The approximate interest rate is calculated as:

$$\left(\frac{500}{10,000} \right) \times \left(\frac{360}{150} \right) \quad = \quad 12\%$$

The effective annual yield calculation is as follows:

$$EAY = \left[1 + \frac{I}{P} \right]^{365/DM} - 1$$

Where:
EAY = Effective Annual Yield
P = Principal
I = Interest amount
DM = Days to maturity

Solution of this equation requires the use of complex algorithms.

$$\left[1 + \frac{500}{10,000} \right]^{365/150} - 1 = 12.61\%$$

To compare the yields on two different investment instruments, it is often necessary to convert from one yield quoting convention to the other.

An easy way to remember the different conventions and how they relate to each other is to appreciate the logic of the sequence above: starting with the discount basis, converting to the simple, annualized (but not compounded) money market yield on a 360-day basis; moving to the still not-compounded bond-equivalent annual yield, calculated on a 365-day basis; and finally moving to the effective annual yield, both compounded and calculated on a 365-day basis. A summary of the yield-quoting conventions is provided in Exhibit 12.3.

EXHIBIT 12.3
Summary of Yield-Quoting Conventions

Yield-Quoting Convention	Characteristics
Nominal Yield	Annualized Not Compounded 360- or 365-Day Basis
Money Market Yield	Annualized Not Compounded 360-Day Basis
Bond Equivalent Yield	Annualized Not Compounded 365-Day Basis
Effective Annual Yield	Annualized Compounded 365-Day Basis

D. Yield Calculations

The following formulas and sample calculations show the relationships among the dollar discount, the discount rate, the purchase price, and the discount rate for a T-bill. The calculations for determining the yield on a commercial paper issue are similar to those of a T-bill.

1. **Purchase Price for a Discounted Instrument** - The dollar discount is equal to the discount rate multiplied by the face or redemption value. This value is then multiplied by the number of days to maturity divided by the appropriate year basis. For T-bills, 360 is used as the year basis.

$$\text{Dollar Discount} = (\text{Discount Rate x Face Value}) \times \frac{\text{Days to Maturity}}{360}$$

The Discount Rate on a period basis is equal to the dollar discount divided by the face value. To annualize that rate, divide by the number of days to maturity and multiply by 360.

$$\text{Discount Rate} = \frac{\text{Dollar Discount}}{\text{Face Value}} \times \frac{360}{\text{Days to Maturity}}$$

The purchase price is equal to the face value minus the dollar discount.

$$\text{Purchase Price} = \text{Face Value} - \text{Dollar Discount}$$

Examples of the calculation of the purchase price and the discount rate for T-bills are provided in Exhibits 12.4 and 12.5.

EXHIBIT 12.4
Example of
T-Bill Purchase
Price
Calculation

The purchase price of a 91-day $100,000 T-bill sold at a 7.91% discount rate is calculated as follows:

$$\text{Dollar Discount} = (\text{Discount Rate x Face Value}) \times \frac{\text{Days to Maturity}}{360}$$

$$\text{DD} = (\text{DR x FV}) \times \frac{\text{DM}}{360}$$

$$= (.0791 \times \$100,000) \times \frac{91}{360} = \$1,999.47$$

$$\text{Purchase Price} = \text{Face Value} - \text{Dollar Discount}$$

$$\text{PP} = \text{FV} - \text{DD}$$

$$= \$100,000 - \$1,999.47 = \$98,000.53$$

EXHIBIT 12.5

*Example
of T-Bill
Discount Rate
Calculation*

The discount rate on a 182-day $100,000 T-bill that is currently selling at a price of $95,875.00 is calculated as follows:

Dollar Discount = Face Value − Purchase Price

$$DD = FV - PP$$

$$= \$100,000 - \$95,875 = \$4,125$$

$$\text{Discount Rate} = \frac{\text{Dollar Discount}}{\text{Face Value}} \times \frac{360}{\text{Days to Maturity}}$$

$$DR = \frac{DD}{FV} \times \frac{360}{DM}$$

$$\text{Discount Rate} = \frac{\$4,125}{\$100,000} \times \frac{360}{182} = 8.16\%$$

2. **Money Market Yield for a Discounted Instrument** - The money market yield (MMY) states the annual yield of a discounted security on a short-term interest-bearing basis with a 360-day year.

$$\text{Money Market Yield} = \frac{\text{Dollar Discount}}{\text{Purchase Price}} \times \frac{360}{\text{Days to Maturity}}$$

This calculation is made in two steps. The dollar discount is divided by the purchase price to obtain the period yield; the period yield is then annualized. A period yield is the effective yield for a particular period such as a week, a month, or a year. A 30-day instrument with a simple annual yield of 12% has a period yield of 1%. An example of this calculation is provided in Exhibit 12.6.

EXHIBIT 12.6

*Example
of Money
Market Yield
Calculation*

The money market yield of a 91-day $100,000 T-bill sold at a discount rate of 7.91 % as presented in Exhibit 12.4 is calculated as follows:

$$MMY = \frac{\text{Dollar Discount}}{\text{Purchase Price}} \times \frac{360}{\text{Days to Maturity}}$$

$$= \frac{DD}{PP} \times \frac{360}{DM}$$

$$DR = \frac{\$1,999.47}{\$98,000.53} \times \frac{360}{91} = 8.07\%$$

3. **Converting to Bond Equivalent Yield From a Discount Rate or Money Market Yield -** Exhibit 12.7 shows how the yield on a discounted security can be converted to the bond equivalent yield (365 days). Note that there are several ways to calculate the bond equivalent yield.

EXHIBIT 12.7
Example of Bond Equivalent Yield Calculations

The bond equivalent yield of the previous 91-day $100,000 T-bill example with a 7.91% discount rate is calculated as follows:

$$\text{BEY} = \frac{\text{Dollar Discount}}{\text{Purchase Price}} \times \frac{365}{\text{Days to Maturity}}$$

$$= \frac{D}{PP} \times \frac{365}{DM}$$

$$= \frac{\$1,999.47}{\$98,000.53} \times \frac{365}{91} = 8.18\%$$

or

$$= \text{MMY} \times \frac{365}{360} = 8.07\% \times 1.0139 = 8.18\%$$

or

$$= \frac{365 \times \text{Discount Rate}}{360 - (\text{Discount Rate} \times \text{Days to Maturity})}$$

$$= \frac{365 \times .0791}{360 - (.0791 \times 91)} = 8.18\%$$

---

4. **Calculation of Commercial Paper Nominal Yield -** The calculation of the yield on commercial paper is similar to that of the BEY for a T-bill. Like T-bills, commercial paper is normally sold on a discount basis, but the nominal yield is calculated using a 365-day basis.

$$\frac{\text{Commercial Paper}}{\text{Nominal Yield}} = \frac{\text{Dollar Discount}}{\text{Purchase Price}} \times \frac{365}{\text{Days to Maturity}}$$

An example of this calculation is provided in Exhibit 12.8.

EXHIBIT 12.8

Example of Commercial Paper Nominal Yield Calculation

The nominal yield of a 45-day, $100,000 commercial paper issue selling at a price of $98,750 is calculated as follows:

$$\text{Dollar Discount} = \text{Face Value} - \text{Purchase Price}$$

$$D = FV - PP$$

$$= \$100,000 - \$98,750 = \$1,250$$

$$\text{Commercial Paper Nominal Yield} = \frac{\text{Dollar Discount}}{\text{Purchase Price}} \times \frac{365}{\text{Days to Maturity}}$$

$$CPY = \frac{D}{PP} \times \frac{365}{DM}$$

$$= \frac{\$1,250}{\$98,750} \times \frac{365}{45} = 10.27\%$$

5. **Algebraic Notation for Yield Equations** - All of the yield formulas presented in this chapter can also be presented in a general algebraic notation format. These formulas are shown in Exhibit 12.9.

EXHIBIT 12.9

Summary of Yield Equations

The yield equations in this chapter expressed in a general algebraic format are as follows:

$$TEY = \frac{TXY}{1 - MT}$$

$$CY = \frac{C}{P}$$

$$P_0 = \frac{C_1}{(1 + YTM)} + \frac{C_2}{(1 + YTM)^2} \cdots \frac{C_n}{(1 + YTM)^n} + \frac{FV}{(1 + YTM)^n}$$

$$D = (DR \times FV) \times \left(\frac{DM}{360}\right)$$

$$DR = \left(\frac{D}{FV}\right) \times \left(\frac{360}{DM}\right)$$

(Continued)

EXHIBIT 12.9
*Summary
of Yield
Equations*

$$PP = FV - D$$

$$MMY = \left(\frac{D}{PP}\right) \times \left(\frac{360}{DM}\right)$$

$$BEY = \frac{D}{PP} \times \frac{365}{DM}$$

or

$$BEY = MMY \times \left(\frac{365}{360}\right)$$

or

$$BEY = \frac{365 \times DR}{360 - (DR \times DM)}$$

$$CPY = \left(\frac{D}{PP}\right) \times \left(\frac{365}{DM}\right)$$

$$EAY = 1\left[+ \frac{I}{P} \right]^{365/DM} - 1$$

Where:

BEY = Bond Equivalent Yield
C = Coupon Amount
CPY = Commercial Paper Nominal Yield
CY = Current Yield
D = Dollar Discount
DM = Days to Maturity
DR = Discount Rate
EAY = Effective Annual Yield
FV = Face Value (redemption value)
I = Interest Amount
MMY = Money Market Yield
MT = Marginal Tax Rate
n = Number of Intervals
P = Price
P_o = Current Market Price
PP = Purchase Price
TEY = Taxable Equivalent Yield
TXY = Tax Exempt Yield
YTM = Yield to Maturity

E. Duration

Duration is the approximate percentage change in the price of a bond for a 1% change in yield. At a yield to maturity of 9%, a bond with a 7% coupon and 10 years until maturity will have a duration of 7.32. If the yield to maturity increases (decreases) by 1%, the price of the bond will increase (decrease) by approximately 7.32%. For most investments, duration will be less than maturity. How much less depends on the instrument's coupon, sinking fund payments, and yield to maturity.

F. The Yield Curve

How the market values a debt instrument in comparison with other similar securities that have longer or shorter maturities is revealed by the yield curve, which expresses the term structure of interest rates. A yield curve depicts the differences in yield of securities that are identical except for their dates of maturity.

The relationship between market yield and maturity is illustrated by Exhibits 12.10 and 12.11.

1.   **Normal Yield Curve** - The most common shape of the yield curve is upward sloping, reflecting the greater return over time that investors require to compensate for the increased price risk.

2.   **Inverted Yield Curve** - An inverted yield curve slopes downward, indicative of a market situation where short term yields are higher than long-term yields. Yield curve inversion happens infrequently and contravenes the usual condition that securities with longer maturities must offer higher yields. One theory explaining an inverted yield curve is that short-term uncertainties, such as an anticipated recession, shift investor preferences away from short-term instruments to those carrying longer maturities, driving down long-term rates.

EXHIBIT 12.10
*Normal
Yield Curve*

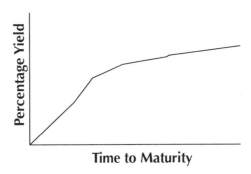

EXHIBIT 12.11
*Inverted
Yield Curve*

VII. INVESTMENT STRATEGIES

A short-term investment strategy may be either passive or active, depending on the company's objectives. In order to increase yield and provide certain fiduciary comfort, many companies hire registered investment advisors.

A. Passive Strategies

Passive strategies make use of static investment approaches. They are appropriate for companies that want safe return of principal, are risk averse, and/or do not want to make the effort necessary to engage in active strategy. There are several types of passive investment strategies.

1. **Replicating an Index or Market** - The objective of an indexed approach to short-term investment management is to replicate, on a dollar-weighted basis, performance of a market for a type of security (or securities) comparable to those in the portfolio, or a suitable market index.

2. **Overnight Sweeps** - A company can sweep excess funds on hand at the end of every day into an account used to purchase repos. Overnight sweep programs can offer investments in Eurodollar time deposits, commercial paper, or money market mutual funds. Such strategies entail minimal risk, time, and effort, and typically produce lower but extremely safe returns.

3. **Matching** - Matching involves purchasing securities that mature when funds are required to meet an expected obligation or obligations.

   • Matching allows companies to invest for extended periods and potentially increase yields.

   • This strategy requires careful forecasting of future cash flows and capital requirements. If cash is needed sooner than expected, the securities purchased to match a specific cash outflow may have to be sold prematurely, perhaps at a loss, due to marketability problems or changes in interest rates.

   • Companies that match tend to do so judiciously, covering a portion, but not the entire amount of the expected capital need.

B. Active Strategies

Active strategies typically are based on expectations regarding the direction of interest rates. Examples of an active investment strategy are dividend capture and riding the yield curve.

1. **Dividend Capture** - Companies may increase the yield on their short-term investment portfolios through a dividend capture or dividend rollover program. Under this type of tax-motivated trading program, a company buys a stock just before the ex-dividend date (the first date on which a new holder of the stock does not receive the last declared dividend). The stock is held for a period long enough to receive the dividend, and at least 46 days to qualify for the 70% intercorporate dividend deduction.

2.   **Riding the Yield Curve** - If a company expects interest rates to remain constant or go down, it can purchase securities that mature beyond the time when funds are needed. The securities are sold prior to maturity, providing a return that exceeds that of the matching strategy. The risk of this strategy is that interest rates may increase, reducing the value of the security at the time it is sold.

3.   **Swaps and Derivatives** - Companies can also use swaps and derivatives as part of their short-term investment strategies. (See Chapter 14, Financial Risk Management.)

Questions

These chapter questions are to test and review the information in the text and are not examples of CCM examination questions, nor are they in the examination format.

Answers can be found at the back of the book on pgs. 379-381.

1. What are the major purposes of having a short-term investment portfolio?

2. What are some of the factors that influence a company's investment policy?

3. What are the three major areas that influence the acceptability of a financial instrument for inclusion in the short-term investment portfolio?

4. What are the two major categories of financial markets?

5. What is meant by "book entry"?

6. What are the three major U.S. Treasury securities?

7. What are federal agency securities?

8. What are the three broad categories of municipal securities?

9. What makes municipal securities an attractive investment?

10. What are Eurodollar CDs?

11. When are banker's acceptances used?

12. What is a repo?

13. What is the maximum time-to-maturity for commercial paper?

14. What is money market preferred stock?

15. What are the four factors that influence yield?

16. What is an inverted yield curve?

17. What is the purchase price of a 182-day, $100,000 T-bill sold at a 4.53% discount rate?

18. What is the bond equivalent yield of the T-bill in Question 17?

19. What bank product is frequently used in an overnight investment strategy?

20. What are the major investment strategies?

21. What characteristics do companies specify in their investment guidelines and how are they determined?

CHAPTER 13

Borrowing

OVERVIEW

This chapter covers borrowing objectives and alternative strategies. It discusses the principal types of borrowing and how they are priced. It also covers the legal considerations and mechanics of borrowing. All borrowing or debt arrangements represent an asset (or security) to one party and a liability (or obligation) to another party. Chapter 12, Short-Term Investments, covers debt instruments from a corporate investor's point of view. This chapter covers them from a borrower's point of view.

LEARNING OBJECTIVES

Upon completion of this chapter and the related study questions, the reader should understand:

1. A company's borrowing objectives and strategies

2. The principal features of borrowing alternatives

3. How to calculate the all-in cost for lines of credit and commercial paper

4. The most common provisions of loan agreements

KEY CONCEPTS

1. Borrowing Objectives and Strategies

2. Borrowing Alternatives

3. Calculating the Costs of Borrowing

4. Common Provisions of Loan Agreements

OUTLINE

I. Corporate Borrowing Strategy and Objectives
   A. Capital Structure and Borrowing Strategy
   B. Short-Term Borrowing Objectives

II. **Variables Affecting the Cost of Borrowing**
    A.   Loan Pricing
    B.   Credit Risk
    C.   Credit Support
    D.   Term or Maturity

III. **Short-Term Borrowing Alternatives**
    A.   Line of Credit
    B.   Revolving Credit Agreement
    C.   Commercial Paper (CP)
    D.   Reverse Repurchase Agreements
    E.   Banker's Acceptance (BA)
    F.   Asset-Based Borrowing
    G.   Securitization
    H.   Loan Syndications and Participations
    I.   Trade Credit
    J.   Export Financing Programs

IV. **Medium- and Long-Term Borrowing Alternatives**
    A.   Medium-Term Notes
    B.   Bonds
    C.   Special Types of Bonds
    D.   Debt-Equity Hybrids
    E.   Term Loan
    F.   Leasing
    G.   Private Placement

V. **Repayment of Principal**
    A.   Amortization
    B.   Sinking Fund

VI. **Legal Aspects of Borrowing**
    A.   Loan Agreements and Bond Indentures
    B.   Promissory Notes

I. CORPORATE BORROWING STRATEGY AND OBJECTIVES

A. Capital Structure and Borrowing Strategy

For a company to realize its long-term financial objectives, it must have access to debt or equity capital. Debt represents a legal liability of the company to repay a creditor for borrowed funds. Equity represents an ownership claim in the company.

Each alternative involves a trade-off between risk and return. The cost of debt is represented by an interest rate; the value of equity is represented by either a stock price or the net value of a company's assets. Interest is a tax-deductible expense; dividends paid on equity shares are not tax-deductible. Debt financings may influence the operation of the company through loan agreement covenants; shareholders exert control through the exercise of specified voting rights.

The mix of debt and equity in a company's capital structure determines its leverage. The greater the debt, the greater the financial leverage and financial obligation. The use of debt increases earnings whenever the return on the capital investment for which the borrowed funds are used exceeds the cost of debt. The converse is also true. For these reasons, a company's borrowing program is often coordinated with its capital budgeting, the process by which a company's management decides how to make capital investments.

In formulating a borrowing strategy, management must decide how much debt to assume, for what purposes, from what sources, and at what cost. To do this it must take into consideration the implications of:

- Debt versus equity financing

- Short- versus long-term borrowing

- Fixed- versus floating-rate interest payments

- Secured versus unsecured debt

- On- versus off-balance-sheet financing

The cash manager needs to be cognizant of the impact of short-term borrowing on the capital structure of the company.

B. Short-Term Borrowing Objectives

On a day-to-day basis, a cash manager is concerned primarily with a company's short-term borrowing needs, the objectives of which include:

- Establishing adequate credit facilities to ensure the availability of borrowed funds sufficient to meet short-term cash requirements

- Minimizing the overall cost of funds, the major component of which is interest

- Minimizing risks such as insolvency due to an excessive debt burden or default due to tightly structured covenants

- Maximizing flexibility by maintaining alternate sources of short-term borrowing

II. VARIABLES AFFECTING THE COST OF BORROWING

Money, like any other commodity, has a cost associated with its use. The total cost of borrowing depends upon the following variables:

A. Loan Pricing

When a company borrows funds from a financial institution in the form of a loan, the key determinant of the cost is the interest rate. Features of interest rates include:

- An interest rate is usually quoted in terms of a base rate plus a spread. The spread includes an adjustment for perceived risk that is related to the overall creditworthiness of the borrower. The sum of the base rate and the spread is called the all-in rate. Typical base rates include:

- ◆ **London InterBank Offered Rate (LIBOR)** - LIBOR is quoted for a full range of short-term maturities including 30, 60, 90, and 180 days. It is the most commonly used base rate for short-term borrowing.

- ◆ **Prime Rate** - Traditionally, prime was the rate at which commercial banks loaned money to their most creditworthy corporate customers. Prime rates vary by financial institution. Prime based pricing is becoming less common for large corporate borrowers, but is widely used for small business and consumer loans.

- ◆ **Other** - The U.S. Treasury Bill rate, the Fed Funds rate, Banker's Acceptance rate, Certificate of Deposit rates, and a financial institution's weighted average cost of funds are examples of other base rates.

- Rates can be fixed or variable. A fixed rate remains unchanged during the term of the debt, whereas a variable rate is subject to periodic adjustments.

- The effective interest rate will be slightly higher than the stated rate if the lender uses a 360-day year basis in calculating the interest due on a loan. When a 360-day year basis is used, the interest expense is calculated based on the actual number of days in the billing period divided by 360 days times the stated annual rate. Banks typically use a 360-day year basis for commercial loans.

- The interest rate on a loan may be lower if the lender is being compensated in other ways, such as loan fees or compensating balance requirements, which are also considerations affecting loan pricing.

B. Credit Risk

Whenever a company borrows from a financial institution or issues debt instruments, a major determinant of the price is the company's overall creditworthiness. For non-public debt issues, creditworthiness is assessed based on a credit analysis performed by the lender.

When a company obtains financing from the capital markets in the form of corporate bonds or commercial paper, it will normally contract with one or more recognized credit rating agencies to obtain a credit rating. A credit rating is assigned based on the perceived risk of the credit issue with higher ratings associated with lower risk. Although a credit rating applies to a specific debt issue, it can be a useful tool in assessing a company's overall creditworthiness. Some of the major credit ratings agencies are Fitch, Duff & Phelps, Moody's, and Standard & Poor's. (See Chapter 12, Short-Term Investments.)

Factors that enter into a lender's credit analysis or the determination of a rating by a credit rating agency include current earnings, leverage, future prospects of the company, and the type of collateral securing the debt. As a rule, lower credit risk correlates with lower borrowing costs.

C. Credit Support

Another key variable affecting the cost of borrowing for a company issuing corporate bonds or commercial paper is credit support or enhancement. Credit support is provided when a third party with a higher credit rating than the borrower guarantees the debt obligations of the borrower. The guarantee may take the form of an indemnity bond, a standby letter of credit, or insurance. A fee is charged for such support. With such support in place, the borrower's debt assumes the credit rating of the guarantor, which may reduce the borrowing cost or enhance the marketability of the debt.

Another way of enhancing or supporting a credit issue is through the use of asset backing. An asset-backed issue is typically collateralized by inventories or assets such as equipment to which instrument holders take title in case of default.

D. Term or Maturity

The life span of a debt instrument is known as its term or maturity. Debt maturities range from overnight to 100 years. Interest rates tend to increase with length of maturity reflecting the greater risk for long-term instruments and investor demands for higher returns.

III. SHORT-TERM BORROWING ALTERNATIVES

Short-term debt instruments mature in less than one year. They are generally used to finance current assets such as accounts receivable and inventory. Any type of loan or credit arrangement can be referred to as a credit facility.

A. Line of Credit

A line of credit is an agreement in which the lender gives the borrower access to funds up to a maximum amount over a specific period of time. A line of credit may be used to provide short-term financing, to back up commercial paper, or to provide a liquidity cushion. Some companies with seasonal borrowing requirements have lines of credit in which the maximum amount available varies over the year.

1. **Key Characteristics** - The key characteristics of a line of credit include:

    - **Commitment** - Lines of credit are either committed or uncommitted. A committed line usually involves a formal loan agreement that specifies the terms and conditions of the credit facility. A committed line of credit typically requires compensation in the form of balances or fees. Under a committed facility, the lender is obligated to provide funding up to the credit limit stipulated in the agreement as long as the borrower is not in default. Money market or demand lines of credit are examples of uncommitted lines. Uncommitted lines are usually made available for a one-year period and can be canceled at any time by the lender.

    - **Revolving** - Lines of credit are usually revolving, meaning the borrower may borrow, repay, and reborrow funds during the commitment period.

    - **Security** - Lines of credit may be unsecured or secured. Secured lines require the borrower to pledge some form of collateral.

- **Clean-up** - To assure the lender that the line is not being used as a permanent source of financing, a clean-up period of 30 to 60 days is sometimes required. No outstanding borrowings are allowed during the agreed upon clean-up period. Typically this requirement is used only for middle market and small companies.

2. **Effective Rate for a Line of Credit** - Pricing for a line of credit is usually negotiable. The lender may take into account various aspects of the overall lender/borrower relationship in pricing the line. There are three basic pricing components for lines of credit:

    - **All-in Rate** - This rate consists of a spread that is added to a base rate such as LIBOR, prime, or the Fed funds rate. This rate is normally variable and will adjust in relation to changes in the base rate.

    - **Commitment Fee** - For committed lines, the lender may charge a percentage fee based either on the total amount of the commitment or on the unused portion of the commitment. Payment is usually made quarterly. Fees vary depending on the creditworthiness of the company, the stated purpose of the line, and the term of the commitment.

    - **Compensating Balances** - Some banks may also require compensating balances, which are maintained in the company's deposit accounts at the bank and do not earn interest or offset other service charges. This practice has become less common. In a compensating balance arrangement, the balance requirement can be specified as a percentage of the total commitment, the unused amount of the commitment, or the outstanding borrowings. If compensating balances are required, their effect is to reduce the amount of the borrowed funds that can be used by the borrower, thereby increasing the effective annual interest rate.

    To compute the effective borrowing rate for a line of credit, the following formula is used:

$$\text{Effective Annual Borrowing Rate} = \left(\frac{\text{Total Interest Paid} + \text{Total Fees Paid}}{\text{Average Usable Loan}} \right) \times \left(\frac{365}{\text{\# of Days Loan is Outstanding}} \right)$$

Where:

- Total Interest Paid is calculated as the all-in rate times the average loan amount outstanding.

- Total Fees Paid include all commitment fees, placement fees, and any issuance costs.

- Average Usable Loan is the net amount of borrowed funds available after any compensating balances are deducted.

- Number of Days Loan is Outstanding is the effective term of the loan or the time over which the funds are borrowed.

This formula can also be represented in an algebraic format as follows:

$$i \quad = \quad \left(\frac{I + F}{L}\right) \quad \times \quad \left(\frac{365}{t}\right)$$

Where:

i = The effective annual borrowing rate

I = Total interest paid (in dollars)

F = Total fees paid

L = Average usable loan

t = Number of days loan is outstanding

An example of this calculation is provided in Exhibit 13.1.

EXHIBIT 13.1

Effective Annual Borrowing Rate Calculation Example

1. Over a one-year period a company has an average loan outstanding of $1,000,000.
2. The commitment is $3,000,000.
3. The lender requires no compensating balances.
4. The commitment fee is 0.25% based on the unused portion of the line.
5. The interest rate charged is set annually with a spread of 2% over prime. (Prime is assumed to be 8%.)
6. Year basis used is 365.

The effective annual borrowing rate is:

$$\text{Effective Annual Borrowing Rate} \quad = \quad \frac{(\text{interest rate} \times \text{average loan outstanding}) \ + \ \text{commitment fee paid}}{\text{usable funds borrowed}}$$

$$= \left(\frac{(.10 \ \times \ \$1,000,000) \ + \ (.0025 \ \times \ \$2,000,000)}{\$1,000,000}\right) \times \left(\frac{365}{365}\right)$$

$$= \left(\frac{\$100,000 \ + \ \$5000}{\$1,000,000}\right) \ \times \ (1) \ = \ 10.5\%$$

The commitment fee in this example adds 50 basis points (1/100 of an interest point) to the interest rate of 10%. If there is a compensating balance requirement, the average amount of compensating balances is subtracted from the amount of funds in the denominator to determine the amount of the usable funds. Given the above assumptions with a compensating balance requirement equal to 10% of the commitment amount, the effective annual borrowing rate becomes 15%, calculated as follows:

(Continued)

EXHIBIT 13.1

Effective Annual Borrowing Rate Calculation Example

$$\text{Effective Annual Borrowing Rate} = \frac{(\text{interest rate} \times \text{average loan outstanding}) + \text{commitment fee paid}}{\text{usable funds borrowed}}$$

$$= \left(\frac{(.10 \times \$1,000,000) + (.0025 \times \$2,000,000)}{\$1,000,000 - (3,000,000 \times .10)} \right) \times \left(\frac{365}{365} \right)$$

$$= \left(\frac{\$100,000 + \$5000}{\$700,000} \right) \times (1) = .15 = 15\%$$

B. Revolving Credit Agreement

A revolving credit agreement, also known as a revolver, is a facility that allows the borrower to borrow, repay, and reborrow up to a defined amount. Revolving credits are contractual commitments with loan agreements, including covenants. Usually there is a commitment fee on the unused portion, as well as a facility fee. While often used for short-term borrowing, the commitment term typically ranges from two to five years and may be followed by a period in which the principal is systematically repaid.

C. Commercial Paper (CP)

CP is an unsecured promissory note issued by a company for a specific amount, with maturities ranging from overnight to 270 days. Limiting the maturity of CP avoids the SEC registration requirement for securities whose maturities exceed 270 days.

The key characteristics of CP include:

1. **Discount Issuance** - CP is generally issued on a discount basis similar to T-bills. The actual rate paid by a company is market-based and is a function of the issuing company's credit rating, the size of the issue, and general market short-term interest rates. Companies with the highest credit ratings can usually raise funds by issuing CP at a lower effective rate than borrowing under a commercial bank line of credit. When CP is issued, there are underwriting or agency fees and charges related to any credit enhancement obtained, but these are usually small relative to the size of the CP issue.

2. **Distribution** - CP is usually sold through dealers, either investment banking companies or commercial banks. Some companies sell CP directly to investors.

3. **Credit Enhancement** - Some CP borrowers arrange back-up lines of credit that may be used if market conditions are not conducive to issuing or refinancing CP. Another alternative to a back-up line is to obtain a bank standby letter of credit.

4. **Credit Rating** - CP of a specific issuer is generally rated by the major credit rating agencies.

5. **Effective Annual Interest Cost for Commercial Paper** - The effective annual interest cost for CP takes into account the discount rate, the dealer fee, and, in some cases, the cost of a back-up line or standby letter of credit. An example of this calculation is provided in Exhibit 13.2.

EXHIBIT 13.2

Effective Cost for Commercial Paper Calculation Example

1. A company issues $20,000,000 of commercial paper with a 30-day maturity at a discount rate of 8%.
2. The paper is sold through a dealer at an annual charge of 1/8 of 1%.
3. The company has a backup line of credit in the amount of $20,000,000, and pays an annual commitment fee of 0.25% on the line.
4. Since this commercial paper is sold at a discount, the company will receive only $20,000,000 less 30 days' worth of interest at 8%.
5. A 360-day-year basis is the U.S. convention for this instrument.

The amount of usable funds is:

$$\text{Usable Funds} = \text{Face Value} \times \left[1 - \left(\text{Discount Rate} \times \frac{\text{Days to Maturity}}{360} \right) \right]$$

$$= \$20,000,000 \times \left[1 - \left(.08 \times \frac{30}{360} \right) \right] = \$19,866,667$$

The interest cost is the difference between the face value of $20,000,000 and the funds received, $19,866,667, which equals $133,333.

In addition to interest cost, the dealer charges and back-up line of credit costs must be considered to determine the total issue costs.

Most commercial paper users issue new commercial paper on a fairly continuous basis, so the prorated figures for both the dealer cost and the cost of the back-up credit line are the most appropriate in determining total issue costs.

$$\text{Prorated Dealer Cost} = .00125 \times \$20,000,000 \times \left(\frac{30}{360} \right) = \$2,083$$

$$\text{Prorated Backup Credit Line Costs} = .0025 \times \$20,000,000 \times \left(\frac{30}{360} \right) = \$4,167$$

Total Issue Costs = Interest Cost + Prorated Dealer Cost + Prorated Back-up Credit Line Costs

$$= \$133,333 + \$2,083 + \$4,167 = \$139,583$$

The effective annual interest cost is determined by dividing the total costs by the amount of usable funds and annualizing this rate. The effective annual cost of the issue to the company is:

$$\text{Effective Annual Cost of Issue} = \left(\frac{\text{Total Issue Costs}}{\text{Usable Funds}} \right) \times \left(\frac{365}{\text{Maturity}} \right)$$

$$= \left(\frac{\$139,583}{\$19,866,667} \right) \times \left(\frac{365}{30} \right) = .0855 = 8.55\%$$

(Continued)

EXHIBIT 13.2

Effective Cost for Commercial Paper Calculation Example

The interest cost paid by the issuer is the interest earned by an investor. The usable funds available to the issuer is the purchase price an investor must pay for the CP. Therefore, the yield to the investor is calculated as follows:

$$\text{Yield to Investor} = \left(\frac{\text{Interest Cost}}{\text{Usable Funds}}\right) \times \left(\frac{365}{30}\right)$$

$$= \left(\frac{\$133,333}{\$19,866,667}\right) \times \left(\frac{365}{30}\right) = .0817 = 8.17\%$$

D. Reverse Repurchase Agreements

In a reverse repurchase agreement (reverse repo), sometimes known as a resale agreement, a company holding securities in its short-term portfolio sells the securities to a dealer with an agreement to buy them back at a specific price at a specific time. In effect, the company is borrowing cash from the dealer and using its securities as collateral for the loan. This is the reverse of a repurchase agreement or repo. (See Chapter 12, Short-Term Investment.)

E. Banker's Acceptances (BAs)

A BA is a negotiable short-term instrument used primarily to finance the import, export, or domestic shipment of goods or the storage of readily marketable staples. (See Chapter 15, International Cash Management.) A BA has the following characteristics:

- It is a debt obligation evidenced by a time draft drawn by the borrower that is accepted by the bank on which it is drawn. By accepting the draft, the bank becomes directly obligated for payment of the draft on the maturity date.

- It is a readily marketable instrument that can be discounted in the money market. The discounted proceeds are advanced to the borrower who is obligated to pay the full draft amount to the accepting bank at maturity. The accepting bank is, in turn, obligated to pay the investor who purchased the BA.

- The pricing compares favorably with other short-term borrowing rates. The all-in rate for acceptance financing includes the discount rate plus the BA commission paid to the accepting bank.

- Acceptance financing is often provided to a buyer or seller in connection with a letter of credit, but acceptances can be created to finance open account transactions as well.

F. Asset-Based Borrowing

Some financial institutions specialize in a form of secured lending based on the pledging of accounts receivable, inventory, or equipment as collateral for a loan. The following are examples of asset-based borrowing:

1. **Collateralizing Accounts Receivable** - Accounts receivable represent the most common form of collateral for asset-based borrowing. In establishing this type of borrowing arrangement:

   - The lender evaluates the type of customers who buy from the borrower by analyzing the volume of customer purchases, delinquency rates, and the level of bad debt write-offs. The lender also monitors the borrower's accounts receivable aging schedule to determine the timeliness of customer payments.

   - An advance rate is determined based on this evaluation. The advance rate is stated as a percentage of accounts receivable outstanding. This percentage, when applied to the amount of pledged accounts receivable, determines the maximum amount that can be borrowed. For example, a lender may restrict a borrower's loan amount to 80% of its accounts receivable.

   - An asset-based lender normally requires the borrower's customers to remit payments directly to the lender. These payments are then applied to the outstanding loan balance.

2. **Collateralizing Inventory** - Inventory represents the other most common form of collateral for asset-based borrowing. As with accounts receivable financing, borrowing is limited by the advance rate and is calculated as a percentage of inventory. In determining the advance rate, the lender has to take into consideration the risk that the borrower will not be able to sell the inventory for reasons such as fluctuating market conditions, changes in commodity prices, spoilage, or obsolescence.

   Generally, inventory lenders are more willing to advance against finished goods and raw materials than work in process. Sometimes different advance rates are determined for these different types of inventories.

3. **Floor Planning** - This type of financing is frequently used to support the inventory of dealers who specialize in high cost durable goods such as automobiles, trucks, farm equipment, and major appliances. The lender advances funds to pay for inventory purchases. To secure the amount owed to it by the dealer, the lender retains legal title to the goods until they are sold. The proceeds from the sale are then used to repay the loan.

4. **Other Asset-Backed Borrowing** - Borrowers sometimes pledge real estate, machinery, or other tangible property as collateral for loans.

5. **Factoring** - Factoring is the sale of or transfer of title to accounts receivable to a third party (factor). A factor is a financing institution that discounts acceptable accounts receivable with or without recourse to the borrower. For this service, the factor charges a percentage commission on the amount of receivables discounted.

G. Securitization

Securitization is a financing technique by which a company issues debt securities backed by a pool of its selected receivables such as mortgages, auto loans, credit card receivables, or equipment leases. Assets suitable for debt securitization usually have a predictable cash flow stream to retire the issue and a low level of historical loss experience.

Securitization is a type of off-balance-sheet financing. Neither the debt nor the assets securing the financing appear on a company's balance sheet. By removing debt financing from the balance sheet, securitization improves some companies' financial ratios.

Sometimes securitized issues are credit enhanced in order to receive a higher credit rating. Typical methods of credit enhancement include:

- Providing over-collateralization with securitized assets that have a higher present value than that of the debt issue they are backing

- Opening a letter of credit from a financial institution

- Establishing a spread account, which is a reserve built from excess cash flow from underlying assets beyond that required for debt service

- Providing recourse to the issuer should the securitized assets not provide the projected cash flow to pay off the debt

H. Loan Syndications and Participations

Loan syndications and participations enable a company to structure large credit facilities with a number of lenders to overcome legal or policy limitations faced by a single lender.

1. In a loan syndication, multiple financial institutions share a single credit facility. The syndicate, or group of lenders, is led by an agent who acts as the intermediary between the company and the syndicate for purposes of negotiating the credit terms and documentation, making advances and payments on the loan, and disseminating information. All the syndicate members share common documentation, but each lender has a promissory note making it a direct lending relationship.

2. With a loan participation, a financial institution purchases an interest in another lender's credit facility. This purchaser is called a participant and the seller is commonly referred to as the lead institution. The participant does not have a separate note and has only an indirect relationship with the borrower. The participation agreement specifies the rights and the obligations of both the participant and the lead institution. In the case of a blind participation, the participation is not disclosed to the borrower and the participant may not directly contact the borrower or disclose the participant's role in the credit facility.

I. Trade Credit

Trade credit is financing that is created when a seller grants credit terms on purchases made by its customers. The most common form is an open account in which the seller gives the buyer a specified period of time to pay for goods or services purchased. Trade credit can be an important part of a company's overall financing strategy. (See Chapter 5, Credit and Accounts Receivable Management.)

J. Export Financing Programs

Export and import financing is available from both commercial lenders and through various programs offered by the Export-Import Bank of the United States. (See Chapter 15, International Cash Management.)

IV. MEDIUM- AND LONG-TERM BORROWING ALTERNATIVES

From an accounting perspective, anything maturing beyond one year is considered long-term. For the purposes of borrowing, however, a distinction is made between medium- and long-term debt. Medium-term debt is generally considered to mature between two and 10 years from the date of issuance. Long-term debt typically has a maturity of more than 10 years. Typically, companies borrow long-term to finance long-term needs such as capital expenditures and borrow short-term for short-term needs such as working capital.

A. Medium-Term Notes

Medium-term notes are a form of debt and are usually sold in two to ten year maturities. Many companies are increasingly using medium-term notes to finance their needs.

B. Bonds

A bond is a form of long-term debt that may be issued at face value and bears interest over its term. Or, it may be issued at a discount and accrete to face value at maturity. The agreement among all the parties to a bond issue is known as an indenture. It defines details of the issue such as terms and conditions, covenants, events of default, subordination, sinking fund, property to be pledged, if any, and the duties of the trustee.

Bonds have the following components or characteristics:

- **Trustee Administration** - Bonds are administered through a trustee. The trustee is a third party who is responsible for ensuring that the bonds are authentic, ensuring that sinking fund and interest payments are properly paid and applied, and administering redemption. In the event of default, the trustee represents the bondholders in legal proceedings.

- **Ratings** - Bonds are often rated by credit rating agencies according to factors such as the financial strength and future prospects of the company and the collateral securing the bond. The ratings apply to the bonds themselves, not the company. (See Chapter 12, Short-Term Investments.)

- **Marketability** - Bonds are usually traded publicly through securities dealers and securities exchanges, but may also be sold directly to institutional investors. Changes in interest rates affect the value of a bond that is traded prior to maturity.

- **Security** - Bonds may be either secured or unsecured. Secured bonds are collateralized by a specific asset or revenues from a specific project. Secured debt gives the investor a lien against an asset. Bonds may be secured by various assets including inventories, real estate, or fixed (capital) assets. Unsecured bonds, called debentures, offer no collateral. Debenture holders have a general claim against a company but not against a specific asset.

- **Ranking** - Bonds may be equal, senior, or subordinated in relation to other debt obligations. In the event of liquidation, holders of secured debt, whether senior or junior, will be paid off before holders of unsecured debt. Then senior unsecured debt holders will be paid out before the subordinated debenture holders. The more junior the debt, the greater the risk to the investor and the higher the borrowing costs to a company.

- **Retirement Before Maturity** - A call feature on a bond allows the issuer to retire the security before maturity. Bondholders must sell the security back to the company at par (face value) or a predetermined premium over face value. A call provision is often useful for the issuer if there is a good possibility that interest rates will fall during the life of the bond. The company can call the bond and refinance with less expensive debt.

C. Special Types of Bonds

Special types of bonds include:

1. **Municipal Bonds** - Municipal bonds are bonds issued by a state or local government entity and are typically repaid out of tax revenue.

2. **Industrial Revenue Bonds** - Industrial Revenue Bonds (IRB) are a special classification of municipal bonds issued by a government entity often for the purpose of financing specific projects that are either publicly or privately managed.

3. **Junk Bonds** - Junk bonds are high-yield, non-investment grade securities. Junk bonds are typically issued by companies which are already highly leveraged.

4. **Zero-Coupon Bonds** - These are bonds which require no periodic interest payments, but only a single payment of face value at maturity. Due to this single payment feature, they are sold at deep discount from their face value.

5. **Eurobonds** - Eurobonds are bonds issued outside the country where the currency of those bonds is domiciled. For example, dollar-denominated Eurobonds are bonds issued in U.S. dollars outside the U. S.

6. **Foreign Bonds** - Foreign bonds are issued in a country's local currency by companies based outside that country—for example, a U.S.-based company that issues Swiss Franc bonds in Switzerland. Foreign bonds are typically used to finance the issuer's operations in that area.

D. Debt-Equity Hybrids

Debt-equity hybrids have both debt and equity characteristics. The following are types of debt-equity hybrids:

- **Convertible Bonds** - Convertible bonds are bonds that are convertible into shares of a company's common stock at a defined price. They generally provide the borrower with a lower interest rate than non-convertible bonds because of the equity conversion option.

- **Bonds with Equity Warrants** - An equity warrant is a long-term option to buy a stated number of shares of common stock at a specified (exercise) price. When a warrant is attached to a bond, the resulting combination provides the same type of hybrid as a convertible bond. However, warrants are usually detachable from the bond so that they may be exercised without having to surrender the bond.

- **Redeemable Preferred Stock** - Redeemable preferred stock is stock that has a predetermined redemption schedule. In addition, redeemable preferred stock normally provides for the accrual or payment of a regular dividend. The dividend and redemption features are essentially the same as the interest and repayment features on bonds.

E. Term Loan

Term loans are made for a fixed period of time, typically two to 10 years, usually to support equipment purchases and more permanent capital financing. Repayment schedules vary depending on the type of loan and the nature of the project being financed. Typical amortization schedules require periodic payments of principal plus interest, but some may require periodic interest payments with repayment of principal upon maturity.

F. Leasing

Leasing, an alternative to term lending, is used extensively as a means of financing equipment. Leasing arrangements are characterized by the following:

* In a typical leasing arrangement, the lessor actually owns the equipment and leases it to the lessee.

* In leasing, typically 100% of the equipment's cost is financed, and payment amounts can be fixed or variable.

* A leasing arrangement can be structured as either on- or off-balance sheet. An on-balance sheet arrangement is referred to as a capital lease; an off-balance sheet arrangement is referred to as an operating lease. Accounting and tax issues must be evaluated to determine the proper classification of lease.

* An operating lease offers tax advantages to both parties. The lessor realizes the benefit of depreciation, and the lessee has tax deductible operating expenses.

* End-of-term options typically allow the lessee to return, purchase, or re-lease the equipment.

G. Private Placement

A private placement is a direct sale of securities by a company to institutional investors such as insurance companies or pension funds. Private placements have the following characteristics:

* Private placements are not registered with the Securities and Exchange Commission (SEC).

* Terms and conditions are often spelled out in an agreement called a note-purchase agreement or a private placement memorandum.

* A private placement can be arranged by an investment banking company, a commercial bank, or the borrower.

* Private placements are usually less costly for the issuer to arrange than publicly issued debt and may offer longer and more flexible terms than commercial bank term loans. However, the interest rate on private placement issues may be higher than public debt of similar credit quality and maturity.

V. REPAYMENT OF PRINCIPAL

Corporate debt can be structured to allow for various principal and interest payment schedules. In general, the repayment of debt should be matched to the cash flows related to the underlying asset or project being financed.

The two most common methods of debt repayment are amortization and sinking fund:

A. Amortization

Amortization is the repayment of the loan principal in installments over the life of the loan. This enables the borrower to pay off the principal gradually, rather than at one point in time. It also reduces the lender's risk by shortening the average life of the loan.

The characteristics and options of amortization schedules include:

- They may be matched to the cash flows expected from the project or equipment being financed and may vary depending on the type and maturity of the loan.

- Some schedules provide for equal principal installments over the life of the loan; others, such as mortgages, have equal payments incorporating both principal and interest over the life of the loan.

- Some schedules allow a grace period whereby the repayment of principal does not begin until some specified future date. For example, an eight-year loan with a two-year grace period would mean that principal payments would not commence until the third year of the loan.

- Some schedules have balloon payments where the principal is amortized over time, but a large "balloon" payment is due at maturity. Balloon payments result when the amortization period exceeds the contractual term of the loan.

- Some loans have bullet maturities in which the entire principal is due on the final maturity date and no amortization occurs.

B. Sinking Fund

A sinking fund assures creditors that adequate funds are available to meet payments at maturity. The borrower makes periodic payments to a separate custodial account that is used to repay the debt.

VI. LEGAL ASPECTS OF BORROWING

A. Loan Agreements and Bond Indentures

Loan agreements and bond indentures are legal documents that spell out the terms and conditions under which the debt is extended. The primary components of a loan agreement or bond indenture include:

1. **Representations and Warranties** - Representations and warranties are the conditions that exist at the time the loan agreement is executed as attested to by the borrower. They include:

    - Affirmation of the valid legal existence of the borrowing company, a resolution by the borrower's board of directors authorizing the borrowing, and the authority of the corporate officers signing the documents

    - The company confirming its compliance with Employee Retirement Income and Security Act (ERISA)

    - An indemnity protecting the lender from environmental liabilities

2. **Covenants** - Covenants are provisions that restrict the borrower's activities in ways that protect the lender during the term of the agreement. Examples of covenants include the following:

    - **Financial Ratios**

        - Maximum debt to equity ratio

        - Minimum interest coverage ratio

        - Minimum tangible net worth

        - Minimum current ratio or working capital

    - **Borrower Limitations**

        - Limitations on capital expenditures

        - Limitations on incurring other debt or lease obligations

        - Limitations on payment of dividends

        - Limitations on mergers and acquisitions

        - Limitations on the sale or pledge of assets

        - Limitations on stock or debt repurchases

    - **Borrower Obligations**

        - Requirement to comply with environmental requirements for properties

        - Requirement to maintain adequate insurance coverage

3. **Events of Default** - An event of default may occur if any term or condition under a debt agreement is breached or violated by the borrower. Events of default are incidents such as non-payment of interest or principal when due, a material adverse change in the condition of the borrower, or violation of a specified covenant. The characteristics of events of default include the following:

- Cure periods, or a period of time in which an event of default may be corrected before the lender is allowed to pursue his default remedies, are often specified in the agreement.

- Remedies available to a lender when a default occurs normally include an acceleration of all principal and interest on the debt.

- Waivers of defaults may be given at the lender's discretion.

B. Promissory Notes

A promissory note is an unconditional promise to pay a specified amount plus interest at a defined rate either on demand or on a certain date. A promissory note can be issued for each individual borrowing or for a total line amount against which multiple borrowings are made.

A master note is a type of promissory note used to simplify the paperwork connected with loans that have a multiple advance feature such as lines of credit and revolvers. A company signs one comprehensive promissory note for the total amount of the line of credit. Any loans or repayments under the note are covered by the terms of the master note.

Questions

These chapter questions are to test and review the information in the text and are not examples of CCM examination questions, nor are they in the examination format.

Answers can be found at the back of the book on pgs. 382-383.

1.   What are the major objectives of a company's borrowing program?

2.   What is LIBOR?

3.   What is credit support or enhancement?

4.   What is a committed line of credit?

5.   A firm has an average loan outstanding of $200,000 on a $500,000 line of credit. There is a commitment fee of 0.25% on the unused portion of the line, and the interest rate on the borrowed funds is 7.0%. If there is no compensating balance requirement, what is the effective annual borrowing rate on the loan?

6.   How are lines of credit used in conjunction with commercial paper?

7.   A company issues $1,000,000 of commercial paper with a 60-day maturity at a discount rate of 6%. The paper is sold through a dealer for a charge of 1/4 of 1%. There is no backup line of credit. What is the effective annual interest cost of issuing the commercial paper?

8.   What is a loan participation?

9.   What are two characteristics an asset should have to be suitable for securitization?

10.   What is a bond indenture?

11.   What is the difference between an operating lease and a capital lease?

12.   What is a sinking fund?

13.   Why will a company issue convertible bonds?

14.   What may the lender do if a default occurs?

CHAPTER 14

Financial Risk Management

OVERVIEW

Uncertainty about the future course of financial prices – such as interest rates, exchange rates, and commodity prices – exposes a company to financial risk. This chapter deals with the basics of financial risk and introduces the reader to the alternative methods and instruments that can be used by organizations to manage this risk.

LEARNING OBJECTIVES

Upon completion of this chapter and the related study questions the reader should understand:

1. Why there is a need for risk management

2. The objectives of financial risk management

3. The definition and types of financial derivatives

4. How financial derivatives are used to manage risk

5. The definition of interest rate exposure and how to manage it

6. The definition of exchange rate exposure and how to manage it

7. The definition of commodity price risk and how to manage it

8. Accounting and tax issues related to financial risk management

KEY CONCEPTS

1. Nature of Financial Risk

2. Identification of Risk

3. Measurement of Risk

4. Risk Management Instruments

5. Monitoring Performance

OUTLINE

I.   WHY RISK MANAGEMENT?

Companies these days are exposed to various sources of financial risk. This financial risk stems from the uncertainty of the future level of interest rates, exchange rates, and commodity prices. Since the late 1960s, there has been a significant increase in the volatility of interest rates, exchange rates, and commodity prices.

There are several examples of industries and companies that have been subjected to the pressures of financial risk.

- **Interest Rate Risk** - The case of the S&L industry in the U.S. during the 1980s is an example of a sector exposed to risk stemming from interest rate changes.

- **Foreign Exchange Risk** - A classic case dealing with exchange rate risk is the story of Laker Airlines. In the late 1970s, the British pound was strong relative to the U.S. dollar. This increased the demand for air travel from Britain to the U.S. Laker Airlines' founder and CEO, Freddie Laker increased the supply of airline seats by buying five DC-10s and financing them with U.S. dollars. Laker Airline's revenues were primarily in pounds while payment for the newly acquired aircraft was in dollars. The result was a mismatch of revenues and expenses exposing Laker Airlines to exchange rate risk. In 1981, the pound weakened relative to the dollar, increasing Laker's expenses (Laker had to pay more pounds to make payments on its dollar debt) and reducing revenues (from a decrease in the demand for air travel to the U.S. because of the weaker pound). The consequence of this foreign exchange exposure was one of the factors that put Laker Airlines into bankruptcy.

- **Commodity Price Risk** - Continental Airlines fell victim to the invasion of Kuwait by Iraq in 1990 when the price of a commodity – oil – changed unfavorably. As a result, the company filed for bankruptcy.

It is this increased volatility of financial prices and the inability to deal with it that has made the financial environment within which companies operate more risky than it has been in the past. This, in turn, created a demand for financial risk management, which sowed the seeds for financial innovation and the growth of a market for financial derivatives (such as forwards, futures, options, and swaps) as instruments in the risk management process.

II. OVERVIEW OF FINANCIAL RISK MANAGEMENT

This section explains the process of managing financial risk. In addition, it explains how changes in a financial price variable will affect the value of the company and indicates how managing the exposure alters the company's risk profile. Finally, the reader is introduced to the concepts of hedging, speculation, and arbitrage.

A. Risk Management Process

The risk management process involves four steps:

1. **Identifying the Exposure** - The interest rate changes, foreign exchange rate changes, or commodity price changes, to which a company is exposed, will depend on its line of business. Because it may be exposed to one or more of these financial price changes, identification of the exposure in each area is necessary.

2. **Measuring the Exposure** - Once the exposure has been identified, measuring and quantifying that exposure is required. Management then needs to decide whether the company is in a position to tolerate the risk, or whether it should reduce or eliminate that exposure via an appropriate risk management strategy.

3. **Implementing an Appropriate Risk Management Strategy** - If the company needs to manage its risk, it must determine an appropriate strategy. Two possible strategies include balance sheet matching and the use of derivative financial instruments. For example, the S&L industry could have created a balance sheet strategy of matching interest-sensitive assets with interest-sensitive liabilities eliminating the exposure to interest rate changes. An alternative would be to maintain a mismatched balance sheet and then manage the resulting exposure with derivatives. The remainder of this chapter develops the strategy approach using derivatives.

4. **Monitoring the Exposure and Evaluating the Strategy** - Finally, the company must periodically monitor the exposure in each financial area. The time interval for monitoring the exposure is decided on an individual basis and may be shortened if volatility in the underlying asset market increases unexpectedly. In addition, the company needs to monitor the effectiveness of the strategy selected.

B. The Risk Profile

The way unexpected changes in a financial price variable such as interest rates, exchange rates, or commodity prices may affect the value of a company can be demonstrated by a company's risk profile. The risk profile of a company is a graphical representation of how the value of the company changes as the financial price variable changes. If the value of the company increases for a positive change in the financial price variable, then the risk profile for the company is upward sloping (see Exhibit 14.1a). On the other hand, if the value of the company decreases for a positive change in the financial price variable, then the risk profile for the company is downward sloping (see Exhibit 14.1b).

The basic idea behind risk management is the implementation of a strategy that has a payoff profile that counteracts the risk profile of the company so that the resulting net exposure is flat. This strategy may involve the use of instruments such as forwards, futures, swaps, and options.

EXHIBIT 14.1a

An upward sloping risk profile relating changes in company value (△CV) to unexpected changes in a financial price (△FP)

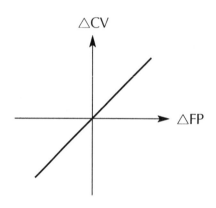

EXHIBIT 14.1b

A downward sloping risk profile relating changes in company value (△CV) to unexpected changes in a financial price (△FP)

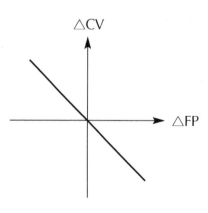

Hence, a company with an exposure given by Exhibit 14.1a may use a risk management tool with a payoff profile similar to Exhibit 14.1b so that the resulting net exposure to the company is flat. Exhibit 14.2 demonstrates this graphically.

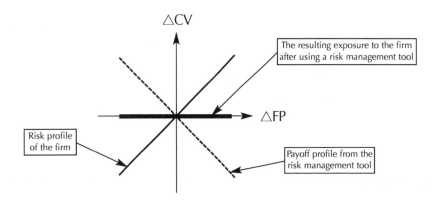

EXHIBIT 14.2

C. Hedging, Speculation, and Arbitrage

1. **Hedging** - Hedging is the process by which a company uses financial instruments to reduce or eliminate the risk associated with the uncertainty about the future price of the asset under consideration.

2. **Speculation** - Speculation involves betting on the direction of the market. Speculators are those market participants who are willing to assume risk. In other words, speculators are betting that the price of the asset will either go up or go down. They have an open position in the asset and unlike hedgers, do not have an underlying exposure they are offsetting.

3. **Arbitrage** - Arbitrage is the process by which buying in one market and simultaneously selling in another leads to a riskless profit. Arbitrageurs do not assume any risk, but attempt to profit from market inefficiencies. Taking advantage of such arbitrage opportunities keeps financial markets efficient.

D. Risk Management, Cash Flow Variability, and Value of the Company

Risk management helps reduce the variability of a company's future cash flows, which in turn adds value to the company. In other words, hedging enables a company to smooth its cash flows over time, while the cash flows of the unhedged company tend to be more volatile.

The company with a lower variability of future cash flows increases its value in several ways:

- As a result of hedging, the company is in a better position to assess its costs and revenues, which lowers the probability of financial distress.

- Shareholders attribute a higher value to companies with less volatile future cash flows.

- The hedged company with less volatile future cash flows is perceived as being less risky and has a borrowing advantage in credit markets.

III. DERIVATIVE INSTRUMENTS USED AS RISK MANAGEMENT TOOLS

A derivative instrument is a financial product that derives value from some underlying asset. The underlying asset could be a financial instrument, a currency, or a commodity. Four basic types of derivative securities are:

A. Forwards

A forward contract is an agreement between two parties to buy or sell a fixed amount of an asset at a future date at a price agreed upon today.

- The asset involved is also referred to as the underlying asset. This underlying asset could be a financial instrument (such as stock index or debt instrument), currency (such as French francs or British pounds sterling), or a commodity (such as gold or coffee).

- The future date is also called the maturity date of the contract.

- The price is the delivery price of the contract.

The party that has agreed to buy the asset is said to be long a forward contract, while the counter-party is short a forward contract. The long position in a forward contract gains value when the underlying asset price rises and loses value when the asset price falls. The short position gains value when the underlying asset price falls and loses value when the asset price rises. Exhibit 14.3a and Exhibit 14.3b depict the payoff profiles from a long and short position respectively in a forward contract.

EXHIBIT 14.3a

Forward Contract – Long Position

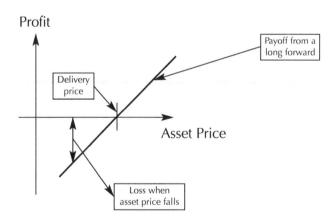

EXHIBIT 14.3b

Forward Contract – Short Position

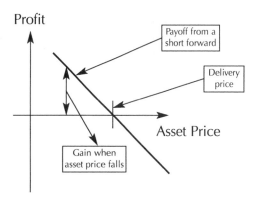

Some notable features of a forward contract are:

- The forward markets are managed and supported by a group of banks, dealers, and traders who act as market makers. Market makers are individuals who will quote both a bid and ask price whenever they are asked to do so. Therefore, forward contracts are private contracts between two parties.

- These contracts are customized to each party's needs and not standardized like a futures contract. In other words, the amount of the underlying asset and the maturity date for the contract are set at the time the contract is negotiated.

- At maturity, delivery of the underlying asset usually takes place.

For example, suppose a U.S. importer needs to pay a 50,000 British pound sterling invoice in 90 days. The importer could purchase a forward contract now for sterling quoted at $1.69 per pound deliverable in 90 days. At the end of 90 days, the importer would pay $84,500 ($1.69 x £50,000) and receive £50,000 in order to pay the invoice. Thus, no matter what fluctuation occurred in the exchange rate of the 90-day time horizon, the purchase of the forward contract would lock in the exchange rate for the future time period.

B. Futures

Futures are similar to forwards. For example, the payoff profile from a long position in a futures contract and a short position in a futures contract looks exactly the same as the payoff from a forward contract (see Exhibit 14.3a and 14.3b). Some of the more notable features of futures contracts are:

- Futures contracts are traded on an organized exchange. In the U.S., futures contracts are traded on the Chicago Board of Trade (grains, metals, financials), the Chicago Mercantile Exchange (livestock, wood, meat) and its International Money Market (IMM) wing (which trades foreign currency futures), and the New York Mercantile Exchange (metals, petroleum, fiber), among others.

- Futures contracts are standardized by the exchanges and have a range of delivery dates. The size of the contract and its maturity date are set by the exchange. An implication of this is that a corporate treasurer may not be able to perfectly hedge an underlying position using a futures contract. For example, the size of a DM (Deutsche mark) contract is for 125,000 DM. If the treasurer has an exposure that is not a multiple of this number, using a futures contract to hedge may exceed or fall short of the exposure.

- Futures trading requires a margin account that is marked-to-market on a daily basis. This means that the investor's/hedger's gains or losses on the position are reflected on a daily basis. If the margin account drops below a specified amount (the maintenance margin), a margin call is issued. This requires the holder of the account to replenish the account to the initial (margin) level or close out the position.

- Futures contracts are rarely settled by actual delivery and are usually closed out prior to maturity. They are used primarily as hedging vehicles.

For example, suppose a company buys wheat as an input to its cereal production process. The company is uncertain as to the future cost of wheat and wishes to protect itself from fluctuations in the commodity price. In such a case the company could purchase a futures contract for wheat now and hold it until it must purchase wheat in the commodity market. If the price of wheat goes up, causing an increase in the company's raw material cost, the company could sell the futures contract, whose price would also rise, for a profit. The profit gained on the futures contract could then be used to offset the higher purchase cost of the commodity.

C. Swaps

A swap is an agreement between two parties to exchange (or swap) a set of cash flows at future points in time. The most common type of swap is an interest rate swap. In such an arrangement, party X may agree to pay party Y a stream of cash flows equal to a floating rate of interest on some mutually agreed-upon amount referred to as a notional principal. At the same time, party Y agrees to pay party X a stream of cash flows equal to a fixed rate of interest on the same notional principal at the same future dates. The principal is notional because it does not exchange hands. Only the interest payments are exchanged. In other words, party X is swapping a fixed rate loan for a floating rate loan, while party Y is doing exactly the opposite.

Consider the following example. Suppose that two parties, X and Y, both wish to borrow $20 million for ten years. Also assume that X has a better credit rating than Y and that each has been offered the borrowing rates given below:

	Fixed Rate	Floating Rate
Party X	10.00%	6-month LIBOR + 0.50%
Party Y	11.00%	6-month LIBOR + 1.00%

Assume Party X wants to borrow at a floating rate, while party Y wants to borrow at a fixed rate due to its own particular financial strategy needs. Because party X has a better credit rating than party Y, it pays a lower rate in both fixed and floating markets. Even though party Y pays more in both markets, it pays relatively less in the floating rate market. So party X has a comparative borrowing advantage in the fixed rate market, while party Y has a comparative borrowing advantage in the floating rate market. This provides the basis for an interest rate swap.

A potential interest rate swap would be the following:

- Party X borrows at a fixed rate of 10.00 percent and party Y at a floating rate of LIBOR + 1.00 percent.

- They then enter into a swap agreement, which ensures that party X receives floating-rate funds and party Y receives fixed-rate funds.

- Assuming that parties X and Y get in touch with each other directly, they may negotiate a swap agreement as shown in Exhibit 14.4.

EXHIBIT 14.4

A Swap Between X and Y

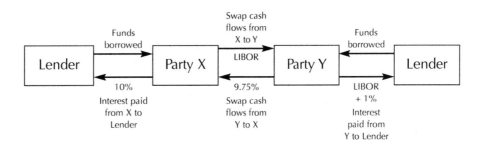

Party X makes payments to a lender at a fixed rate of 10.00 percent. It makes payments based on LIBOR to party Y and receives payments from party Y at a fixed rate of 9.75 percent. The net effect of this for party X is that it ends up paying LIBOR + 0.25 percent, which is 25 basis points less than what it would have paid if it borrowed directly from the floating-rate market. On the other hand, party Y makes payments to a lender at a fixed rate of LIBOR +1.00 percent. It makes payments based on a fixed rate of 9.75 percent to party X and receives payments based on LIBOR from party X. The net effect of this for party Y is that it ends up paying a fixed rate of 10.75 percent, which is 25 basis points less than what it would have paid if it borrowed directly from the fixed-rate market.

There are several other types of swap arrangements. Among the more common ones are:

- Currency swaps, where the agreement is to convert an obligation in one currency to an obligation in another currency, and

- Commodity swaps, where a floating price for a commodity is exchanged for a fixed price.

D. Options

An option is a contract between two parties wherein the buyer of the contract has the right (but not the obligation) to either buy or sell a fixed amount of some underlying asset at a fixed price, on or before a specified date.

- If the contract gives the owner the right to buy the underlying asset at a fixed price, the option is a call option.

- If the contract gives the owner the right to sell the underlying asset at a fixed price, the option is a put option.

The fixed price is called the strike/exercise price of the contract and the specified date is the maturity date (or exercise date) of the contract.

If the contract allows the buyer to exercise (buy/sell the underlying asset) the option only at maturity, then the contract is called a European option contract. If the contract allows the owner to exercise the option at any time prior to maturity, then the contract is called an American option contract. There are American calls and puts as well as European calls and puts.

Unlike forwards and futures, options have a premium associated with them. The seller of the option (also called the writer of the contract) receives a premium from the buyer (or holder) of the contract. In return, the writer has the obligation to fulfill the contract (that is, sell or buy the underlying asset) if the buyer chooses to exercise the contract.

- **Call Option Example** - Consider an investor who buys a three-month European call option on XYZ with a strike (or exercise) price of $110 and pays $5 for it. The payoff (or profit and loss) from this would look like Exhibit 14.5a. If at maturity the market price of XYZ is less than or equal to the strike price of $110, the investor does not exercise the option (because it is cheaper to buy XYZ at the market price than by exercising the option) and has a loss (of $5) equal to the option premium. When the market price is greater than the strike price plus the option premium (i.e., $110 + $5 = $115), the investor makes a profit.

- **Put Option Example** - Consider an investor who buys a one-month European put option on XYZ with a strike (or exercise) price of $100, and pays $4 for it. The payoff (or profit and loss) from this would look like Exhibit 14.5b. If at maturity the market price of XYZ is greater than or equal to the strike price of $100, the investor does not exercise the option (because the investor will receive more by selling XYZ at the market price than by exercising the option) and takes a loss (of $4) equal to the option premium. If at maturity the market price of XYZ is less than the strike price the investor exercises the option. When the market price is less than the strike price minus the option premium (i.e., $100 - $4 = $96), the investor makes a profit.

EXHIBIT 14.5a

Payoff from a long (buy) call

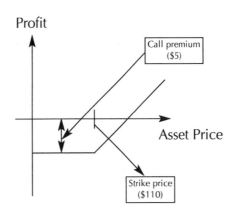

EXHIBIT 14.5b

Payoff from a long (buy) put

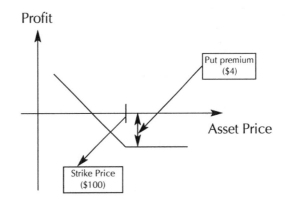

There are a variety of payoff possibilities with options:

- An option is at-the-money if the underlying asset price is equal to the strike price of the option.

- A call option is out-of-the-money if the asset price is less than the strike price of the option.

- A put option is out-of-the-money if the asset price exceeds the strike price of the option.

- A call option is in-the-money if the asset price is greater than the strike price of the option.

- A put option is in-the-money if the asset price is less than the strike price of the option.

An important feature of using options to manage financial risk is that they allow the hedger to participate in a favorable market. Forwards and futures lock the hedger into a price independent of market changes.

IV. INTEREST RATE EXPOSURE

Many companies face financial risk due to exposure to interest rate changes. This exposure may arise from the inherent nature of their business or from their financing activities. This section outlines some examples of interest rate exposure and the types of instruments used to manage interest rate risk.

A. Examples of Interest Rate Exposure

1. **Falling Rates** - Companies with variable interest rate investments face the possibility of lower earnings when interest rates fall. Such companies have a positively sloped risk profile as in shown in Exhibit 14.1a.

2. **Rising Rates** - Companies with debt tied to variable interest rates face higher borrowing costs when interest rates rise. The risk profile of such companies will have a negative slope as shown in Exhibit 14.1b.

B. Different Types of Interest Rate Derivatives

There are several types of interest rate derivative instruments used by companies to manage their exposure to interest rate changes. The rest of this section defines some of the more commonly used instruments.

1. **Forward Rate Agreements (FRAs)** - A FRA is a forward contract on interest rates in which two parties agree that a certain interest rate will apply to a certain principal during a specified future period of time. The notional principal amounts are agreed upon but never exchanged. If at settlement the actual rate is different from the rate agreed in the contract, then one party pays the other a cash amount equal to the present value of the difference between the interest in the contract rate and the actual rate. The majority of FRAs are based on Eurodollar rates, although others are available.

2. **Interest Rate Futures** - Interest rate futures are futures contracts on an underlying asset whose price is solely dependent on the level of interest rates. The most popular short-term (90-day) interest rate contracts are the T-bill, the Eurodollar contracts traded on the Chicago Mercantile Exchange (CME), and bank certificates of deposit (CDs). In the T-bill futures contract the underlying asset is the 90-day Treasury bill. In the Eurodollar futures contract, the underlying asset is a 3-month Eurodollar deposit. The interest earned on a Eurodollar deposit is the 3-month London Interbank Offer Rate (LIBOR). The most actively traded long-term interest rate contracts are the 5-year and 10-year US Treasury notes and the 30-year US Treasury bonds.

3. **Interest Rate Swaps** - A common type of interest rate swap is the exchange of a fixed interest rate cash flow for a floating interest rate cash flow – both cash flows being in the same currency. If both interest rates are floating, then the exchange of the cash flows is called a basis-rate swap. An example of a basis-rate swap is the exchange of interest payments based on LIBOR for interest payments based on the commercial paper rate.

4. **Interest Rate Options** - Interest rate options are options where the payoff depends on the level of interest rates. There are three basic types of interest rate options:

- **Interest Rate Cap** - Interest rate caps ensure that the borrower of a floating rate loan receives a ceiling rate if interest rates rise above a specified level. This level is known as the cap rate. If rates fall, the borrower is not obligated to exercise the option and can still enjoy the benefits of the lower borrowing costs. The price of this insurance is the premium paid for the cap.

- **Interest Rate Floor** - A company with a floating rate asset can use an interest rate floor to hedge against rates dropping below a certain level. If rates fall, the floating rate asset is protected by this put option on interest rates. If interest rates rise, the company can still benefit, as it is not obligated to exercise the option. Again, the cost of this insurance is the premium paid for the interest rate floor.

- **Interest Rate Collar** - A combination of an interest rate cap and an interest rate floor is called an interest rate collar. A company that buys a cap and sells a floor is effectively locking in a range for its borrowing costs. The cap establishes a maximum borrowing rate, thereby protecting the company against higher interest rates, while the floor sets a minimum borrowing rate. A collar can be costless if the income received from selling the floor matches the premium paid for the cap. Costless collars are popular hedging vehicles, as they provide some interest rate protection at no cost.

Besides caps, floors, and collars there are several other types of interest rate options. As an example, an option on an interest rate swap is called a swaption, where the buyer of the option has the right to enter into an interest rate swap at a future date.

V. EXCHANGE RATE EXPOSURE

Companies that deal with foreign currencies are faced with different kinds of exposure. This section explains the types of currency exposure and the alternate currency derivatives that can be used to manage foreign exchange exposure.

A. Types of Foreign Exchange Exposure

Companies dealing in foreign currencies face three kinds of exposure: transaction, translation, and economic exposure.

1. **Transaction Exposure** - If a company's balance sheet, either receivables or payables, is affected in value by changes in foreign exchange rates, then the company has a transaction exposure. Transaction exposure usually occurs if the receivables and payables are in different currencies. Adjusting the selling price for adverse changes in the exchange rate does not necessarily eliminate transaction exposure. For example, a U.S. exporter sells merchandise to a French buyer agreeing to accept payment (in francs) three months from now. The exporter records the transaction as an accounts receivable. However, the exporter is exposed to a possible loss in value if, in three months, the French franc depreciates relative to the U.S. dollar (because the receivables would convert into fewer dollars).

2.   **Translation Exposure** - Companies with foreign subsidiaries or foreign operations are exposed to translation exposure. Translation exposure is created when a foreign subsidiary's financial statements are converted (or translated) into the parent company's home currency to consolidate the parent's financial statement.

3.   **Economic Exposure** - Economic exposure is the long-term effect of exchange rate changes on the present value of future cash flows to the company. Multinational corporations that do business in several different currencies will, in the long run, always be subject to fluctuations in cash flows because of exchange rate changes. Even purely domestic companies are exposed to economic exposure. For example, a company that purchases its supplies and sells its product locally is clearly not affected by transaction exposure. However, if there is foreign competition within the local market and the local currency appreciates against the competitor's, then the company's earnings in the long run may be affected as demand shifts towards the relatively cheaper foreign competitor's product.

B. Currency Derivatives used to Hedge Foreign Exchange Exposure

Once a company has identified and quantified its exposure to exchange rate changes, it decides whether or not to hedge that exposure. There are several instruments that a company can use if it decides to manage its exchange rate risk.

1.   **Currency Forwards** - A currency forward is a commitment to buy or sell a specified amount of foreign currency at a future date at an exchange rate that is agreed upon today. Foreign exchange forwards are traded in most major currencies with standard maturities of 1, 2, 3, 6, 9, and 12 months. Since forwards are credit instruments (and entail credit risk), the dealers in foreign exchange forwards are usually banks. Also, most of the documentation concerning foreign exchange forwards involves credit issues.

2.   **Currency Futures** - Currency futures contracts are similar to currency forwards except that they are traded on an exchange and are therefore standardized contracts in terms of amount and maturity date. Currency futures are available for only a relatively few major currencies.

3.   **Currency Swaps** - A currency swap involves the exchange of a floating-rate cash flow denominated in one currency with a fixed-rate cash flow denominated in another currency, in addition to an exchange of principal.

4.   **Currency Options** - A foreign currency option gives the buyer the right to buy (call option) or sell (put option) a fixed amount of a foreign currency at a fixed exchange rate (strike price), on or before a specific future date. A foreign currency put option establishes a floor value (in terms of the domestic currency) for the foreign currency, which is the exercise price less the premium on the put. Similarly, a foreign currency call option sets a ceiling cost (in terms of the domestic currency) for the foreign currency. The ceiling cost is the strike price plus the premium paid for the call.

For example, an importer with an accounts payable due in three months in British pounds can ensure a maximum cost for the pounds by going long (buying) a call option on the pound. If at the time of payment the spot market price of the pound is less than the strike price of the call option, the importer does not exercise the option and loses only the premium. The net cost of the pounds to the importer is the spot price of the pound plus the option premium. The option acts as insurance against the spot price of the pound rising above a specific level; for this, the importer pays a premium which is the option price.

VI. COMMODITY EXPOSURE

Markets exist for several commodities which are either used by companies in their production process or which are sold by companies to customers. The most common commodities markets are in the areas of agricultural and meat products, oil and gas, minerals, and metals. This section provides examples of commodity price exposure and the different commodity derivatives used to manage that exposure.

A. Examples of Commodity Exposure

There are two types of commodity exposure:

1. **Price Exposure** - The primary commodity price exposure faced by companies is the potential for changes in the price of that commodity. If a company utilizes commodities in the input process, rising prices create an exposure for the company (the risk profile of the company is negatively sloped). Conversely, if a company sells the product (the risk profile is positively sloped), then falling prices would create an exposure.

2. **Delivery Exposure** - For some companies (mainly energy users) regular supply of the commodity is crucial. In addition to price exposure, these companies also face delivery exposure. Entering into a long-term agreement with an energy producer can mitigate this exposure.

B. Derivative Instruments Used to Hedge Commodity Exposure

As with interest rate risk and foreign exchange risk, commodity-price risk can also be managed using forwards, futures, swaps, and options, or even combinations of these basic tools. The following are two examples:

- In an oil swap, the parties would agree on a notional principal that is expressed in barrels of oil (not dollars) and, similar to currency or interest rate swaps, make regular settlements on the basis of fixed and floating oil prices. The floating price used in an oil swap is usually the average price of oil over a specified period.

- To reduce the uncertainty associated with the change in a commodity price, the company may decide to use a zero cost collar (a combination of a cap and a floor).

VII. ACCOUNTING AND TAX ISSUES

A. Accounting Issues

Due to the nature of the instruments used in financial risk management, there are special accounting issues that must be considered. Many of these issues are addressed by the Financial Accounting Standards Board (FASB). Some of the critical FASB pronouncements related to financial risk management include:

1. **Financial Instruments Disclosure** - The pronouncements concerning disclosure have

resulted in FASB Statement No. 105, which deals with the disclosure of information about the use of instruments with off-balance-sheet risk and instruments with a concentration of credit risk, and FASB Statement No. 107, which concerns the disclosure of the fair market value of financial instruments. Additional requirements concerning disclosure are provided in FASB Statements No. 114 (Accounting by Creditors for Impairment of a Loan) and No. 115 (Accounting for Certain Investments in Debt and Equity Securities).

2. **Other Accounting Issues** - Hedge accounting is an accounting technique that is applied to the components of a hedge, so that the fair value of the hedged asset and the hedging vehicle are included in earnings for the same period. As a result of the tremendous growth in alternative hedging instruments, no standard accounting guidelines have been established for financial derivatives. Although hedge accounting has been addressed in FASB Statements No. 80 (Accounting for Futures Contracts) and No. 52 (Foreign Currency Translation), they contain certain conceptual inconsistencies. Statement No. 52 limits hedge accounting for currency transaction to those future transactions that are firmly committed, while No. 80 extends hedge accounting to those anticipated future transactions that are not firmly committed, provided certain hedge criteria are met.

B. Tax Issues Related to Hedging

Since the U.S. tax system differentiates between ordinary income and capital gains, the main issue for tax treatment here is whether the gains/losses on a hedge should be treated as ordinary gains/losses or capital gains/losses. As of October 1993, the Temporary Regulations on Hedging Transactions of the IRS considers the gains/losses on "most business" hedges as ordinary gains/losses. If the loss on the hedge is treated as a capital loss, then the company can deduct the loss only to the extent that it offsets other capital gains in the business. If the gains are not sufficient, then there can be a situation in which the loss on the hedge cannot be deducted against income.

QUESTIONS

These chapter questions are to test and review the information in the text and are not examples of CCM examination questions, nor are they in the examination format.

Answers can be found at the back of the book on pgs. 383-385.

1. What is financial risk management, where does it stem from, and why is it important?

2. Outline the steps involved in the financial risk management process.

3. What is the risk profile? How does it differ for a firm that hedges and for one that does not hedge?

4. How can risk management increase the value of a firm?

5. What is the difference between hedging, speculation, and arbitrage?

6. What are the four basic types of contracts or instruments used in financial risk management?

7. What is a derivative instrument?

8. What are the differences between a forward contract and a futures contract?

9. What are the primary types of interest rate exposure.

10. What are caps, floors, and collars?

11. What is the difference between transaction exposure and translation exposure?

12. Explain how a firm wishing to invest in floating rate investments can use a swap to manage its interest rate exposure. Explain how a company selling oil in the spot market can use futures contracts to hedge the future selling price of its product.

13. What are the two types of commodity exposure?

14. What are the accounting issues that are related to hedging primarily concerned about?

15. What are the tax issues related to hedging transactions?

CHAPTER **15**

International Cash Management

OVERVIEW

This chapter describes the principal methods of international cash management including the application of cash management principles to the business environment of other countries and techniques specific to cross-border cash management. It describes the principal international trade payment methods such as letters of credit and documentary collections, and introduces export financing and insurance.

LEARNING OBJECTIVES

Upon completion of this chapter and the related study questions, the reader should know:

1. The importance of international cash management

2. The objectives of international cash management

3. The basics of foreign exchange rates and markets

4. The differences between various countries' payment and banking systems

5. How cross-border check payments and wire transfers are made

6. The techniques used to help manage international cash flows

7. The types and uses of letters of credit and documentary collections

8. The principal methods of export financing and credit management

9. The tax considerations of international cash management

KEY CONCEPTS

1. Objectives of International Cash Management

2. Differences Between Various Countries' Payment and Banking Systems

3. Cross-Border Check Payments and Wire Transfers

4. Managing International Cash Flows

5. Letters of Credit and Documentary Collections

6. International Tax Implications

OUTLINE

I. Introduction to International Cash Management
A. Increased Globalization of Business
B. Increased Competition in the Domestic Marketplace
C. Need for Cash Management Services on a Global Basis

II. Objectives of International Cash Management
A. International Cash Management Issues
B. Foreign Exchange
C. International Cash Management Organization

III. Characteristics of International Banking Systems
A. Central Bank
B. Bank and Company Relationships
C. Number of Banks
D. Restrictions on Corporate Demand Deposit Accounts
E. Value Dating
F. Characteristics of Banks and Banking Systems in Some Other Countries

IV. Characteristics of International Payments Systems
A. Paper-Based Payments Systems
B. Electronic Payments Systems

V. International Trade Financing Methods
A. Open Account
B. Documentary Collections
C. Letters of Credit (L/C)
D. Other Trade Payment Methods
E. Banker's Acceptances (BA)
F. Trade Acceptances

VI. International Cash Management Issues and Techniques
A. Credit Management
B. Accounts Receivable Management
C. Cash Concentration
D. Leading and Lagging
E. Reinvoicing
F. Internal Factoring
G. Multi-Currency Accounts
H. Information Reporting Services

VII. International Financing, Taxes, and Other Considerations
A. Export Financing
B. Financing International Operations
C. Tax Considerations
D. Legal and Ethical Issues

I. INTRODUCTION TO INTERNATIONAL CASH MANAGEMENT

International cash management is becoming increasingly important as companies expand their presence in the global marketplace. This global marketplace, however, is a constantly changing and complex environment in which to do business. Each country operates under different sets of laws, business practices, and banking systems. The U.S. banking and payments system, with which most cash managers are familiar, is significantly different from those used elsewhere in the world.

A. Increased Globalization of Business

Almost every company in the U.S. is affected by events on a global basis. Even small, localized companies use supplies with some foreign content or sell goods that compete with imported products. Organizations such as the World Trade Organization (WTO) and agreements such as the North American Free Trade Agreement (NAFTA) have facilitated trade between countries, increasing the level of international business activity.

B. Increased Competition in the Domestic Marketplace

Increased competition in the domestic marketplace has caused many companies to look internationally for sources of additional revenue, either through export sales or expansion into foreign markets. The same competitive forces and costs have also caused many companies to seek non-domestic suppliers for their product or raw material needs.

C. Need for Cash Management Services on a Global Basis

Companies expanding abroad have a need for the same kinds of cash management services they have in the U.S. Companies operating multinationally have many of the same concerns related to collection, concentration, disbursement, and information management they have in the U.S., but these issues may have to be dealt with on a very different basis. The selection of financial service providers to assist a company in its international operations is a critical part of the international cash management process.

II. OBJECTIVES OF INTERNATIONAL CASH MANAGEMENT

The objectives of international cash management are similar to those for U.S. cash management. The main objective is the efficient utilization of a company's global cash resources in a manner consistent with its strategic goals. International cash management is the application of basic functions such as collection, concentration, disbursement, investment, borrowing, and information management to each international environment. International cash management is also concerned with cross-border funds movement, foreign exchange, and cash management practices within countries outside the U.S.

A. International Cash Management Issues

International cash management involves many of the same issues as domestic cash management, with several additional challenges:

1. **Cash Flow Complexity** - A multinational company must deal with cash flows from subsidiaries, suppliers, and customers in each of the countries in which it operates. As a result of widely differing regulations, banking systems, and information availability, companies operating internationally must manage a complex series of cash flows that are typically in different currencies and that often cross national boundaries.

2. **Foreign Exchange Exposure** - International companies dealing in various foreign currencies are exposed to foreign exchange rate risk. A company must assess the types and levels of its exposure to foreign exchange rate fluctuations and volatility for the specific currencies in which it operates. (See Chapter 14, Financial Risk Management.)

3. **Political Issues** - Multinational companies are exposed to varying degrees of political risk as they become corporate citizens of different sovereign nations. Companies with operations in foreign countries must be knowledgeable about the laws, regulations, and customs that will govern their business activities. They should also be aware of the overall political and social dynamics of the various countries in which they have invested their capital.

B. Foreign Exchange

International cash management requires a basic understanding of foreign exchange rates and markets.

1. **Foreign Exchange Rates** - Foreign exchange rates are quoted in several ways, depending on the currencies and the markets involved.

   • **Rate Quoting Conventions** - A foreign exchange rate is the equivalent number of units of one currency per unit of a different currency. From a U.S. perspective, there are two ways to quote foreign exchange rates: the U.S. dollar equivalent of a unit of the foreign currency, or the amount of the foreign currency per U.S. dollar. The following example shows those quotation formats for selected foreign currencies. (Decimals have been rounded.)

EXHIBIT 15.1
Rate Quoting Conventions

CURRENCY	U.S. $ EQUIVALENT	CURRENCY PER U.S. $
British Pound (£)	1.626	0.615
German Deutschemark (DM)	0.55	1.818
Japanese Yen (¥)	0.008	125.00

EXHIBIT 15.2
Foreign Exchange Calculation Example

Using the information provided in Exhibit 15.1, £250,000 would be equivalent to US$406,500:

$$£250,000 \text{ X } 1.626 = \$406,500$$

Or, to use another example, DM250,000 would be equivalent to US$137,514 (rounded):

$$\frac{DM250,000}{1.818} = US\$137,514$$

- **Bid-Offer Spreads** - Banks and other dealers quote both bid and offer rates for foreign currency. The bid rate is the rate at which a dealer is willing to purchase currency. The offer rate is the rate at which a dealer is willing to sell currency. The spread between the bid rate and the offer rate provides income for the dealer.

EXHIBIT 15.3

Bid-Offer Spread Calculation Example

Assume:

A dealer provides a bid-offer quote of DM 1.82 - 1.83 US$. This means the dealer is willing to buy (bid) one US$ at DM 1.82 and sell (offer) one US$ at DM at 1.83.

Example:

If a U.S. cash manager wanted to sell a dealer US$50,000 in exchange for DM, the dealer would buy (bid) the US$50,000 from the cash manager for DM 91,000.

$$\$50,000 \times 1.82 = DM91,000$$

However, if the same U.S. cash manager turned around and sold back the DM 91,000 to the dealer in exchange for US$, the dealer would sell (offer) the cash manager US$49,727 (rounded):

$$\frac{DM91,000}{1.83} = US\$49,727$$

The difference of $273 (US$50,000 - US$49,727) illustrates the dealer's spread on this transaction.

---

2. **Foreign Exchange Markets** - For foreign exchange, there are two basic markets, the spot market and the forward market.

- **Spot Market** - A rate quoted in the spot market for currency is called a spot foreign exchange rate (spot rate). These rates are generally quoted for delivery one or two business days from the date of the trade. Faster delivery may be possible, but at the expense of a rate higher than the quoted spot rate.

- **Forward Market** - The forward foreign exchange market is one in which an exchange rate for a future delivery of currencies can be fixed today.

  - A forward foreign exchange rate (forward rate) is an exchange rate established today for a currency transaction with delivery occurring beyond two days in the future. Deliveries under most forward foreign exchange contracts occur within a year from the trade date. However, delivery dates beyond one year are available for actively traded currencies.

- ◆ Forward exchange rates are based on the spot exchange rate and the difference in interest rates between two countries. The terms par, discount, and premium describe the relationship between spot and forward exchange rates. The interest rate differential between two countries will determine if their respective currencies will trade at par, at a discount, or at a premium in the forward market. This concept is known as interest rate parity.

- ◆ If the spot rate and forward exchange rate are the same, then the forward rate is at par to the spot rate. In theory, this would imply that the interest rate structure between the two countries is exactly the same. As this is rarely the case, currencies will generally trade at a discount or premium.

- ◆ A currency is at a discount if it is worth less in the forward market than in the spot market. The currency with the higher interest rate will sell at a discount in the forward market against a currency with the lower interest rate.

- ◆ A currency is at a premium if it is worth more in the forward market than in the spot market. The currency with the lower interest rate will sell at a premium in the forward market against a currency with the higher interest rate.

C. International Cash Management Organization

The organization of the international cash management function may be centralized, decentralized, or a combination of both.

1. **Centralized Control** - Centralized control over international cash management gives relatively little autonomy to field office personnel. A company that operates overseas sales offices with limited personnel will typically centralize control of its treasury functions at its head office. A centralized function can result in economies of scale for services and lower a company's operating costs.

2. **Decentralized Control** - A company with relatively autonomous international subsidiaries is more likely to have a decentralized treasury structure. Here field personnel are responsible for delegated treasury functions and are typically required to submit management reports summarizing bank balances, loans, investments, and other indicators of performance. Headquarters personnel may make periodic visits to international offices to audit and train treasury staff.

3. **Combined** - Some large multinational companies have combined some of the features from both of the above structures and operate regional treasury centers. These regional centers are responsible for providing treasury services to specific subsidiaries within a designated geographic area.

III. CHARACTERISTICS OF INTERNATIONAL BANKING SYSTEMS

Each country's banking system is structured differently and has different regulations and capabilities, and offers different services.

A. Central Bank

The central bank or monetary authority of a country usually establishes the conditions under which both domestic and foreign banks can operate. Changes in these conditions and restrictions are occurring rapidly in many countries. In general, recent changes have tended to create more competition and to have a positive impact on the efficiency of all financial institutions operating within the country.

Many central banks perform functions similar to those of the U.S. Federal Reserve system, which operates the payments system, regulates banks, acts as lender of last resort, and controls the money supply.

B. Bank and Company Relationships

In many countries, banks are permitted to own minor or controlling ownership positions in corporations through equity investments. In the U.S., commercial banks are, by law, precluded from such corporate stock ownership.

C. Number of Banks

Foreign banking systems are often less fragmented than the U.S. system. In the U.S., there are thousands of independent financial institutions, ranging from those with extensive branch networks to those with a single location. In most other countries, the banking system is characterized by only a few banks operating nationwide.

D. Restrictions on Corporate Demand Deposit Accounts

In the U.S., legislation prevents payment of interest on corporate demand deposit accounts offered by banks (there are current legislative initiatives that could change or lift this restriction). In most other countries, banks pay interest on corporate demand deposit accounts with positive balances and charge interest on accounts with negative balances. This makes many of the cash management services offered by U.S. banks, such as zero-balance and sweep-accounts, unnecessary overseas.

E. Value Dating

Outside of the U.S., banks typically use value dating as compensation for services provided to their customers. Under a value dating system, the bank sets the dates upon which it grants credit for deposits or it debits the account for checks written.

- The forward value date is the date upon which the firm will be granted credit for deposited items. This practice is similar to the concept of determining availability for deposited items in the U.S. banking system.

- The back value date is the date upon which checks written on an account are debited from that account. For example, if a check is back valued, the date of the debit reflected on a customer's account will be earlier than the date the item was presented. Back value dating can also be applied to other services that result in a debit to a customer's account such as outgoing wire transfers.

Value dating policies may be negotiable depending upon the bank and the country.

F. Characteristics of Banks and Banking Systems in Some Other Countries

Banks and banking systems vary widely from country to country and generally are different from the U.S. banking system. Following are general overviews of the financial systems that exist in countries that are the major trading partners of the U.S.

1. **Canada** - Canada is the largest U.S. trading partner. It is joined with the U.S. and Mexico in the North American Free Trade Agreement (NAFTA). The characteristics of the Canadian banking system and other financial institutions include:

    *   The major financial institutions provide nationwide banking through their branches.

    *   The Canadian Payments Association (CPA) developed and operates the national clearing and settlement system. Typically, all deposits receive same-day availability. The CPA also is spearheading the introduction of the Large Value Transfer System, an electronic mechanism to handle large or time-sensitive national and international payments.

    *   Cross-border settlement between U.S. and Canadian banks is available via automated clearing house (ACH).

    *   Lockboxes are used less frequently in Canada. They are used primarily to reduce mail and processing float or for reductions in processing costs. Lockboxes have no impact on availability float since all deposits receive same-day availability.

    *   Canadian financial institutions offer a variety of electronic services, including support for electronic data interchange (EDI).

    *   Many Canadian financial institutions offer support for cross-border transactions such as U.S.-dollar check settlements via U.S.-dollar accounts in Canada or via U.S. Fed banks or branches.

2. **Mexico** - Recently, the Mexican government opened its financial industry to foreigners, and there are no longer any currency restrictions. There is a real-time electronic check clearing system called Sistema de Pagos Electronicos de Uso Ampliado (SPEUA). The National Automated Clearing House Association (NACHA) in the U.S. is working with Mexico to implement an international cross-border payments system among all NAFTA members.

3. **United Kingdom (UK)** - There are many similarities between the UK and U.S. banking and payment systems. Among these similarities are the following:

    *   The UK has a highly developed banking system that provides a full spectrum of financial and transactional services to customers in wholesale and retail markets.

    *   London, like New York, is one of the major financial centers of the world, and it features one of the largest international real-time, high-value clearing and settlement systems of the world: the Clearing House Automated Payment System (CHAPS). Beginning in 1999, CHAPS will be the major clearing system for the euro, enabling payments to be made both between parties within the UK and cross-border through its link to the Trans-European Automated Real-Time Gross Settlement Express Transfer System (TARGET). (See the information on the euro in the next section.)

- Payments systems in the UK parallel those in the U.S. Checks are the primary method of payment. However, there is increasing use of a wide range of electronic banking services by consumers, such as telephone banking, home banking, and an ACH-like system called the Bankers Automated Clearing Service (BACS).

There also are several aspects of the UK banking and payments system that appear similar to those in the U.S. but have some subtle differences. Among them are the following:

- The Bank of England (founded in 1694) performs a regulatory and supervisory role similar to that of the Federal Reserve, but unlike the Fed, the Bank of England does not operate the clearing system. Also, in its monetary role, the Bank of England was only recently (1997) granted authority to establish interest rates.

- Both the corporate and consumer banking systems have been historically dominated by only four major UK banks that operate the clearing system for England, Scotland, Wales, and Northern Ireland. Recently, a series of mergers among Building Societies, the UK equivalent of the U.S. mutual savings banks, have begun to challenge the dominant status of these four major UK clearing banks.

4. **Europe** - Northern European banks generally are efficient and offer a full array of electronic services. However, banking systems in such countries as Italy, Portugal, and Greece tend to be somewhat less efficient. Banking in Eastern Europe continues to evolve in conjunction with political reform efforts and the general trend toward market-driven economies. Traditional U.S. cash management services are typically unavailable in Eastern Europe or are in the early states of development.

The banking systems and financial markets will be dramatically affected by growing economic integration within Europe. One of the chief aims of EMU (Economic and Monetary Union) is the introduction of a single currency, the euro, in January 1999. In early May 1998, the Council of the European Union finalized the launch of EMU by officially naming the following 11 nations that will join the union and adopt irrevocable conversion rates for the euro in January 1999: Austria, Belgium, Finland, France, Germany, Ireland, Italy, Luxembourg, the Netherlands, Portugal and Spain. The UK has decided to defer its entry until at least 2002.

The European Central Bank (ECB), which was established in July 1998, will oversee a single monetary policy for all EMU members. Initially, the euro will be used primarily in capital markets by the central banks, commercial banks and corporations. Smaller companies and consumers will convert to the euro over a three-year period. Euro banknotes and coins, however, will not be released until January 1, 2002. The national currencies of participating countries will cease to be legal tender no later than July 1, 2002.

To encourage acceptance and use of the euro, new government-issued debt will be denominated in euros, as will operation of interbank, monetary, capital, and exchange markets. The effects of a transition to the euro will include:

- Elimination of currency exposures between the EMU countries

- Reduced transfer and foreign exchange transaction costs

- Consolidation of banking relationships

- Simplification of certain international cash management techniques such as pooling and netting. (These techniques are presented later in this chapter.)

- Reduced foreign exchange exposure, resulting in simplified exchange risk management

There will be four primary mechanisms for the settlement of euro payments and transfers:

- Beginning in January 1999, Trans-European Automated Real-Time Gross Settlement Express Transfer System (TARGET) will provide real-time settlement for cross-border payments, similar to the Fedwire in the U.S. The system will be used primarily for urgent, high value payments. An important function of TARGET is to enable central banks to mobilize liquidity around Europe in order to manage monetary policy objectives as determined by the ECB.

- Correspondent banking, the traditional clearing method, will likely remain the most common method of cross-border payment for many banks, primarily for low value, bulk payments.

- European network banks will continue to use their own networks and access local clearing systems directly.

- The ECU Bankers Association (EBA), an association of 49 major clearing banks, currently operates a net settlement system similar to the CHIPS settlement procedure in the U.S., but it is used primarily for financial, rather than commercial, transactions. This system is projected to convert to euro-denominated transactions by January 1999.

5. **Japan** - The Japanese banking system is highly developed, with many banks having extensive international operations or alliances throughout the world. The following are some characteristics of the Japanese financial system:

    - The Bank of Japan (BOJ) is Japan's central bank and performs many of the same activities as the Fed in the U.S. BOJ is responsible for implementing monetary policy, examining financial institutions, and serving as the lender of last resort. It also provides payment settlement through direct entries to the deposit accounts maintained by financial institutions.

    - The nucleus of the banking system is comprised of approximately 140 city and regional commercial banks. In addition, the Japanese post offices provide some financial services, similar to giros in Europe, including the receipt of funds for postal savings, insurance, and pension accounts.

    - Clearing of paper-based items in Japan is handled through local and regional clearing houses. The largest is the Tokyo Clearing House, which also facilitates operation of an automated clearing house system. Unlike the ACH system in the U.S., this system currently handles only credit transfers.

- The Zengin Data Telecommunications System (Zengin System) is the on-line network through which most domestic funds transfers are initiated. In 1990, the Zengin System went to a real-time basis and established a cap on intra-day net debit positions for each participating institution. Nichigin Net is the inter-bank settlement system operated by BOJ. Financial institutions that maintain accounts with BOJ are provided on-line access to initiate settlement transfers between accounts.

- The banking and financial markets are highly regulated, with both the Ministry of Finance and BOJ playing major roles. There are efforts underway to deregulate certain aspects of the financial marketplace, but involvement of foreign financial institutions remains somewhat limited.

IV. CHARACTERISTICS OF INTERNATIONAL PAYMENTS SYSTEMS

When describing international payments systems there are two important considerations to keep in mind. Different systems or methods are used for intra-country payments versus cross-border payments. Payments may be denominated in a country's local currency or the currency of another country. These issues have a significant impact on settlement procedures.

A. Paper-Based Payments Systems

International paper-based systems involve payment and clearing of checks, also referred to as drafts, within and between countries. There are several key issues in international check clearing. They include:

1. The check clearing process within a country varies significantly from country to country. Some countries have nationwide clearing, others do not. The clearing of checks may be accomplished by the central bank (as the Fed does in the U.S.), by several of the major banks acting as clearing agents, or by correspondent relationships between different banks.

2. The clearing of checks between countries (cross-border clearing) is often a slow and complicated process. Inter-country checks generally clear as collection items which must be presented back to the bank in the country where they are drawn. Settlement is typically accomplished through correspondent bank accounts. For smaller value items the drawee bank may replace the original check for one that can be cleared in the payee's country. This check is then returned to the payee's bank for deposit.

3. Some financial institutions offer specialized international check clearing services that speed up the process of collecting cross-border payments.

B. Electronic Payments Systems

Many countries offer different types of electronic systems for both corporate and consumer payments.

1.   **Company-to-Company Electronic Payments Systems** - Electronic payment of company obligations is more common in some areas of the world than it is in the U.S. The actual structure and operation of these payments systems vary from country to country, but they also have some common characteristics:

   • **Credit-Based Transactions** - Most company-to-company electronic payments are credit transactions, where the payor initiates a transfer of funds to the payee. In this sense, these payments are similar to ACH credits or Fedwire transactions in the U.S. The method by which a company accesses its bank to initiate payment varies widely by country, bank, and company. Generally, the payment initiation systems are provided by the banks to their customers on a proprietary basis.

   • **Transactions are Cleared Through Correspondent Balances** - The majority of electronic payments systems outside the U.S. are cleared through correspondent balances of the banks involved in the transfers. Between countries, this clearing is usually done bank-to-bank on a bilateral basis. Within a country, the clearing may be done on a bilateral basis, or through a netting system run by a few clearing banks. These systems are different from the Fedwire system in the U.S., where value is transferred by debits and credits to bank reserve balances at the Federal Reserve.

   • **Role of the Society for Worldwide Interbank Financial Telecommunications (S.W.I.F.T.)** - S.W.I.F.T. is an interbank telecommunications network that enables banks to send authenticated electronic messages in standard formats. These communications, initiated and received by member banks, cover a wide variety of international banking services. A company can request its bank to initiate a balance transfer or foreign payment through S.W.I.F.T. It should be noted that S.W.I.F.T. communications contain payment-related information but do not transfer value. The actual clearing and settlement of S.W.I.F.T. messages regarding the transfer of funds are accomplished through correspondent bank balances. Standardized S.W.I.F.T. messages have also been developed for other international service needs including balance reporting, letters of credit, foreign exchange transactions, and documentary collections.

2.   **Consumer Electronic Payments Systems** - The use of electronic payments systems by consumers is more common in many areas of the world than in the U.S. These types of payments include those from consumers to companies and governments, as well as consumer-to-consumer payments. As in the case of company-to-company payments, the structure and operation of the payment systems vary from country to country. Some of the most common systems and applications are as follows:

   • **Use of Giros** - Many European countries have giro systems which operate through their postal systems. Giro systems allow payments from one giro account to another using direct debits and credits. Payments from consumers to companies and to governments (for taxes) represent the bulk of payment volumes in these systems. Consumers use the giro system in place of checks for payment of their monthly bills and statements. In some countries, consumers access these systems via PCs, terminals, or telephone. Though these systems are primarily used for consumer initiated payments, there is experimental use of giros for corporate-to-corporate and corporate-to-consumer payments in some countries.

- **Debit Cards** - Debit cards outside the U.S. operate similarly to U.S. cards. As consumers use these cards for purchases, the funds are debited from their bank or giro account and credited to the seller's account.

- **Smart Cards** - These cards are similar to debit cards but contain a microchip with additional information and security protection. Smart cards may be used for prepaid value transactions, where the consumer prepays the bank, giro, or company issuing the card. The card then keeps track of purchases and any remaining balance.

V. INTERNATIONAL TRADE FINANCING METHODS

In the U.S., it is customary for a seller to check the credit standing of a buyer prior to selling on open account. Invoices are often sent with each shipment and included in a statement of amounts due at the end of the month. Exporting goods to a non-domestic buyer necessitates more credit risk protection, particularly for a new business relationship.

The most frequently used international trade payment mechanisms – open account, documentary collections, and letters of credit (L/C) – can be explained in terms of increasing levels of protection, complexity, and cost. Open account terms are the simplest and the least costly, but they offer the least protection. Documentary collections are more complex and costly and offer more protection to both parties. L/Cs are the most complex, costly, and secure vehicles for international trade. (Exhibit 15.4 shows the hierarchy of trade payment mechanisms.)

Regardless of the method of trade payment, the currency to be used must be agreed upon by the buyer and seller. Payment is generally specified in either the buyer's currency or the seller's currency, but it may be in a third currency if mutually acceptable to both parties.

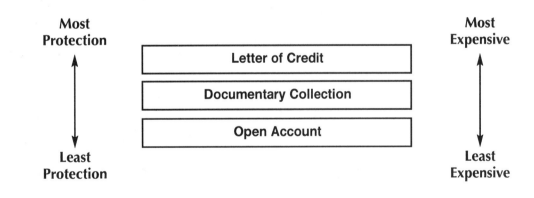

EXHIBIT 15.4
Hierarchy of International Trade Payment Methods

Most Protection — Least Protection

Letter of Credit

Documentary Collection

Open Account

Most Expensive — Least Expensive

A. Open Account

Under the open account method, the seller ships the merchandise and sends an invoice to the buyer. The buyer is then responsible for initiating payment to the seller in accordance with any agreed upon credit terms. The open account is the most frequently used method of payment for well established relationships.

B. Documentary Collections

Documentary collections are another method of payment used in international trade. The characteristics and uses of this method follow:

1. **Definition** - A documentary collection is a payment method that processes the collection of a draft and accompanying shipping documents through international correspondent banks. Instructions regarding the specifics of the transaction are contained in a collection letter or form which accompanies the documentation. It is the responsibility of the exporter to determine the specific instructions to be used in the collection letter.

2. **Role of Banks** - The banks involved in a documentary collection act only as collecting and paying agents and, unlike an L/C, assume no direct obligation for ensuring that payment will be made. Banks involved in these transactions may play the following roles:

   • **Remitting Bank** - The remitting bank is the seller's (exporter's) bank that prepares the collection letter and forwards documents to a correspondent bank in the buyer's (importer's) country.

   • **Collecting Bank** - The collecting bank is the remitting bank's correspondent and is responsible for contacting the buyer (importer), collecting the amount due, and releasing the documents as instructed.

3. **Collection Letter** - A collection letter specifies the exact procedures to be followed before shipping documents are released to the importer. The importer usually requires physical possession of the shipping documents in order to obtain the merchandise. Documents are typically released either against payment or acceptance as follows:

   • Documents against payment use a sight draft, which is a draft payable on demand, and require that the collecting bank receive full and final payment of the amount owed prior to releasing the documents.

   • Documents against acceptance use a time draft, which is a draft payable on a specified future date that must be accepted by the importer before the collecting bank may release documents. Upon maturity of the time draft, it is presented to the importer for payment.

4. **Payment** - Once full and final payment is received, the collecting bank transfers the funds to the remitting bank, as instructed, for payment to the exporter.

5. **Non-Payment or Non-Acceptance** - In the event of non-payment or non-acceptance, the exporter bears the risk and cost of re-marketing the goods to another buyer or, possibly, returning the merchandise. The exporter may have the collecting bank initiate formal action against the importer for non-performance. Exhibit 15.5 illustrates a documentary collection.

EXHIBIT 15.5

Illustration of a Documentary Collection

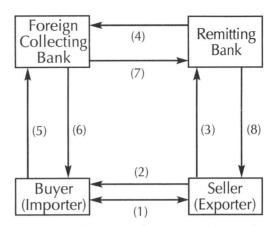

Step 1.   Buyer and seller agree to a sales contract requiring the use of a documentary collection.

Step 2.   The seller/exporter ships merchandise to the buyer/importer.

Step 3.   The seller/exporter delivers the draft and documents to the remitting bank.

Step 4.   The remitting bank forwards the documents and collection letter to the buyer/importer's bank, the foreign collecting bank.

Step 5.   The buyer/importer makes payment to the foreign collecting bank in the case of a sight draft, or accepts a time draft.

Step 6.   The foreign collecting bank releases the documents so that the buyer/importer may take delivery of the merchandise.

Step 7.   The foreign collecting bank transfers funds to the remitting bank.

Step 8.   The remitting bank pays the seller/exporter.

C. Letters of Credit (L/Cs)

An L/C is a document issued by a bank, guaranteeing the payment of a customer's draft up to a stated amount for a specified period provided certain conditions are met. An L/C substitutes a bank's credit for that of the buyer, virtually eliminating the seller's credit risk. L/Cs are a widely used method of payment for import and export shipments. L/Cs can also be used as a financing vehicle for international trade transactions.

1.   **Commercial L/C** - A commercial L/C is issued by a bank in relation to a trade transaction involving the domestic or international shipment of merchandise. It is the intended mechanism of payment and typically requires presentment of a draft, commercial invoice, and related shipping documents.

2.   **Documentary Nature of L/C** - It is important to realize that an L/C is documentary in nature. This means that a bank's role in an L/C transaction is the examination of documents, not the underlying merchandise. Since a bank deals solely with documents, it is the responsibility of the importer (buyer) to specify the documentation required for payment that will reasonably ensure their receipt of the exact merchandise ordered.

3.   **Role of Banks** - Banks may have the following roles in L/C transactions:

- **Issuing Bank** - The issuing bank is the buyer's (importer's) bank that issues the L/C in favor of the beneficiary (seller/exporter).

- **Advising Bank** - The advising bank advises the beneficiary of an L/C in its favor.

- **Negotiating Bank** - The negotiating bank examines the documents presented by the beneficiary, receives payment from the issuing bank, and pays the beneficiary. The advising and negotiating bank are often the same bank.

- **Confirming Bank** - If requested, the advising bank may add its confirmation to an L/C. In doing so, the confirming bank commits to the beneficiary that payment will be made if documents meet the terms and conditions of the L/C, regardless of the issuing bank's ability to pay. If an L/C is confirmed, the confirming bank will also be the negotiating bank.

Exhibit 15.6 illustrates a typical international commercial letter of credit transaction.

EXHIBIT 15.6

Illustration of a Letter of Credit Transaction (Sight Draft)

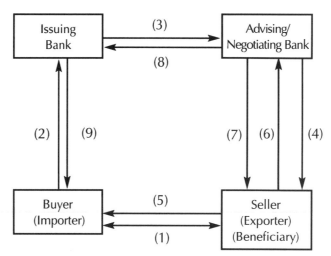

Step 1.   The buyer and the seller agree to a sales contract in which the buyer is required to open an L/C in favor of the seller.

Step 2.   The buyer chooses a bank in its country and opens an L/C in favor of the seller.

Step 3.   The issuing (buyer's) bank sends the L/C to a bank in the seller's country. The latter bank becomes the advising bank.

Step 4.   The advising bank sends details of the credit to the seller, who is the beneficiary of the credit.

Step 5.   The seller ships the merchandise to the buyer.

Step 6.   The seller presents the draft and documents to the advising/negotiating bank.

Step 7.   The advising/negotiating bank examines the documents and pays the seller if the documents meet the terms of the L/C.

(Continued)

Step 8.   The advising/negotiating bank sends the documents to the issuing bank and charges the issuing bank's account.

Step 9.   The issuing bank examines the documents, charges the buyer's account, and releases the documents to the buyer. With the documents, the buyer is able to claim the merchandise.

---

4.   **Commitment** - Most L/Cs are irrevocable, meaning that the L/C cannot be canceled nor amended without the agreement of all parties to the transaction. The parties that must agree are the buyer, beneficiary (seller), issuing bank, and, if the L/C is confirmed, the confirming bank.

5.   **Payment Timing** - Once conforming documentation has been presented, the L/C may provide for either immediate or deferred payment to the beneficiary (seller/exporter).

- When the L/C requires the presentment of a sight draft, which is a draft payable on demand, the negotiating bank pays the seller immediately, and is reimbursed by the issuing bank.

- The L/C may require presentment of a time draft which provides for payment at a future date. The use of a time draft is a way for the seller to provide credit terms to the buyer. The seller may be able to receive payment prior to maturity by discounting (selling for its discounted value) the time draft to a local bank.

- A deferred payment L/C provides for presentation of one or more sight drafts at specified dates in the future, and this sometimes extends over several years. When medium-term financing is provided for the export of capital goods, a deferred payment L/C may be used in conjunction with a term loan agreement.

6.   **Standby Letter of Credit** - A standby L/C is a variant of a commercial L/C. They are issued primarily by U.S. banks which are legally prohibited from issuing formal guarantees. Once issued, the standby L/C serves as a vehicle to ensure the financial performance of a bank's customer to a third-party beneficiary. Standby L/Cs typically require presentation of a sight draft and documentation that supports the beneficiary's claim of non-performance on the part of the issuing bank's customer. Standby L/Cs are frequently used as credit enhancement for commercial paper programs or to guarantee a bid tender or financial performance on a contract.

D. Other Trade Payment Methods

Other less frequently used international trade payment mechanisms include the following:

1.   **Cash Before Delivery (CBD)** - CBD is when the seller requires the total protection of receiving payment before shipment of goods.

2.   **Consignment** - Consignment involves the shipment of goods to a foreign agent where the exporter (seller) retains legal title to the goods. When the goods are sold by the agent, payment is due to the exporter and title transfers to the buyer. Regaining possession of unsold goods may be difficult and costly.

3.   **Barter** - Barter involves the direct exchange of goods or services between two end users without using money. It is most frequently used when funds cannot be repatriated.

4.   **Countertrade** - Countertrade is a method of payment used by companies that do not have access to sufficient hard currencies (internationally traded currencies) to pay for imports from other countries. For example, a U.S. exporter ships merchandise to the countertrading country and takes in exchange merchandise that can be sold elsewhere in the world for U.S. dollars.

5.   **Forfaiting** -Forfaiting is a specialized form of export financing which provides both short- and medium-term financing. The seller accepts a note from the buyer which may have a maturity of up to three years. The note can be discounted in a specialized market in London. It may be useful in situations where confirmed letters of credit are not available.

6.   **Trading Companies** - Trading companies are used when an exporter (seller) can also sell its products at a discount to an export trading company which, in turn, resells the products internationally.

E. Banker's Acceptances (BAs)

A BA is most often used to finance the import, export or domestic shipment of goods, but it can also be used to finance storage of properly titled goods. BAs are commonly, but not necessarily, used in conjunction with L/Cs requiring a time draft drawn on a bank.

A BA is a time draft on the face of which the drawee bank has written the word "accepted" over its signature. The date and place payable are also indicated. The bank accepting and agreeing unconditionally to pay the draft at a particular time and place is known as the acceptor.

By accepting the draft, the bank creates a BA indicating its commitment to pay the face amount of the draft at maturity. Through its acceptance of the payment risk, the bank creates a short-term negotiable instrument. Therefore a bank can fund a BA transaction by selling it to an investor or by holding the BA in its own portfolio.

1.   **Cost** - The cost of acceptance financing has two components: the discount rate (the rate earned by the investor) and the bank's acceptance commission.

2.   **Eligibility** -Most acceptance financing is done with eligible acceptances. An eligible BA is an acceptance that may be discounted at the Federal Reserve. To be eligible for discount, the acceptance may not have a maturity of more than 180 days. Eligible underlying transactions include the following:

- Import or export of goods

- Domestic storage transactions with documents conveying title attached

- Storage of readily marketable staples secured by warehouse receipts.

F. Trade Acceptances

A trade acceptance is another instrument that may be used in international transactions. It is similar to a BA except that it is typically drawn on and accepted by a company, usually the buyer (importer). It can be used to evidence a buyer's obligation to pay for purchased merchandise where the seller (exporter) is satisfied with the credit risk.

VI. INTERNATIONAL CASH MANAGEMENT ISSUES AND TECHNIQUES

A. Credit Management

Managing and evaluating credit can be more difficult in foreign countries where unsecured consumer credit is less prevalent and where rating agencies and credit information systems are less evolved. Whenever this is the case, companies generally require stricter credit terms.

B. Accounts Receivable Management

Companies typically are more careful about managing accounts receivable in foreign countries because defaulted receivables there are more difficult to collect than those in the U.S.

C. Cash Concentration

Companies concentrate cash internationally for the same reason they do domestically: to utilize cash more efficiently. However, international operations often necessitate employing other measures in addition to those used domestically, such as pooling and netting.

1. **Pooling** - In some European countries, banks offer a procedure known as pooling. In pooling, any excess funds in the accounts of a company or its subsidiaries may be used to offset any deficits in other accounts of the parent or its subsidiaries. This type of pooling arrangement typically is offered for a variety of currencies.

   - Pooling requires a company and all its subsidiaries to maintain their accounts at the same bank.

   - Credit facilities of some kind are usually required by the bank to support any negative balances in the pool.

   - Positive and negative balances may be aggregated each day for the calculation of interest earned or due. Normally, funds are not actually transferred; they are merely totaled for the purpose of calculating interest. This practice is known as notional pooling.

2. **Netting** - Netting is an internal company system designed to reduce the number of cross-border payments among units of a company through the elimination or consolidation of individual funds flows denominated in different currencies. Many countries impose restrictions on the use of netting systems, and formal approval may be required.

   - **Bilateral Netting** - In a bilateral netting system, purchases between two subsidiaries of the same company are netted against each other so that periodically – typically once a month – only the net difference is transferred. If the payments to be netted are in different currencies, the total due each subsidiary is converted to a common reference currency to determine the net amount due.

For example, subsidiaries of a multinational company, one located in France and another in Germany, hold payments until one or two regularly scheduled times during the month. Prior to the settlement date, the payments in both directions are totaled, the net due one of the subsidiaries determined, and a single transfer is scheduled.

- **Multilateral Netting** -This system is similar to bilateral netting but with more than two subsidiaries. Each subsidiary informs a central treasury management center of all planned cross-border payments. To determine netting transactions, the payments between all subsidiaries are converted into a common, reference currency. Payments are combined into fewer, but larger, transactions and each unit is informed prior to the settlement date of the net amount to pay or to be received in its own currency. The netting center makes the necessary foreign exchange conversions. Although multilateral netting is used primarily for intra-company transactions, some companies include third-party payments or receipts in their systems.

The mechanics of multilateral netting are illustrated in Exhibit 15.7.

EXHIBIT 15.7

Illustration of Multilateral Netting

Intercompany Cash Flows Before Netting

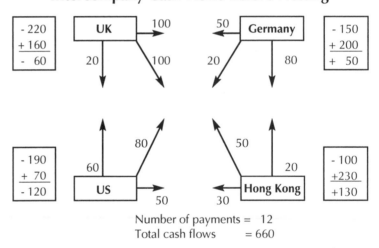

Number of payments = 12
Total cash flows = 660

Cash Flow with Multilateral Netting Center

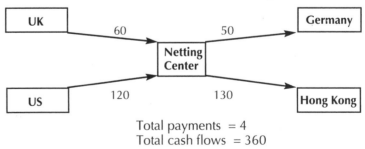

Total payments = 4
Total cash flows = 360

3.   **Benefits** - The benefits of netting include:

- Reduction of the number of foreign exchange transactions and cross-border wire transfers.

- Availability of more favorable foreign exchange rates for the larger foreign exchange trades resulting from consolidation.

- Improved cash forecasting for both the subsidiary and the parent as a result of the ability to pre-plan cross-border payments.

4.   **Costs** - There are setup and maintenance costs which must be considered when starting and operating a netting system.

D. Leading and Lagging

Netting systems may be used to implement leading and lagging. Leading and lagging involve making cross-border payments between subsidiaries either ahead of schedule (leading) or behind schedule (lagging). Liquidity is moved from one subsidiary to another. Leading can be helpful when a currency is expected to depreciate, while lagging will be used when the currency is expected to appreciate relative to the parent's home currency.

E. Reinvoicing

Reinvoicing is a method of centralizing the responsibility for monitoring and collecting international accounts receivable and more effectively managing the related foreign exchange exposure. A reinvoicing center is a company-owned subsidiary that buys the goods from an exporting subsidiary and resells the goods to an importing subsidiary. The exporting unit invoices and receives funds from the reinvoicing subsidiary in its own currency, while the importing unit is invoiced and pays funds to the reinvoicing subsidiary in its own currency. Although title to the goods passes through the reinvoicing center, usually the actual goods are shipped directly from the exporting subsidiary to the importing subsidiary. Establishing a reinvoicing center requires local government approval and negotiation on how the subsidiary will be taxed.

1.   **Benefits** - The benefits of a reinvoicing center include:

- Centralization of foreign exchange exposure in the reinvoicing center where it can be more effectively managed.

- Improvement in a company's worldwide short-term liquidity management by providing flexibility in inter-subsidiary payments. For instance, reinvoicing enables leading and lagging arrangements to be implemented easily, improves export trade financing and collections, reduces bank costs, and improves foreign exchange rates by enabling larger trades.

2.   **Costs** - Reinvoicing center expenses include physical location and administration costs as well as costs specifically associated with netting centers.

Reinvoicing is illustrated in Exhibit 15.8.

EXHIBIT 15.8
Illustration of Reinvoicing

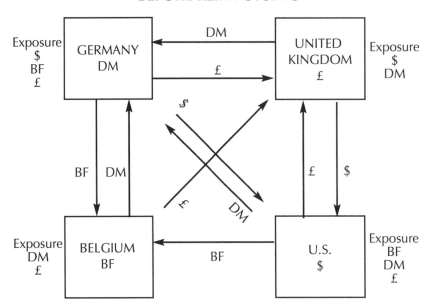

TRANSACTION EXPOSURES
BEFORE REINVOICING

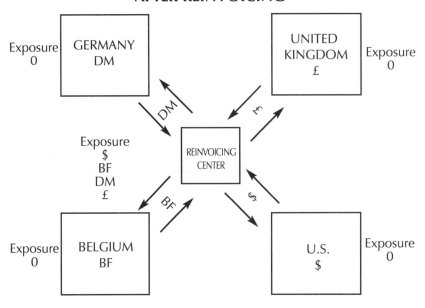

TRANSACTION EXPOSURES
AFTER REINVOICING

Management of foreign exchange exposure is now centralized in the reinvoicing center.

F. Internal Factoring

The purpose of an internal factoring center is similar to that of reinvoicing. Rather than taking actual title to the goods as with reinvoicing, the internal factoring unit buys accounts receivable from the exporting unit and collects from the importing unit. The benefits of internal factoring are the same as they are for reinvoicing.

G. Multi-Currency Accounts

Multi-currency accounts are a special arrangement between a bank and its corporate customer whereby the bank allows the customer to receive or make international payments in a range of currencies from a single account. The agreement generally specifies the following:

- The base currency in which the account will be denominated

- The portfolio of currencies that will be accepted

- The spread or margin over the spot rate that will be used for purposes of exchanging each currency back to the base currency

- The value date that will be applied to debits and credits for each transaction type and currency

H. Information Reporting Services

Major banks in Europe and Asia offer electronic reporting services that provide information on balances and previous day transaction detail. Such reporting services allow both local and international access. For example, the balances and debit and credit details for a Dutch subsidiary of a U.S. company can be reported to local management in the Netherlands as well as to the parent. Major international banks and third-party service providers can consolidate reporting by a company's banking network, both foreign and domestic operations, into a single daily report.

VII. INTERNATIONAL FINANCING, TAXES, AND OTHER CONSIDERATIONS

Export financing, export credit insurance, offshore financing alternatives, and tax implications are important considerations for a multinational company.

A. Export Financing

A critical issue for many companies selling internationally is how to finance their sales to foreign buyers. For U.S.-based companies, the primary sources of financing are commercial banks and the Export-Import Bank of the U.S.

1. **Commercial Banks** - Some commercial banks in the U.S. specialize in providing direct financing to the foreign buyers of U.S. exports.

2. **Export-Import Bank of the U.S.** -The Export-Import Bank of the U.S. (Eximbank) is an independent agency of the U.S. government established to finance and guarantee payment for U.S. exports. The Eximbank is directed by its corporate charter to:

- Develop export financing programs that are competitive with those offered by other countries

- Ensure that financing or repayment guarantees are made to borrowers with a reasonable capacity to repay

- Enhance or supplement financing offered by private commercial banks

3. **Export Credit Insurance** - A common method of insuring payment of foreign accounts receivables is through the purchase of export credit insurance. This insurance is provided by the Eximbank and by certain private insurers. Export insurance can cover both political (sovereign) risk and commercial risk. Insurance coverage is available for shipments to almost every country with which the U.S. has diplomatic relations. The insurance obtained through the Eximbank is backed by the U.S. government.

    The Eximbank's programs also include a working capital program aimed at small businesses, a loan guarantee program to encourage private-sector loans, and a direct loan program used in situations in which foreign competitors receive government subsidized financing.

B. Financing International Operations

Offshore financing involves raising funds outside a company's home country. Companies may finance outside their country for the following reasons:

1. **Diversification of Funding** - A company may want to diversify its funding sources rather than depend on one market for several reasons:

    - Too much debt in a particular market may saturate investors' desire for a company's debt and therefore raise the cost of borrowing additional amounts.

    - In times of tight credit, it is helpful to have relationships with a number of different lenders.

2. **Hedging in Foreign Currencies** - Liabilities in a foreign currency can hedge a similar term asset in the same currency. For example, if a U.S. company had accounts receivable denominated in British pounds, it may consider short-term debt denominated in pounds. In this case, if foreign currency-denominated assets depreciate, liabilities denominated in the same foreign currency depreciate as well, thereby minimizing foreign exchange translation exposure. (See Chapter 14, Financial Risk Management.)

3. **Lower Borrowing Rates for Parent Company** - A U.S. parent company may be able to borrow in a foreign currency at a lower borrowing rate than its U.S. borrowing rate, even after hedging.

4. **Lower Borrowing Rate for Foreign Subsidiaries** - An international subsidiary may be able to borrow in its local market from one of its local banks at lower rates than it can through its parent company.

5. **Tax Advantages** - There may be tax advantages available in the subsidiary's home country.

Companies may also establish offshore financing subsidiaries to obtain funding and benefit from favorable tax regulations. A company may fund the needs of a number of subsidiaries in different countries through its offshore finance company, thus taking advantage of lower rates by borrowing in large amounts. Companies can also invest in short-term foreign financial instruments through offshore subsidiaries.

C. Tax Considerations

Multinational companies must deal with tax codes in all the countries in which they have operations or sales. Some of the more important considerations include:

1. **Foreign Tax Credits** - A U.S. company's income derived from its foreign operations is typically included in its tax return to determine the amount of the U.S. income tax due. If this foreign source income has already been subject to foreign income taxes, the same income is being taxed twice.

    To relieve the effect of this double taxation, the U.S. tax law allows a U.S. company a dollar-for-dollar tax credit against its total U.S. income tax liability for those foreign income taxes paid by the parent and its subsidiaries. This credit is called the foreign tax credit. It is allowed only for those foreign taxes that are income taxes and and do not exceed U.S. tax rates.

2. **Foreign Tax Planning** - The complexity of the law regarding the taxation of non-domestic income makes it important for treasury personnel to work with tax experts.

3. **Tax-Advantaged Business Centers** - To attract multinational businesses and related employment opportunities, a number of countries offer tax incentives for subsidiaries that perform certain administrative and financial functions.

D. Legal and Ethical Issues

In many countries, "commissions" or "fees," which would be considered bribes in the U.S., are deeply ingrained in the commercial culture. However, the Foreign Corrupt Practices Act forbids U.S. companies to engage in such practices.

Questions

These chapter questions are to test and review the information in the text and are not examples of CCM examination questions, nor are they in the examination format.

Answers can be found at the back of the book on pgs. 385-386.

1.   Why is international cash management becoming increasingly important for companies?

2.   What are some of the key characteristics in which international banking systems differ?

3.   What is value dating?

4.   What must a payee do if it receives a check drawn in a different country?

5.   How do payment practices vary outside the U.S.?

6.   What is pooling, as applied in non-U.S. banking systems?

7.   What is a multi-currency account?

8.   What are the major benefits of using a netting system?

9.   What is a reinvoicing center, and how does it differ from internal factoring?

10.   What risk is eliminated by the use of a letter of credit?

11.   What is an irrevocable letter of credit?

12.   What is a standby letter of credit?

13.   What is the major difference in the role of the banks under a documentary collection as opposed to a letter of credit?

14.   What is counter-trade?

15.   What is the maximum maturity for a banker's acceptance to remain eligible for discount at the Federal Reserve?

16.   What is the Eximbank?

17.   Why do companies use offshore financing?

CHAPTER **16**

Relationship Management

OVERVIEW

This chapter describes the objectives of relationship management. It explains the various issues involved in selecting financial service providers. It explains the role of account analysis in financial institution compensation and the different methods of compensating financial institutions.

LEARNING OBJECTIVES

Upon completion of this chapter the reader should know:

1. The objectives of relationship management

2. How companies select and evaluate financial institutions and other service providers

3. What an account analysis statement is and how it is used in relationship management

4. How to perform collected balance and earnings allowance calculations

5. The options for compensating financial institutions

KEY CONCEPTS

1. Objectives of Relationship Management

2. Selection and Evaluation of Financial Institutions

3. Account Analysis Statement

4. Collected Balance and Earnings Allowance Calculation

5. Financial Institution Compensation

Essentials of Cash Management 6 • **311**

OUTLINE

I.   OBJECTIVES OF RELATIONSHIP MANAGEMENT

The objectives of relationship management generally include:

- **Access to Credit** - A company requires access to credit facilities to meet short-term working capital needs and longer-term financing requirements.

- **Access to Non-Credit Services** - A company requires access to services such as cash management, investments, trust, international services, and risk management.

- **Management of Costs and Quality** - A company selects and monitors financial institutions and other service providers to ensure that the relationship is cost-effective, and that services provided are consistent with agreed upon standards.

- **Monitoring Risks** - A company monitors the risk of a disruption in a financial institution relationship arising from changes in management policy, merger, acquisition, or failure.

- **Development of a Partnership Approach** - A partnership approach means that the relationship is mutually beneficial.

II.   SERVICE PROVIDER SELECTION

Consolidation and specialization among financial institutions and other service providers have made the selection process critical for many companies. Consolidation reduces the number of providers in certain product areas. Specialization raises the importance of matching a given company's needs with a particular provider's strengths.

A. Selection Process

1. **Informal** - Selecting a financial institution or service provider does not always involve a formal process. Sometimes a company may already have established a relationship with a particular service provider or financial institution or may have targeted specific candidates. In such cases, the selection process does not involve a formal written proposal.

2. **Request for Information** - In some cases, a Request for Information (RFI) may be used in the selection process. An RFI is often used by a company simply to confirm that use of a current provider of a service is justified, or to narrow the field of potential providers before issuing a Request for Proposal (RFP). An RFI is also used to solicit ideas from service providers on how to solve a particular business or operational problem.

3. **A Request for Proposal** - A Request for Proposal is a formal document prepared by a company which outlines its objectives and service requirements. An RFP can be used to obtain bids for everything ranging from one particular service to a company's entire relationship. By law, some government entities are required to prepare RFPs on a periodic basis, usually every three to five years, to ensure that they are receiving comparable services at competitive prices. Many private sector companies also periodically prepare RFPs for similar reasons. Outside consultants are sometimes used to assist in the preparation of RFPs and evaluation of responses. There are now standard formats which allow for electronic submission and comparison of proposals. TMA and the Bank Administration Institute (BAI) have published standard RFP formats for common banking services.

   A typical RFP requests the following:

   • Background information on the provider

   • Objectives to be met

   • Summary of the proposed solution

   • Service descriptions

   • Service features and benefits

   • The provider's commitment to support and enhance services

   • A price schedule and a cost/benefit analysis

   • Pro forma account analysis statement (financial institutions only)

   • Sample service commitments or agreements

   • Customer references

B. Selection Criteria

Selecting service providers involves assessing capabilities based on the following criteria:

- Knowledge of a specific industry or business

- Responsiveness to questions asked in the selection process and understanding of the company's needs and objectives

- Quality of customer service

- Pricing of services

- Willingness to provide credit on flexible terms and at competitive rates

- Ability to provide financial advice or consulting services

- Financial strength of service provider

- Commitment to a company, industry, or service

- Quality and expertise of relationship managers and technical specialists

- Ability to customize services and develop new services

- Geographic and other convenience considerations

- Ability to meet future needs of the company

III. ISSUES IN FINANCIAL INSTITUTION RELATIONSHIP MANAGEMENT

When assessing the suitability of a financial institution, companies consider the following factors:

A. Creditworthiness

The creditworthiness of financial institutions is a concern of corporate treasurers and cash managers – particularly since the 1980s when some financial institutions failed or were acquired in lieu of being liquidated. Failures and acquisitions affect access to credit and other services that are crucial to a company's business operations.

The ratings that agencies give financial institutions have become increasingly important. Ratings are a proxy for creditworthiness, and a number of agencies offer ratings services. Some offer ratings only, while others also offer detailed backup reports that provide both quantitative financial analyses and qualitative assessments of management. (See Chapter 14, Short-Term Investments.)

Among the most common methods of rating depository financial institution strength is the CAMELS rating, a system widely used by regulators. CAMELS is the acronym for Capital Adequacy, Asset Quality, Management Capability, Earnings, Liquidity, and Sensitivity to

Market Risk. Although banks are prohibited from disclosing their CAMELS ratings, rating agencies such as Standard & Poor's and Moody's evaluate the same factors in their assessment processes.

- **Capital Adequacy** - A financial institution is expected to maintain capital commensurate with the nature and extent of its risks and the ability of management to identify, measure, monitor, and control these risks.

- **Asset Quality** - The asset quality rating reflects the existing and potential credit risk associated with the loan and investment portfolio, other assets, and off balance-sheet items.

- **Management Capability** - This rating reflects the capability of the board of directors and management, in their respective roles, to identify, measure, monitor, and control the risks of an institution's activities and to ensure the institution's safe, sound, and efficient operation in compliance with applicable laws and regulations.

- **Earnings** - This rating indicates the level of earnings, earning trends, and sustainability. A bank's profitability, asset quality, and credit risk management can affect its earnings ratings.

- **Liquidity** - This aspect of the rating pertains to current and future levels of liquidity in comparison with funding needs. It also indicates the adequacy of funds management practices relative to an institution's size, complexity, and risk profile.

- **Sensitivity to Market Risk** - This is the degree to which changes in interest rates, foreign exchange rates, commodities prices, or equities prices can adversely affect a financial institution's earnings or capital.

B. Number of Relationships

Typically, the number and nature of financial institution relationships a company maintains depends on the following considerations:

- **Credit Accessibility/Adequacy** - Many companies establish multiple relationships to ensure that they have adequate credit facilities or to diversify service providers.

- **Costs** - There are internal and external costs for each financial institution relationship, resulting in an incentive to optimize the number of relationships. There has been a trend among large companies toward fewer financial institution relationships.

- **Strategic Implications** - Each institution should serve a purpose in the company's business strategy. Because of increasing financial institution consolidation and specialization, there is a trend toward establishing and maintaining relationships based on a particular need.

- **Relative Strength and Capabilities** - When a company has multiple financial institution relationships, often one is designated a lead institution. There may be different lead institutions for credit and other services.

C. Negotiation and Pricing

Negotiation plays an important part in managing relations with financial institutions, particularly since financial institutions have developed more sophisticated methods for measuring relationship profitability.

For example, pricing of loans is often based on interdependent factors such as the cost of funds, risk, total loans committed and outstanding, service fees, deposit balances, and the range of other services used. Likewise, pricing of services is often based on such factors as business strategy, volume, customization, exception handling requirements, costs of providing the service, deposit balances, operational overhead, and other services used.

D. Relationship Documentation

The important documents associated with the establishment of a financial institution relationship include:

1.   **Account Resolution** - This document is the basic account authorization and is usually a board of directors' resolution. It specifies:

     - What functions can be performed by specific individuals or job titles, authorized signers on the account, and the liability of each party.

     - The scope and limitations of the relationship. It may be very general or very specific regarding actions that the financial institution may take on behalf of the company.

The resolution can be a standard one used by all commercial customers of a given financial institution, or it can be customized for a given company. Some companies have developed their own standard resolutions that they use for all their financial institution relationships, and their banks' use of the company standard is a matter of negotiation.

2.   **Signature Cards** - Financial institutions require companies to furnish signatures of authorized signers or specimens of facsimile or computerized signatures.

3.   **Terms and Conditions** - Financial institutions may provide terms and conditions to companies when depository accounts are established. This document will detail the responsibilities of the bank and the account holders in the maintenance of accounts. Some of the important areas contained in the document may include information on funds availability, timeframes during which errors must be reported, and the bank's right of offset against accounts related to fees owed. These terms are amended from time to time, and notice is generally mailed out with account statements.

4.   **Service Agreements** - Financial institutions or companies may require service agreements. The agreements may be standardized or customized. The elements of a service agreement can include:

     - Operational policies and procedures including the detailed processing requirements for the service, information needs, and people who are authorized to make changes

     - Performance standards that define agreed upon levels of service performance and quality

- Compensation policies, including pricing, method of payment, payment frequency, excess/deficit balance arrangements, contract length, and adjustments

- Liability clauses defining responsibilities for specified risks

- Terms and conditions

E. Audit and Control

The audit and control issues facing a company in managing its relationships with financial institutions include the following:

- Establishing and updating policies and procedures for opening accounts that cover such matters as:

    - Approval required for opening accounts
    - Corporate resolution(s)
    - Individuals authorized to open accounts or contract for services
    - Individuals authorized as signatories

- Timely reconciliation of account statements and timely reporting of problems and exceptions. (Under UCC4, a company has 30 days to report any unauthorized activities. This timeframe can be extended by agreement between both parties.)

- A clear separation of transaction initiation, accounting, and reconciliation duties

- Maintenance of account documentation and record keeping, including corporate resolutions, contracts for services, and signatories on accounts

- Tracking of unresolved discrepancies

F. Performance Measurement and Evaluation

Service quality is a very important aspect of relationships with financial institutions. An important task for a company is to determine exactly what quality standards it wants and what error rates are reasonable for the various services. The company's performance expectations should be based on the service levels stipulated in its agreements with the bank. Two of the most common types of performance measurement techniques are report cards and relationship reviews.

1. **Report Cards** - A report card is a tool companies use to obtain a quantitative rating of a bank's level of service and responsiveness to problems. Criteria commonly found in report cards include:

- Number of errors by service

- Reporting times for information services

- Responsiveness to questions

- Timeliness of error resolution

- Effectiveness of personnel

Companies prepare report cards monthly, quarterly, or annually. Some companies that deal with many financial institutions and other service providers rank them by their ability to meet the companies' quality criteria on a service-by-service basis.

2. **Relationship Review** - A relationship review is another procedure companies use to qualitatively assess the service levels and personnel responsiveness. Reviews can be either formal or informal. Formal reviews typically involve a quarterly, semi-annual, or annual meeting of the senior management representatives of both parties. Informal reviews typically involve weekly or monthly contacts by individuals who are responsible for the day-to-day management of the relationship.

   Financial institutions also initiate relationship reviews by preparing summaries of services, fees, error rates, and other relationship information. Relationship reviews also enable financial institutions and companies to discuss future strategies and needs.

   The BAI has developed standards for measuring performance quality in cash management services.

IV. FINANCIAL INSTITUTION COMPENSATION AND ACCOUNT ANALYSIS

A. Relationship Approach

Mutual success in every long-term relationship involves the accommodation of both parties. The factors that increase the mutual benefit and profitability of the relationship include:

- Open and frequent two-way communications

- Regular and timely feedback

- Clear expectations as established by agreements and legal contracts

- Fair compensation of the financial institution by the company, and fair pricing of services by the financial institution

- Complete disclosure by both parties of information essential to the success and ethical basis of the relationship

B. Account Analysis

The account analysis statement is a paper or electronic report a bank provides to its commercial customers specifying services provided, volumes processed, and charges assessed. It is essentially an invoice for services provided. However, banks often use varying terminology in describing these services. Services and fees can be detailed and itemized, or bundled into a single line item, or some combination of the two. Fee structures are varied and complex, as are the account analysis formats banks use to report them.

1. **TMA Account Analysis Standard** - In 1987, the Treasury Management Association (TMA) developed a standard format for account analysis that included a standard set of service codes. The latest version of the standards was published in 1998.

    The current TMA standard account analysis consists of sections which provide:

    - Customer information

    - Balance and compensation information

    - Rate information

    - Service information

    - Adjustment detail

    - Summary of accounts

    - Optional historic balance and compensation information

2. **TMA Service Codes** - The six-character alphanumeric TMA service codes provide standard, uniform references and terms for identifying, describing, and reporting bank services and associated charges. By simplifying and organizing the varied and complex terminology often used to identify bank services, the codes also help resolve errors in volume and pricing. Examples of the TMA service code product families (indicated by the first two characters of the service code) are:

    - **Lockbox Services (05)** - This product family includes services associated with whole-sale and retail lockbox processing and covers document handling, data capture, and programming as well as lockbox deposit reporting and information delivery.

    - **Depository Services (10)** - This product family includes services associated with the processing of coin and currency, encoded and unencoded check deposits, branch and vault deposits, supplies of coin and currency, and services related to domestic collections and return item processing. It also includes deposit reconciliation services, reports, and software.

    - **Paper Disbursement Services (15)** - This product family includes services associated with the issuance, control, and processing of checks and drafts paid against an account, controlled disbursement, positive pay, and payable through draft services. It also includes check inquiries and stop payments, returned checks, teller services, check sorting, microfilming and retention, and disbursement information reporting and software.

    - **General ACH Services (25)** - This product family includes services associated with the origination and receipt of ACH transactions, ACH input processing, ACH activity reporting, master file maintenance, ACH returns and exception processing, and ACH software.

3. **ASC X12 822 Account Analysis Format** - The American National Standards Institute (ANSI) has developed a standardized format (ASC X12 822 Customer Account Analysis) for financial institutions to use in sending account analysis statements to companies electronically. The ASC X12 822 transaction set can accommodate the TMA Standardized Account Analysis format and incorporates TMA service codes.

4. **Account Analysis Terminology** - Common terms used in account analysis statements include:

    - **Service Charges** - The explicit fees or prices charged for services provided by a financial institution. Service charges are usually expressed in the form of a per item or per unit price. The unit price is multiplied by the volume.

    - **Average Net Ledger Balance** - The sum of the daily ending ledger balances (both positive and negative) divided by the number of days in the analysis period. Balances are net of current period adjustments.

    - **Average Float Balance** - The sum of the daily dollar amount of items in the process of collection divided by the number of days in the analysis period.

    - **Average Collected Balance** - The sum of the daily ending collected balances (both positive and negative) divided by the number of days in the analysis period.

    - **Reserve Requirement Balances** - Non-interest-bearing deposits that must, by law, be maintained by financial institutions at the Federal Reserve. The reserve requirement is one of the key components of U.S. monetary policy. (See Chapter 3, The U.S. Financial Environment.) For compensation purposes, a financial institution may use a reserve percentage other than that which is required by the Federal Reserve.

    - **Earnings Allowance Rate (EAR)** - The rate used to calculate the earnings allowance. While the method of determining this rate varies by financial institution, the most commonly-used measure is the 90-day T-bill rate. If a bank utilizes a reserve-adjusted EAR, the impact of the reserve requirement is included in the EAR calculation. (The examples in this book do not use reserve-adjusted EAR.)

    - **Investable Balance** - Balance on which the earnings allowance rate is applied. This value can be either positive or negative. A negative balance indicates a shortage of investable funds. Some banks calculate the investable balance as the average collected balance reduced by the reserve requirements balance. Other banks reduce the EAR by the reserve requirement so that the investable balance equals the average collected balance. (In the examples in this book, the EAR is not reduced by the reserve requirement.)

    - **Earnings Allowance** - The total allowance which can be used to offset service charges incurred during the period. It is calculated by multiplying the collected balances (adjusted for the reserve requirement) by the earnings allowance rate for the period.

5. **Earnings Allowance Calculation** - The formula for converting collected balances into the earnings allowance is:

$$\frac{\text{Earnings}}{\text{Allowance}} = \frac{\text{Collected}}{\text{Balances}} \times \left(1 - \frac{\text{Reserve}}{\text{Requirement}} \right) \times \left(\frac{\text{Earnings Allowance}}{\text{Rate}} \times \frac{\text{Days in Month}}{365} \right)$$

$$EA = CB \times (1 - RR) \times \left(EAR \times \frac{D}{365} \right)$$

Where:

EA = Earnings allowance
CB = Actual collected balances
RR = Reserve requirement
EAR = Earnings allowance rate
D = Number of days in the month

Note: Some banks use the earnings allowance rate divided by 12 instead of using the actual number of days to determine this monthly calculation.

An example of the earnings allowance calculation is provided in Exhibit 16.1.

EXHIBIT 16.1
Earnings Allowance Calculation Example

Assumptions:

Average ledger balance	$250,000
Deposit float	$30,000
Reserve requirement	10%
Earnings allowance rate	5%
Service charges for the month	$1,000
Days in month	30

Average Collected Balance Calculation:

Average ledger balance	$250,000
Less: deposit float	($ 30,000)
Equals: average collected balance	$220,000

$$\frac{\text{Earnings}}{\text{Allowance}} = \frac{\text{Collected}}{\text{Balances}} \times (1 - \text{Reserve Requirement}) \times \left(\frac{\text{Earnings}}{\text{Allowance Rate}} \times \frac{\text{Days in Month}}{365} \right)$$

$$EA = CB \times (1 - RR) \times \left(EAR \times \frac{D}{365} \right)$$

$$= \$220{,}000 \times (1 - .10) \times \left(.05 \times \frac{30}{365} \right) = \$220{,}000 \times .90 \times .0041 = \$811.80$$

The answer above assumes that intermediate calculations are rounded as shown.

If the current service charges are $1,000, but the amount of earnings allowance is only $811.80, the company did not keep sufficient collected balances on deposit to cover the cost of services over the period. In effect, the company has a compensation deficit of $188.20 which is owed to the financial institution.

6. **Calculation of the Collected Balances Required** - The collected balances required is the daily average balance needed to offset service charges for the current analysis period. The formula for this computation is:

Collected Balances Required $= \dfrac{\text{Monthly Service Charges, Fees, or Costs}}{\left(\dfrac{\text{Earnings Allowance Rate}}{} \times \dfrac{\text{Days in Month}}{365}\right) \times (1 - \text{Reserve Requirement})}$

$$CB = \frac{SC}{\left(EAR \times \dfrac{D}{365}\right) \times (1 - RR)}$$

Where:
CB = Collected balances required for services
SC = Service charges, fees, or costs
EAR = Earnings allowance rate
RR = Reserve requirement
D   = Number of days in the month

Note: Some banks use the earnings credit rate divided by 12 instead of using the actual number of days to determine this monthly calculation.

An example of the collected balances required calculation is provided in Exhibit 16.2.

EXHIBIT 16.2
Collected Balances Required Calculation

A company uses services with charges that total $10,000 per month. The earnings allowance rate is 5%. The reserve requirement is 10%. Assuming a 30-day month, the average collected balances required to compensate the financial institution for the services used is as follows:

$$\text{Collected Balances Required} = \frac{\text{Monthly Service Charges, Fees, or Costs}}{\left(\text{Earnings Allowance Rate} \times \dfrac{\text{Days in Month}}{365}\right) \times (1 - \text{Reserve Requirement})}$$

$$CB = \frac{SC}{\left(ECR \times \dfrac{D}{365}\right) \times (1 - RR)}$$

$$= \frac{\$10,000}{\left(.05 \times \dfrac{30}{365}\right) \times (1-.10)} = \frac{\$10,000}{(.0041 \times .90)} = \frac{\$10,000}{.0037} = \$2,702,703$$

The answer above assumes that intermediate calculations are rounded as shown.

Note: If $1.00 is used as the service charge in the above formula, the balance multiplier is calculated. This number, 270.27, multiplied by the service charges, gives the collected balances required to pay for services.

C. Financial Institution Compensation Practices

Compensation practices vary among financial institutions. Some of the principal features include:

- **Compensation for Excess Collected Balances** - If a company has collected balances in excess of the amount required for compensation, interest cannot be paid on the balances according to Regulation Q. (See Chapter 4, Payments System, for a discussion of Regulation Q.) Policies vary on how financial institutions treat the excess. Institutions may or may not allow these excesses to be carried forward to future periods.

- **Collection of Deficit Service Charges** - Deficit service charge amounts are collected by the financial institution either by direct debit of a customer's account or by invoicing the customer.

- **Calculation of Earnings Allowance** - Most financial institutions calculate the earnings allowance on collected balances net of reserve requirements (net collected balances). Some apply the EAR to the monthly average net collected balance. Others apply it to the daily net collected balance. If it is applied to the daily amount, this may result in a borrowing rate being charged on days when there is a negative net collected balance.

- **Basis for Compensation** - Accounts may be considered individually or on a combined basis for compensation. If accounts are combined, all balances are averaged together. This approach is helpful for a company that has excess balances in some accounts but deficit balances in others. By combining the balances for purposes of compensation, overall service charges can be reduced.

- **Analysis Consolidation** - A company that has multi-state locations may use a financial institution that has facilities in each of the states. In some cases, the financial institution will prepare a combined account analysis for all of the company's accounts in all states. The practice of preparing a combined account analysis statement may become more common as interstate branching increases.

D. Comparing Service Charges

Companies compare financial institution service charges both during the initial selection process and during periodic relationship reviews. Service charge comparisons are difficult to make for the following reasons:

- Financial institutions have different pricing strategies.

- Service charges may be bundled or unbundled. Bundling is the practice of charging for a group of related services. Unbundling is charging individually for each service used. For example, with controlled disbursement, one provider may have all charges combined in a single per item price. Another provider may have a charge for each check paid, one for account reconciliation services, another for reporting the amount of checks clearing each day, and another for funding the account. As a result, to make valid comparisons between providers it is necessary to know all the service charge components that make up a service. Some companies rebundle unbundled prices in order to facilitate comparison of total charges.

- Prices may vary depending on the level of service provided to a company. Some services or agreement provisions can influence bank compensation in ways that do not show up on a schedule of service charges. These include earnings allowance for balances, deficient balance fees, and availability schedules.

E. Fee versus Balance Compensation

Financial institutions allow companies to pay for services in fees, collected balances, or by combining both. The advantages and disadvantages of each method vary depending on whether they are viewed from a company or a financial institution perspective.

1. **Fee Compensation: Company Perspective** - Among the reasons companies favor fee compensation are:

    - **Opportunity Cost** - A company can generally earn more interest on its investments than it can obtain in earnings allowance on net collected balances. The primary reasons for this are the deduction for the reserve requirement when balance compensation is calculated and the fact that the EAR is typically tied to short-term investment instruments with lower rates.

- **Explicit Cost Control** - Fees can be budgeted and compared with other costs, while balances are not as directly comparable.

2. **Fee Compensation: Financial Institution Perspective** - Financial institutions often favor fee compensation for the following reasons:

   - **Capital Requirements** - Because deposit balances increase the liabilities on a financial institution's balance sheet, they can lead to a need for additional capital to meet regulatory or other requirements.

   - **Annuity Factor** - Compared to interest income from loans, fees from services are a recurring – and generally lower risk – source of earnings for a financial institution.

3. **Balance Compensation: Company Perspective** - Factors favoring balance compensation for a company include:

   - **Transaction Balance Levels** - Daily transaction requirements or unanticipated deposits often result in some collected balances in deposit accounts. If a company's concentration system does not mobilize all of these funds, the collected balances can be used for compensation.

   - **Relationship Considerations** - Some financial institutions price loans and other services more favorably if collected balances are maintained.

   - **Soft Dollar Budgeting** - Balance compensation is not as visible as fees for budgeting purposes.

   - **Differential Charges for Fee Compensation** - Some financial institutions' preference for deposit balances is so strong that they charge less if services are paid in balances rather than fees.

4. **Balance Compensation: Financial Institution Perspective** - The factors prompting financial institutions to favor balance compensation include:

   - **Funding Strategies** - Some financial institutions' strategy involves attracting deposits to fund their loans and investments.

   - **Potential Investment Returns** - Because of the spread between the EAR it pays and the investment rates earned, services may be more profitable to a financial institution when paid in balances rather than fees.

5. **Compensation by Both Fees and Balances** - If collected balances can be used as the compensation base with any deficiencies paid in fees, a company can maximize the value of transaction balances and may reduce its overall service costs.

Questions

These chapter questions are to test and review the information in the text and are not examples of CCM examination questions, nor are they in the examination format.

Answers can be found at the back of the book on pgs. 386-389.

1. What are the major objectives of relationship management?

2. What are some of the criteria for selecting service providers?

3. What are the six components commonly used to measure a depository financial institution's strength?

4. Why does a company seek to optimize the number of financial institutions with whom it has relationships?

5. What are the major documents associated with the establishment of a relationship with a financial institution?

6. What are the major audit and control issues regarding managing financial institution relationships?

7. What types of performance are commonly graded on a service provider report card?

8. What are the key factors in ensuring a successful relationship between a company and its financial institutions?

9. What is an account analysis?

10. What are some of the basic product families of TMA Service Codes for account analysis?

11. A company uses services with charges that total $4,000 per month. The bank's earnings allowance rate is 6% and the reserve requirement is 10%. Assuming a 30-day month, what is the average collected balance required to compensate the bank for services used?

12. The following information is provided:

Average ledger balance	$100,000
Deposit float	19,000
Reserve requirement	10%
Earnings Allowance Rate	6%
Service charges for the month	$650
Days in the month	30

    Is the earnings allowance sufficient to cover the service charges?

13. What is bundling of service charges?

14. How may financial institutions be compensated?

15. What are the major factors favoring fee compensation to a financial institution from the company perspective?

ACRONYMS

ABA - American Bankers Association or American Bar Association

ACH - Automated Clearing House

AICPA - American Institute of Certified Public Accountants

ANSI - American National Standards Institute

ASC - Accredited Standards Committee

ATM - Automated Teller Machine

BA - Bankers Acceptance

BACS - Bankers Automated Clearing Service

BAI - Bank Administration Institute

BEY - Bond Equivalent Yield

BOJ - Bank of Japan

CAMELS - Capital, Asset Quality, Management, Earnings, Liquidity, Sensitivity to Market Risk

CBD - Cash Before Delivery

CBOT - Chicago Board of Trade

CCD - Cash Concentration or Disbursement

CCD+ - Cash Concentration or Disbursement Plus Addendum

CD - Certificate of Deposit

CD-ROM - Compact Disk-Read Only Memory

CEO - Chief Executive Officer

CFO - Chief Financial Officer

CHAPS - Clearing House Automated Payment System

CHIPS - Clearing House Interbank Payment System

CME - Chicago Mercantile Exchange

CMO - Collateralized Mortgage Obligation

CO - Consolidated Obligation

COD - Cash on Delivery

COP - Certificate of Participation

CP - Commercial Paper

CPA - Certified Public Accountant or Canadian Payments Association

CPU - Central Processing Unit

CTX - Corporate Trade Exchange

DDA - Demand Deposit Account

DIDMCA - Depository Institutions Deregulation and Monetary Control Act (1980)

DM - Deutsche Mark

DSO - Days Sales Outstanding

DTC - Depository Transfer Check

EAR - Earnings Allowance Rate

EBA - European Banking Association

EBIT - Earnings Before Interest and Taxes

ECB - European Central Bank

ECCHO - Electronic Check Clearing House Organization

EC - Electronic Commerce

ECP - Electronic Check Presentment

EDI - Electronic Data Interchange

EDT - Electronic Depository Transfer

EFAA - Expedited Funds Availability Act (1988)

EFT - Electronic Funds Transfer

EFTA - Electronic Funds Transfer Act (1978)

EFTA - Electronic Funds Transfer Association

EFTPS - Electronic Federal Tax Payment System

EMU - Economic and Monetary Union

ERISA - Employee Retirement Income and Security Act

EU - European Economic Union

FAS - Financial Accounting Standards

FASB - Financial Accounting Standards Board

FDIC - Federal Deposit Insurance Corporation

FEDI - Financial Electronic Data Interchange

FFCB - Federal Farm Credit Bank

FFIEC - Federal Financial Institution Examination Council

FHLB - Federal Home Loan Bank

FHLBB - Federal Home Loan Bank Board

FHLMC - Federal Home Loan Mortgage Corporation (Freddie Mac)

FIRREA - Financial Institutions Reform, Recovery and Enforcement Act (1989)

FNMA - Federal National Mortgage Association (Fannie Mae)

FOMC - Federal Open Market Committee

FRA - Forward Rate Agreement

FRR - Financial Reporting Releases

FTC - Foreign Tax Credit

FTD - Federal Tax Deposit

FX - Foreign Exchange

GAAP - Generally Accepted Accounting Principles

GAAS - Generally Accepted Auditing Standards

GATT - General Agreement on Tariffs and Trade

GIC - Guaranteed Income Contract

GNMA - Government National Mortgage Association (Ginnie Mae)

GSE - Government Sponsored Enterprise

HDGS - High Dollar Group Sort

IBBEA - Interstate Banking and Branching Efficiency Act

ICR - Intelligent Character Recognition

IMM - International Money Market

IRB - Industrial Revenue Bond

IRR - Internal Rate of Return

IRS - Internal Revenue Service

ISDA - International Swap Dealers Association

JIT - Just In Time

LAN - Local Area Network

L/C - Letter of Credit

LIBOR - London Interbank Offered Rate

LVTS - Large Value Transfer System

MAC - Message Authentication Code

MBS - Mortgage Backed Security

MICR - Magnetic Ink Character Recognition

MIS - Management Information System

MMY - Money Market Yield

NACHA - National Automated Clearing House Association

NAFTA - North American Free Trade Agreement

NASD - National Association of Security Dealers

NCHA - National Clearinghouse Association

NCUA - National Credit Union Administration

NCUSIF - National Credit Union Savings Insurance Fund

NOCH - National Organization of Clearing Houses

NOW - Negotiable Order of Withdrawal

NPV - Net Present Value

NSF - Not Sufficient Funds

NYSE - New York Stock Exchange

OCC - Office of the Comptroller of the Currency

OCR - Optical Character Recognition

ODFI - Originating Depository Financial Institution

OTS - Office of Thrift Supervision

PAD - Preauthorized Debit

PC - Personal Computer

PID - Payable if Desired

PIN - Personal Identification Number

POD - Proof of Deposit

POS - Point of Sale

PPD - Prearranged Payment or Deposit

PTD - Payable Through Draft

RCPC - Regional Check Processing Center

REPO - Repurchase Agreement

RFI - Request for Information

RFP - Request For Proposal

S&L - Savings and Loan Association

SEC - Securities & Exchange Commission

SIA - Securities Industry Association

SLMHC - SLM Holding Corporation

SPEUA - Sistema de Pagos Electronicos de Uso Ampliado

S.W.I.F.T. - Society for Worldwide Interbank Financial Telecommunication

TARGET - Trans-European Automated Real Time Gross Settlement Express Transfer System

TIE - Times Interest Earned

TMA - Treasury Management Association

TMIS - Treasury Management Information System

TR - Transit Routing

TXP - Tax Payment Format

UCC - Uniform Commercial Code

UK - United Kingdom

UN/EDIFACT - United Nations Rules for EDI Administration, Commerce and Transport

VA - Veterans Administration

VAB - Value-Added Bank

VAN - Value-Added Network

VRDB - Variable-Rate Demand Bond

WACC - Weighted Average Cost of Capital

WAN - Wide Area Network

WTO - World Trade Organization

YTM - Yield to Maturity

ZBA - Zero Balance Account

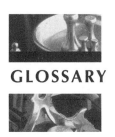

GLOSSARY

Account Analysis – A statement, essentially an invoice for services, that a financial institution provides to its commercial customers specifying services provided, volumes of transactions processed, and charges assessed.

Accounts Receivable – Assets resulting from the extension of trade credit to a company's customers.

Accounts Receivable Balance Pattern – The percentage of credit sales in a time period (usually a month) that remains outstanding at the end of each subsequent time period.

Account Resolution – A board of directors' resolution granting authorization for the establishment of an account in the name of the company and specifying those individuals or officers authorized to transact business in relation to the account.

Accrete – The process whereby a bond issued at a discount to par increases to face value as it approaches maturity.

Accrual Accounting – A type of financial record keeping in which a company records revenues as they are earned and expenses as they are incurred, regardless of when the related cash flow occurs. Most larger companies use accrual accounting, and even companies that keep day-to-day records on a cash basis can adjust to accrual accounting at the end of financial periods.

ACH Credit Transaction – An Automated Clearing House (ACH) transaction that involves the transfer of funds from an originator's account to a receiver's account.

ACH Debit Transaction – An Automated Clearing House (ACH) transaction that moves funds from the receiver's account to the originator's account.

ACH Operator – An Automated Clearing House (ACH) association or Federal Reserve bank that processes and distributes ACH transactions received from an originating financial institution.

Active Investment Strategies – Short-term investment strategies that involve a fair amount of planning, work, and risk assessment such as dividend capture and riding the yield curve; these can also involve the use of swaps and derivatives.

Adjustable-Rate Preferred Stock – Preferred stock with a dividend rate that varies.

Advising Bank – In transactions involving letters of credit (L/C), an institution advising the beneficiary (exporter), of an L/C opened in its favor.

Agency – A role in which a bank or trust institution manages assets in which the title remains with the owner.

Agency Issues (Agency Securities) – Securities issued by federal agencies, those chartered by the federal government, or those considered to be backed by the federal government.

Agent – A designation in which a financial institution manages assets to which the owner retains title.

Aging Schedule – At a given point in time, a list of the percentages and/or amounts of outstanding accounts receivable classified as current or past due in 30-day increments.

All-In Rate – The rate on a credit facility or debt obligation equal to the sum of the base rate plus the spread.

American National Standards Institute (ANSI) – The recognized coordinator and clearing house for information on national and international standards including those for electronic transaction formats that are used in electronic data interchange (EDI).

American Option Contract – An option contract that can be exercised from the date of purchase until the maturity date.

Amortization Schedule – The schedule of principal payments on a debt obligation.

Anticipation – The initiation of a transfer before cash becomes available at the depository financial institution.

Arbitrage – The process by which buying in one market and simultaneously selling in another leads to a risk-free profit.

ASC X12 822 – The American National Standards Institute (ANSI) standardized format for financial institutions to use in sending account analysis statements to companies electronically.

As-Of Adjustment – Adjustment of the value date of a transaction in order to calculate collected balances to a date different from the date the transaction occurred.

Asset-Based Borrowing – Lending based on the pledging of accounts receivable, inventory, or other assets as loan collateral.

Asset-Backed Securities – Corporate debt obligations secured by specific assets, such as accounts receivable.

Automated Clearing House (ACH) System – A domestic electronic funds transfer system.

Availability – When funds deposited will become available for use.

Availability Float – The time interval or dollar amount outstanding between the time a check is deposited and the time the company's account is credited with collected funds.

Availability Schedule –A schedule that specifies when a bank or the Federal Reserve grants credit for deposited checks in the form of an increase in the depositor's available or collected balance.

Available Balances – The amount of funds available for withdrawal from an account.

Back Value Date – Compensation practice of non-U.S. banks where debits to a customer's statement of account will reflect a date prior to the actual outflow of funds.

Balance and Transaction Activity – Information on current ledger and collected balances, one- and two-day float, debit and credit detail, and adjustment items. Average balances and a balance history may also be reported.

Balance Sheet – One of the standardized financial statements that companies and individuals use to show assets, liabilities, and equity (or net worth) at a given point in time.

Balance Sheet Matching – The matching of interest-sensitive assets with interest-sensitive liabilities eliminating the exposure to interest rate changes.

Balloon Payment – The majority of the principal balance is due in the final years of the loan term.

Bank Insurance Fund (BIF) – A fund administered by the Federal Deposit Insurance Corporation (FDIC), which insures the deposits of commercial banks and mutual savings banks.

Bank Notes – Subordinated debt instruments with yields that are close to those of similarly rated commercial paper that banks issue.

Banker's Acceptance (BA) – A time draft drawn on and accepted by a bank thereby obligating the bank to pay the face amount of the draft at maturity.

Barter – The direct exchange of goods and/or services without using money.

Base Rate – A widely recognized and quoted interest rate—such as the Fed funds rate, the prime rate, or the London InterBank Offered Rate (LIBOR)—on which a rate of interest is based.

Basis Point – One one-hundredth of a percentage point (.0001).

Bearer Security – A security where the holder can collect interest or principal at maturity as well as sell the security. The security is not registered to the holder.

Benchmarking – The practice of comparing performance of a business operation, typically against the best practice standard in a given field or industry.

Bid-Offer Spreads – The difference between the price banks and foreign currency dealers are willing to buy and sell currencies.

Bid Rate – The price for which banks and foreign currency dealers are willing to buy currencies.

Bilateral Netting – System in which purchases between two subsidiaries of the same company are netted against each other so that over time, typically one month, only the difference is transferred.

Board of Governors of the Federal Reserve System – The seven-member body that oversees the U.S. Federal Reserve and supervises the U.S. banking system.

Bond – A long-term debt instrument administered by a trustee.

Bond Equivalent Yield – Yield quoted on a 365-day basis for debt instruments.

Bond Indenture Agreement – Formal agreement between an issuer of bonds and the bondholder(s).

Book Entry – Securities are stored at the Federal Reserve Bank of New York and electronic entries are made when ownership changes; book entry securities do not physically move when traded.

Bullet Maturity – A loan where the entire principal amount is due on the final maturity date.

Call Back – A return call to a company to ensure that a transaction has been authorized; a call is placed after the transaction has been entered, but before it is executed.

Call Option – The right, but not the obligation, to buy an asset for a specified price (the strike price) over an interval or at a fixed point in the future.

Call Provision – Part of a bond indenture giving the issuer the right to redeem the instrument before maturity.

CAMELS – A depository financial institution rating system. CAMELS is an acronym for capital adequacy, asset quality, management capability, earnings, liquidity and susceptibility to market risk.

Capital Budgeting – The process businesses go through to assess their long-term investment alternatives.

Capital Lease – An on-balance-sheet leasing arrangement.

Capital Market – A financial market that consists of both equity and debt instruments that mature in more than one year.

Captive Finance Company – An affiliate or subsidiary of a company that finances the purchases customers make on credit.

Cash-Basis Accounting – A type of financial record keeping in which revenues and expenses are recorded as cash is received and disbursed. Typically, small businesses keep their records on a cash basis, while larger businesses use the alternative, accrual accounting.

Cash Application – The process of matching and applying customer payments against outstanding accounts receivable.

Cash Before Delivery (CBD) – Credit terms requiring payment, often in the form of a check, a cashier's check, or a certified check before the order is shipped.

Cash Concentration – The movement of funds from outlying depository locations to a central bank account where they can be utilized and managed most effectively.

Cash Concentration or Disbursement (CCD) – An Automated Clearing House (ACH) payment format for concentration and disbursement of funds within a company or between companies.

Cash Concentration or Disbursement Plus Addendum (CCD+) – An Automated Clearing House (ACH) format used for U.S. Treasury Vendor Express Program and company-to-company payments.

Cash Flow Timeline – The graphic representation of a company's cash inflows and outflows that occur in conjunction with its operating cycle.

Cash Forecasting – The process of predicting cash flows for the purposes of liquidity management and financial control.

Cash Letter – A bundle of checks accompanied by a list of individual items and control documents.

Cash on Delivery (COD) – Credit terms in which goods are shipped and the buyer must pay upon delivery.

Cash Terms – Credit terms in which the buyer generally has a week to 10 days to make the payment.

Cash Transfer Scheduling – The decision on when and how much cash to transfer.

Cashier's Check – A check drawn by a bank on its own funds signed by an officer.

Certificates of Deposit (CDs) – Negotiable or non-negotiable bank time deposits.

Certificates of Participation – Debt securities with proceeds that finance specific capital investments and/or projects of municipal and state governments.

Certified Check – A check drawn by a depositor on his own checking account and certified by the drawee bank that funds will be available for payment.

Check – A demand instrument that transfers funds from the payor to the payee.

Check Clearing – The process by which a check is presented to and accepted by the drawee bank, the institution on which it is drawn.

Check Retention – Also known as check safekeeping, a service financial institutions perform by retaining paid checks for periods that typically range from one to six months. Companies can receive microfilm, microfiche, or CD-ROM image records of the checks.

Check Truncation – The process by which essential information contained on a conventional paper check is captured electronically and the electronic information, not the paper check, is sent through the clearing system.

City Items – Checks drawn on banks located in federal reserve cities.

Clearing Float – The delay between the time the check is deposited by the payee and the time the payor's account is debited.

Clearing House – A formal or informal association of banks in a geographic area that facilitates the exchange of items drawn on participants.

Clearing House Automated Payment System (CHAPS) – A U.K.-based payment system for high-value, same-day settlement of transactions.

Clearing House Interbank Payment System (CHIPS) – An independent message-switching system that permits international financial transactions to be settled among New York banks. CHIPS is operated by the New York Clearing House Association.

Collateralized Mortgage Obligations (CMOs) – Securities that are formed from portions of mortgage pools.

Collected Balances – Balances in an account for which the bank of deposit has received settlement.

Collecting Bank – In a transaction involving a documentary collection, the remitting bank's correspondent, which is responsible for contacting the buyer (importer), collecting the amount due, and releasing documents as instructed.

Collection Float – The interval between when a check is mailed and the time the payee receives available funds in its account.

Collection Letter – In documentary collections, a letter putting forth the exact procedures to be followed before shipping documents are released to the importer.

Commercial Letter of Credit – See trade or commercial letter of credit.

Commercial Paper (CP) – Unsecured promissory notes that companies issue to finance short-term capital needs with a maturity of 270 days or less.

Commitment Fee – A component of pricing for a line of credit. A percentage fee, either on the total amount of the commitment or on the unused portion of the commitment.

Commodity Swaps – A contract between two parties to exchange commodities at an agreed upon price in the future.

Company Processing Center – A collection system in which the company does its own processing and depositing of payments.

Compensating Balances – Balances held by a company in the form of collected balances to pay for bank services.

Confirming Bank – In a transaction involving a letter of credit (L/C), a bank that adds its confirmation to the L/C, committing to the beneficiary that it will ensure payment regardless of the issuing bank's ability to pay.

Consignment – A transaction in which a seller ships goods to a third party, but retains legal title to the goods until they are sold to an end user.

Consumer Advisory Council – A committee that advises the Fed board. It represents the interest of consumers.

Controlled Disbursement – A cash management service that provides same-day notification, usually by early or mid-morning, of the dollar amount of checks that will clear against the controlled disbursement account that day.

Convertible Bond – A type of bond convertible into shares of the company's common stock at a defined price.

Corporate Trustee – A financial institution that ensures compliance with indenture agreements between issuers and investors in corporate bond or preferred stock issues.

Correspondent Balances – Demand deposits held by one bank at another bank to facilitate check clearing, securities, letters of credit, or other transactions.

Correspondent Bank – A financial institution that regularly performs services for other banks.

Counter-Trade – Method of payment, typically an exchange of merchandise, used by companies lacking access to sufficient hard currency to pay for imports.

Country Items – Checks drawn on banks located outside areas serviced by a federal reserve city or a regional check processing center (RCPC).

Covenants – Provisions in loan agreements that restrict a borrower's activities in ways that protect the lender during the term of the agreement.

Credit Enhancement – Use of an indemnity bond or letter of credit to back a debt issue, thereby substituting the creditworthiness of the guarantor for the borrower's creditworthiness.

Credit Facility – Any type of loan or credit arrangement.

Credit Rating – A standardized assessment, expressed in alphanumeric characters, of a company's or individual's creditworthiness.

Credit Scoring – Statistical analysis used to estimate the creditworthiness of credit applicants.

Credit Support – See credit enhancement.

Currency Forward Contract – An agreement to buy or sell a specified amount of a foreign currency at a future date for a price agreed upon today.

Currency Futures Contracts – Standardized contracts for future delivery of currencies that are traded on various exchanges.

Currency Swaps – The exchange of a floating rate cash flow denominated in one currency with a fixed rate cash flow denominated in another currency in addition to an exchange of principal.

Current Assets – Assets that are likely to be converted into cash within a year or a normal accounting cycle.

Current Liabilities – Liabilities that are likely to be settled within a year or a normal accounting cycle.

Current Yield – Yield determined by the coupon payment of a debt instrument, in dollars, divided by its price.

Daily Cash Position – A report which assists a cash manager in determining a company's cash needs. Information about incoming and outgoing wire transfers, collection of large accounts receivable, clearing of large disbursement items, and Automated Clearing House (ACH) credits and debits is compiled to prepare a daily cash position.

Data Exchange – An arrangement in which a financial institution or a third-party reporting service gathers and consolidates account balances and transactions from various financial institutions with which the company has accounts.

Daylight Overdraft – An intra-day exposure of a bank when an account is in an overdraft position at any time during the business day.

Days' Sales Outstanding (DSO) – A credit measurement ratio calculated by dividing accounts receivable outstanding at the end of a time period by the average daily credit sales for the period.

Debit Card – An instrument that allows a transaction to post to bank deposit accounts as a withdrawal. On-line settlement requires a Personal Identification Number (PIN) to initiate the transaction.

Debt-Equity Hybrids – Securities that have both debt and equity characteristics.

Demand Deposit Accounts (DDAs) – A type of bank account from which the depositor can transfer funds to a third party via a check, wire transfer, or an Automated Clearing House (ACH) transfer.

Deposit Deadline – The time of day, based on an item's drawee endpoint, by which an item must be at the depository bank's processing center ready for transit in order to qualify for the availability stated on that bank's availability schedule.

Deposit Float – The sum of each check deposited multiplied by its availability in days.

Deposit Reconciliation – Service that enables deposits from multiple locations credited to a single corporate account to be identified and reported. Also called branch consolidation services.

Depository Bank – The bank that accepts a check for deposit and credit to a customer's account.

Depository Institutions Deregulation and Monetary Control Act (DIDMCA) (1980) – A federal law that requires all deposit-taking institutions to maintain reserves at the Fed, requires the Fed to eliminate or price Fed float, and charge for its services.

Depository Transfer Checks (DTCs) – A pre-printed, unsigned, restricted-payee instrument used by a company to transfer funds from one of its outlying depository locations to its concentraton account.

Derivative – A security whose value depends on that of another security or index.

Direct Send – An alternative to other check clearing processes in which banks send cash letters directly to a non-local Fed or the paying bank.

Disbursement Float – The time interval or dollar amount outstanding between the time a payor mails a check and the time the bank debits the payor's account.

Disbursement Network – A system of check mailing locations and drawee banks based on disbursement studies and designed to maximize disbursement float.

Discount – The face value multiplied by the discount rate times the number of days divided by 360.

Discount Instruments – Securities that are sold at a discount to face value.

Discount Rate – The rate used to discount future cash flows to determine present value.

Discounting – The application of a discount rate to projected future cash flows or payments to adjust for the time value of money. Alternatively, the practice of purchasing a financial asset at a price that is less than face value.

Distribution Method – A forecasting technique used in cash scheduling wherein the distribution of cash flow over a given time period is estimated.

Diversification – The practice of investing in an array of securities or other assets in order to modify risk and return characteristics of a portfolio.

Diversification of Funding – The practice of capitalizing a company or project with several sources of capital to ensure access to different creditors.

Dividend Capture – An active investment strategy that tries to boost yield by capturing the dividend of preferred issues.

Documentary Collection – An international payment method that processes the collection of a draft and accompanying shipping documents through international correspondent banks.

Dollar-Days – The usual measurement for collection float, calculated by multiplying the time lag in collections by the dollar amount being delayed.

The Douglas Amendment (1956) – A federal law which allowed banks to merge across state lines if each state permitted but did not allow bank holding companies to acquire banks in other states.

Drawdown – A request sent by a company to a bank to initiate a wire transfer from its own or another party's account.

Duration – The approximate percentage change in the price of a bond for a 1% change in yield.

Dutch Auction – An auction process in which the price of the goods being sold is lowered in increments until it prompts a bid; used by the U.S. Treasury for pricing new issues.

Drawee Bank – The bank on which a check is drawn, the payor's bank.

Earnings Allowance – The total allowance which can be used to offset service charges during the period.

Earnings Allowance Rate – The rate used to calculate the earnings allowance.

Economic Exposure – The long-term effect on the company of exchange rate changes on the present value of future cash flows.

Edge Act (1919) – A federal law that permits U.S. banks to invest in corporations located in other geographic areas that engage solely in international banking and finance.

Effective Annual Yield – Annual yield calculation based on a 365-day year that includes the effect of compounding of interest payments.

Electronic Benefit Transfers – Government-sponsored programs that distribute benefit payments through Automated Teller Machines (ATMs) and Point of Sale (POS) terminals.

Electronic Check Presentment (ECP) – Electronic transmission of data captured by a check reader/sorter to a drawee bank to effect settlement of a check.

Electronic Commerce (EC) – The exchange of business information from one organization to another in an electronic format in some mutually agreed standard. EC includes unstructured electronic messaging such as facsimile (fax) or electronic mail (E-mail) as well as Electronic Data Interchange (EDI) formats.

Electronic Data Interchange (EDI) – The movement of business data electronically between or within companies (including their agents or intermediaries) in a structured computer-processable data format that permits data to be transferred without re-keying.

Electronic Depository Transfer (EDT) – An ACH transaction used for concentration of funds.

Electronic Federal Tax Payment System – The primary method that the U.S. government uses to collect taxes.

Electronic Funds Transfer (EFT) – The movement of funds by non-paper means (i.e., electronically), usually through a payment system such as the ACH network or Fedwire.

Electronic Funds Transfer Act (EFTA) (1978) – A federal law that defined the rights and responsibilities of individuals using EFT services.

Electronic Lockbox – A collection service that records the receipt of incoming wire transfer and ACH payments, reformats the data, and transmits it to the company in whatever format it desires.

Eligible Banker's Acceptance (BA) – A BA with a term of 180 days or less that may be discounted at the U.S. Federal Reserve Bank.

Encryption – A process which electronically scrambles a message so that only persons who have compatible decryption hardware and/or software can interpret the message.

Endpoint – The drawee bank or location established by the clearing agent at which a check is presented for settlement.

Equity – Ownership, in many cases evidenced by shares of common stock.

Equity Warrant – A long-term option to buy a specific number of shares of common stock at a specific price.

Eurobond – A bond issued outside the country where the currency of the bond is domiciled.

Eurodollar CD – U.S. dollar-denominated CD issued by banks, including branches of U.S. banks, outside the U.S.

Eurodollar Deposits – U.S. dollar-denominated deposits in banks or bank branches located outside the U.S.

Eurodollar Time Deposits (Euro-TDs) – Non-negotiable, fixed-rate time deposits with maturities from overnight to several years, issued by non-U.S. banks and branches of U.S. banks outside the U.S.

European Option Contract – An option contract that can be exercised only on the maturity date.

Evaluated Receipts Settlement (ERS) – A payment method designed to eliminate the need for a supplier to provide an invoice to the customer.

Event of Default – The breaching or violation of any term, covenant, or condition in a debt agreement by a borrower.

Excess Bank Balances – Average collected balances in a company's bank account above the average required for bank compensation, or above the level a company has chosen to maintain at a bank.

Eximbank – The Export-Import Bank of the U.S. is an independent agency of the U.S. government established to finance and guarantee payment for U.S. exports.

Expedited Funds Availability Act (1988) – A federal law that defined maximum funds availability time periods and established return procedures for checks and payable through drafts, etc.

Exponential Smoothing – A time series forecasting technique that assigns declining weights to past values.

Export Credit Insurance – A common way of insuring payment of foreign receivables that is provided by Eximbank and private insurers. Coverage can be obtained for both political and commercial risk.

Extranet – A wide area network (WAN) in which two or more organizations share information using Internet protocols with access limited to the participants.

Factoring – The sale or transfer of title of the accounts receivable to a third party (factor).

Factors – Financial companies that purchase or manage other companies' receivables.

Fed Funds – Funds deposited by commercial banks at Federal Reserve banks, including funds in excess of bank reserve requirements. Banks may lend federal funds to each other on an overnight basis at the federal funds rate to help the borrowing bank satisfy its reserve requirements or liquidity needs.

Federal Advisory Council – A 12-member council comprised of commercial bankers from the 12 Federal Reserve Districts that advise the Fed Board of Governors.

Federal Deposit Insurance Corporation (FDIC) – Independent federal agency that insures deposits in member banks. It has its own reserves and can borrow from the U.S. Treasury.

Federal Deposit Insurance Corporation Improvement Act (FDICIA) (1991) – A federal law that established standards for financial institution safety and soundness, mandated the FDIC to declare insolvent any bank or thrift that failed to maintain certain levels of capital adequacy, and required the FDIC to charge deposit insurance premiums on a risk-adjusted basis.

The Federal Financial Institution Examination Council (FFIEC) – The U.S. government entity that coordinates the activities of the Fed, the Office of the Comptroller of the Currency (OCC), the Federal Deposit Insurance Corporation (FDIC), and the Office of Thrift Supervision (OTS) to ensure consistency in the implementation of regulatory policy.

Federal Open Market Committee – The 12-member committee that implements the Fed's monetary policy through open market operations.

The Federal Reserve Act – The federal law which set up the Federal Reserve Bank and directs it to conduct monetary policy in such a way as to maximize employment, promote price stability, and maintain moderate long-term interest rates.

Federal Reserve Bank – A bank that is part of the U.S. Federal Reserve System.

Federal Reserve District Banks – The Federal Reserve Banks that serve geographic districts in the U.S. These 12 banks have 25 branches and Regional Check Processing Centers (RCPCs).

Federal Reserve System (Fed) – An independent agency of the U.S. government that plays a central role in monetary policy, domestic payments systems, and the regulation of financial institutions.

Federal Reserve Float (Fed Float) – The difference in timing between the availability granted a clearing bank by the Fed and the actual presentment of the item to the drawee bank.

Federal Agency Securities (Agencies) – Discount and coupon obligations of federal agencies that were established by Congress to provide credit to specific sectors of the economy.

Fedwire – The same-day value electronic funds transfer system operated in the U.S. by the Fed.

Fee Compensation – Compensation for bank services by direct, explicit fee payment.

Fiduciary – An individual or institution to whom property is given to hold according to agreed upon terms.

Financial Accounting Standards Board (FASB) – The entity that promulgates Generally Accepted Accounting Principles (GAAP) in the U.S.

Financial Electronic Data Interchange (FEDI) – A type of Electronic Data Interchange (EDI) in which financial information is transferred including electronic format for invoices, initiation of payments, lockbox deposit reports, and remittance information.

Financial Institutions Reform, Recovery, and Enforcement Act (FIRREA) (1989) – A federal law that consolidated the Federal Savings and Loan Insurance Corporation (FSLIC) under the FDIC, and set up the Office of Thrift Supervision (OTS) to supervise thrifts and Savings and Loans (S&Ls), and established the Resolution Trust Corporation (RTC) to handle the assets of failed savings and loans.

Financial Leverage – The use of debt to finance a company.

Financial Ratios – Standardized measures of financial and operational performance.

Fixed Assets – Property used for production of goods and services.

Float – Time interval, or delay, between the start and completion of a specific phase or process that occurs along the cash flow timeline. Certain types of float can be quantified and expressed in dollar amounts.

Float Balance - The sum of the daily dollar amount of items for collection.

Floor Planning – A type of financing frequently used to support an inventory of high cost durable goods.

Foreign Bonds – Bonds issued in the country of their currency by non-residents of that country.

Foreign Currency Option – The right, but not the obligation, to buy or sell a fixed amount of a foreign currency at an agreed upon price before or on a specific day.

Foreign Currency Swap – A transaction in which specific amounts of two different currencies are exchanged and the amounts repaid over time.

Foreign Exchange (FX) Rate—The equivalent number of units of one currency per unit of a different currency.

Foreign Tax Credits – Tax credits U.S. companies can take against domestic taxes for those taxes paid to foreign governments.

Forfaiting – Specialized form of export financing in which the seller accepts a note from the buyer which can be discounted; useful where confirmed letters of credit are not available.

Forward Contract – An agreement between two parties to buy or sell a fixed amount of an asset at a specified price at a future date or time interval.

Forward Foreign Exchange Contract – A contract to purchase or sell a specified quantity of a foreign currency at an exchange rate established today for delivery on a specific date in the future.

Forward Foreign Exchange Rate – An exchange rate established today for a currency transaction that settles more than two days in the future.

Forward Market – A market on which prices for the future exchange of assets can be fixed today.

Forward Rate Agreement – Forward contract in which two parties agree on the interest rate to be paid at a future settlement date.

Forwards – Contracts that require some specific action at a later date and allow lock-in of a future price or rate; forwards are typically used to provide a hedge against future price fluctuation.

Forward Value Date – Compensation practice of non-U.S. banks where credits to a customer's account statement will reflect a date later than the actual date funds were received.

Fractional Availability – Availability granted in fractions of days that represent a bank's experience in final settlement of items drawn on that particular endpoint.

Freight Payments – Specialized payment services offered by banks and third parties that effect payment for the client directly to freight carriers and offer data bases that assist in determining cost-efficient freight distribution methods.

Full Reconciliation – A financial institution service that matches checks paid against the file of checks issued by the company. The bank supplies a listing, either as a paper report or electronically, of checks paid and outstanding in check serial number order.

Future Value – The value, at some specific point in the future, of money invested today using a projected rate of return.

Futures Contract – A standardized, normally exchange-traded contract for future delivery of a financial or real asset.

Garn-St. Germain Depository Institutions Act (1982) - A federal law that established lending limits of banks, allowed the FDIC to arrange mergers of banks in different states, and allowed banks to offer accounts that would offer rates of interest comparable to money market mutual funds.

General Obligation Securities – Municipal securities backed by all of the issuer's resources and its authority to levy taxes.

Generally Accepted Accounting Principles (GAAP) – The accounting conventions promulgated by the Financial Accountings Standards Board (FASB) in the U.S. They do not have the force of law but are required by government regulatory bodies, such as the Securities and Exchange Commission (SEC), to be followed.

The Glass-Steagall Act (also known as the Banking Act of 1933) – The federal law that prohibits financial institutions engaged in deposit taking and lending from underwriting, and vice versa.

Government-Sponsored Enterprises – Private, shareholder-owned companies with a relationship with government agencies, e.g., Fannie Mae and Freddie Mac.

Grace Period – Permits repayment of principal beginning at some specified future date. For example, an eight-year loan with a two-year grace period would mean that principal payments would not commence until the third year of the loan.

Hedging – The process whereby a company uses financial instruments such as forwards and futures to reduce or eliminate the impact of fluctuations in the price of credit, foreign exchange, or commodities on its profits or company value.

High Dollar Group Sort (HDGS) – A program of the Federal Reserve to expedite the processing of high-dollar checks through the system.

Hybrid Lockbox – A collection system that has characteristics of both retail and wholesale lockboxes and can process both consumer and company-to-company mail receipts. Sometimes referred to as a whole-tail lockbox.

Imprest Accounts – An account maintained at a prescribed level for a particular purpose or activity; it is periodically replenished to the prescribed level.

Income Statement – One of the standardized financial statements companies and individuals use to show revenues and expenses over a certain interval of time.

Indenture – The agreement among parties to a bond issue.

Industrial Revenue Bonds (IRBs) – A special class of municipal bonds issued to provide funds for a facility the municipality is trying to attract to the area.

Information Reporting Services – A service that major Asian, European and U.S. banks offer to provide information on clients' account balances and transactions.

Integrated or Comprehensive Accounts Payable – An accounts payable service that allows a company to outsource all or part of its accounts payable and/or disbursement services.

Interest – The cost, usually expressed as an annual percentage (but sometimes implied by a discount), charged for borrowing money or earned on an investment.

Interest-Bearing Instruments – Securities that pay interest at a specified rate either at periodic intervals or at maturity.

Interest Rate Cap – A ceiling on the maximum interest rate for a loan or variable-rate security. Caps on loans limit the amount of interest that a borrower will pay while caps on investments limit the interest that will be paid to an investor.

Interest Rate Collar – The combination of an interest rate floor and an interest rate cap giving the holders ranges of minimum and maximum interest rates.

Interest Rate Exposure – The vulnerability of a company's earnings to interest swings that impact a company's floating rate assets or liabilities.

Interest RateFloor – Minimum interest rates for a loan or variable-rate security.

Interest Rate Futures – Legally binding commitments to sell financial instruments at a specified future date and price.

Interest Rate Option – An option contract with a value dependent on interest rate movements.

Interest Rate Parity – The tendency of interest rate differentials between countries to influence whether their currencies trade at parity, discount, or a premium in the forward versus the spot market.

Interest Rate Swaps – The exchange of fixed interest rate payments or cash flows for variable interest rate payments or cash flows.

Internal Factoring – A factoring arrangement in which a designated corporate affiliate or subsidiary buys accounts receivables from an exporting subsidiary and collects from an importing subsidiary.

Internal Rate of Return – A calculation of the return of a project or capital investment found by setting the net present value (NPV) of cash inflows equal to zero.

Internet – A Wide Area Network (WAN) to which anyone with the appropriate hardware, software, and communication links has access.

The Interstate Banking and Branching Efficiency Act (1994) – A federal law that phased out prohibition of barriers against multi-state branching established by the McFadden Act.

Intranet – A Local Area Network (LAN) or Wide Area Network (WAN), typically belonging to one company, that uses the open standards of the Internet rather than proprietary software for communication among computers.

Inverted Yield Curve – A downward sloping yield curve, which happens only occasionally, where yields on shorter term securities exceed yields on similar longer term securities.

Investable Balance – The balance on which the earnings allowance rate is applied.

Invoicing Float – The time interval between the purchase of goods and services and the receipt of an invoice by the payor.

In-Sample Validation – Tests using historical data from which a model was developed to show how well a forecasting model works.

Issuing Bank – In transactions involving a letter of credit (L/C), the buyer's(importer's) bank, that issues the L/C in favor of the beneficiary (seller/exporter).

Junk Bonds – High yielding, non-investment-grade debt securities.

Lagging – Delaying cross-border payments between corporate subsidiaries to take advantage of expected foreign exchange rate movements.

Leading – Accelerating cross-border payments between corporate subsidiaries to take advantage of expected foreign exchange rate movements.

Ledger Balance – Balance in a bank account that reflects all items that have been deposited or cleared through the account.

Ledger Cutoff or Ledger Cutoff Time – The time of day when a check must be received to be posted to the depositor's account.

Letter of Credit (L/C) – A document issued by a bank guaranteeing the payment of a customer's draft up to a stated amount for a specified period provided that specified terms and conditions are met.

Leverage – The use of borrowed funds or high fixed costs to amplify the impact of revenues on net or operating profits. Also the amount of debt capital relative to the amount of equity capital.

Line of Credit – An agreement between a bank and a customer under which the customer can borrow up to a specified amount during a specified time period.

Liquidity – The ability to turn an asset into cash quickly without significant loss of market value. Also refers to a company's ability to pay its obligations when they become due.

Loan Agreements – Legal documents that set forth the terms and conditions under which credit is extended.

Loan Participation – A bank agreement to share part of an existing bank loan with another lender.

Loan Syndication – The process whereby a group of financial institutions extends a credit facility to a borrower.

Local Area Network (LAN) – A network connecting computers within the same organization.

Lockbox – A collection system in which a bank or a third party receives, processes, and deposits a company's mail receipts. Also known as a lockbox processor.

Lockbox Networks – Collection systems that offer multiple locations to receive customer remittances through one organization.

London InterBank Offered Rate (LIBOR) – The interest rate on eurodollar borrowings that banks offer each other; a benchmark or base rate on short-term borrowings.

Long-Term Liabilities – Obligations that are expected to be settled beyond one year or a normal accounting cycle.

Magnetic Ink Character Recognition (MICR) Line – The lower part of a check, deposit ticket, or other item, that contains the special character information necessary to read the item by electronic scanning.

Mail Float – The time interval outstanding between the time a check is mailed and its receipt at the designated address.

Market Makers – Individuals or firms who will quote both a bid (buying) and an offered price (selling) for a financial instrument or other type of asset.

Marketability – The ability to sell something readily without making a substantial price concession.

Master Account – Account used to fund zero balance accounts automatically.

Master Note – A type of promissory note used for loans with multiple advance features such as lines of credit and revolvers.

Matching – Purchase of a security with a maturity on the date that funds are required to meet an obligation.

The McFadden Act (1927) – A federal law that established state boundaries as the primary limits for bank expansion, prohibiting banks from accepting deposits, and engaging in branching across state lines without state government approval.

Memo Posting – Posting an ACH credit or debit early in the day when the actual credit or debit will not be posted until later in the day.

Merchant's Processor – Service provider that has entered into an agreement with a merchant to process credit card transactions. Also referred to as a merchant acquirer.

Message Integrity – The process whereby parties sending messages utilize a digital signature to protect the messages from tampering.

Money Market – Financial markets consisting of debt instruments that mature in one year or less.

Money Market Deposit Accounts – A deposit account which pays a floating interest rate based on the rates that short-term highly liquid financial instruments pay.

Money Market Mutual Funds – Funds that commingle investors' capital and invest exclusively or primarily in short-term, highly liquid instruments.

Money Market Preferred Stock – A variable rate preferred stock with a dividend rate based on money market instruments.

Money Market Treasury Funds – Money market mutual funds made up exclusively or principally of short-term U.S. Treasury obligations.

Money Market Yield – Yield of short-term instruments quoted on a 360-day basis.

Money Order – A pre-paid paper instrument issued by a party such as a company, a bank, or the post office to transfer value to a specified payee.

Multi-Bank Reporting – An arrangement in which a financial institution or third-party reporting service gathers, consolidates, and reports account balances and transactions from various financial institutions with which the company maintains accounts.

Multicurrency Accounts – An account that allows for the transfer of payments in any readily convertible currency to and from one designated account.

Multilateral Netting – A netting system that consolidates the cross-border payments of various subsidiaries after conversion into a common, reference currency.

Multiple Drawee Checks – Checks that can be presented for payment at a bank other than the drawee bank; both bank names appear on the check. Also called payable-if-desired (PID) checks.

Municipal Securities or Bonds – Debt securities issued by a state or local government authority.

National Automated Clearing House Association (NACHA) – A membership association that provides market and education assistance and establishes rules, standards, and procedures for Automated Clearing House (ACH) payments.

National Credit Union Share Insurance Fund (NCUSIF) – The entity that insures deposits in most U.S. credit unions.

Negotiable Order of Withdrawal (NOW) Accounts – A type of checking account that pays interest.

Negotiating Bank – In an international transaction involving an L/C, the bank that examines the documents presented by the beneficiary of the credit, receives payment from the issuing bank, and pays the beneficiary. (The advising and negotiating bank are often the same.)

Net Present Value – The discounted value of future cash inflows and outflows.

Net Working Capital – Current assets minus current liabilities.

Netting – A system designed to reduce the number of cross-border payments among international affiliates of a company through the elimination or consolidation of funds flows typically denominated in different currencies.

Nominal Yield – The quoted yield on an annual basis for most instruments as an annual rate.

Non-Repetitive Transfers – One time Fedwire transfers that may be sent to differing parties in varying amounts.

Normal Yield Curve – An upward sloping yield curve where yields on long-term securities exceed yields on similar short-term securities.

North American Free Trade Agreement (NAFTA) – An agreement between the U.S., Canada, and Mexico that reduces and eliminates tariffs, thereby helping to unite their economies.

Offer Rate – The rate at which a foreign exchange dealer is willing to sell a currency.

The Office of the Comptroller of the Currency (OCC) – The federal government office that grants charters to, regulates, supervises, and examines national banks.

The Office of Thrift Supervision (OTS) – The federal government office that oversees thrifts and savings and loans in the same way the Office of the Comptroller of the Currency (OCC) oversees national banks.

Ongoing Validation – The continuing comparison between projected and actual data that allows ongoing re-evaluation and refinement of a forecasting model.

On-Us Check – A check that is deposited in an account held at the same bank on which it is drawn.

Open Account (Open Book Credit) – Type of commercial trade credit in the U.S. in which the seller issues an invoice, which is formal evidence of an obligation, and records the sale as an account receivable.

Open Market Activities – The purchase and sale of securities from the Federal Reserve's portfolio respectively increasing or decreasing the money supply.

Operating Cycle – A company's ongoing activities relating to the acquisition of raw materials or resources, their conversion into goods or services, and subsequent sale to customers.

Operating Lease – An off-balance-sheet leasing arrangement.

Opportunity Cost – The foregone return of available investment alternatives.

Options – The holder has the right, but not the obligation, to sell (put option) or buy (call option) financial instruments at a specified price (strike price) within a fixed period of time.

Originating Depository Financial Institution (ODFI) – The institution that receives an ACH transaction instruction from its customer and forwards the transaction to the ACH operator.

Out-of-Sample Validation – The use of data not involved in a forecasting model's development for testing or validation.

Outsourcing – The practice of having an outside entity perform all or part of a business operation previously handled in-house.

Over-the-Counter/Field Deposit – Collection system in which funds are received and deposited by local operating units in the field in the form of cash, checks, or credit card vouchers.

Paid-On-Production – The process by which a payment record is created for goods and/or services when they are used rather than when they are shipped or delivered.

Partial Reconciliation – A listing or file of checks paid in numerical order by check serial number or date paid.

Passive Investment Strategies – Approaches to short-term investments that are not actively managed, such as index or market replications and overnight sweeps.

Payable-If-Desired (PID) – See multiple drawee checks.

Payable Through Draft (PTD) – A payment instrument resembling a check that is drawn against the payor, not the bank, for which the payor has a period of time in which to honor or refuse payment.

Payee - The party to which a check is made payable.

Paying Agent – Agent, usually a bank, that receives funds from an issuer of bonds or stock and in turn pays principal and interest to bondholders and dividends to stockholders.

Payment Finality – The Federal Reserve's guarantee of funds received. For example, on Fedwire, the Fed guarantees the transferred funds to the receiving bank if the sending bank fails to settle.

Payment Float – The interval between the receipt of an invoice by the payor, including the credit period, and the time the payor's account is charged for funds sent in payment of the invoice. May also be quantified and expressed in dollar amounts.

Payor – The party that issues a check.

Payor Bank Services – An information service in which the Federal Reserve electronically notifies controlled disbursement banks early in the morning of all checks that will be presented that day.

Percentage-of-Sales – A forecasting method in which financial statements are projected based on future sales and the historical relationship between sales and balance sheet items.

Period Yield – The effective yield for a particular period, such as a week, a month or a year.

Personal Identification Number (PIN) – A sequence of alphanumeric characters that identifies someone accessing an electronic information system.

Pooling – A procedure common to some European countries in which excess funds in the accounts of a company or its subsidiaries are used to offset deficits in other company accounts for the purpose of determining interest earned or owed.

Positive Pay – Also known as match pay, a service used to combat check fraud. The bank pays only those checks with serial numbers and dollar amounts that match those in an issue file supplied by the company.

Prearranged Payments or Deposits (PPD) – An Automated Clearing House (ACH) format companies use to effect a transfer of funds to or from a consumer account.

Pre-Authorized Debit – A payment method in which the payor approves in advance the transfer of funds from the payor's bank account to the payee's bank account. The payee initiates the transaction.

Pre-Authorized Draft/Check – A transaction in which the payor authorizes the payee to draw a draft/check against the payor's account.

Pre-Encoding – The encoding of the dollar amount on the MICR line prior to depositing.

Preferred Stock – A corporate equity that enjoys seniority over common equity; all accrued preferred dividends must be paid before common dividends can be distributed.

Prenotifications (Prenotes) – Optional zero-dollar entries that are sent to the Automated Clearing House (ACH) system to verify instructions prior to sending live entries.

Present Value – The discounted value today of cash flows at specific points in the future.

Presentment – The delivery of a check to the payor's bank.

Prime Rate – The interest rate banks charge to their most creditworthy customers; it applies primarily to middle-market companies.

Private Placements – Equity or debt securities that companies issue that do not have to be registered with the Securities and Exchange Commission (SEC) because they are offered to a limited number of investors.

Processing Float – The delay between the time the payee or processing site receives a check and the time the check is deposited.

Promissory Note – An unconditional promise to pay a specified amount of principal plus interest.

Proof of Deposit (POD) – A bank procedure for assigning availability to a check based on time of deposit and endpoints. Also called item-by-item, this is the method most banks use to assign availability.

Provisional Credit – The granting of credit to a payee when a check is deposited subject to final settlement of the item.

Purchasing/Procurement Card – A type of credit card companies issue to employees for routine, typically small dollar, procurements.

Put Option – The right, but not the obligation, to sell an asset for a specified price (the strike price) over an interval or at a fixed point in the future.

Rate-Quoting Conventions – The way in which foreign currencies are quoted in the U.S. (in the number of units per dollar or the number of dollars per unit) or in other countries.

RCPC Items – Checks drawn on banks served by Federal Reserve Regional Check Processing Centers (RCPCs).

Receipts and Disbursements Method – Basic method for short-term cash forecasting that uses schedules of cash receipts and cash disbursements.

Receiving Depository Financial Institution (RDFI) – The financial institution that receives an Automated Clearing House (ACH) transaction for one of its customers.

Redeemable Preferred Stock – Preferred stock that has a predetermined redemption schedule.

Re-engineering – The radical redesign of a particular business process or procedure.

Registered Securities – A treasury security registered in the name of an investor, and only that party can collect interest and principal or sell the security.

Registrar – A party responsible for maintaining names and addresses of stockholders and bondholders of record.

Regression Analysis – A statistical technique that establishes the best linear relationship between the variable to be predicted from one or more input or explanatory variables.

Regulation CC – A U.S. Federal Reserve Bank regulation that covers procedures regarding collecting, depositing, granting availability, and returning checks and payable through drafts.

Regulation D – A U.S. Federal Reserve Bank regulation that imposes uniform reserve requirements on all depository institutions with different levels of reserves for different types of deposits.

Regulation E – A U.S. Federal Reserve Bank regulation that establishes the rights, liabilities, and responsibilities of parties to consumer-related electronic funds transfers (EFT) and protects consumers involved in Automated Teller Machine (ATM), Automated Clearing House (ACH), and credit card transactions.

Regulation J – A U.S. Federal Reserve Bank regulation that establishes the procedures, duties, and responsibilities for check collection and settlement through the Federal Reserve system.

Regulation Q – A U.S. Federal Reserve Bank regulation that prohibits depository institutions from paying interest on corporate demand deposit accounts.

Reinvoicing – A method of centralizing responsibility for monitoring and collecting international accounts receivable and improving foreign exchange exposure management.

Reject Items – Checks that are rejected by a bank's automated processing equipment.

Relationship Review – An informal or formal procedure companies use to assess the service levels and responsiveness of a financial institution.

Repetitive Transfers – Repeated Fedwire transfers in which the debit and credit parties and transaction description remain the same and only the amount and date of the transfer changes.

Report Card – A quantitative ranking of a financial institution's level of service and customer responsiveness.

Representations and Warranties – Conditions that borrowers attest they have agreed to or will continue to maintain in a loan agreement.

Repurchase Agreement (Repo) – A transaction between a securities dealer and an investor in which the dealer sells the security to the investor with an agreement to buy the security back at a specific time and price that will result in a predetermined yield for the investor.

Request for Information (RFI) – A formal request that a company uses to confirm that use of a service provided is justified or to solicit ideas on how to solve a particular business or operational problem.

Request for Proposal (RFP) – An official request or format used to facilitate selection of a service or goods provider.

Reserve Requirements—Federal Reserve balances that must be maintained by depository financial institutions.

Retail CDs – Interest-bearing deposits that financial institutions offer to retail customers with original maturities that range from seven days to several years.

Retail Lockbox – Lockboxes characterized by a large number of relatively small-dollar remittances, usually from consumers.

Return Item – A check which the drawee bank rejects and returns to the depository bank.

Revenue Securities – Securities that represent a claim on specific government revenues, such as tolls or user fees.

Reverse Positive Pay – A service that transmits to the issuing company a file of checks presented for payment that the company matches to its register data for check fraud control. The company contacts the financial institution if any items are to be returned. See also Positive Pay.

Reverse Repurchase Agreement (Reverse Repo) – A borrowing arrangement between a customer who owns securities and a securities dealer in which the borrower/investor sells the securities to a dealer with an agreement to buy back for a specific price at a specific time.

Revolving Credit Terms – A form of trade and consumer credit in which credit is granted without requiring specific approval for each transaction as long as the account is current and below the maximum limit.

Revolving Line of Credit – A line of credit under which a borrower may borrow, repay and reborrow funds over the term of the facility.

Riding the Yield Curve – An investment strategy to improve investment returns. The investor buys highly liquid and marketable securities that mature on a day beyond the time when investment proceeds are needed. This investment has a higher yield than one with a shorter maturity.

Risk Profile – The vulnerability of a company's value to changes in interest rates, exchange rates, and/or commodity prices.

Robinson-Patman Act – Federal law that prohibits price discrimination among customers when a cost basis cannot be demonstrated as the reason for price differences.

Same-Day Settlement – Fed rule designed to improve competition in check collection services. It requires a drawee bank to settle in same-day funds by the close of Fedwire on checks presented by 8 a.m. local time.

Seasonal Dating – Credit terms that require payment near the end or after the buyer's selling season.

Seasonality – An attribute of certain businesses with revenues and/or profits that fluctuate during the year due to the inherent nature of the business; for example, retail operations during the Christmas holiday season or a swimwear company in the spring and summer.

The Securities and Exchange Commission (SEC) – The U.S. government regulatory entity empowered to regulate the selling of securities.

Securitization – A financing technique in which a company issues securities backed by selected financial assets.

Semi-Repetitive Transfers – Fedwire transfers in which debit and credit parties remain the same, but descriptions may be changed along with the date and dollar amount.

Sender Net Debit Cap – Limits set by the Federal Reserve and based on a bank's self-evaluation. These limits set the maximum intraday overdraft that a bank can incur in its Federal Reserve account.

Service Charges – The explicit fees or prices charged for services that financial institutions provide.

Settlement Dates – Dates of ACH transactions that determine the availability of funds.

Sight Draft – An instrument payable on demand that is usually presented in combination with other documents in a letter of credit or documentary collection transaction.

Signature Cards – The cards or electronic representations on file at a financial institution that contain the signatures of authorized check and document signers.

Simple Moving Averages – Extrapolative methods that base a forecast on a simple average of past values of the variable to be predicted.

Sinking Fund – A fund that is built up by periodic payments to a custodial account that ensures that adequate funds are available to repay a bond at its maturity or specified payment dates.

Smart Cards – Stored value cards. Plastic cards with embedded integrated computer chips capable of storing data, including monetary value, that can be electronically replenished.

Society for Worldwide Interbank Financial Telecommunications (S.W.I.F.T.) – The major international financial telecommunications network that transmits international payment instructions as well as other international financial instruments or messages.

Sovereign Risk – The risk that a foreign country's government will not allow an obligation to be paid. Also referred to as political risk.

Speculation – Any purchase of securities or derivatives that is a bet on the direction of the market versus the hedging of an existing risk.

Spot Market – A market in which a currency or commodity is traded for settlement, usually within two business days.

Standby Letter of Credit (L/C) – A type of letter of credit issued to ensure the financial performance of a bank's customer to a third party beneficiary and is drawn upon only in the event of non-performance.

Statement of Cash Flows – One of the standardized financial statements companies use that shows cash inflows and outflows over a given period of time. This statement relates to a company's operating, investing, and financing activities. It is prepared in accordance with applicable accounting standards.

Statement of Shareholders' Equity – One of the standardized financial statements companies use to show changes in equity over a period of time. It is prepared in accordance with applicable accounting standards.

Statistical Forecasting – Describes the relationship between the cash flow component to be predicted and one or more input variables. It is useful when there is a large population to be sampled, and it can be applied to the analysis of trends. Two of the more important statistical techniques are time series forecasting and regression analysis.

Stop Payment – An instruction by a payor to the drawee bank to not pay a check when presented.

Strike Price – The price over the life of an option for which the owner can buy or sell the underlying security or asset.

Subordination – The establishment of priority of one claim over another.

Swap – An agreement between two parties to exchange (or swap) a set of cash flows at future points in time.

Swaption – An option on an interest rate swap where the buyer of the option has the right to enter into an interest rate swap at a future date.

Sweep Account – A bank account that automatically transfers excess balances into an overnight interest-earning investment with the same bank.

S.W.I.F.T. – See Society for Worldwide Interbank Financial Telecommunications.

Target Balance – Average collected balance that must be maintained to compensate a bank for all the services provided to the company. Targets are often set monthly and monitored daily.

Target Concentration – All funds above a target balance level are transferred to the concentration account.

Tax Payment Format (TXP) – An Automated Clearing House (ACH) format that is a modified version of the CCD+ format designed for the electronic payment of taxes to state and federal governments.

Term Loan – A loan, usually used to support capital investments, that has a fixed term of typically two to ten years.

Threshold Concentration – Depository balance levels are allowed to build up to a predetermined level. Then most or all funds are transferred to the concentration account.

Thrift Institutions Advisory Council – A council that advises the Fed Board of Governors in matters pertaining to savings and loan associations, mutual savings banks, and credit unions.

Time Deposit Accounts – A type of interest-bearing account in which the depositor cannot withdraw funds in advance of an agreed upon time without incurring a penalty.

Time Draft – An instrument that is similar to a sight draft but is not payable until a specified future date.

Time Series Forecasting – Forecasts a variable based only on past observations of that variable. Primary types of time series forecasting are simple moving average and exponential smoothing.

Time Value of Money – Concept that the value of money is different at different points in time because of its capacity to earn interest over time.

TMA Service Codes – Six-figure, alphanumeric codes that provide standard references and terms for identifying, describing, and reporting bank services and associated charges.

Trade Acceptance – An instrument similar to a banker's acceptance (BA) used in international transactions. Whereas a BA is drawn on a bank, a trade acceptance is typically drawn on and accepted by a company, usually the buyer (importer).

Trade Credit – A form of credit granted to a company's customers through the extension of credit terms for purchases.

Trade or Commercial Letter of Credit (L/C) – A document issued by a bank guaranteeing the payment of a customer's draft up to a stated amount for a specified period provided certain terms and conditions are met. It is typically used in international commercial transactions.

Transaction Balances – Depository balances held by a company for collection and disbursement activities.

Transaction Exposure - The vulnerability of a company's earnings accounts including receivables or payables to changes in exchange rates from the time a transaction is recorded until it is completed.

Transaction Sets – The electronic equivalent of a paper business document or form.

Transfer Agent – An individual or company that keeps a record of the sale and purchase of a company's stocks and bonds and maintains records of the shareholders of a company by name, address, and shares held.

Transit Routing Number – The number that is part of the MICR line of a check or payable through draft that allows the depository bank to route the check back to the drawee bank.

Translation Exposure – The vulnerability of a company's balance sheet accounts to exchange rate fluctuations when a foreign subsidiary's financial statements are converted into the parent company's home currency to consolidate the parent company's financial statements.

Treasury Bills (T-Bills) – Short-term discount debt instruments issued by the U.S. Treasury in maturities of 13, 26, and 52 weeks.

Treasury Bonds (T-Bonds) – Coupon securities issued by the U.S. Treasury with interest paid semi-annually in original maturities of ten to 30 years.

Treasury Management Information System (TMIS) – Configurations of hardware, software, and information sources designed to assist in the collection and formatting of information and routine calculations.

Treasury Notes (T-Notes) – Interest-bearing securities issued by the U.S. Treasury with original maturities of two to ten years.

Treasury Securities – "Full faith and credit" obligations of the U.S. Government issued by sale at periodic auctions, and delivered and cleared electronically.

Treasury Workstation – A personal computer that has software that gathers information from both internal and external sources and compiles the data to be analyzed for decision-making purposes. It is also capable of initiating transactions such as wire transfers or ACH transfers.

UN/EDIFACT Standards – United Nations Rules for EDI for Administration, Commerce and Transportation. UN/EDIFACT comprises a set of internationally agreed-upon standards, directories, and guidelines for the electronic interchange of structured data related to trade.

Uniform Commercial Code (UCC) – A uniform set of laws governing commercial transactions enacted separately and sometimes differently by each state.

Value-Added Bank (VAB) – A bank that provides VAN services for information related to payments as well as non-financial EDI services.

Value-Added Network (VAN) – A communications intermediary that provides various services to users of EC.

Value Dating – A technique employed by non-U.S. banks to obtain compensation for services provided to their customers.

Vendor Express – The U.S. Department of the Treasury program to pay government agency vendors electronically through the ACH.

Weighted Average Cost of Capital – A calculation of the cost of capital based on the relative mix and cost of equity and the after-tax cost of debt.

Wholesale Lockboxes – Lockboxes characterized by a moderate number of large-dollar remittances, usually from company payors.

Wide Area Network (WAN) - A network that connects computers and LANs in several locations.

Working Capital – Funds invested in a company's current asset accounts, accounts receivable, inventory, etc.

Yankee CD's – U.S. dollar-denominated CD's issued in the U.S. by foreign banks through their U.S. branches.

Year Basis – A factor affecting pricing is the lender's use of either a 360-day or 365-day year in calculating interest cost. Certain methods of borrowing have traditionally used one year basis over the other.

Yield – The gain, expressed in a percentage, an investor derives from a financial asset.

Yield Curve – The relationship between current market interest rates (or yields) and time to maturity of similar securities.

Yield to Maturity (YTM) - The measure of yield on a bond from the current date until maturity that takes into account the capital gain on a discount bond, or loss on a premium bond.

Zero Balance Account (ZBA) – A disbursement bank account on which checks are written even though the balances in the accounts are maintained at zero. Debits are covered by a transfer of funds from a master account at the same bank.

Zero-Coupon Bonds – Debt instruments that are issued at a deep discount to face value, pay no interest and accrete to par as they approach maturity.

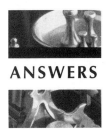

ANSWERS

Chapter 1: The Role of Cash Management in Corporate Finance

1. The major objectives of cash management are:

   - Maintaining liquidity
   - Optimizing cash resources
   - Obtaining short- and long-term financing
   - Monitoring and controlling financial risk exposure
   - Coordinating decision-making with other departments in the firm

2. The cash flow timeline comprises the total time interval from the time resources are purchased at the beginning of a company's operating cycle until the time payment is received for goods or services at the end of a company's operating cycle.

3. The three general types of cash flows are as follows:

   Cash Inflows - These are funds collected from customers, obtained from financial sources, or from other payors.

   Concentration and Liquidity Management Flows - Concentrated funds are those that are systematically transferred to create a centralized inventory of liquid reserves held as cash or invested in cash equivalents. Concentration funds include internal transfers among operating units of a company and between various bank accounts owned by a company.

   Cash Outflows - These funds are disbursed from liquid reserves to vendors, employees, lenders, shareholders, and other payees of the company.

4. The tools of cash management are designed to synchronize a company's cash flows, thereby promoting the efficient operation of the cash flow timeline. Products used in the collection, concentration, and disbursement of funds reduce unfavorable float that occurs along the cash flow timeline.

5. The principal roles of the finance function are:

   Accounting - reporting and record-keeping function
   Funding - raising capital to finance projects
   Capital Budgeting - determining the projects in which to invest

6. The major decision areas are:

   - Capital structure
   - Investment decisions
   - Financing decisions
   - Dividend decisions

7.   The key players in the finance function (other than the cash manager) are:

 • Chief Financial Officer (CFO)
 • Treasurer
 • Controller
 • Internal Auditor
 • Credit Manager

8.   The typical cash management functions and responsibilities include:

 • Funds management
 • Banking systems administration
 • Liquidity management
 • Forecasting
 • Systems design, implementation, and evaluation

9.   *Float* - The time interval, or delay, between the start and completion of a specific phase or process occurring along the cash flow timeline.

10.   The 1970s saw the introduction of remote disbursement and controlled disbursement.

11.   Depository Institutions Deregulation and Monetary Control Act of 1980 had a major impact on bank services and prices.

12.   The key issues in the current treasury environment are:

 • *Quality concerns* - Treasury departments are being challenged to provide a high level of quality results at an acceptable cost.

 • *Reorganization of treasury operations* - Many companies have restructured their treasury operations using such tools as: re-engineering, benchmarking, and outsourcing.

Chapter 2: Accounting and Financial Concepts

1.   GAAP (Generally Accepted Accounting Principles) are the detailed rules, developed by the Financial Accounting Standards Board, that govern financial reporting and record-keeping in the U.S.

2.   A company may avoid reporting it by combining cash and marketable securities on its balance sheet or by reporting checks written but not yet presented as a current liability.

3.   The three basic financial statements are the balance sheet, the income statement, and the statement of cash flows.

4. The present value of $1,500 two years from now at an opportunity cost of 5% can be computed as follows:

$$\text{Present Value} = \frac{\text{Future Value}}{(1 + \text{Interest Rate})^{\text{Number of Periods}}}$$

$$= \frac{\$1,500}{(1 + .05)^2} = \$1,500 \times (1 + .05)^{-2}$$

$$= \frac{\$1,500}{(1.1025)} = \$1,500 \times (.9070) = \$1,360.50$$

5. Companies use debt for two basic reasons: 1) debt is less expensive due to its tax-deductibility, and 2) the use of debt does not dilute the equity position of the shareholders.

6. A company needs liquidity for transaction requirements, precautionary requirements, and speculative requirements.

7. The ratios typically used to measure liquidity are the current ratio, quick ratio, cash flow to total debt ratio, cash conversion cycle, and cash turnover.

8. The cash conversion cycle measures the time it takes a company to convert a cash outflow (for payment of inventory purchases) into a cash inflow (collection of accounts receivable). This measure uses the average age of the inventory, the average days of accounts receivable, and the average age of the accounts payable to indicate how efficiently a company is using its current assets and liabilities.

9. Among the disadvantages of traditional ratio measures are the following:

    • Traditional ratio measures usually reflect accounting rather than economic values.
    • Ratios express static relationships that do not take the variability of cash flows into account except to the extent that the ratios themselves may vary.
    • Financial ratios provide indications but not answers. The evaluation of the company's worth is a matter of judgment.
    • Ratios are affected by differing methods of depreciation and by window dressing, the practice of adjusting certain accounts just prior to the end of the accounting period to make financial statements look better.

10. In cash accounting, all accounting entries are directly related to a cash inflow or out-flow. In accrual accounting, revenues are recognized as they are earned and expenses as they are incurred, regardless of when the related cash flows occur.

11. The auditor can render four types of opinion: unqualified, qualified, disclaimed, or adverse.

12. If a company is leveraged with high levels of debt or other fixed costs, earnings will change at a more rapid rate than revenues.

Chapter 3: The U.S. Financial Environment

1. The major products of commercial banks are:

    - Deposit Accounts
    - Credit Services
    - Investment Banking Services
    - Payments and Collections
    - Trade Services
    - Credit Enhancement or Payment Guaranty
    - Acting as Agent or Fiduciary
    - Consulting Services
    - Risk Management Services
    - Broker/Dealer Services

2. Underwriting is the principal function of an investment banking firm. It ensures the issuer of stock or bonds of a definite sum of money for the issue at a definite time. The investment banker assumes the risk of price and marketability.

3. Savings and mutual savings banks have traditionally been state chartered. The Garn-St. Germain Act of 1982 allows mutual savings banks to switch to a federal charter.

4. Unlike banks, credit unions are not-for-profit financial institutions with restricted membership.

5. The five major roles of the Federal Reserve are:

    - Supervising and regulating banks
    - Conducting monetary policy
    - Providing services for banks
    - Acting as the fiscal agent for the U.S. Treasury
    - Acting as a consumer protection agency

6. National bank charters are granted by the Office of the Comptroller of the Currency (OCC).

7. The Office of Thrift Supervision is the primary regulator of nationally chartered S&Ls.

8. The Edge Act allows U.S. banks to invest in corporations engaged in international banking.

9. The McFadden Act originally prohibited banks from accepting deposits across state lines. The Douglas Amendment allowed banks to merge across state lines if each state permitted it, but did not allow bank holding companies to acquire banks across state lines. The Interstate Banking and Branching Efficiency Act (1994) phases out, over a three-year period, the state barriers against branching established by the McFadden Act. Full interstate branching was achieved in June 1997, except for Texas and Montana

10. The Glass-Steagall Act separates commercial banking from investment banking.

11. The Depository Institutions Deregulation and Monetary Control Act (DIDMCA) of 1980 included mandates that the Federal Reserve reduce and/or price float.

12. The Financial Institutions Reform Recovery and Enforcement Act (FIRREA) consolidated the two financial institution insurance funds under the FDIC.

13. The Interstate Bank and Branching Efficiency Act of 1994 has the following primary provisions:

    - Permitted bank holding companies to acquire a bank located in any state effective September 1995.
    - Allowed banks in one state to merge with banks in another state beginning June 1997, so long as neither state had taken legislative action to prohibit interstate mergers between the date of enactment and the end of May 1997.
    - Allowed banks to establish new branches in states where they do not maintain a branch if the host state passed a law expressly permitting such branches.

14. The payment of interest on corporate demand deposits is prohibited by Regulation Q.

15. Federal Reserve Regulation CC established rules for handling return of checks and payable-through-drafts.

16. Article 3 of the Uniform Commercial Code (UCC) permits avoidance of inadvertent accord and satisfaction.

17. Under UCC Article 4A, banks are not responsible for consequential damages, which are losses resulting from the action or error made by the bank beyond the simple loss of funds. A bank incorrectly executing a payment order remains liable for interest losses or incidental expenses. The bank is liable for consequential damages only if it agrees to assume this liability in a written agreement with the customer.

Chapter 4: The Payments System

1. The payee is the receiver of a check and party to whom a payment is made. The payor is the party who writes or draws the check to remit funds.

2. The purpose of the Magnetic Ink Character Recognition (MICR) is to clear checks back to the bank on which the check is drawn and, when received by the drawee bank, to debit the payor's account.

3. Checks can be cleared through the following channels:

    - On-us clearing
    - Clearing house
    - Federal Reserve Bank
    - Correspondent bank

4. A cash letter is a bundle of checks accompanied by a list of individual items and other control documents.

5. A direct send is a cash letter that bypasses the local Federal Reserve. A bank sends it directly to the paying bank or a non-local Federal Reserve bank.

6. An on-us item is a check deposited in the same bank on which it is drawn.

7. High Dollar Group Sort (HDGS) is the Fed's program to expedite the processing of high-dollar checks through the system. The HDGS program automatically involves making a second presentment to banks with more than $10 million of checks presented daily from outside their Fed districts.

8. A ledger balance reflects accounting entries to a bank account while collected balances reflect the balance in an account for which the bank of deposit has received settlement.

9. Deposit float is the sum of the deposited items that are in the process of collection.

10. Factors that determine availability include:

    - Drawee's location
    - Time of deposit
    - Pre-encoding by the customer
    - Checks rejected during processing

11. Federal Reserve float represents the difference between the availability granted the clearing bank and the time required to debit the drawee bank's account.

12. PTD is drawn against the payor and not a bank.

13. A sight draft is payable when presented while a time draft is payable at a specified future date.

14. The most commonly used ACH formats are:

    - Prearranged Payment or Deposit (PPD) used for consumer transactions
    - Cash Concentration and Disbursement (CCD) used to move funds within or between companies
    - Cash Concentration and Disbursement plus Addendum (CCD+) used for the U.S. Treasury Department's Vendor Express program and corporate-to-corporate payments
    - Corporate Trade Exchange (CTX) used for corporate-to-corporate payments

15. In an ACH transaction settlement occurs one or two days after transmission of the payment information to the ACH operator, with the debit and credit occurring simultaneously.

16. Settlement through Fedwire is immediate rather than on a one- or two-day cycle like the ACH.

17. A repetitive wire transfer is used when a company makes frequent transfers between the same debit and credit parties. A unique identifier is used to identify each transfer with only the date and dollar amount allowed to be changed. A non-repetitive wire requires that all information for a wire transfer be given when making the wire.

18. CHIPS is both a message and a settlement system, while S.W.I.F.T. is not a funds transfer network. S.W.I.F.T. sends payment instructions, while settlement occurs through another means like Fedwire, CHIPS or a correspondent bank account.

19. A daylight overdraft is an intra-day exposure that occurs when an account is overdrawn during a business day. Because the Federal Reserve is guarantor of a wire transfer to the receiving bank, it could be forced to make good a wire transfer initiated by a bank that subsequently fails. The Federal Reserve has set a cap on the daylight overdraft allowed for each financial institution to lessen the risk.

20. Among examples of the types of security procedures that are commonly used are the following:

- Physical security and limited access at both the company and the bank
- Passwords and Personal Identification Numbers (PINs) to identify authorized users
- Test keys or codes to validate wire transfers
- Repetitive wires to limit where funds can be transferred
- Dual approval (one person enters the wire and another reviews and releases it)
- Electronic security methods such as encryption (the scrambling of a message by the sender and the unscrambling of the message by the receiver) and message authentication (a digital signature which prevents an unauthorized person from changing a wire)

Chapter 5: Credit and Accounts Receivable Management

1. The major objectives of credit management are:

- Establishing and communicating a company's credit policies
- Establishing terms of sale consistent with overall company objectives
- Evaluating customer creditworthiness and setting customer credit lines
- Ensuring prompt and accurate customer billing in conjunction with the customer service or billing departments
- Creating, preserving, and collecting accounts receivable
- Maintaining up-to-date records of accounts receivable
- Following up on overdue accounts and initiating collection procedures when necessary

2. A credit policy consists of setting credit standards, specifying credit terms, and establishing a collection policy.

3. The formula for calculating the effective cost of not taking a discount is as follows:

$$\text{Annualized Cost of Trade Credit} = \frac{\text{Early Pmt Discount}}{(1 - \text{Early Pmt Discount})} \times \frac{365}{(\text{Net Pmt Period} - \text{Discount Pmt Period})}$$

Given terms of 3/20, Net 60, the cost of not taking the discount (i.e., paying the net amount on day 60, rather than the discounted amount on day 20) can be calculated as:

$$\text{Cost of Trade Credit} \ = \ \frac{.03}{(1-.03)} \ \text{x} \ \frac{365}{(60-20)} \ = \ 28.22\%$$

4. The five C's of credit are:

    - *Character* - willingness to pay
    - *Capacity* - ability to pay
    - *Capital* - financial strength
    - *Collateral* - protection for the lender
    - *Conditions* - economic environment

5. Credit scoring is a technique used to estimate creditworthiness of credit applicants based on statistical profiles of prior credit applicants. Various elements on the applications are weighted and compared to historical profiles.

6. Revolving credit terms involve the granting of credit without requiring specific approval of each transaction as long as the credit limit is not exceeded and required minimum payments are made on time.

7. Seasonal dating is a special credit term used in industries with highly seasonal sales. Payment is due near the end of the buyer's selling season although sliding discounts may be offered to encourage early payment.

8. Days' sales outstanding (DSO) in this question is determined as follows:

$$\frac{\text{Average Daily}}{\text{Credit Sales}} \ = \ \frac{(\$75,000 + \$100,000 + \$90,000)}{90} \ = \$2,944.44$$

$$\text{DSO} \ = \ \frac{\text{Outstanding Accounts Receivable}}{\text{Average Daily Credit Sales}} \ = \ \frac{\$125,000.00}{\$2,944.44} \ = \ 42.45 \text{ Days}$$

9. Factoring is the sale or transfer of title of an accounts receivable to a factoring company.

10. The Robinson-Patman Act is federal legislation that prohibits price discrimination.

11. The Truth-in-Lending Act is federal legislation that requires disclosure of the true cost of a loan.

Chapter 6: Collections

1. The major objectives of a collection system are to mobilize funds, provide timely and accurate information, update accounts receivable, and support audit trails for both internal and external auditors.

2.   Companies may collect through the following methods:

- through an over-the-counter/field deposit system
- by mail payments to the company or to a lockbox
- electronically via a wire transfer or through the ACH system

3.   In designing a collection system, a company must take into consideration the following issues:

- commonly accepted payment practices
- the nature of the payments system
- the nature of its own business
- characteristics of the payment instrument used
- the cost of float and system administration
- the differences between wholesale and retail businesses

4.   Collection float is composed of mail float, processing float, and availability float.

5.   Availability float is determined by the depository bank's availability schedule.

6.   The average daily cost of float and the annual cost of float are determined as follows:

- Average daily float = $2,120,000 / 30 = $70,667
- Annual cost of float = $70,667 x .07 = $4,947

7.   The selection of either a company processing center or a lockbox is a function of the volume of checks processed and the dollar size of the checks. For example, a low volume of checks with large-dollar amounts usually supports the use of a lockbox system.

8.   A lockbox system reduces mail, processing, and availability float; provides economies of scale in processing; and establishes an audit trail outside the company.

9.   A wholesale lockbox is used primarily for corporate-to-corporate payments where large-dollar remittances are involved. A retail lockbox is used for large-volume, small-dollar remittance payments like consumer payments.

10.   The determination of the net benefit of the lockbox is as follows:

- Average float with lockbox = $1,010,000 / 30   = $ 33,667
- Annual cost of float with lockbox = $33,667 x .07   =   2,357
- Float savings with lockbox = $4,947 - 2,357   =   2,590
- Fixed lockbox cost   =   (1,000)
- Variable lockbox cost = (6,000 x .30)   =   (1,800)
- Savings of internal processing cost = (6,000 x . 20)   =   1,200
- Net benefit of lockbox   = $ 990
- A lockbox is profitable in this situation.

11. An electronic lockbox allows companies to receive customer payments by wire transfer or through the ACH.

12. An over-the-counter field deposit system is a collection system in which funds are received and deposited by local operating units of the company such as division offices or retail stores.

13. A pre-authorized debit involves the advance approval of a payor for the payee to transfer funds from the payor's account. An example of this application is the automatic withdrawal of insurance premiums from a policyholder's account.

14. Net settlement systems benefit companies in the same industry that buy and sell from each other on a regular basis by requiring only periodic transfers of the net amount due to other companies.

15. Image technology is used to facilitate processing of both wholesale and retail payments. This technology allows paper documents to be scanned, converted to a digital image, and stored for subsequent handling and processing. The documents scanned can be both checks and remittance advices. Potential benefits of applying image technology to the remittance processing function include reduced overall processing costs, increased productivity, improved accuracy, and the ability to capture data for automated posting to accounts receivable.

16. The major types of retail collection systems include credit cards, debit cards, automated teller machine (ATM) networks, telephone banking, bill paying services, home banking, agents, and smart cards.

Chapter 7: Cash Concentration

1. The objectives of a cash concentration system include:

   - Simplifying cash management
   - Improving control of funds
   - Pooling funds for investment or debt reduction
   - Minimizing excess balances
   - Reducing transfer expenses

2. EDT stands for electronic depository transfer, which is an ACH transaction used to concentrate funds.

3. Wire transfers may also be used for concentration. They are generally used when the amounts are large enough to justify their cost.

4. The major cost components of a cash concentration system are excess balances in the company's banks, costs to transfer funds, and the administrative costs of operating the concentration system.

5. Excess balances may arise through delays in deposit reporting, clearing, or the initiation of transfers.

6. Anticipation is the initiation of a transfer before funds become available at the deposit bank. Availability anticipation initiates the transfers on the basis of actual deposit information, while deposit anticipation is done on the basis of unreported, expected deposits.

7. Threshold concentration allows bank balances to build to a predetermined level and then a transfer is initiated to the concentration bank.

8. The minimum wire transfer required to break even is determined as follows:

$$\text{Minimum Transfer} = \frac{\text{Wire Cost} - \text{EDT Cost}}{\text{Days Accelerated} \times \dfrac{\text{Opportunity Cost}}{365 \text{ Days}}}$$

$$= \frac{\$22.00 - \$1.00}{1 \text{ Day} \times \dfrac{.08}{365 \text{ Days}}}$$

$$= \$95,812.50$$

9. Fraud may be prevented by having different reports prepared by different people, by conducting surprise audits, by requiring daily reporting, and by instructing banks to allow no overdrafts.

10. Pooling funds is a valuable objective of cash concentration because it permits a company to buy larger blocks of short-term securities which tend to earn higher yields. Alternatively, pooled funds can be used to reduce debt or take advantage of supplier discount opportunities.

11. Among a company's concentration system considerations are its collection system, disbursement system, funds transfer alternatives, and banking network.

Chapter 8: Disbursement and Accounts Payable Management

1. The five major objectives of a disbursement system are:

   - Cost reduction
   - Disbursement float management
   - Information access
   - Fraud prevention
   - Relationship maintenance

2. Disbursement systems may be centralized, decentralized, or a cimbination of both. In a centralized system check writing and account reconciliation are controlled from headquarters, while in a decentralized system checks are drawn on a local bank and account reconciliation is performed at the local level. It is also possible for check issuance and account reconciliation to be performed at the local level but drawn on a centralized disbursement account.

3. Disbursement float is composed of mail float, processing float, and clearing float.

4. Control and fraud prevention measures include the following:

   • Developing and implementing written policies and procedures for the creation and distribution of disbursement checks.
   • Separating functional authority for collection and disbursement of funds.
   • Separating expense approval, check-signing authority, and account reconciliation responsibilities.
   • Using safety paper and watermarks that are difficult to reproduce on check stock.
   • Using reputable printing companies.
   • Storing checks and signature plates in separate secure areas with controlled access.
   • Using printing processes that do not require preprinted check stock (i.e., laser printing of checks and MICR lines).
   • Using Positive Pay, a service that matches check serial numbers and dollar amounts against the company's issue file to determine the checks to be paid.
   • Setting a specific amount limit on checks issued from each type of account. Checks issued above this limit are returned to the depositor as unauthorized.
   • Increasing the use of electronic payment methods and utilizing appropriate security features
   • Using an electronic payment authorization service (similar to Positive Pay for checks) to protect against fraudulent ACH debits.

5. Controlled disbursement is a bank service that provides notification of the dollar amount of checks that will clear against the controlled disbursement account that day. This information is usually available by early or mid-morning. The disbursement bank must receive its final cash letter of the day from the local Fed early in the morning so that the checks can be sorted and the company notified of its funding requirement. Payor bank services are often used to aid in this process.

6. A zero balance account is an account on which a company writes checks, even though the balance in the account is maintained at zero. The checks are covered by a transfer of funds from the company's master account in that bank.

7. EFTPS is the primary method for collecting and accounting for taxes withheld by employers from individuals' salaries and wages, as well as corporate business and excise taxes. Most companies have been mandated to make these deposits electronically.

8. Payor Bank Services is an information service of the Fed that electronically notifies controlled disbursement banks early in the morning of all checks that will be physically presented later that day.

9. A controlled disbursement bank should be evaluated on the following criteria:

    - Timeliness of reporting of disbursement banks
    - Processing accuracy
    - Volume capacity
    - Reporting detail and reconciliation services
    - Price
    - Customer service support

10. Positive Pay is a service used for fraud control. The company transmits a file of checks issued. The bank matches serial numbers and dollar amounts and pays only those checks that match.

11. In a partial reconciliation service, a bank lists all checks paid in numerical order by check serial number, or in chronological order by date paid. For each item, the paid report generally shows the check serial number, dollar amount, and date paid. The listing is available as a paper report, on CD-Rom, and/or via electronic form. With a full reconciliation service, a company supplies an electronic file of checks issued to its bank and the bank matches checks paid against the file. The bank supplies a listing, either as a paper report and/or in an electronic format, of checks paid and outstanding in check serial number order.

12. There are two situations in which a bank has credit exposure. These are:

    - With delayed funding, there is risk that an ACH debit may be returned by the bank on which it is drawn. By the time the returned debit reaches the disbursement bank, it may be too late to return any disbursement checks being funded by the ACH debit. The disbursement bank is owed funds and becomes a creditor of the company.
    - With the use of an affiliated bank for disbursing with funding through the parent bank, there is no problem if the affiliate bank is funded directly on a same-day basis by a wire transfer. However, if the company funds the parent bank and the parent bank automatically funds the affiliate with immediate funds, there is a potential overdraft problem at the parent bank. Since the affiliate bank does not have an overdrawn account, it cannot legally refuse to pay the checks even though there may be an overdraft at the parent bank, unless this option is provided for in the service agreement.

13. The two basic approaches to managing an integrated or comprehensive accounts payable service are:

    - A company sends a single data file to a third-party service provider containing a list of all its payments to be made. The file contains information on when to issue a disbursement and to whom, as well as instructions on the payment method to be used (check, wire, or ACH).
    - Alternatively, the third-party provider maintains a database of a company's payees that includes detailed information such as preferred payment methods, specific remittance information, and receiving financial institutions. The database is periodically updated as new payees are added or an existing payee's remittance profile

changes (for example, if a payee switches to ACH instead of check for its standard payment type). In such cases, as a company makes a disbursement, it sends to the third party only limited payment information.

14. Purchasing cards are credit cards used by a company for the small-dollar purchase of supplies, inventory, equipment, and service contracts. Advantages of a purchasing card include:

- Cost savings
- Improved control
- Better vendor relations
- Improved reporting

15. Image technology is a major component of many disbursement services. Both the front and the back of a check may be captured and converted into digital information using optical scanning. Check images (all of them or selected ones) may be transmitted to a company's computer and stored there or sent to a fax machine. The check images may also be stored in a bank database which a company can access to view or retrieve the images. Any of these methods allows a company faster access to check information. Imaging services are particularly useful in conjunction with Positive Pay services.

Chapter 9: Electronic Commerce

1. The primary benefits of electronic commerce (EC) include the following:

- Improved productivity
- Reduced cycle time that may result in lower inventory
- Lower error rates
- Improved cash forecasting
- Improved communication capabilities

2. The three basic types of electronic data interchange (EDI) are cross-industry EDI, industry convention EDI, and proprietary EDI.

3. Electronic networks used for EDI include a LAN, a WAN, an intranet, an extranet, and the Internet.

4. EDI is a vehicle for the electronic movement of business data in a standard format from one company's application system to another company's application system. FEDI and EFT are subsets of EDI. FEDI is the electronic transmission of payments and payment-related information in standard formats between company trading partners and/or their banks. EFT is the exchange of value, which requires the involvement of financial intermediaries such as banks to send and receive electronic payments.

5. The costs that must be considered in an EC or EDI implementation are as follows:

- Software
- Hardware

- Communications
- Encryption and message authentication
- Education and training
- Trading partner selling and support
- Negotiating with trading partners

6. In addition to the costs of EDI, additional barriers are:

    - Convenience of paper-based systems
    - Tradition of paper-based systems
    - Dual systems may be required initially
    - EDI capabilities of banks

7. Parallel efforts in EDI standards development have been proceeding in many countries leading to the development of the UN/EDIFACT standards (United Nations EDI for Administration, Commerce and Transportation). UN/EDIFACT comprises a set of internationally agreed-upon standards, directories, and guidelines for the electronic interchange of structured data that relates to trade in goods and services between independent computerized information systems. UN/EDIFACT standards are widely used in Europe and some Asian countries.

8. The primary ASC X12 financial transaction sets are the following:

    - 810 Invoice
    - 820 Payment Order/Remittance Advice
    - 821 Financial Information Reporting
    - 822 Customer Account Analysis
    - 823 Lockbox Information
    - 824 Application Advice
    - 828 Debit Authorization
    - 835 Health Care Claim Payment/Advice
    - 997 Functional Acknowledgement

9. The primary NACHA formats for ACH payments are the following:

    - *PPD* - Prearranged Payments or Deposits
    - *CCD* - Cash Concentration or Disbursement
    - *CCD+* - CCD plus Addenda
    - *TXP* - Tax Payment Format
    - *CTX* - Corporate Trade Exchange

10. The basic steps performed by EDI software are file conversion, translation, and communication.

11. The services offered by VANs to their customers are the following:

    - Communications capacity
    - Mailboxing
    - Protocol conversion

- Standards conversion
- Line speed conversion
- Gateway to other VANs or VABs
- Implementation assistance

12.   VABs offer VAN services related to payments. They may also provide EDI services that are not directly related to payments or Financial EDI.

13.   EDI enables companies to complete paper processing more rapidly. This along with EFT generally results in faster payments, which are a disadvantage to buyers and an advantage to sellers. To compensate for changes in the cash flow timeline, companies are beginning to negotiate new EDI-based credit terms.

14.   Evaluated Receipts Settlement (ERS) is a payment method designed to eliminate the need for a supplier to provide an invoice to the customer. The dollar amount for ERS payments is based not on an invoice, but on a calculation of the quantity actually received by the customer multiplied by the price on the purchase order. The supplier does not send an invoice, but is simply paid by the customer on an agreed date after receipt of the shipment.

Chapter 10: Information and Technology Management

1.   The objectives of information management include the following:

- Determining cash requirements
- Tracking activity
- Identifying opportunities
- Updating forecasts
- Updating management information

2.   The typical tasks a cash manager performs on a daily basis include the following:

- Obtaining account balances and transaction detail from external sources
- Obtaining internal information that impacts the cash flow timeline
- Consolidating the external and internal information into the cash position worksheet
- Integrating data on current-day transfers
- Determining the cash position
- Initiating funds transfers
- Executing investment and/or borrowing decisions
- Updating the cash position worksheet and the short-term cash forecast

3.   The types of internal data exchanged between the treasury area and other areas of the company include the following:

- Sales summary reports
- Purchasing summary reports
- Cash receipts and disbursements
- Aging schedules

- Investment schedules
- Debt repayment schedules

4. The sources of current-day information for the cash manager include the following:

    - Lockbox deposits and remittance detail
    - Controlled disbursement
    - Cash concentration reports
    - Wire transfers
    - ACH transactions
    - Money market and foreign exchange rates
    - Investments
    - Return items
    - Positive Pay exception items

5. Multi-bank reporting is a service used by companies with two or more banking relationships. An arrangement is established by which one of the company's financial institutions or a third-party reporting service gathers and consolidates the account balances and transaction activity from each of the company's financial institutions. The arrangement is commonly referred to as data exchange.

6. The five most common types of reporting mechanisms are personal computers, direct high-speed connections, telephone, facsimile (fax), and the Internet.

7. A treasury workstation is typically a PC which has software that gathers information from both internal and external sources, then compiles the data for purposes of analysis and decision-making. A treasury workstation can either be stand-alone or part of a LAN or WAN.

8. The modules typically found in treasury workstation systems include the following:

    - Account balance report
    - Target balance report
    - Cash position worksheet
    - Transaction detail report
    - Investment
    - Borrowing
    - Letters of credit

9. The types of transactions which can typically be initiated through a treasury workstation include the following:

    - Wire transfers
    - ACH debits and credits
    - Stop payments
    - Letters of credit
    - Investment purchases and sales
    - Loan drawdowns and repayments
    - Foreign exchange transactions

10. The benefits associated with TMIS technology include the following:

- Improved productivity
- Expedited data gathering, compilation, and analysis
- Increased forecasting accuracy
- Reduced borrowing expense
- Improved short-term investment returns
- Improved management reporting

The costs associated with TMIS technology include the following:

- Hardware and software selection, purchase, and installation
- Start-up and personal training expense
- Administration, maintenance, and overhead
- Telecommunications charges
- Transaction service charges
- System security expenses

11. The three most common types of security risks related to TMIS are loss of data, unauthorized user access, and computer viruses.

12. The basic types of security safeguards for TMIS are as follows:

- Creating a security officer/system administrator position
- Developing written policies and procedures
- Establishing physical security
- Instituting basic access requirements
- Establishing different levels of user access
- Requiring backup storage
- Instituting computer virus protection methods
- Using electronic security

13. A disaster recovery plan should include the following steps:

- Indentifying internal and external threats
- Assessing business risks
- Determining what is needed to perform critical tasks
- Developing backup or alternative systems and sites
- Obtaining management approval
- Keeping the plan current

Chapter 11: Forecasting Cash Flows

1. The objectives of cash forecasting are:

- Liquidity management
- Financial control

- Meeting strategic objectives
- Capital budgeting
- Managing costs
- Managing currency exposure

2. The steps in the forecasting process include the following:

- Determine the forecast horizons
- Understand the company's cash flow cycle
- Divide the cash flows into their major components
- Categorize the cash flows by their degree of certainty
- Identify and organize the data to be used in the forecast
- Select a forecast method and validate the forecast

3. Short-term forecasts can be prepared using either the receipts and disbursements method or the distribution method.

4. A pro forma statement is prepared using the percentage-of-sales method. This presumes the next financial statement period will retain the same relationship between sales and other income statement and balance sheet items as it did in the prior period.

5. The primary types of time series forecasting are simple moving average and exponential smoothing.

6. The moving average forecast is: (100+150+250+210) / 4= 177.5

7. Exponential smoothing is a variation on the simple moving average that weights each observation with more recent observations given heavier weights. This enables trends and seasonality to be captured in the forecast.

8. The steps in selecting a forecasting method are as follows:

- Establish data relationships
- Select a method
- Test and validate the relationship

9. The three types of forecast validation are in-sample validation, out-of-sample validation, and ongoing validation.

10. Regression analysis is a statistical technique that systematically identifies the relationship between a variable to be predicted (the dependent variable) and other data that may be available (explanatory or independent variables).

Chapter 12: Short-Term Investments

1. A firm has a short-term investment portfolio in order to hold temporary surplus funds, maintain a liquidity reserve, and generate income with an acceptable degree of risk.

2. A company's investment policy is influenced by:

   - Purpose and objectives for short-term investments
   - Maturity and segmentation
   - Tax status of the company
   - Staffing
   - Legal or internal restrictions
   - Financial reporting requirements

3. A company will examine the time to maturity, credit quality, and marketability of a financial instrument in order to determine its fit with the company's short-term investment portfolio.

4. Financial markets may be divided into long-term or capital markets with instruments that mature in more than one year, and the money market, which consists of short-term debt instruments maturing in one year or less.

5. In a book entry transaction, the physical securities do not move when traded. Treasury securities, for example, remain in a vault at the Federal Reserve Bank of New York, and book entries are made when ownership changes.

6. The U.S. Treasury issues T-bills with maturities of three months to one year, T-notes with maturities from 2 to 10 years, and T-bonds with maturities of 10 to 30 years.

7. Federal agency securities are debt instruments issued by agencies with some degree of backing by the U.S. Government. Agencies act as financial intermediaries in certain credit markets. For example, the Federal National Mortgage Association (Fannie Mae) helps provide liquidity to the mortgage market.

8. Municipal securities are classified as general obligation securities, certificates of participation, or revenue securities. General obligation securities are backed by the taxing power of the issuing entity, certificates of participation are securities used by municipal issuers to finance certain equipment purchases and capital projects, and revenue securities pay their principal and interest from proceeds of a specific project.

9. The income from municipal obligations is exempt from federal income tax and is often exempt from taxes in the state in which they are issued.

10. Eurodollar CDs are U.S. dollar-denominated certificates of deposit issued by banks, including branches of U.S. banks, outside the U.S.

11. Bankers' acceptances are short-term obligations of a bank created in financing an international or domestic trade transaction.

12. Repo is an abbreviation for a repurchase agreement, which is a transaction between a securities dealer and an investor in which the dealer sells securities to the investor with an agreement to repurchase them at a specific time and price to produce a pre-determined yield to the investor.

13. Commercial paper is an unsecured promissory note that matures in 270 days or less.

14.   Money market preferred is preferred stock in which the dividend rate is adjusted every 49 days on the basis of current Treasury yields.

15.   Yield is influenced by:

   • *Marketability* - securities without an active secondary market tend to have higher yields
   • *Default Risk* - the lower the credit rating of the instrument, the higher its yield
   • *Price Risk* - a reduction in a security's price increases its yield; normally the shorter the time to maturity, the lower the yield
   • *Tax-Status* - tax-exempt securities, like municipal securities, will have a lower pre-tax yield than a taxable instrument of similar risk

16.   An inverted yield curve means that yields on long-term securities are not as high as those of short-term securities. This is due to investor expectations of falling interest rates.

17.   The purchase price of a 182-day, $100,000 T-bill sold at a 4.53% discount rate is calculated as follows:

$$\text{Dollar Discount} = (\text{Discount Rate x Face Value}) \times \frac{\text{Days to Maturity}}{360}$$

$$= (.0453 \times \$100,000) \times \frac{182}{360} = \$2,290.17$$

$$\text{Purchase Price} = \text{Face Value - Dollar Discount}$$

$$= \$100,000 - \$2,290.17 = \$97,709.83$$

18.   The bond equivalent yield of the T-bill in Question 18 is calculated as follows:

$$\text{Bond Equivalent Yield (BEY)} = \left(\frac{\text{Dollar Discount}}{\text{Purchase Price}}\right) \times \left(\frac{365}{\text{Days to Maturity}}\right)$$

$$= \left(\frac{\$2,290.17}{\$97,709.83}\right) \times \left(\frac{365}{182}\right) = 4.70\%$$

19.   Banks provide sweep accounts, which automatically transfer excess balances into an interest-earning account.

20.   The two categories of investment strategies are (1) passive strategies and (2) active strategies. Passive strategies include replicating an index, overnight sweeps, and matching investment maturities with funding needs. Active strategies include dividend capture, riding the yield curve, and the use of swaps or other derivatives.

21.   The development, implementation, and periodic review of investment guidelines are critical factors in the management of short-term investments. They are usually determined by the CFO and/or the board of directors. The important considerations are: acceptable instruments, diversification, acceptable dealers/issuers, investment authority, and custody requirements.

Chapter 13: Borrowing

1. The objectives of a company's borrowing program include:

    - Maintaining availability of credit
    - Minimizing the cost of funds
    - Minimizing risk
    - Maintaining flexibility

2. The London Interbank Offered Rate (LIBOR) is the most commonly used base rate for short-term borrowing.

3. Credit support or enhancement is a process in which a bank or an insurance company guarantees the debt obligation of the borrower using an indemnity bond or letter of credit. The borrower's debt is traded at a level that reflects the credit rating of the guarantor.

4. A committed line of credit usually involves a formal loan agreement and obligates the bank to provide funding up to the established credit limit, provided the agreement is not in default.

5. The effective annual borrowing rate (interest cost) of the loan can be determined as follows:

$$\text{Effective Annual Borrowing Rate} = \left(\frac{(.07 \times \$200{,}000) + (.0025 \times \$3{,}000{,}000)}{\$200{,}000} \right) \times \left(\frac{365}{365} \right)$$

$$= \left(\frac{\$14{,}000 + \$750}{\$200{,}000} \right) \times (1) = 7.38\%$$

6. Some commercial paper issuers have lines of credit to be used if market conditions are not conducive to issuing commercial paper.

7. The effective annual interest cost of issuing the commercial paper can be determined as follows:

$$\text{Usable Funds} = \text{Face Value} \times \left[1 - \left(\text{Discount Rate} \times \frac{\text{Maturity}}{360} \right) \right]$$

$$= \$10{,}000{,}000 \times \left[1 - \left(.06 \times \frac{60}{360} \right) \right] = \$990{,}000$$

$$\text{Interest Cost} = \text{Face Value} - \text{Usable Funds} = \$1{,}000{,}000 - \$990{,}000 = \$10{,}000$$

$$\text{Pro-Rated Dealer Cost} = (\text{Annual Dealer Charge} \times \text{Face Value}) \times \left(\frac{\text{Maturity}}{360} \right)$$

$$= (.0025 \times \$1{,}000{,}000) \times \left(\frac{60}{360} \right) = \$417$$

$$\text{Total Issue Costs} \quad = \text{Interest Cost} + \text{Pro-Rated Dealer Cost}$$

$$= \$10,000 + \$417 = \$10,417$$

$$\text{Effective Annual Cost of Issue} \ = \left(\frac{\text{Total Issue Costs}}{\text{Usable Funds}} \right) \ x \ \left(\frac{365}{\text{Maturity}} \right)$$

$$= \left(\frac{\$10,417}{\$990,000} \right) \ x \ \left(\frac{365}{60} \right) \ = 6.40\%$$

8. A loan participation is an arrangement whereby a bank purchases an interest in another lender's credit facility.

9. An asset suitable for securitization should have a predictable, steady cash flow and a low level of historical loss experience.

10. A bond indenture is the formal agreement among all parties to a bond issue defining the details of the issue, such as the collateral, if any, and the duties of the trustee.

11. A leasing arrangement can be structured as either on- or off-balance-sheet. On-balance sheet is referred to as a capital lease; off-balance sheet is referred to as an operating lease. Accounting and tax issues must be evaluated to determine a lease's proper classification.

12. A sinking fund is used to insure that adequate funds are available to pay a bond issue at its maturity. Periodic payments are accumulated in a separate custodial account that is used to redeem the securities.

13. A company may issue convertible bonds to obtain a lower interest rate.

14. If a default occurs the lender may demand repayment of the debt prior to maturity.

Chapter 14: Financial Risk Management

1. Financial risk management involves the identification, measurement, hedging, and monitoring of risk stemming from changing interest rates, foreign exchange rates, and/or commodity prices. Management of financial risk is important because it impacts the value of the company.

2. The four steps of financial risk management involve: 1.) identifying the exposure, 2.) measuring the exposure, 3.) implementing an appropriate risk management strategy, and 4.) monitoring the exposure and evaluating the strategy.

3. The risk profile of a company demonstrates graphically how the value of the company is impacted by unexpected changes in a financial price variable such as interest rates, exchange rates, or commodity prices. The risk profile of a company that does not hedge is either positively sloped or negatively sloped. The risk profile of a hedged company is horizontal.

4.   Risk management helps reduce the variability of a company's future cash flows, which in turn adds value to the company.

5.   Hedging is typically defined as utilizing financial instruments or contracts to reduce or eliminate the risk from future changes in rates or prices. The purpose of speculation, in contrast, is to profit from a change in a future rate or price. Arbitrage is the process of buying in one market and simultaneously selling in another in order to earn a riskless profit.

6.   The four basic types of contracts or instruments used in financial risk management are forwards, futures, swaps, and options.

7.   A derivative is a financial product that derives value from some underlying assets.

8.   Though futures are similar in purpose to forwards, there are several important differences:

   • Futures are based on standardized contracts, with standard underlying assets.
   • Futures are normally bought and traded on organized exchanges and require both margin accounts and instant adjustment of the value of the future to the market.
   • The existence of margin accounts on futures allows investors in the market to benefit from leverage on their holding of futures.
   • Futures are rarely settled by actual delivery of the underlying assets and normally are closed out prior to their maturity

9.   The primary types of interest rate exposure are from falling rates and rising rates.

10.   Caps, floors, and collars are option-like instruments that allow companies to benefit from the low cost of adjustable-rate financing while protecting themselves against interest rate movements.

11.   Transaction exposure is the exposure of balance sheet accounts such as accounts receivable, accounts payable or loans to a change in foreign exchange rates between the time a transaction is recorded and the time it is paid. Companies with foreign subsidiaries are exposed to translation exposure when the subsidiary's financial statements are converted (translated) into the parent company's home currency for consolidation purposes.

12.   **Interest rate swap:** a company desiring a floating rate investment but with a comparitive advantage in the fixed rate market can invest in a fixed rate investment and contract with a counterparty to pay the counterparty a fixed rate return in exchange for a floating rate return.
      Futures contract: a company selling oil may wish to hedge the futures price by selling a futures contract. The company can deliver the oil at the price the contract was sold for if the expiration date of the contract matches the delivery date of the oil. If not, the contract can be bought back prior to expiration and then the oil sold at the prevailing market price. If the commodity price has decreased, the price of the futures contract will have also decreased and a profit will be made on the future contract transaction. This profit can be used to offset the price decline in the commodity market.

13.   The two basic types of commodity exposure are price exposure and delivery exposure.

14. The primary accounting issues deal with disclosure of information about the use of derivatives. In addition, hedge accounting is a technique that is applied to the components of a hedge so that the fair value of the hedged asset and the hedging vehicle are included in earnings for the same period.

15. The primary tax issues related to hedging transactions deal with whether the gains/losses on a hedge should be treated as ordinary gains/losses or capital gains/losses.

Chapter 15: International Cash Management

1. International cash management is becoming increasingly important due to the increased globalization of business, increased competition in the domestic market-place, and the need for cash management services on a global basis.

2. The key characteristics in which international banking systems differ are the following:

   • Central bank operations
   • Bank and company relationships
   • Number of banks and branching
   • Restrictions on corporate demand deposit accounts
   • Value dating

3. In most countries other than the U.S., banks use value dating as compensation for services provided to their customers. Under a value dating system, the bank sets the dates upon which it grants credit for deposits or it debits the account for checks written.

4. The clearing of checks between countries is often a slow and complicated process. Inter-country checks generally clear as collection items that must be presented back to the bank in the country where they were drawn.

5. The check clearing process within a country varies significantly from country to country. Some countries have nationwide clearing; others do not. The clearing of checks may be accomplished by the central bank (as the Fed does in the U.S.), by several of the major banks acting as clearing agents, or by correspondent relationships between different banks. Other differences include the significant use of electronic payments for both corporate and consumer payments.

6. Pooling is the practice of allowing excess balances in the accounts of some subsidiaries to be used to offset deficits in the accounts of other subsidiaries.

7. Multicurrency accounts are a special arrangement between a bank and its corporate customer whereby the bank allows the customer to receive or make international payments in a range of currencies from a single account.

8. A netting system reduces the number of foreign exchange transactions and therefore lowers the transaction cost. There is favorable pricing for larger foreign exchange transactions, and cash forecasting is improved. Netting can eliminate float and result in greater certainty regarding value dating.

9.	A reinvoicing center is a company-owned subsidiary that buys goods from the exporter and sells goods to the importer. Each party conducts the transaction in its own currency. Unlike a reinvoicing center, internal factoring does not involve a title transfer of goods. Internal factoring involves the purchase and collection of accounts receivables between subsidiaries.

10.	A letter of credit substitutes a bank's credit for that of the buyer. Consequently, it eliminates the risk of non-payment to the seller.

11.	An irrevocable letter of credit requires the issuing bank to honor all drafts presented by the seller as long as all necessary documentation is provided.

12.	A stand-by letter of credit states that a bank will pay the beneficiary upon presentation of a signed statement by the beneficiary that the bank's customer has not fulfilled the terms of the contract.

13.	Banks under a documentary collection do not assume credit risk but act only as agents in the collection process.

14.	Counter-trade is a method of payment in which a purchaser in a country with an insufficient amount of hard currency agrees to exchange merchandise that can be sold elsewhere by the seller to obtain payment in the required hard currency.

15.	To be eligible for discount at the Federal Reserve, a banker's acceptance may not have a maturity of more than 180 days.

16.	The Export-Import Bank of the United States (Eximbank) is an independent agency of the United States government established to finance and guarantee U.S. export loans.

17.	A company may seek offshore financing in order to:

- Diversify its funding sources
- Hedge foreign currency assets thereby reducing translation exposure
- Lower borrowing rates for its parent company
- Lower borrowing rates for foreign subsidiaries
- Gain tax advantages

Chapter 16: Relationship Management

1.	The major objectives of relationship management include:

- Access to credit
- Access to non-credit services
- Managing costs and quality
- Monitoring financial institution risk
- Development of a partnership approach

2.	The criteria for selecting service providers include:

- Willingness to be a reliable provider of credit at competitive rates

- Ability to structure flexible loan terms and conditions and provide financial advice
- Knowledge of a company and/or a specific industry
- Responsiveness to questions and understanding of needs
- Quality of customer service
- Pricing of services
- Commitment to a company, industry, or service
- Quality and expertise of relationship managers and technical specialists
- Financial strength of service provider
- Ability to customize services and innovation in developing new services
- Geographic considerations and convenience

3. The six components commonly used to measure a depository financial institution's strength are referred as a CAMELS rating. CAMELS is an acronym for Capital adequacy, Asset quality, Management capability, Earnings, Liquidity, and Sensitivity to market risk.

4. A company will want to optimize the number of financial institutions with which it has a relationship because there are internal and external costs for each relationship. As a result, there is an incentive to avoid having more relationships than are necessary.

5. Among the major documents associated with a financial institution relationship are the account resolution, signature cards, terms and conditions, and service agreements.

6. Among the audit and control issues facing a company in managing its financial institution relationships are the following:

- Establishing and updating policies and procedures for opening accounts
- Establishing and updating policies and procedures for timely reconciliation of account statements and timely reporting of problems and exceptions
- Establishing and updating polices and procedures for account documentation and record-keeping, including corporate resolutions, contracts for services, and signatories on accounts

7. A service provider report card often includes the following items:

- Number of errors by service
- Reporting times for information services
- Responsiveness to questions
- Timeliness of error resolution
- Effectiveness of personnel

8. Among the factors that increase the success and profitability of a relationship for both parties are the following:

- Open and frequent two-way communications, both formal and informal
- Regular and timely feedback, both formal and informal
- Clear expectations as established by letters of agreement and legal contracts
- Fair compensation of the financial institution by the company and fair pricing of services by the financial institution

- Complete disclosure by both parties of information that is essential to the success and ethical basis of the relationship

9. The account analysis statement is a bank's paper or electronic report to its commercial customers of services provided, volumes processed, and charges assessed. It is essentially an invoice. Services and fees can be detailed and itemized, or bundled into a single line term, or some combination of the two.

10. The basic product families of TMA Service Codes for account analysis include the following:

- Lockbox Services (05)
- Depository Services (10)
- Paper Disbursement Services (15)
- General ACH Services (25)

11. The average collected balance required to compensate the bank for services used are computed as follows:

$$\text{Collected Balances Required} = \frac{\text{Monthly Service Charges, Fees, or Costs}}{\left(\text{Earnings Allowance Rate} \times \dfrac{\text{Days in Month}}{365}\right) \times (1 - \text{Reserve Requirement})}$$

$$= \frac{\$4,000}{\left(.06 \times \dfrac{30}{365}\right) \times (1 - .10)}$$

$$= \frac{\$4,000}{.0044383} = \$901,246$$

12. Given the information in this problem, the earnings allowance can be calculated as follows:

$$\text{Earnings Allowance} = \text{Collected Balances} \times \left(1 - \text{Reserve Requirement}\right) \times \left(\text{Earnings Allowance Rate} \times \frac{\text{Days in Month}}{365}\right)$$

$$= (\$100,000 - \$19,000) \times (1 - .10) \times (.06 \times 30/365)$$

$$= \$81,000 \times .90 \times (.0049315)$$

$$= \$359.50$$

In this example, the earnings credit of $359.50 is not sufficient to cover the $650 of bank services for the month. The company will owe the bank $290.50.

13. Service charges may be bundled or unbundled. Bundling is the practice of charging for a group of related services. Unbundling is charging individually for each service used.

14. Financial institutions may allow companies to pay for services in fees, balances, or a combination of both.

15. The major factors favoring fee compensation from the company perspective are the following:

    • A company can generally earn more interest on its investments than a financial institution pays on collected balances.
    • Fees can be budgeted and compared with other costs, while balances are not as directly comparable.

INDEX

A

acceptance commission, 302

acceptance financing, 256

account analysis, 145, 313, 318-323

    consolidation, 324

    service codes, 319-320

    terminology, 320

account reconciliation services, 164-165

account resolution, 316

accounting

    accrual, 21

    capital and dividends, 22

    capitalized assets, 21

    cash, 21

    cost recognition, 21

    deferred taxes, 22

    depreciation and amortization, 22

    derivatives, 282

    financial instruments, 282

    income recognition, 21

    management discretion, 22

Accounting Standards Board, 28

accounts payable, 25, 154-166

accounts receivable, 89-109

    aging schedule, 101

    and EDI, 108

    asset-based borrowing, 256-257

    balance patterns, 103

    carrying costs, 92

    factoring, 106, 257

    financing of, 104-106

    international, 302

    management of, 90

    monitoring and control, 100-104

    securitization, 105

Accredited Standards Committee, 177

accrual accounting, 21

ACH, 13, 74-80, 172

    associations, 74

corporate trade payments, 13

credit transactions, 75-76

cross-border settlement, 292

debit transactions, 75, 77

direct deposit of payroll, 13

in collection systems, 117, 130-133

NACHA standard formats, 178-179

operators, 74

payment formats, 77-78

prenotification (prenote) entries, 79

regulations, 56, 58, 59-60

risk issues, 77

settlement, 78

system structure, 74

transaction participants, 75

active investment strategies, 243

adjustable-rate preferred stock, 232

advance rate, asset-based borrowing, 257

advising bank, letters of credit, 299-300

agency securities, 227-228

agent, 48

all-in rate, 249, 252

alpha, 215

American Institute of Certified Public Accountants (AICPA), 28

American National Standards Institute, 177

American option, 276

American Stock Exchange, 224

amortization, 22

amortization schedule, 261, 262

annuity factor, 325

anticipation notes, as investments, 228

anticipation, availability, 147

application advice transaction set, 178

arbitrage, 271

as-of adjustments, 73

ASC X12 financial transaction sets, 177

ASC X12 standards, 177

ASC X12 structure, 177

C

W

Y

Z

NOTES